The American Civil War

Gary W. Gallagher, Ph.D.

THE
GREAT
COURSES®

PUBLISHED BY:

THE GREAT COURSES
Corporate Headquarters
4840 Westfields Boulevard, Suite 500
Chantilly, Virginia 20151-2299
Phone: 1-800-832-2412
Fax: 703-378-3819
www.thegreatcourses.com

Gary W. Gallagher, Ph.D.

Professor of History of the American Civil War
University of Virginia

Professor Gary W. Gallagher is the John L. Nau Professor in the History of the American Civil War at the University of Virginia. Before coming to UVA, he was Professor of History at Pennsylvania State University—State College flagship campus. He graduated from Adams State College of Colorado and earned both his master's degree and doctorate in history from the University of Texas at Austin. His research and teaching focus are on the era of the Civil War and Reconstruction.

Recognized as one of the top historians of the Civil War, Dr. Gallagher is a prolific author. His books include *The Confederate War*, *Lee and His Generals in War and Memory*, and *Stephen Dodson Ramseur: Lee's Gallant General*. He has also coauthored and edited numerous works on individual battles and campaigns, including Antietam, Fredericksburg, Chancellorsville, Gettysburg, Wilderness, Spotsylvania, and the 1864 Shenandoah Valley campaign, and published over eight dozen articles in scholarly journals and popular historical magazines. Virtually all his books have been History Book Club selections.

He has received numerous awards for his research and writing, including, most recently, the Laney Prize for the best book on the Civil War (1998), The William Woods Hassler Award for contributions to Civil War studies (1998), the Lincoln Prize (1998–shared with three other authors), and the Fletcher Pratt Award for the best nonfiction book on the Civil War (1999).

Additionally, Professor Gallagher serves as editor of two book series for the University of North Carolina Press ("Civil War America" and "Military Campaigns of the Civil War"). He has appeared regularly on the Arts and Entertainment Network's series *Civil War Journal* and has participated in other television projects. Active in historic preservation, Professor Gallagher was president of the Association for Preservation of Civil War Sites (APCWS) from 1987 through mid-1994, has served on the Board of Directors of the Civil War Trust, and has testified before Congress on battlefield preservation on numerous occasions. ■

Table of Contents

Table of Contents

Table of Contents

The American Civil War

Scope:

This course examines the era of the American Civil War with emphasis on the period from 1861 to 1865, four years during which the United States endured its greatest national trauma. The lectures address such questions as why the war came, why the North won (or the Confederacy lost), how military campaigns unfolded, and how the war affected various elements of American society. The principal goal is to convey an understanding of the scope and consequences of the bloodiest war in our nation's history—a struggle that claimed more than 600,000 lives, freed nearly 4,000,000 enslaved African Americans, and settled definitively the question of whether states had the right to withdraw from the Union. The course also will address issues left unresolved at the end of the conflict, most notably the question of where former slaves would fit into the social and political structure of the nation.

Leading participants on both sides will receive extensive attention. Interspersed among discussions of military and nonmilitary aspects of the war will be biographical sketches of Abraham Lincoln, Robert E. Lee, Ulysses S. Grant, Frederick Douglass, "Stonewall" Jackson, William Tecumseh Sherman, Thaddeus Stevens, and several dozen other prominent figures. Although this is not a course on Civil War battles and generals per se, approximately half of the lectures will be devoted to the strategic and tactical dimensions of military campaigns. It is impossible to understand the broad impact of the war without a grasp of how military events shaped attitudes and actions on the home front, and there will be a special effort to tie events on the battlefield to life behind the lines.

Part I traces the prelude to the war by discussing the key issues of the antebellum period, starting with the Missouri Compromise of 1820 and continuing for 40 years to the election of 1860. The secession crisis that election precipitated turned into armed conflict in early 1861. Early lectures size up the two opposing sides of the military conflict, including a consideration of the men who manned the armies. The final five lectures of Part I trace the early fortunes of war from the Battle of Bull Run (First Manassas) through the Peninsula and Shenandoah Valley campaigns of early 1862, when first one side, then the other seemed to be in ascendancy.

Part II picks up the military narrative with the pivotal Seven Days' Battles before Richmond, when the Union advance in the East was halted by the newly appointed General Robert E. Lee, and continues up to the crucial Battle of Antietam in September. Lectures on the issue of emancipation, military conscription, and financing of the war provide a look at political and social issues that came to the fore in this period. Part II concludes with more discussion of major campaigns and battles, including Gettysburg and Chickamauga, bringing the narration up to the fall of 1863.

Part III begins with the campaign for Chattanooga that saw the ascendancy of Ulysses S. Grant as the top Union general. The emphasis shifts to the diplomatic front, as both sides vied to present their case before the world (i.e., European) audience. The war from the African American perspective comes next, followed by a discussion of Northern wartime "reconstruction" policies. We devote two lectures to the naval war, both that conducted on the high seas involving the Northern blockade and Southern commerce raiding, as well as that which took place on the "brown water" of rivers and bays. Two lectures cover the experience of women in the war, on the home front, as medical workers on the field, and even (in a few cases) as soldiers. The focus then shifts back to the military events of 1864, moving the narrative forward to the Overland campaign up to the battles of the Wilderness and Spotsylvania in the spring of 1864.

Part IV brings us to the finale of the Overland campaign and the siege of Petersburg and Richmond. This offers an excellent opportunity to discuss the home front, in both the North and the South, and consider the differences in the wartime experience between the two sections. After one lecture on the issue of prisoners of war, we turn back to the military front to investigate how Grant's strategy to envelope the South and eliminate its ability to fight militarily played out in Sherman's Atlanta campaign and his inexorable pressure on Lee at Richmond. With the conclusion of the war in April 1865 came the chance for peace and reconciliation, but the assassination of Abraham Lincoln dominated the immediate period after the cessation of hostilities. A final lecture sums up the lessons and legacies of this great national trauma and reminds us that, in a larger context, the issues that divided the nation during the era of the Civil War continue to resonate in modern America. This course will attempt to make those issues clear while providing a sense of the drama and tragedy of this tumultuous period in the life of the nation. ■

Prelude to War
Lecture 1

In this lecture we'll first look at the ways in which the North and South developed along different paths in the four decades before the conflict erupted. Then we'll see how the issue of territorial expansion into the Federal lands in the West proved especially poisonous. And finally we will look very briefly at some of the mileposts along the road to sectional disruption.

Between 1788 and 1860, the North developed into a society that embraced the idea of modern capitalism. The population grew rapidly and was more urban, with more immigrants than the South. The economy was diversified: It was about 40 percent small-farm agricultural, with strong industrial and merchant sectors. Religion helped to encourage economic growth. Yankee Protestantism was dominant; the political and economic leadership largely came from this segment. A Catholic minority stood somewhat out of the mainstream.

Reform movements also thrived in the North during this period. Temperance stood among the more important movements. Public education received widespread support. Abolitionism was the most important reform movement, with its roots in the "free labor" idea. And many people in the North held negative perceptions about the South: They thought it was holding the nation back.

The South between 1788 and 1860 offered many contrasts to the North. The population grew less rapidly. The South was not as urban, and public works were not as extensive. The biggest city in 1861 was New Orleans, with 160,000 people. Because of its smaller population, the South was falling behind in the House of Representatives.

About 80 percent of the economy in the South was focused on agriculture, and slavery exerted a major influence on economic development. Leaders were large, wealthy landowners and slaveholders. Only 25 percent of the population held slaves, and only about 12 percent had twelve or more slaves. However, all Southern whites had a stake in slavery, because it gave them status, regardless of their economic position. Agrarian dominance was based on cash crops, and "King Cotton" was the most important.

Southern religion differed from that in the North in important ways. It was more personal. It was less interested in societal reform and more interested in personal salvation. And education and reform movements did not thrive in the South. Many people in the South held negative perceptions about the North. They viewed Northerners as cold, grasping people. They thought Northerners were more interested in money than anything else.

The issue of territorial expansion poisoned national politics. Expansion helped to determine national political representation. The South saw the North gaining seats in the House of Representatives because of the increase in its population. The South wanted to protect its social system by keeping parity in the Senate and allowing expansion of slavery into the territories, but the Northern "Free Soil" movement opposed this expansion of slavery.

[B]y 1859, a great many people, both North and South, had worked themselves into such a state that compromise would be very difficult if another great crisis did arise.

In 1831, two major events occurred. The first was the most important slave rebellion in the United States's history: Nat Turner's insurrection in Southside, Virginia. Nat Turner, a black preacher, and a handful of followers rose up and killed several dozen white people—some by hacking. The insurrection sent an enormous shock across the white South. This is, of course, a great Southern nightmare, slaves rising up and slaughtering masters.

The same year, William Lloyd Garrison began publication of *The Liberator*, an abolitionist newspaper. And nullification in South Carolina, ostensibly over tariffs, caused a national crisis. The admission of Texas to the Union in

1845, and then the Mexican War in 1846 to 1847, brought vast new Western lands into the nation that fanned the sectional tensions.

Crisis followed crisis fairly rapidly after 1848, a year in which the Free-Soil Party ran a presidential candidate. The Free-Soil Party was for keeping slavery out of the territories. The Wilmot Proviso, although voted down in the Senate, alienated slaveholders by barring slavery from any territory acquired as a result of the Mexican War. Land acquired from Mexico—now California, Utah, New Mexico, Arizona, and parts of Colorado and Nevada—thus became the focus of hot debate. The Compromise of 1850 helped to avert a crisis but satisfied neither the North nor the South. It allowed California to enter the Union as a free state, breaking parity in the Senate. However, it contained tough Fugitive Slave laws.

Prints and Photographs Division, Library of Congress.

Dred Scott, the slave whose Supreme Court case denied slaves the rights of citizens and helped propel the country toward civil war.

Two years later, Harriet Beecher Stowe published *Uncle Tom's Cabin*. Hundreds of thousands of people in the United States and abroad quickly bought the controversial book, which deepened national divisions. Many Northerners who really hadn't cared before became empathetic about the awful situation of black people living under slavery.

Two years after *Uncle Tom's Cabin* was published, the Kansas-Nebraska Act of 1854 deepened national divisions even further. The doctrine of "popular sovereignty" appealed to some as a solution to the slavery expansion problem: It would allow residents of the territories to decide the issue of slavery.

Many Northerners said that this doctrine violated the Missouri Compromise because it would potentially open up to slavery some of the territories that the Missouri Compromise had said would be closed to slavery forever. The compromise went beyond the stage of mere debate. There was tremendous violence associated with the Kansas-Nebraska Act, as pro-slavery people and antislavery people fought and killed each other in Kansas and along the Kansas-Missouri border. There was virtually a minor civil war that broke out to win control of the area.

In 1856, one of the more dramatic things that have ever happened on the floor of the House or the Senate occurred. Senator Charles Sumner of Massachusetts, after giving a powerful speech condemning what he called the "Crime against Kansas" (that is, perhaps allowing slavery into Kansas), was caned by Preston Brooks of South Carolina, confirming negative perceptions on both sides.

In 1857, The *Dred Scott* decision seemed to guarantee slavery's spread throughout the United States and alienated a large part of the North. It declared that slaves were not citizens. It found that the Missouri Compromise violated the Fifth Amendment prohibition against governmental "taking." Congress had a responsibility to protect slaves as "property."

National institutions failed to perform as stabilizing forces during this period. Several churches divided into Northern and Southern branches (e.g., Southern Baptists). The Whig and Democratic parties also split along sectional lines. The Whig Party died out altogether in 1852. And the Democratic Party became a Southern party. Then, in 1856, the Republican Party was founded and became a sectional (Northern) party. The national parties were no longer influential in holding things together, just as the churches were not.

Many people looked to the Supreme Court as the last hope for an institution that really would be above the sectional controversy. But *Dred Scott* showed that that was not the case either. The Supreme Court seemed to favor the slaveholding South. Even major Northern politicians, such as Franklin Pierce and James Buchanan, seemed to favor the South in their policies and actions; for this, they and their ilk were derisively termed "dough faces" by their political opponents. These are Northern men doing the bidding of their Southern masters, said many who opposed them. Many in the North worried that they were almost hopeless in the face of the powerful slaveholding influence.

So many Northerners and Southerners had developed such strong antithetical views of the other by 1859 that any sort of compromise would be nearly impossible should another great crisis arise—which it did when the election of 1860 brought to power the Republican Party, which had called for closing off the territories to slavery. An important thing to keep in mind when reviewing this period is that perception was more important than reality in the sectional crisis. ■

Essential Reading

McPherson, *Battle Cry of Freedom: The Civil War Era*, chapters 1–5.

Potter, *The Impending Crisis, 1848–1861*, chapters 1–12.

Supplementary Reading

Cooper, *The South and the Politics of Slavery, 1828–1856*.

Donald, *Charles Sumner and the Coming of the Civil War*.

Questions to Consider

1. Did the North and South have good reasons to fear each other's influence over the course of national affairs?

2. Would a serious crisis have been possible in the absence of slavery?

Prelude to War
Lecture 1—Transcript

We're going to spend 48 lectures exploring various aspects of the American Civil War. Although 48 may seem to be a large number, we'll be able to do no more than scratch the surface of a subject so vast, complex, important, and engaging that it has inspired a literature that conservatively runs to more than 50,000 books and pamphlets. More than one book or pamphlet a day has been published since April 1861, when the firing on Fort Sumter helped precipitate the conflict.

The course will provide a narrative thread supplemented by a number of lectures that look at topical aspects of the war. We'll devote considerable attention to both the military and the civilian spheres, and we'll take time for brief biographical sketches of several dozen key actors. We'll not be able to spend much time on the coming of the war, and we'll look at Reconstruction only within its wartime context, the beginning of the process of Reconstruction that took place while the war was still raging.

Now both the coming of the war and Reconstruction easily could be the subject of separate courses, but we're not going to be able to spend that much time on them. Having said that, I'll add that some background is necessary to set the stage for the war, and that's what we'll do in this first lecture.

Time prevents our employing anything but the broadest of brush strokes, and I'll say at the outset that we should not fall into the trap of trying to understand the outbreak of fighting by bringing everything we know to our consideration of why the war came. Most Americans did not wake up every morning during the antebellum years thinking only about sectional tensions. They didn't wake up with the first thought on their minds, "What's going on in the North?" or "What's going on in the South?"

They got on with their lives. They were concerned with the type of mundane activities that occupy our attention most of the time. They didn't know that a gigantic war lurked a few years ahead, and thus they generally had no sense of time ticking away for a young republic destined to undergo a trauma of unimagined proportion. They often looked, for example, at local or state rather than national politics as their main focus when they were engaged in the political system, yet we can trace the unfolding of sectional tensions that contributed to a situation where war could come in 1861.

In this lecture we'll first look at the ways in which the North and South developed along different paths in the four decades before the conflict erupted. Then we'll see how the issue of territorial expansion into the federal lands in the West proved especially poisonous. And finally we will look very briefly at some of the mileposts along the road to sectional disruption.

There's been a great deal of debate among historians about whether the North and South had developed by the midpoint of the nineteenth century into societies that were different from one another. Some scholars have argued that they had become essentially two different civilizations, divided across a fault line delineated by the institution of slavery. Other scholars point to a common language, a common history—most obviously the struggle for independence in the late eighteenth century—and other shared characteristics. These scholars insist that differences were minor compared to commonalities between Northerners and Southerners.

I believe much of this debate misses a major point, and that is that most Americans, in my view, by the mid-1850s at the latest, believed that there were major differences between Northerners and Southerners, white Northerners and white Southerners. Northerners looked south and saw people made different by slavery. Many white Southerners, I would say most in turn, considered Northerners an almost alien people bent on interfering with Southern society. The key thing to understand is that it doesn't matter whether there were really major differences. If the people thought there were and acted accordingly, that is the most important thing, and I believe that was the case. People looked north if they were in the South and saw a people they believed was different, and the same thing happened in the other direction.

It's always risky to generalize about large groups of people, whether in the United States or anywhere else, but I think it is possible to make some generalizations about the two sections. All these generalizations could be qualified. There're always exceptions to everything that I'm going to say, but let's plow ahead fearlessly and make some generalizations about each side, starting with the North.

The North was increasing far more rapidly in population during the antebellum decades than was the South. There was more immigration by far. It was a far more urban area, although certainly not an urban area by our modern standards. It was far more developed commercially and industrially than the South was. There was also a very strong agricultural sector in the North. Forty percent or more of the entire labor force in the North was engaged in agriculture. But it was far more urban, far more commercial, and far more industrial than the South.

If we had to pick out the single dominant element of the Northern population, it would be what we would probably call yeoman farmers, independent farmers who worked their own land, relatively small parcels of land. The North had a strong strain of Yankee Protestantism that urged citizens to be thrifty and to work hard and to avoid alcohol or excess of any kind.

Now, again, not all Northerners fit into this pattern. There were millions of Catholics in the North—many Irish Catholics and German Catholics in cities and elsewhere. There were many non-Catholics who lived especially in the southern regions of the North, what was called the Little Egypt region of the Midwest, down along the Ohio River, who did not subscribe to this notion of Yankee Protestantism. But among the political and economic leaders of the North, Yankee Protestantism was very strong, and this strain of Protestantism helped fuel economic expansion and pointed the way toward an emerging capitalist, industrial, and commercial giant.

The North also embraced reform movements. Again, these were supported in a major way by this strain of Yankee Protestantism, this Yankee Protestant ethic. Temperance was a major reform movement in the North, as was public education, and, most importantly, abolitionism.

What historians called a "free labor" ideology had taken strong hold in the North by the mid 1850s, an ideology that argued that there is no inherent antagonism between labor on the one hand and capital on the other. It argued an individual could begin owning nothing but his labor, and they would have put it within the context of *his* labor, nothing but his labor: Work, use that labor to acquire a small amount of capital, and eventually become a member of the middle class or even more. Abraham Lincoln was a perfect example of this, someone who began with virtually nothing but his labor and ended up as a very successful member of the middle class. The Republican Party believed fervently in the notion of a free labor society.

Many in the North looked south and saw a section that they believed was holding the nation back. They saw a land of lazy, cruel, violent people who did not subscribe to the ideas that would make the United States great. That is the view many in the North had of the South.

Let's shift to the South now. The South was losing ground in population and thus clout in Congress. The railroad, canal, and road networks in the South were underdeveloped compared to those in the North. Cities were fewer and smaller. New Orleans, at a 160,000 people plus or minus a few in 1860, was by far, by far, the largest city in the South. There were many cities in the North that dwarfed most of the cities in the South.

The South was overwhelmingly agricultural. Eighty percent of its labor force engaged in agriculture. The vast majority of Southern wealth was invested in land and in slaves. Wealthier slaveholders dominated the region politically and socially, and their lands produced key cash crops. They produced cotton and sugar and tobacco and rice. Cotton was the key. Cotton fed Northern and European textile industries. Cotton exports alone gave the United States a favorable balance of trade in the 1850s.

Southern religion was also of course predominantly Protestant, overwhelmingly Protestant. But it was a more personal kind of Protestantism, concerned less with reforming or improving society and more with individual salvation. Reform movements did not really take root in the South. There's very little of the Temperance Movement. There is virtually no abolitionist sentiment in the South, at least not spoken sentiment by the 1850s, or really even before that. Education lagged far behind Northern standards across most of the South. Now, many white Southerners looked to the North as a region of cold, grasping people who cared little about family and subordinated everything to the process of making money.

Slavery was not only a form of labor control in the South but also the key to the South's social system. Only about a quarter of white Southern families owned slaves, and most of those held five or fewer. Only 12 percent of the slaveholders, that is 12 percent of the 25 percent who owned slaves, had 12 or more slaves, which is one way to divide slaveholders between relatively large and more modest slaveholders. All Southern white people, however, had a stake in the system of slavery because as white people they were automatically part of the controlling class in the South. No matter how poor they were, how wretched their condition might be, they were superior in their minds and, according to the legal and social structures of their society, to the millions of enslaved African Americans among them.

In an ironic way, all Southern whites, regardless of economic status, were made equal by the fact of slavery. For this reason, and because there was genuine fear of what would happen if large numbers of free black people were to be set loose, as they would put it, to live among them, Southern whites, almost all of them, saw slavery as a necessary and generally good institution, and they reacted very defensively when Northerners attacked it.

Now I think it's important to separate notions about slavery from notions about race. Most white Southerners were intensely racist. Most white Northerners were intensely racist during the mid-nineteenth century. The difference was that virtually all of the black people in the United States lived in the South at this time. I mean virtually all of them lived in the South. Whenever enough black people would congregate some place in the North to pose a threat to the white population of that area, white Northerners often responded almost precisely as white Southerners did. So do not assume that racism is somehow a Southern phenomenon during the nineteenth century. It's national.

So there are differences between the North and the South in the way they're developing. Let's move on and look at the question of expansion into new federal territories and how it became an especially aggravating question.

The South was aware of the fact, obviously, that the North was outstripping it in population. The House of Representatives was clearly dominated by the North well before the Civil War because, as you know, that's representation based on population there. The Senate was something the South tried to maintain parity in. We'll talk more about that in just a minute, but because the South knew the North was outstripping it in population, the white Southerners believed it was necessary on their part to do anything possible to try to erect safeguards to their social system and the ability of their social system to expand, in other words, the ability of slavery to expand. One of the ways to do that was to try to keep parity in the Senate, as I said.

Now, the North is equally aware of its preponderance of population. It believed that since there were more people in the North, the North should have more clout in the United States. There are more of us. Why should we not be able to do what we want to do if we outnumber, and increasingly outnumber the South? White Southerners felt that the peculiar institution, as they called slavery, had to go into new federal territories or their economy would stagnate. They'd be caught in a situation where slavery was boxed in. Slave populations would grow in that area, and it would be a problem, potentially not only socially but also economically.

Northerners, on the other hand, increasingly came to call for territories being reserved for free men only who would work their own farms. The "Free Soil" movement that gained strength through the 1840s and 1850s argued for this. Reserve the Western territories for free men. Many of these Northerners calling for Free Soil in the West, I will emphasize, couldn't care less about the black people who were caught in slavery. They wanted Free Soil for white men in the West. They didn't want Free Soil for black freed slaves in the West. They wanted the territories reserved for white men.

So this was an issue—whether or not slavery would be allowed to expand into the territories—that became a greater and greater and greater area of dispute between the sections as we go toward 1860. And, of course, it was a problem because the United States was acquiring more and more land as we go toward 1860.

Let's shift now to some of the key mileposts along the road of sectional friction. Now most of these, I suspect, are very familiar to you, but we'll go through some of the more important ones just to have them fresh in your minds. And again, I don't want to convey, by going through this list of sectional tensions, that there was a sense beginning in 1820 or so that we're pointing toward an inevitable civil war, that all of these things are just leading to a point where we're going to be killing each other. Most people did not believe that. Some would argue that, but that isn't the main thing on everybody's mind. Nonetheless, these things occurred, and they upped the level of tensions, and they made more possible an explosion at some point.

Let's start in 1820 with the Missouri Compromise. It restricted slavery in the old Louisiana Purchase country to land below the 36°30' line. It allowed Missouri to come in as a slave state, and Missouri would be balanced by Maine very shortly thereafter coming in as a free state. Until 1850, free states and slave states would alternate coming into the Union, which preserved the balance of power in the Senate. So for 30 years after the Missouri Compromise, you'll have states essentially coming in in pairs in the United States, one slave and one free.

In 1831, two major events occurred. The first was the most important slave rebellion in the United States's history. Nat Turner's insurrection or rebellion in Southside, Virginia, where Nat Turner, a black preacher, and a handful of followers rose up and killed several dozen white people—hacked some of them to death, killed others—sent an enormous shock across the white South. This is, of course, a great Southern nightmare, slaves rising up and slaughtering masters.

That same year, 1831, William Lloyd Garrison began publication of *The Liberator*, which would become the most famous abolitionist newspaper. That also set off alarms in the South. Here's somebody publishing a newspaper, getting a lot of attention, saying all of our slave property should be swept away. These events are both in 1831.

There was a nullification controversy in South Carolina that really spread over from the very later 1820s into the early 1830s, ostensibly about the tariff but really about slavery, I believe, and whether the federal government, if it were given the power in the area of tariffs, might not step in and interfere with state institutions such as slavery later on (a fear of too much federal power). In 1840, the Liberty Party first ran a presidential candidate. The Liberty Party had one issue, the end of slavery.

15

The admission of Texas to the Union in 1845, and then the Mexican War in 1846 to 1847, brought vast new Western lands into the nation that fanned the conflict, the sectional conflict, during the 1840s. In response to these huge new areas brought in—and they included California and Utah, or what are now California, Utah, New Mexico, Arizona, and parts of Colorado and Nevada—the North staked out a clear position with the 1846 Wilmot Proviso offered by a Democrat from Pennsylvania named, interestingly enough, David Wilmot.

Wilmot's Proviso said, all right, we'll take all this land from Mexico, we'll bring all of this land into the Union, but we will bar slavery from any lands acquired as a result of the war with Mexico. That passed in the Northern-dominated House of Representatives, the Wilmot Proviso did, but it was voted down in the Senate. It gave a clear warning to the South of the intention of a good part of the North to seal off new territories to slavery. Many people in the North, even some Democrats, said white Southerners like David Wilmot want to keep our slave property out of the territories.

Crisis followed crisis fairly rapidly after 1848, a year in which the Free-Soil Party ran a presidential candidate in a major effort. The Free-Soil Party, obviously, was for keeping slavery out of the territories. The Compromise of 1850, together with the Missouri Compromise, are two of the most famous efforts in the antebellum years to dampen sectional tensions and animosities. The Compromise of 1850 arose in response to a number of issues, and it really consisted of a cluster of pieces of legislation that didn't really please anybody but did manage to quiet things down for a while.

The key elements of the Compromise? California came in as a free state, and that broke parity in the Senate. From the admission of California forward, the North would control the Senate as well as the House of Representatives. On the Southern side, the Compromise included a very tough Fugitive Slave Law that put the United States government in the position of having to help slave owners recover slaves who managed to run away to free territory. So much of the North wasn't happy with the Fugitive Slave Law, and much of the South was not happy with California coming in as a free state under the Compromise of 1850.

Two years later, Harriet Beecher Stowe published *Uncle Tom's Cabin,* and it really is impossible, I think, for us to grasp the effect that *Uncle Tom's Cabin* had. It was an enormous best-seller. It sold hundreds of thousands of copies very quickly. That is at a time when the nation had only about 25 million people. It sold thousands of copies overseas as well. It really did bring home to a vastly increased proportion of the white North some notion about the awful situation of black people living under slavery. Many Northerners, who really hadn't cared before, became sensitive to the issue because of *Uncle Tom's Cabin* and Harriet Beecher Stowe.

There's a wonderful story about Abraham Lincoln meeting Harriet Beecher Stowe during the Civil War. It may be apocryphal, but it may not. He is introduced to her and he says, "Oh, so this is the young lady who brought on this great Civil War." Her book did have a good deal to do with increasing, in some ways, sectional tensions. It was a book loathed in the South. In fact, a couple of books, a couple of novels in the South, were written as answers to *Uncle Tom's Cabin.* It's a very important book, I think easily the most important novel in American history.

Two years after *Uncle Tom's Cabin*, the Kansas-Nebraska Act of 1854 was passed, which included a provision for "popular sovereignty." Popular sovereignty meant that the people of a territory should decide for themselves whether or not they would want slavery in their territory. Don't let Congress decide. Let the people who are living there decide. It was the brainchild, to a degree, of Steven A. Douglas of Illinois, although the notion had come up earlier. Louis Cass had brought it up back in the Campaign of 1848.

Many Northerners said, this violates the Missouri Compromise. This means that you're going to potentially open up some areas to slavery, some of the territories that the Missouri Compromise had said would be closed to slavery forever. It went beyond the stage of just debating this. There was tremendous violence associated with Kansas-Nebraska as pro-slavery people and antislavery people fought and killed each other in Kansas and along the Kansas-Missouri border. There was virtually a minor civil war that broke out to win control of the area.

In 1856, one of the more dramatic things that ever happened on the floor of either the House or the Senate occurred when Senator Charles Sumner of Massachusetts, after giving a powerful speech condemning what he called the "Crime against Kansas," that is, perhaps allowing slavery into Kansas, was caned on the floor of the Senate by Preston Brooks, a Representative from South Carolina. Beaten into insensibility, literally covered with blood, he collapsed on the floor. Charles Sumner, who was an abolitionist, left the Senate for three years as a result of this beating, and Massachusetts left his seat vacant.

So there was Charles Sumner's empty seat in the Senate, a constant reminder, said people in the North, to the brutality and tendency toward violence on the part of white Southerners. In the white South, they reacted by sending new canes to Preston Brooks and saying that he had upheld the honor of the South against a man who not only was impugning the whole region in his speech but also had attacked personally a relative of Preston Brooks. So the caning of Sumner was a major national event. That's 1856.

In 1857, one of the most important Supreme Court cases in our history was decided, the *Dred Scott* decision, handed down by the Supreme Court presided over by Roger B. Taney. The *Dred Scott* decision in effect said that no black person could be a citizen. It said that the Missouri Compromise violated the Fifth Amendment's prohibition against taking property from people without due process, that is, by saying someone couldn't take their slave property into a part of the old Louisiana Purchase country. It also in effect said that Congress must protect slave property. What was at issue was the case of a slave named Dred Scott, who was taken to free territory by his master, who then returned to slave territory. The question was whether Scott should have become free because he had lived on free territory. The Taney Court said no.

This case alienated a significant part of the North. The abolitionists in the North went absolutely crazy about this. They said, this is a perfect example of how a slave power conspiracy controls our government. The Court, the Supreme Court, which should be standing above special interest, has here weighed-in directly on the side of the slave owners, said people in the North and that, they argued, is a bad situation. The slave power conspiracy, they said, is holding sway even though we outnumber them, and we're outnumbering them more and more. Something is wrong here. We have to curb this conspiracy.

Part of the problem as we move through the 1840s and 1850s is that the national institutions that generally had been looked to to bring the nation together were failing. The churches split over the issue of slavery, many of them dividing in the 1840s and later. We get Northern Baptists and Southern Baptists, Northern Methodists and Southern Methodists, rather than just Baptists and Methodists. The Whig and Democratic parties broke down. Those parties had been national parties, also tending to hold things together because the parties would try to find compromises so they would have voters in both North and South.

The second party system, the Whigs and Democrats—the first party system had been the Federalists and the Jeffersonian Republicans—this second national party system broke down under the strain of sectionalism. The Whigs ran their last serious presidential candidate in 1852, and the Democratic Party became an almost completely Southern-dominated sectional party as well, with most of its national policies favoring the South.

The Republican Party first ran a candidate in 1856, the Army officer and famous explorer, John C. Frémont. The Republican Party is a sectional party. It has no appeal in the South—none. Its platform called for the banning of slavery from the territories. In Southern minds, the Republicans quickly became associated with abolitionists though the two were by no means synonymous. But the party system then is breaking down. The national parties are no longer an influence holding things together, just as the churches are not.

And finally, many people have grasped that the Supreme Court is the last hope for an institution that really would be above the sectional controversy, but *Dred Scott* showed that that was not the case either. Many in the North worried that they were almost hopeless in the face of this powerful slaveholding influence in the nation. They would point even to Northern men who were powerful politicians: Franklin Pierce, a Democratic president from New Hampshire, James Buchanan, a Democratic president from

Pennsylvania, but their policies were all pro-Southern, said many in the North who opposed them, Republicans and others. They're "dough faces." That was the expression, the derisive expression, applied to what were called Northern men of Southern principles. These are Northern men doing the bidding of their Southern masters, said many who opposed them.

And here's a key element in the whole sectional controversy. Perceptions on each side had reached a point by the mid-1850s that scarcely allowed many Northerners and Southerners to view the other section in anything like sympathetic or even realistic terms. Each side expected the worst from the other. The white South looked north and saw a nation of abolitionists trying to kill the institution that was the foundation of the South's economic and social order. The North looked south and saw a land of aggressive slaveholders who, through the national courts and with "dough face" allies in Congress and the White House, frustrated the nation's progress in the modern world. There isn't much common ground in a sense as we move toward the end of the 1850s.

I'll close with the observation that, by 1859, a great many people, both North and South, had worked themselves into such a state that compromise would be very difficult if another great crisis did arise. When the election of 1860 brought to power a party that had called for closing off the territories to slavery, the Republican Party, just such a crisis had arrived, and how each side dealt with that crisis will be the subject of our next lecture.

The Election of 1860
Lecture 2

Today we're going to shift forward and look at the presidential election of 1860, really the most momentous presidential election in United States history, an election around which more was at stake than at any other time in our national past.

The presidential canvass of 1860 and Abraham Lincoln's election as the first Republican to occupy the White House precipitated the secession crisis of 1860–1861. Against a backdrop of sectional antagonism fueled by John Brown's raid on the Federal arsenal at Harpers Ferry, Virginia (now West Virginia), on October 16, 1859, voters mobilized to decide which party would hold power in Washington. There was a mixed response in the North: The majority did not approve of Brown's action, but there was some praise for it. Most white Southerners, recalling Nat Turner's earlier revolt, reacted to the raid with horror as a failed attempt to foment a slave uprising. In particular, the mixed praise in the North was perceived in the South as broader than it really was. Then a series of unexplained fires in Texas in the summer of 1860 further rocked the white South. They were attributed to slaves, which fed the fear among white Southerners.

[In the 1860 election], there was a clear choice. If you vote for the Republicans, there will be no more slavery in the territories. … If you vote for Breckinridge, there will be an absolute guarantee for slavery.

The initial convention at Charleston, South Carolina, was divided between the pro-slavery, pro-Southern Yancey platform and the pro-Northern Douglas platform that favored popular sovereignty in the territories. The convention failed to agree on a candidate, as 49 Southern delegates walked out. A second convention in Baltimore saw the final breakup of the Democratic Party: The majority of delegates nominated Stephen A. Douglas of Illinois and Hershel V. Johnson, while the Southern minority nominated John C. Breckinridge of Kentucky and Joseph Lane in mid-May 1860.

The Republican Party, aware of the disarray in the Democratic Party, selected a moderate candidate. Several principal contenders failed in early ballots: William Henry Seward (too radical), Salmon P. Chase (too radical), and Edward Bates (ex-Whig; too conservative).

Supporters of Abraham Lincoln of Illinois crafted a winning strategy to secure his nomination. Their platform accepted slavery where it existed but called for barring it from the Federal territories. It deplored John Brown's raid and called for a Homestead Act, internal public improvements, and protective tariffs. This platform represented a Northern, progressive, mercantile philosophy.

The Constitutional Union Party, growing out of the earlier American Party and "Know-Nothing" movement, attempted to avoid the issue of slavery. John Bell and Edward Everett won the nomination. The platform ignored slavery and called for support of the Constitution and the Union.

The campaign offered the spectacle of a nation in trauma. All four candidates professed devotion to the Union. The canvass took on the character of two contests: Lincoln and Douglas contended for Northern votes; Douglas, Breckinridge, and Bell contended for Southern votes. Lincoln was not even on the ballot in several Southern states. Many Southerners, especially in the lower tier of states, threatened secession should the Republicans win; they associated Republicans with abolitionists and John Brown. Slavery, race, and economics were the principal campaign issues but were not equally important in every section of the nation. Abolitionists were not satisfied with the Republican platform, but they generally supported

Abraham Lincoln, president of the United States from 1861 to 1865.

the Republican Party. Lincoln did not campaign; Douglas did, even in the South.

The campaign of 1860 ranks as the most important and one of the most complex in United States history. The election yielded a divided result. Lincoln lost the popular vote by a wide margin (2.8 million votes to 1.9 million), but he won the Electoral College by an even wider margin (an absolute majority of 180-123).

A united Democratic Party would not have won the election. Douglas polled 1.35 million popular votes and 12 Electoral votes. Breckinridge received 675,000 popular votes and 72 Electoral votes, mostly in the South. Bell won 600,000 popular votes and 39 Electoral votes, in the upper South and border states.

Lincoln's support was not evenly distributed across the North. The Upper North (strongly antislavery in sentiment) provided the strongest Republican turnout. Antislavery Northerners viewed the election as a major step toward throwing off the "slaveocracy" of the South.

The year of 1860 was a momentous one in American political history. Voters had a clear choice on the issues of slavery and the economy. In only their second national campaign, the Republicans elected their candidate as president. ■

Essential Reading

McPherson, *Battle Cry of Freedom: The Civil War Era*, chapters 6–7.

Potter, *The Impending Crisis, 1848–1861*, chapters 14–16.

Supplementary Reading

Donald, *Lincoln*, chapters 8–9.

1. What does the election of 1860 tell us about whether the American people believed there were true differences between the North and South?

2. Can you imagine a modern election in which the candidate of either the Democratic or Republican Party did not appear on the ballot in several states (as was the case with the Republicans in 1860)?

The Election of 1860
Lecture 2—Transcript

In our opening lecture the last time, we took a look, a comparative look, at the North and South in the late antebellum period. We looked at mileposts along the road to secession, key arguments relating to the issue of slavery in the late antebellum years. Today we're going to shift forward and look at the presidential election of 1860, really the most momentous presidential election in United States history, an election around which more was at stake than at any other time in our national past.

There will be four main parts to the lecture today. We'll start out by looking at John Brown's raid and its importance as one of the precipitants of the final phase of the secession crisis. We'll then move on to four nominating conventions in 1860. There were four candidates fielded in 1860 rather than the two or perhaps three that we're more generally used to. We'll then take a look at the progress of the campaign itself and then assess the results.

But first let's start in Harper's Ferry, Virginia, now West Virginia, for what was one of the opening scenes of the election of 1860 and of the entire crisis of 1860-1861. It's mid-October, 1859. On the 16th of that month, John Brown and a small group of followers seized the federal arsenal there as part of a plan to gather slaves and move south through the mountains, deeper and deeper into Virginia and eventually beyond Virginia. John Brown's intention was to gather slaves to his Army of Liberation as he marched south, and in the end he hoped to free all of the slaves in the entire South through one vast uprising that would begin there, where the Shenandoah and Potomac Rivers flow together at Harper's Ferry.

But his plan went wrong very quickly. Robert E. Lee and a small group of Marines came out to Harper's Ferry from Washington. Brown and his followers barricaded themselves but were quickly subdued, a number of them killed, John Brown himself wounded. Brown was put on trial by the state of Virginia. He was found guilty of treason, and he was hanged.

But it's the reaction to John Brown that is most important. He had comported himself with great dignity, both during the trial and as he went to the gallows. He handed one of his jailers a note near the end that said, "I, John Brown, am now quite certain that the crimes of this guilty land will never be purged away but with blood." Many people in the North praised Brown. Churches' bells pealed in his honor. After his death a number of newspapers praised him, and it seemed to many in the white South that a significant part of the North, if not most of the white North, actually approved of what John Brown had done. Now that wasn't the case. A majority of the North almost certainly didn't approve of what John Brown had done, but there was enough of a mixed reaction to send tremors through the white South. This was the greatest nightmare of the white South. We talked about Nat Turner's Rebellion last time. That was scary enough to white Southerners, the notion that a black man would lead confederates in an effort to win their freedom through violence. But this was even worse because this is a Northern white man who's coming south and trying to incite what white Southerners would have considered servile insurrection.

So it's a tremendous shock to the white South, a white South that could, in their nightmare, see a full-scale bloodbath all across their section, a bloodbath led, precipitated, by white abolitionists from the North. Many white Southerners equated John Brown with abolitionists, abolitionists with Republicans, and Republicans with the whole North. A wave of near hysteria swept across many of the Southern states, the greatest since that that had been triggered by Nat Turner's Rebellion nearly three decades before. Militia companies drilled more regularly and more seriously. Volunteer military companies beefed up their numbers in the wake of John Brown. Support for secession mushroomed.

As one Southern Unionist, that is, a man who valued the Union above section, sadly observed after John Brown's raid, "This has wrought almost a complete revolution in the sentiments, thoughts, and hopes of the oldest and steadiest conservatives in the Southern states." And by conservatives he meant people who were more devoted to the Union than to the idea of Southern rights.

Several months after John Brown's raid there was another shock to the white South, and that came in the form of a series of unexplained fires in Texas. These fires were attributed to slaves who, like John Brown's followers, had in mind a general slave insurrection. There were fires in other parts of the South as well, and this helped feed this growing feeling that the white South was under siege. John Brown's raid, these fires in Texas—there was tremendous emotional capital invested in these kinds of things, and these events had a direct impact on the upcoming election of 1860.

William L. Yancey of Alabama was one of the most extreme Secessionist fire-eaters. The fire-eaters were way over toward one end of the political spectrum in the South. They were men who insisted on state rights, insisted on a very strong defense of slavery, the right to take slaves wherever you wanted to take them in the United States. The fire-eaters were agitators who were always pushing and pushing against any perceived threat from the North, always trying to rally whites in the South to take the strongest possible stance in favor of slavery and in favor of Southern state rights.

Well, William Yancey was one of these men, an Alabamian, and he persuaded the Alabama Democratic Party in January 1860 to instruct its delegates to the upcoming national presidential convention to insist that the national Democratic Party give complete protection to slavery in the territories. He said, if they don't give us that, if the Democratic Party does not go on record as absolutely protecting our right to carry our slave property into all the federal territories, we should walk out of the convention and refuse to be part of it. There was ample evidence at the time that several other Southern states would follow Alabama's lead.

So in the fall of 1859 and on into early 1860, in the summer of 1860, there is a good deal of quite volatile sectional emotion at work, and there is this group of fire-eaters in the South who are going to make their pitch for a very strong stance in favor of slavery with the Democratic Party.

Let's move on now to the conventions that selected presidential nominees in 1860, and we'll start with the Democrats, the great majority party since the time of Thomas Jefferson. The Democratic Party had always been the majority party, had elected more presidents than anyone else, had controlled Congress to a far greater degree than anyone else. Here the Democrats are in 1860, in this volatile year, and they're meeting in one of the worst imaginable places, Charleston, South Carolina, which is among the most radical of the hotbeds of Southern sentiment. It's not a location conducive to calm debate.

When the delegates met, they were immediately confronted with the choice of choosing between two platforms. The Yancey platform was put forward, which called for a slave code plank, an absolute protection of slavery in the territories. The rival platform was what was called the Douglas platform. It was named after Senator Steven A. Douglas of Illinois, the most prominent Democratic politician in the country at this point, the man who defeated Abraham Lincoln in a famous senatorial election in Illinois in 1858.

The Douglas platform was much more moderate than the Yancey platform. It called for popular sovereignty holding sway in the territories, that is, allowing the people of the individual territories to vote and decide whether they wanted to have slavery within their borders or not. Coupled with that, the Douglas platform promised to abide by a definitive decision from the Supreme Court on the question of whether the territories would be able to decide their own fate regarding whether or not they would have slavery. Northern Democrats would not go farther than the Douglas platform: That's it. We are not willing to give more than that, they said. We're willing to let the Court decide. We're willing to embrace popular sovereignty, but we will not do what the Yancey platform asks us to do.

The two platforms came up for a vote, and the Douglas platform won on an almost straight sectional vote with Northerners voting for the Douglas platform and Southerners voting for the Yancey platform. Forty-nine delegates from eight Southern states walked out of the convention, and they met in another hall. They adopted the Yancey platform, and they waited to see what would happen. Steven A. Douglas proved unable to get two-thirds of the remaining delegates to support his platform. You needed two-thirds in the Democratic Party. That had been a sop to the South as well because it protected the South against just a strict majority, which the North almost always would be able to have.

The convention, in the end, after 57 ballots, the main part of the convention adjourned and agreed to meet in Baltimore a few weeks later. They reconvened in Baltimore. The same fissures appeared between the Southern

Democrats and the Northern Democrats, and there was another walkout on the part of Southern delegates. This time 110 left, more than a third of the whole, and you had the phenomenon of the Democratic Party split in two and nominating two slates for president and vice president.

The regular Democrats nominated Douglas and a moderate from Georgia named Hershel V. Johnson to be his running mate. The Southern Democrats nominated John C. Breckinridge of Kentucky, vice president under James Buchanan and later a Confederate general and Confederate Secretary of War for part of the Civil War. Breckinridge is the Southern Democratic candidate. The running mate is Joseph Lane of Oregon, who will be the vice presidential nominee. The Democratic Party, in short, is in a shambles as the election approaches in 1860.

The Republicans met in Chicago in mid-May. They met in between the Charleston convention and the Baltimore convention of the Democrats, and they were upbeat. They understood very well what was going on with the Democratic Party. They knew that they would carry most of the North, and they knew that to win the electoral college they needed only to carry the states they had carried in 1856 plus Pennsylvania and either Illinois or Indiana. All three of those last states had gone Democratic in 1856.

The Republicans sensed victory, but they were going to be careful in this election. They were facing the prospect of choosing from a number of potential candidates. Most of the party wanted to play it safe and pick someone who would appeal to the widest possible spectrum of Northern voters. In other words, don't embrace anyone considered too radical on the question of slavery. The frontrunner was William Henry Seward of New York, a longtime politician, powerful Whig politician, and then a Republican. But he was considered unsafe on slavery—too far in advance, too far toward the abolitionist end of the spectrum to appeal to more moderate voters in the North.

Salmon P. Chase of Ohio was another man that in the end the convention considered too radical on the slavery issue to appeal to the broad spectrum of Northern voters. They were both considered, especially Seward, to be men with histories that were too long as well. Their political careers had simply gone on so long that they had managed to alienate a good number of people along the way. So they were considered iffy candidates on those grounds as well.

A conservative named Edward Bates from Missouri was also put forward. He was another ex-Whig. He was supported by Horace Greeley, the powerful editor of the *New York Tribune*. But Bates was considered too conservative by many of the delegates to the convention. Weaknesses in all of these men's appeal strengthened the candidacy of Abraham Lincoln of Illinois. Lincoln had only held national office very briefly back in the 1840s as a one-term member of the House of Representatives, but he had a fairly high national profile because of some lectures he had given in the late 1850s and in 1860 and because of the famous senatorial contest in Illinois in 1858 with Steven A. Douglas.

Lincoln had very bright managers. He was supported only by Illinois initially, but his managers moved around from delegation to delegation and said, we understand that you're in favor of candidate X or candidate Y as your first choice. What we hope you will do is make our man Lincoln your second choice, and if your candidate doesn't make it, we hope you will shift your votes to support Abraham Lincoln on subsequent ballots.

Lincoln was a very good second choice. He was a moderate. He was against the extension of slavery. No slavery in the territories, said Lincoln, but he was not for immediate emancipation. Now, personally, he was antislavery, but his political stance was, the Constitution protects slavery where it exists, and therefore we must respect that. But no slavery in the territories, said Lincoln. He was also safe on the Republican economic issues, which I'll talk about more in just a minute. And he was potentially strong in the Lower North, those areas of southern Illinois and southern Ohio and southern Indiana, parts of Pennsylvania, where abolitionist sentiment, sentiment relating to the issue of slavery, was not nearly as strong as it was in New England and parts of the Upper North. Lincoln seemed to be ideal in many ways.

It took the Republican Convention just three ballots to decide on Abraham Lincoln. A former Democrat from Maine, Hannibal Hamlin, was nominated for the vice presidential slot. Again, that will broaden appeal of the party during the election: a former Democrat and Abraham Lincoln, a former Whig, heading the ticket for the Republican Party.

The Republican platform called for, first, no slavery in the federal territories, and that's the most important plank. No extension of slavery into the federal territories. Second, it deplored John Brown's raid, the platform did. Third, it said that it would not strike against slavery where it already existed. We do not want to kill slavery in the Southern states where it already exists, said the Republican platform. They're officially on record in that regard. And, finally, the platform called for a Homestead Act. It called for internal improvements, that is, government support for things such as railroads, harbor improvements, canals, and so forth, big public works projects.

It called for a transcontinental railroad as part of that, and it also supported protective tariffs to help fledgling industry in the United States compete with products from abroad. Take all of these economic parts of the platform and put them together, and you see a clear expression of what we talked about last time as well, the mercantile business, free labor sentiments of the modernizing North. The Republican Party clearly represents that kind of sentiment.

So we have three candidates in the field now: the two Democrats and Abraham Lincoln for the Republicans. A fourth party also put forward a ticket, a party called the Constitutional Union Party. This was essentially the old American or Know-Nothing Party of the mid-1850s without the fiercely nativist element of that party, without the vicious anti-Catholic, anti-immigrant rhetoric of the American or Know-Nothing Party.

Many of these Constitutional Union supporters would have been Know-Nothings or American Party people. They took a middle-of-the-road course. They didn't even mention slavery in their official platform. What they tried to do was appeal to the nation strictly on the basis of the Union. They said, we love the Union. The Union is more important than anything else in our political life, and we should put aside our sectional differences and support the Union and the Constitution and our national laws. The candidates were John Bell of Tennessee and Edward Everett of Massachusetts. So there are the four candidates: Lincoln and Douglas and Breckinridge and John Bell of Tennessee.

Let's move on to the campaign itself now. The campaign offered the interesting spectacle, really, of a couple of campaigns going on at the same time. Four men with very different platforms and constituencies all profess to love the Union, and their rhetoric, I think, should not be viewed as just rhetoric. I think they really did love the Union each in his own way, each of the parties in its own way, but it shows the degree to which the nation had divided in terms of how it understood what the best interest of each part of the nation was.

Now let me just quote from each of them. Douglas said, "The Federal Union must be preserved." Breckinridge said that the Constitution and the equality of the states are symbols of everlasting Union. To Lincoln, what he called the perpetual Union, indivisible and eternal, was an article of faith, and, of course, for John Bell and the Constitutional Union Party, Union was all there was. That is what they were running on. They were running on Union.

The canvas quickly became a race in the North and a race in the South. It was Lincoln versus Douglas in the North and Bell versus Breckinridge in the South. Lincoln and Douglas had no chance for electoral votes in the slave states; Bell and Breckinridge no chance for electoral votes in the free states. Lincoln wasn't even on the ballot. The Republican candidate for president was not even on the ballot in a number of Southern states. That's very hard for us to imagine now that a major candidate of one of the great parties would not even appear on our ballot if we lived in certain states, but that was the situation in 1860.

It became clear very early on that Lincoln could lose only if the other three candidates somehow managed to fuse their tickets and pool their support, and of course that was impossible. The notion that defeat was almost certain brought great gloom to the Democratic efforts.

The South worked itself into another state of hysteria during the campaign as rumors of slave insurrections and of what might happen if the Republicans won swept across many of the Southern states. Remember that, to many white Southerners, Republican meant abolitionist, and abolitionist had all kinds of awful connotations. A Republican victory might let loose a flood of John Browns on the South. That kind of fear, I think, helped make this canvas all the more emotional in much of the South.

In fact, during the course of the campaign, just about every leader from the Lower South, that is, that bottom tier of Southern states—Texas, Louisiana, Mississippi, Alabama, Georgia, South Carolina, and Florida—just about every major leader from those Lower South or Deep South states said that secession might well follow a Republican win. As one of these people put it, "This government and Republicanism cannot live together." That is in the words of a Georgian.

Now, Republicans tended to discount the talk of secession because they'd heard it before. They'd heard it in the early 1830s from South Carolina. They had heard it again in the early 1850s. To them it seemed a case of the little boy crying wolf again. If we don't get our way, we're going to do this, we're going to do that. We'll secede if we don't get our way. That kind of rhetoric had been present before, and the South had not acted on it. South Carolina hadn't even acted on it. And so many Republicans, most Republicans, I think, simply didn't believe that the South would do anything here.

Lincoln stayed in Springfield. He made no public statements during the campaign—none. He said, my record is clear. If you want to know what my stance is on any issue, look at what I've said. I stand by what I've said. I don't need to add to what I already have placed in the public record.

Douglas did take threats of secession seriously. He's the only candidate who campaigned throughout the United States. It was really an act of bravery on his part because he met extremely, extremely hostile crowds in much of the South. There were threats against him in parts of the South. Nonetheless, he campaigned everywhere, calling for union, trying to calm Southern fears. It was a performance, however, that had very little effect in the South, and when he stopped in Mobile, Alabama, the day before the election, his secretary noted, "The Senator is more hopeless than I have ever seen him before." Douglas gave it his best effort, but it was to no avail.

Democratic campaigners in the South, the Breckinridge people, stressed the slavery issue to the exclusion, really, of all others. Democrats in the North concentrated on race. They laid out a range of awful things that they said would happen if the Republicans won. There'd be racial amalgamation, they said. There'd be tremendous competition for white labor by black labor. They put out cartoons of black people and white people kissing each other while Lincoln and Greeley looked on smiling. It was the most virulent and base kind of racial appeal by the Democratic Party across much of the North.

Republicans in the Upper North, the more abolitionist, the more antislavery parts of the North, stressed the issue of slavery. In the Lower North, they tended to focus on economic issues—the tariff in Pennsylvania, internal improvements in the Homestead Bill in the West and California. So we have different Republican messages in different parts of the nation.

The Democrats, the Republicans were quick to point out, had opposed all of these economic measures, and if we can only win this election we can finally begin to enact our program, they said. They said, the fact that dough face lackeys like Buchanan, that is, Northern men who tended to side with the South on issues of slavery and on economic issues, those kinds of Northerners had been in league with the South for too long, said the Republicans. It's time to throw them all overboard and try to get our program in place.

Now, most abolitionists in the North, black and white, were not thrilled with the Republican Party platform. It didn't go nearly far enough to suit them. It accepted slavery where slavery existed, and of course they didn't want that. It did keep it out of the territories, which was good, but it didn't go nearly as far as the abolitionists would have had it go. Still, the vast majority of abolitionists supported the Republican Party because, among the four choices, it was clearly the party that was most attuned to what the abolitionists hoped to achieve. By the end of the campaign there was a good deal of genuine enthusiasm across the North for Lincoln, his candidacy, and the Republican Party.

There were massive marches and rallies that recalled to many the great log cabin and hard cider campaign of William Henry Harrison in 1840, when many of the trappings of modern campaigning first made their appearance on the American stage. The image of Lincoln the rail-splitter was perfect for those who subscribed to the free labor ideology, the notion that we owned our labor and we could use that labor to move up into the property-owning class. Lincoln was a perfect example of that. He began splitting rails and otherwise working with his hands and soon became a member of the property class and then a prominent member of the property class. Here is a poster child, as it were, for free labor in Abraham Lincoln, and the Republicans made a great deal of that in the North.

Meanwhile, a fearful South expecting the worst watched the canvas unfold. A confident Republican Party in the North eagerly anticipated the day when the ballots would be cast, and so they were cast, and let's move on to see what the results were. They were nothing unanticipated. It was pretty clear what was going to happen, and that is exactly what did happen. Abraham Lincoln won 180 electoral votes and nearly 1.9 million popular votes.

He carried every free state except New Jersey, which he split with Steven Douglas. Lincoln got four of the electoral votes; Douglas got three in New Jersey. In every state of the North except California, Oregon, and New Jersey—with those three exceptions—Lincoln outpolled all of his opponents put together. His 180 electoral votes were an absolute majority. Even if all of his opponents had pooled their electoral votes, Lincoln still would have won the election of 1860 and by a fairly comfortable margin.

The other three candidates won a much larger popular vote, about 2.8 million. Nearly a million more votes were cast for the other three candidates than were cast for Abraham Lincoln. Lincoln's percentage was just under 40 percent of the popular vote, but their electoral votes, all those other candidates put together, only amounted to 123. If all the other candidates had run together under one banner they would have carried just three more states. They would have carried California and Oregon and New Jersey, and they still would have lost decisively in the electoral college.

When we break down the non-Lincoln votes, Steven A. Douglas received about 1.35 million votes. He was the second largest vote getter in the canvas, but he only won 12 electoral votes—second most popular votes, only 12 electoral votes. He got those three from New Jersey, and he got Missouri's nine. John C. Breckinridge tallied about 675,000 popular votes. He carried 72 electoral votes. He did very well among the slave states. He carried all of the Lower South, the entire tier of the seven Lower South states. He also carried Maryland, Delaware, Arkansas, and North Carolina—all slave states, of course. John Bell won the border and Upper South states of Tennessee, Virginia, and Kentucky. That gave him 39 electoral votes. He had just under 600,000 popular votes.

Lincoln's greatest strength came from the upper sections of the North, the most staunchly antislavery sections of the North and in the Yankee counties of Ohio, Indiana, Illinois, and Iowa. In those parts of the North, New England and the Upper North, he polled about 60 percent of the vote. In the other parts of the free states, he barely managed a majority of the popular vote. Thus, the strongly antislavery portion of the North was the key to his victory, and that meant influence for that segment of Northern society in the next Congress and within the Lincoln administration.

Although many abolitionists had been cool toward the Republican Party during the election and before the campaign actually began, most of them rejoiced at the Republican victory. Charles Francis Adams, the son and grandson of United States presidents and an abolitionist himself, a founder of the Free-Soil and Republican Parties in Massachusetts, sat back and assessed the results of the campaign, and he spoke for many other abolitionists when he said, with Lincoln's election, the great revolution has actually taken place. The country has thrown off the domination of the slaveholders.

So 1860 was a momentous political year in United States history. In the wake of seismic events at Harper's Ferry in 1859, the nation had gone to the polls. They had been presented with a stark choice. We're often given choices that don't seem really to be choices. The candidates often seem to be very similar in modern elections. That wasn't the case in 1860. There was a clear choice. If you vote for the Republicans, there will be no more slavery in the territories. There'll be a different economic agenda. If you vote for Breckinridge, there will be an absolute guarantee for slavery and so forth. There was a real choice in 1860.

The Republicans won. They quite astonishingly won. They'd only been a party for a few years, and here in their second contest they had elected a man president. The great question left hanging after the votes were counted was, what next? What will the South do? What will the Southern reaction be? And that's the topic we'll turn to in our next lecture.

The Lower South Secedes
Lecture 3

[W]ith Abraham Lincoln and the Republicans triumphant in the presidential canvas of 1860, the great question facing the United States in mid-November 1860 and the topic that we'll take up in this lecture is how the South would react to the verdict at the polls.

Many white Southerners considered the Republican victory in 1860 a triumph for those in the North who hoped to kill the institution of slavery. This was especially true in the seven states of the Deep (or Lower) South (South Carolina, Alabama, Mississippi, Louisiana, Georgia, Texas, and Florida), where pro-secessionist forces quickly organized. Beginning with South Carolina in December 1860, all the Lower South states passed ordinances of secession by the first week of February 1861. They sent delegates to a convention in Montgomery, Alabama, where they wrote a constitution and established a government for a new nation called the Confederate States of America.

Self-consciously modeling themselves on their revolutionary forebears and claiming to be their successors, the founders of the Confederacy chose moderate leaders and sought to entice the eight slaveholding states still in the Union (Arkansas, Delaware, Kentucky, Maryland, Missouri, North Carolina, Tennessee, and Virginia) to join them. This first phase of the secession movement represented a risky effort on the part of the Lower South to protect the institution of slavery—this in the face of a defeat at the polls that promised, by their reading of events, to undermine the economic and social bases of their society.

Jefferson Davis was named president of the Confederacy in 1861.

Prints and Photographs Division, Library of Congress.

The Montgomery Convention in early February 1861 established the Confederacy. The Confederate and United States constitutions offer an interesting comparison:

- There were many similarities of thought and language.

- There were key differences regarding slavery and Federal versus state power.

- The Confederate Constitution outlawed congressional outlays for internal improvements and prohibited protective tariffs.

- Ironically, the Confederate Constitution also prohibited secession.

The Convention produced essentially moderate work. William L. Yancey and other radical secessionists were absent. Moderates Jefferson Davis (Mississippi) and Alexander H. Stephens (Georgia) were chosen as provisional President and Vice President, respectively, pending general elections. Both Davis and Stephens were "reluctant" secessionists. The Convention avoided radical actions in an attempt to appeal to the eight slave states of the Upper South and refused to allow the re-introduction of the African slave trade. This represented the sentiment in the Lower South.

It will not come as a surprise that one thing the Confederate Constitution did was explicitly protect the institution of slavery.

Immediate secessionists (e.g., Breckinridge supporters) wanted each state to act at once. Cooperationists (e.g., Bell and some Douglas supporters) favored joint action regarding secession. Unionists (typically in the Upper South and border states) favored working out a compromise with the North. Many Northerners—including Lincoln—thought the Cooperationists were against secession and expected a backlash in the South against secessionist sentiment.

Southerners took different stances about whether Montgomery represented a revolutionary or legal response to Lincoln's election. Initially, secession was compared to the American Revolution of 1776 as an exercise in throwing off the yoke of an onerous central power. Although the hope was for peaceful separation, the Confederate States of America took several military actions during this period. They seized Federal forts and arsenals, activated the militia, and authorized an army of 100,000 men. Later arguments insisted that the Lower South had acted legally under the United States Constitution by asserting state sovereignty.

Secession cannot be disentangled from the institution of slavery. The Lower South embraced secession as a means to stave off Northern efforts to strike at slavery. White Southerners feared that their social and economic fabric would be destroyed by a dominant North, and the Republican Party's victory in 1860 focused their fears. Postwar Southern arguments tried to shift focus away from slavery. One argument revolved around constitutional issues, and both Davis and Stephens wrote lengthy tomes on this issue. In studying this era and this question, we need to note what people said at the time to properly evaluate retrospective comments. ■

Essential Reading

McPherson, *Battle Cry of Freedom: The Civil War Era*, chapter 8.

Potter, *The Impending Crisis, 1848–1861*, chapters 17–18.

Supplementary Reading

Davis, *"A Government of Our Own": The Making of the Confederacy*.

Thomas, *The Confederate Nation, 1861–1865*, chapter 3.

1. Did the secessionists of the Lower South make a good case that they were the heirs of the American revolutionary generation? Support your answer.

2. Would secession have been likely in 1860–61 without the presence of slavery?

The Lower South Secedes
Lecture 3—Transcript

We left off in our last lecture with Abraham Lincoln and the Republicans triumphant in the presidential canvas of 1860. The great question facing the United States in mid-November 1860 and the topic that we'll take up in this lecture is how the South would react to the verdict at the polls. We'll consider five aspects of this broad topic.

We'll look first at the Lower South's immediate move toward secession. Then we'll move on to the Montgomery Convention that had delegates from the Lower South states that established the new nation, the Confederate States of America. We'll then look at the degree to which the convention in Montgomery represented the people of the states of the Lower South. We'll move on to the question of whether this should be considered a revolution on the part of the Deep Southern states in reaction to the Republican victory. Finally, we'll address the question of how important slavery was in the secession movement in December 1860 through March 1861.

Let's start with the Lower South's reaction to Lincoln's election. Most white Southerners, certainly most white Southerners in the Deep South or the Lower South, read the election returns as a clear-cut victory for those in the North who hoped to put an end to slavery, "the peculiar institution," as it was called in the nineteenth century. A Richmond newspaper summed up the feelings of many across the South in these words: "A party founded on the single sentiment of hatred to African slavery is now the controlling power. No claptrap about the Union can alter this or weaken its force." Republicans will get after slavery, is the feeling on the part of this newspaper and on the part of much of the white South.

Now, contrary to what most Republicans expected and in contrast to how the white South had reacted in the past to perceived threats from the North, the Lower South states moved very quickly toward secession in the wake of Lincoln's election. South Carolina called immediately for a convention to consider secession, and, within another six weeks, the rest of the Lower South had followed suit. And each of the seven Lower South states voted to leave the Union within a very brief period.

South Carolina was first, passing its ordinance of secession on December 20, 1860. The official vote was 169 to 0 in South Carolina to leave the Union. Next was Mississippi on January 9, 1861, the vote 85 to 15. Then came Florida the next day on January 10, the vote 62 to 7. Alabama followed on January 11, the vote 61 to 39—a much closer vote that reflected the divisions within that state. There're tremendous geographical divisions in terms of how Alabamians viewed the sectional crisis. The up country, the hill country of northern Alabama, reacted very differently than the Black Belt counties did, for example, and that vote reflects the fact that there were divisions in Alabama.

Georgia was next on January 19, its vote 208 to 89. Next out was Louisiana, which left on January 26, the vote 113 to 17. The final Deep South state to take up the issue and to vote to leave was Texas, which voted on the 1st of February 1861 to leave the Union. Texas left over the strenuous objections of Governor Sam Houston, the most famous man in the state, the most famous Texan, the great hero from the days of the Texas Revolution.

Sam Houston was a staunch Unionist, and his behavior, I think, illustrates the fact that we should never fall into the trap of thinking that everybody in the Deep South favored secession. Even in the Deep South there were a number of people who did not favor secession, and Sam Houston exemplified those people. He was governor of the state during the secession crisis. He fought it as hard and as long as he could. He said, this is a mistake. If we go down this road it's going to weaken our society rather than strengthen it. We're going to lose the things that we think we're going to safeguard by embracing secession. Don't do it, said Sam Houston.

Houston refused to recognize the Secession Convention, which met in Austin in January 1861. He just said, I'm not even going to acknowledge that you're doing this, and he went along his way as governor. But after the state voted to go out of the Union, Houston's days were numbered. He was removed from office. Houston continued to insist that Texans owed no allegiance to the Confederacy, or to any confederacy that would be formed, I should say. But he was a voice in the wilderness, so to speak, or at least he was in a distinct minority in Texas as the secession movement rolled on there.

He was removed from office, as I said. He retired to his home a very unhappy and embittered man because of the road that Texas had taken in this crisis after Lincoln's election. The Secession Convention in Texas simply declared the governor's office vacant and named the lieutenant governor to replace Houston.

So here by February 1, very quickly by February 1, there're seven states out of the Union. The entire tier of Deep South states had decided very quickly that each of them could not remain in the Union, and they were gone. They all then sent delegates to a convention to meet in Montgomery, Alabama, which will be our second topic in this lecture. They gathered in Montgomery, Alabama, to draft founding documents for a new slaveholding republic.

Delegates from those seven seceding states met in early February 1861, their task was to draft a constitution and put in place a provisional government that would control the country until regular elections could be held. Montgomery would be the seat of the government for this incipient Confederate States of America. The delegates used the United States Constitution as their model. In fact, you can picture them holding the U.S. Constitution in one hand and having a blank piece of paper in the other hand and then simply transferring most of what is in the U.S. Constitution into their new document.

That's one reason they could work so quickly. Unlike the delegates to the Philadelphia Convention back in that steamy summer of 1787, these men in Montgomery had a clear blueprint from which to work, and that's what they did, and they worked very expeditiously. They made only a few changes in the United States Constitution, changes that reflected the state rights, pro-slavery concerns that had caused them to secede in the first place.

The final Confederate Constitution was completed in March after acceptance in February, and here's the new founding document. Here are a couple of the changes between the Confederate Constitution and the United States Constitution. It will not come as a surprise that one thing the Confederate Constitution did was explicitly protect the institution of slavery. The word "slavery" or "slave" does not appear in the United States Constitution, of course, although there are euphemisms used. The Confederate Constitution explicitly guaranteed slavery in the states and in all the territories.

It also forbade passage of protective as opposed to revenue tariffs and outlawed congressional appropriations for internal improvements. That's the antithesis of the Republican program, of course, as put forward in the Republican 1860 platform. There won't be government money for internal improvements. There won't be protective tariffs. The Confederate Constitution also omitted the general welfare clause from the United States Constitution and stated that, in ratifying the document, each state acted "in its sovereign and independent character."

Other changes included limiting the president to a single six-year term and giving the president a line item veto. Those are things that have been debated as possible amendments to our Constitution over the years. Interestingly, the Confederate Constitution also said that states that entered into this compact couldn't leave, which is very unusual. They've just left the United States, but now they're saying that once you're on our team, you're not going to leave our team.

The extreme fire-eaters, men such as William L. Yancey, who was not even a delegate to the convention, had very little to say in the deliberations in Montgomery. They are not a major presence in Montgomery. This is often the case. The more radical individuals who precipitate a crisis and who provide the leadership in the revolutionary phase of a movement or the violent phase of a movement often are not the ones who sit down around the table to undertake the hard work of writing constitutions or putting in place governments that will work.

Our revolutionary generation is an excellent example of this. The Washingtons and Hamiltons and Jeffersons and Adamses who played such prominent roles in drafting our great founding documents are not the same ones who were out in the street, so to speak, during the crisis with Britain. The John Hancocks and the Sam Adamses and those men were not the ones who were present to write the great documents.

The same thing is true on the Confederate side. Much more moderate men held sway in Montgomery than the William L. Yanceys and others who had agitated for a long time to have some kind of break from the United States. The delegates in Montgomery selected Jefferson Davis of Mississippi and

Alexander Hamilton Stephens of Georgia to be the provisional president and vice president, respectively, of this new nation. Later legislation called for election of permanent officers in November of 1861 and their inauguration in February of 1862, but until that happened, until the general elections were held later in 1861, the provisional Congress would be made up of the delegates in Montgomery, and Davis and Alexander Stephens would be the provisional president and provisional vice president of the Confederacy.

Now it's significant, I think, that both Davis and Stephens were considered to be very moderate. Jefferson Davis was, in many ways, a logical choice to be the new president. He was probably the most eminent Southern statesman of the late antebellum years. He occupied a position somewhat like that that John C. Calhoun had held for many years, although he was not as great a thinker as John C. Calhoun, certainly not as original a thinker as Calhoun, and didn't inspire quite the admiration among white Southerners that Calhoun had.

Having said all of that, Jefferson Davis was a man of significant stature in the late antebellum South and a man who made sense as a leader of this new nation. A senator from Mississippi, he'd been Secretary of War, and he had occupied a number of other important positions. He was at best a lukewarm secessionist. He had not been in the vanguard of the secession movement in Mississippi or for the South as a whole. He had embraced it reluctantly as he saw the situation coming to a point where the South might really be at a disadvantage, at least in his mind.

Alexander Stephens was a former Whig. Davis had always been a Democrat. Alexander H. Stephens was a former Whig. He was an even more reluctant secessionist than Jefferson Davis. He was a Georgian. Georgia had been tremendously divided over the question of secession. There were bitter, bitter debates in Georgia during the secession crisis, and Alexander Stephens had been a moderate voice in Georgia during those debates after the election of Abraham Lincoln. He steadfastly had sought a way out of the crisis of secession, but here he was as the provisional vice president of this new Confederate States of America.

I think that the convention selected these men first of all because they were able. As I said, no question about that. Stephens was brilliant, quirky, very quick to take offense. He was a tiny man. He only weighed about 100 pounds. Not much there except a powerful intellect but clearly a man of substance. Jefferson Davis was a man of substance as well. That is the most important reason they were chosen. But they were also chosen, I think, to send a message to the Upper South, to the eight slave states that were still in the Union.

Never forget that fewer than half the slave states are gone at this stage. No one knows how many other states are going to go. Don't ever fall into the trap of reading backward into history everything we know to try to understand what's going on. No one knew how many states would end up seceding. All they knew was that seven were gone, and these men in Montgomery want to send a message to the eight slave states that are still in the Union that were moderates. They're saying, we're selecting moderate leaders. We are responsible. We're setting up a reasonable government that could accommodate the wishes and needs of you less strident states, slave states, that have chosen not to leave at this point.

I think that same kind of thinking, that same kind of moderate thinking, caused the convention to refuse to reopen the African slave trade. A number of the fire-eaters pushed for that. Reopen the slave trade. We're proudly a slaveholding republic now. Let's go ahead and start importing slaves again.

The convention said no. They knew that they would lose some of the militant secessionists on that point, but they also knew that many in the Upper South had been against the slave trade for years and that foreign observers, especially England and France, were against the slave trade, very strongly. They'd abolished slavery, both of them, England and France. The British Navy, the Royal Navy, tried to stop the slave trade. These men in Montgomery knew that if they sought to reopen the slave trade it would send a very radical message not only abroad but to the states of the Upper South, and they did not want to do that. So, in all, I think we have a very moderate group at work in Montgomery, Alabama.

Let's move on to the question of whether these moderates in Montgomery, or generally moderate men, represented accurately their constituencies in the Deep South states. Are these men indicative of what's going on in the Deep South? The process had gone so quickly from the first calling of secession conventions to the meeting of the convention in Montgomery, Alabama, that it sometime seems that there must have been near unanimity in the Deep South states on the issue of secession. Let's get out; let's get out now. We all agree on this. That's sort of the portrait that emerges of the Deep South.

The whole process had taken considerably less than four months from when South Carolina voted to leave the Union until there's a Confederate government in place. Now that's less time than it took, as I said earlier, for the Philadelphia Convention to draft our Constitution, but I don't think we should be confused by that apparent swiftness. There was a range of opinion in the South, in the slaveholding South, and even in the Deep South as to what the best course of action should be in response to the Republican victory.

For our purposes, I think we can break opinion down into three broad camps in the slaveholding South. The first camp would be the immediate secessionists, those who wanted individual action by each state now. Each state should decide and either go or not go. That was their attitude. Let the chips fall where they will. Breckinridge backers were very prominent in this group.

A second group we'll call cooperationists favored waiting until the South could act as a whole, until they could act in union with one another—in other words, correspond with each other, try to decide what the best policy would be, and then do something as a group rather than just going off one state at a time. Many of the upland counties with fewer slaves and some Bell and Douglas supporters would fall into the cooperationist camp. Alexander H. Stephens was a cooperationist during the debates over secession.

A third group would be called the unconditional Unionists. These are people who opposed secession, period. They believed that the South had a better chance of achieving what it wanted by staying in the Union. After all, the Constitution still protected slavery. Slave property had always been safe within the United States. These Unionists said, we should stay in the United States and try to do the best we can there. These men were strongest in the Upper South and the border states, although there were some of them, witness Sam Houston, who were in the Deep South states as well. So we have the immediate secessionists, the cooperationists, and the Unionists.

Now, outside of South Carolina, where secessionists were a very large majority, about 40 percent of the Lower South was made up of cooperationists. It's a significant chunk of that population, but many Northerners tended to confuse cooperationists with Unionists, and Abraham Lincoln was one of those in the North who did that. They tended to think that cooperationists were not in favor of secession just as Unionists weren't, but, in fact, cooperationists were generally in favor of secession but in favor of united action on secession rather than the action of individual states. So it's a misreading of Southern opinion on the part of many Northerners.

Many Northerners, including Lincoln, counted on a backlash against secessionists. They thought this great Unionist majority in the South would assert itself and push aside the secessionist leaders and bring the Southern states back to their senses, so to speak. It was an incorrect expectation on the part of Lincoln and many other observers in the North because cooperationists would have demanded things that the Republican Party could not accept. They would have demanded a federal slave code for the territories or some guarantee of slavery in the territories, and the Republicans could not do that. It had been too important to their being elected.

By mid-January 1861, Republican leaders had made it very clear that they were not going to make any concession on the question of slavery in the territories, and, in fact, they said, we're not going to make any other concessions, period. The white South has been placated too long, the slaveholding South, and we are not going to make any more efforts to placate the white South.

With state after state leaving the union, cooperationists joined the secessionists, and you had a very strong majority in the Deep South in favor of getting out of the Union. And, as I said earlier, Alexander Hamilton Stephens is the best example of that. He accepted the vice presidency of the

Confederacy and showed clearly by doing that that there was little chance of working out a deal that most white Southerners would consider palatable. It is not a question of there being this great hidden Union sentiment in the Deep South. It's not there, although many people thought that it was.

Let's move on to the question of whether what these seceding states were doing should be considered revolutionary. Are these revolutionaries at work in the Deep South? At first many white Southerners spoke of secession as the Revolution of 1861. You see that again and again: This is our Revolution of 1861. They compared what they were doing to what the American colonists had done in throwing off the British yoke in 1776. And it was a tremendous release for passions, this secessionist movement was, passions that had built up over several decades of wrangling over questions relating to slavery. Finally, there's a release. Finally we're doing something instead of just calling each other names. And of course that pressure had built up especially since John Brown's raid back in the fall of 1859.

Now, most people hoped there would be a peaceful separation. Again, secession doesn't necessarily mean war. We know a war came now, but they didn't know a war was coming then, and we shouldn't ever assume that they did. They hoped that they would be allowed to go peacefully, but they did begin to prepare for war. Federal forts and other installations were seized. State militias were beefed up in the Confederate states, and the provisional Confederate Congress authorized an army of 100,000 men—100,000 men. To put that in perspective, the Unites States army at this stage had about 15,000 men, between 15,000 and 16,000 men. So the Confederacy is saying, we can have an army of six or seven times as large as the United States Army.

In time, most Southerners came to argue that they had not precipitated a revolution, at least not in the accepted sense of the word that suggests armed revolt against a sitting government. They argued instead that they had acted under the Constitution, that, in fact, they were the true inheritors of the revolutionary tradition. We're the true inheritors of what the founders had tried to do, they argued. The founders set up a slaveholding republic. We're trying to set up a slaveholding republic where our rights as protected under the Constitution would be made safe.

The original Union, they said, had been a compact of sovereign states that had come together to act as a nation. Those states as a group had authorized the federal government to act as their agent, but they hadn't given up their sovereignty in 1787, argued the Confederates in 1861. They had retained that sovereignty, and now the Southern states were merely reasserting that sovereignty when they left the Union and came together to form a new nation.

By contending that secession was legal rather than revolutionary, these Confederates hoped to place their nation on an equal footing with other nations in the Western world and thereby gain legitimacy. They quoted from the Declaration of Independence, and they quoted from the Constitution. They quoted from the Declaration that part that said you could dissolve an old government that was unjust and create a new one. They didn't quote the part dealing with the equality of all men, which the Republicans liked to point out to them.

Some Southerners, in fact, turned the argument around and accused Republicans of being the true revolutionaries. They're the ones who are trying to depart from the architectural plan of the founders, they said. They're the ones who are going to strike at slavery, something that the founding generation protected. If you want to know who the radicals are here, look to the Republicans—don't look to us. All we're trying to do, they argued, is safeguard our right to hold our property and to do the other things that the founders envisioned all Americans would be able to do.

I think the important point is that if we're going to say that the South, the Deep South, was pursuing a revolution, it was clearly a conservative one if such a thing is possible, if you can have a conservative revolution, because they're trying to protect what they already have. They're not trying to create something new. They're not trying to get something they don't have in founding their new Confederate nation. They're trying to protect what they already had under the old Constitution.

And that was the key as we move on to our last section, the question of whether slavery was really at the heart of this or not. I think the key is that the secession of the Lower South was about whether they would be able to maintain their social system that was so inextricably bound up with the institution of black slavery. Secession was a gambling effort to protect the institution of slavery in the face of a defeat at the polls that promised, in Southern minds at least, white Southern minds at least, to unravel the economic and social fabric of their section.

The white South looked down the road and saw ever-increasing numbers of free states coming into the Union, controlling both houses of Congress. They saw Republican justices on the Supreme Court, put forward by Abraham Lincoln and maybe other Republican presidents. They saw a federal government willing to tolerate or even encourage men like John Brown. They may actually foster that kind of activity, the Republicans, believed many people in the white South. All of those things, all of those bad things, from a white Southern point of view, loomed in a future where the Republican Party would play a key role in the national government, where Abraham Lincoln and William Henry Seward and others would be in control.

After the war, after their utter defeat, many white Southerners looked back and argued that slavery wasn't very important in this whole process. In the myth of the Lost Cause, which we'll talk about later in the course, many of the writers said that it wasn't slavery we were concerned about, it was constitutional principle. We were trying to uphold the principles of the Constitution and the founding generation, and slavery was just one of many issues that were bound up in that. State sovereignty was another one. There were many that were important; it was not about slavery, argued many former Confederates after the war. Prominent among them were both Jefferson Davis and Alexander Hamilton Stephens, each of whom wrote a big, and I mean big, two-volume set of memoirs. Davis's is called *The Rise and Fall of the Confederate Government.* Alexander Stephens's is called *A Constitutional View of the Late War Between the States.*

Both of them are very difficult to read. In fact, Stephens's is impossible to read, I think. Anyone who can read that from front to end is a very tough person indeed. But in these two big works the two top officeholders of the Confederacy argued the straight constitutional view of why the war had come. It had been about the Constitution; it had been about state sovereignty. It had not been about protecting slavery. Slavery was almost incidental to what was going on at that point. I think it was important for them to distance themselves from slavery after the war because they knew that slavery was not embraced by the Western world. They were out of step with the Western world, and it would cast them in a bad light if they were perceived as primarily interested in slavery.

This is a perfect example of why it is important to see what people wrote at the time to understand what was really going on rather than what they wrote in retrospect because in 1861 the white South was not confused about how important slavery was. Let me just quote from a couple of people here, and I'll use Stephens and Jefferson Davis. Stephens said, "Our new government is founded upon the great truth that the Negro is not equal to the white man, that slavery, subordination to the superior race, is his natural and moral condition. This, our new government, is the first in the history of the world based upon this great physical, philosophical, and moral truth." That's Stephens in the midst of the secession crisis. Slavery seems awfully important to him there.

As for Davis, in his message to the Confederate Congress in late April 1861, he said, "The labor of African slaves was and is indispensable to the South's economic development. With interests of such overwhelming magnitude imperiled," he added, "the people of the Southern states were driven by the conduct of the North to the adoption of some course of action to avert the danger with which they were openly menaced." We're protecting our social system based on slavery, is what Jefferson Davis was saying there.

The Mississippi state convention put it even more bluntly, "A blow at slavery is a blow at civilization. We have no choice but submission to the mandates of abolition or dissolution of the Union." And testimony of that kind is very easy to find during the secession crisis itself.

My point is that if you want to know what was going on during the secession crisis, read what people were saying then. Davis and Stephens and the Mississippi state convention for secession, and most other Deep South whites, were not confused about how central slavery was to the process of secession. It absolutely was imbedded near the center.

So here we are in March 1861. We have seven states out of the Union, a slaveholding republic established with its capital at Montgomery. Everyone watched closely now to see if some or all of the remaining slave states would follow the lead of the Lower South. The reaction of those eight slave states and the crucial role in determining that reaction by events at Fort Sumter will be the subject of our next lecture.

The Crisis at Fort Sumter
Lecture 4

Between December 1860 and April 1861, James Buchanan and Abraham Lincoln, in turn, had to try to deal with the greatest crisis that the United States had ever faced, a crisis utterly unprecedented in American history. ... That crisis came to center on Fort Sumter in Charleston Harbor, which assumed enormous psychological importance to people in both the North and the South.

The period between the secession of the Lower South and the outbreak of war saw the United States and the Confederacy eye each other warily and contend for the support of eight slave states that remained in the Union. Lame-duck President James Buchanan and other Democrats sought to appeal to slaveholders with a range of compromises relating to slavery in the territories, but the Republicans stood firm in their demand for a total ban. Buchanan did not recognize the secession and stated that he would enforce the laws; however, he refused to coerce the seceding states. He proposed a constitutional amendment protecting slavery in the territories and the repeal of "personal liberty" laws in the North (these laws reflected a Northern states rights response to slavery and were given headlines by the Anthony Burns affair). Buchanan even proposed a movement to acquire Cuba and turn it into a slave state or states.

Senator John J. Crittenden of Kentucky offered the most famous compromise regarding the territories. Crittenden's constitutional amendment proposal favored the slaveholding South. For example, he proposed the extension of slavery in all territories below 36°30'. Republicans in the Senate defeated the bill twice. But because each side had a minimum demand on which it would not yield, there was no real hope for a compromise.

Lincoln pursued a careful path regarding the crisis before and after taking office. He remained quiet before succeeding Buchanan in March of 1861. He initially believed that Unionist sentiment in the South would assert itself. His inaugural address sought to place responsibility for the start of any hostilities on the Confederates. He stated that the Federal government would hold, occupy, and protect its installations in the South and continue to carry out governmental functions, such as the collection of customs tariffs. And he said that he would not use force but would enforce the laws.

The fate of Fort Sumter in Charleston Harbor came to be the focal point of the crisis, with many in the North insisting that it be retained as a United States installation and many Confederates arguing that it stood on South Carolina soil and should be seized. Abraham Lincoln's decision in April 1861 to resupply the fort triggered an aggressive response from Jefferson Davis's government. The resultant shelling and capture of the fort caused Lincoln to call for 75,000 volunteers to suppress the rebellion and that, in turn, prompted Virginia, North Carolina, Arkansas, and Tennessee to join the Confederacy.

James Buchanan, president of the United States from 1857 to 1861.

The Fort Sumter crisis unfolded as follows: Lincoln decided to resupply the fort with an unarmed vessel. An earlier attempt by Buchanan to do this had failed. The fort became a symbol for both sides. On March 5, 1861, the commanding officer of the fort sent a message saying that he was running out of provisions. In deciding to resupply the fort, Lincoln went against many of his advisers, including William Seward (secretary of war) and General Winfield Scott. Lincoln believed that Northern public opinion favored holding the fort.

The Davis Administration reacted by firing on the fort. Davis faced a range of poor options. He didn't want to appear to be the aggressor, so he asked the fort to surrender. Public opinion in the Confederacy supported seizing the fort; on April 15, gun batteries opened fire and bombarded the fort for 36 hours. News of the firing on Fort Sumter ignited passions across both the North and the South. The next day, President Lincoln called for 75,000 volunteers to put down the rebellion.

The Upper South seceded in reaction to Lincoln's call for volunteers. Virginia, North Carolina, Arkansas, and Tennessee decided that they must secede rather than supply troops to be used against the Confederacy. Public opinion in each state had been divided about secession. Lincoln's call convinced a majority in each state to support secession.

The war is imminent at this point. It's imminent, and there's no way to get around it in the view of most quite reasonable people on both sides.

The loss of the Upper South greatly complicated the task of restoring the Union. There were now eleven states in secession. The Upper South (especially North Carolina, Virginia, and Tennessee) supplied most of the Confederacy's soldiers. The Upper South contained vital industrial and agricultural resources for the Confederacy. The capital of the Confederate States was moved from Montgomery, Alabama, to Richmond, Virginia (which had 40 percent of the South's manufacturing capacity), in recognition of Virginia's importance. ■

Essential Reading

McPherson, *Battle Cry of Freedom: The Civil War Era*, chapters 8–9.

Potter, *The Impending Crisis, 1848–1861*, chapters 19–20.

Supplementary Reading

Current, *Lincoln and the First Shot*.

Potter, *Lincoln and His Party in the Secession Crisis*.

Stampp, *And the War Came: The North and the Secession Crisis, 1860–61*.

For more insight into President Lincoln and his political development, as well as a close look at his First Inaugural Address, we recommend the Great Course *Abraham Lincoln: In His Own Words* by Professor David Zarefsky of Northwestern University.

Questions to Consider

1. Were there any possible grounds for compromise between Republicans and Democrats that might have averted the crisis of 1861?

2. To whom would you assign primary responsibility for the outbreak of war in mid-April 1861?

The Crisis at Fort Sumter
Lecture 4—Transcript

As we saw in our last lecture, by February 1, 1861, seven states, seven slave states, had left the Union. That left eight slave states loyal to the Union: a tier of border states, Missouri, Kentucky, Maryland, and Delaware, and a tier of what were called the Upper South states, Arkansas, Tennessee, Virginia, and North Carolina.

Between December 1860 and April 1861, James Buchanan and Abraham Lincoln, in turn, had to try to deal with the greatest crisis that the United States had ever faced, a crisis utterly unprecedented in American history. They did so in very different ways. That crisis came to center on Fort Sumter in Charleston Harbor, which assumed enormous psychological importance to people in both the North and the South.

In this lecture we're going to do four things. We're going to examine efforts to diffuse the crisis during the last weeks of the Buchanan administration. We're going to explore Abraham Lincoln's path regarding the crisis, both before and right after he took office. We're going to describe events at Fort Sumter and the key Northern and Confederate decisions regarding its fate as the Unites States installation in Charleston Harbor. Finally, we're going to address the impact of Sumter's fall on the Upper South and the importance of the Upper South's movement to join the Confederacy. How much of a difference did it make that these four states of the Upper South—Arkansas, Tennessee, Virginia, and North Carolina—joined the Confederate States of America?

Let's begin with James Buchanan. Buchanan had a number of weeks in office before Abraham Lincoln would succeed him. Remember, Lincoln was elected in November of 1860, but under the old system he wouldn't take office until early March 1861. So you have this period during which the lame-duck Buchanan is presiding over an unfolding crisis regarding secession and eventually regarding what to do with Fort Sumter.

James Buchanan is a classic politician in that he began in the lower ranks of the Democratic Party and then very slowly and systematically made his way up through the ranks until he was the man obviously to select to carry the banner of the party in the 1856 presidential election. A hack might be too harsh a word to use for Buchanan, but he'd certainly been a good, loyal Democratic soldier. He'd been one of the most prominent of the "dough faces" in the North, that is, the Northern men of Southern principles, as they were called, Northern Democrats who did their best to try to smooth over differences between North and South, usually by taking positions favorable to what the slaveholding interests of the South wanted.

Poor Buchanan. You really have to pity him in one sense because he'd waited his whole life to be president, punched all the tickets he should have punched to become president, and, then, as soon as he did become president, this enormous sectional strife heated up. And he had to deal with problems in Kansas and Nebraska—violence there. He had to deal with the *Dred Scott* case before the Supreme Court. In fact, he had urged Roger B. Taney to make as broad a decision as possible in the *Dred Scott* case, as we talked about in our opening lecture.

Then came John Brown, and then came the election of 1860 and secession, and there's poor James Buchanan sitting in the White House. You can just see him hoping that he will be able to play out his string before absolute catastrophe befalls the nation. There he is, our old "dough face" friend, and he says, on the one hand, I refuse to accept the legitimacy of secession. You cannot secede, he said. He said he was going to enforce all the laws in those states, all of the federal laws in his capacity as the person who should oversee that, but he also said he would do nothing to coerce the seceded states back into the Union.

That statement upset Republicans tremendously, such as William Henry Seward and many, many others, never mind abolitionists. They said, well, Buchanan's trying to have it both ways. He said you can't secede, but he says he won't do anything to coerce those states back into the Union. Seward sarcastically noted that Buchanan's distinction between enforcement and coercion meant that "No state has the right to secede unless it wishes to and that it is the President's duty to enforce the laws unless somebody opposes him."

So the Republicans are very unhappy with James Buchanan. Buchanan blames the Republicans. He's unhappy with them. He thinks they have brought on the crisis, and what he tries to do in his last days in office as he watches so much happening in the South is come up with a way to placate yet again the slaveholding interests of the South. He puts forward a number of suggestions. He says, well why not a constitutional amendment protecting slavery in the territories, a firm protection for slavery in the territories forever? That would be one way to do this. He said, we could also annul the "personal liberty" laws in the North.

The personal liberty laws had been enacted in the mid-1850s. They had arisen out of a famous case involving a slave named Anthony Burns who escaped from Virginia to freedom in the North, in Massachusetts. He made the mistake of writing a letter home to his brother. The letter was found out. His master found out Anthony Burns was in Boston, and he moved to regain possession of Anthony Burns. He asked the federal government to help him regain his slave property.

Under the Fugitive Slave provision of the Compromise of 1850, the federal government was on record and was obligated to try to help recover escaped slave property. So the administration of Franklin Pierce, another "dough face" Northern Democrat, in this instance from New Hampshire, decided to make an example of this and to put the full weight of the federal government behind the effort to recapture Anthony Burns and return him to his master in the South.

Pierce eventually sent troops and spent about $100,000 in federal money, which would be several million in modern American dollars, to see that Anthony Burns was returned, and he was returned on a United States vessel to Virginia. A year later, a committee of Northerners raised the money to purchase Burns's freedom, and eventually he was freed. He moved to the North. He lived in Canada for a while, and he died in 1862.

He's primarily important because of the reaction across the North to the spectacle of the United States government throwing its full weight behind an effort to return a man to bondage who had escaped to freedom. The North, nine northern states, passed what were called "personal liberty" laws, and they said that someone in Anthony Burns's position should have the right to counsel, should have the right to a jury trial, should not be held in a government building, a public building as a fugitive, so that a slave master could come and take him back. In other words, they tried to put as many obstacles as possible in the way of a master trying to recover an escaped slave.

It's an absolutely fascinating case of Northern states invoking state rights to try to block the application of a federal statute. We usually think of the Southern states always hollering state rights. We're for state rights. We want state rights. But here you have Northern states trying to interpose a level of state power between a federal law that they don't like and what they see as a victim of that law in Anthony Burns. It's a nice turnaround of the usual thinking about state rights and, of course, one of the many ironical elements of the sectional controversy and the Civil War.

Now, the Supreme Court weighed in and upheld the constitutionality of the Fugitive Slave Law in 1859 in a case titled Abelman v. Booth. So the Court eventually made its feeling on this known. But the key thing is that there was passed a series of laws in the mid-1850s that tried to frustrate the workings of the Fugitive Slave Law, and James Buchanan says, let's get rid of those. That would make the South think that we're honest in our efforts to protect their slave property. Get rid of the Fugitive Slave laws. Pass a constitutional amendment to protect slavery. Get rid of the personal liberty laws.

Or, he said, why not acquire Cuba? That would be another thing that would send the right message to our friends in the South. We could acquire Cuba and turn it into a slave state, or more than one slave state maybe eventually, which would also make them know that we see a longtime future for slaveholders in the United States.

Well, other compromises were put forward, but almost all of them, like these that Buchanan mentioned, called on the North to make all the concessions. All of these things are aimed to placate the South. None of them takes into account the fact that the Republican Party had just won an election based on a plank that said, no more slavery in the territories. We will not countenance that. So all this talk of various ways to get around that was sure to fall on deaf ears among Republicans in the North.

The Republicans could not give on the issue of extension of slavery into the territories. It was the heart of their platform. They would have broken faith with everyone who voted for them if they agreed to concede anything in that direction, and they made it clear that they were not going to do so. They also thought, we won the election. Why should we have to make all the concessions? We won. Why do the winners make all the concessions? Why shouldn't the slaveholding South, which has had its way in national government for so many years, why shouldn't they make some concessions now that the democratic verdict has been that we are in control?

The most promising compromise in the eyes of many at the time came in the form of what was called the Crittenden Compromise. It was named after an old senator from Kentucky, John J. Crittenden, a man who in some ways had inherited the mantle of Henry Clay, the great pacificator of earlier in American history—someone who was always looking to find a way to reconcile differences between the sections. Many pointed out that it was right that Kentuckians would be doing that because there's Kentucky, between the South and the North, a state that's on the great border land, and here these statesmen from Kentucky are trying to find a way to hold it all together.

Crittenden certainly was acting that way in December of 1860 and on into the spring of 1861. What he came up with was a series of constitutional amendments, the most important of which would allow slavery south of the old 36°30' line of the Missouri Compromise. Reinstate that line, extend it all the way to California, and allow slavery in existing territories below that line and in any territories that the United States might later acquire below that 36°30' line. Republican votes killed the Crittenden legislation twice in the Senate—once in December and again in January. Republicans were not going to go along with that.

The key thing here is that there's really no ground on which to fashion a compromise because each side has a minimum demand that the other will not accept. The South wants an absolute guarantee of their slave property in the territories. The Republicans want an absolute ban on slavery in the territories. Neither side is willing to compromise on that issue, and therefore, there really isn't any kind of ground on which to explore a compromise that both sides would expect to last and to be effective. So you have this discussion and debate and suggestions put forward, but really, I think, none of them had a realistic chance of success because of the minimum demands of each side.

Let's see what Lincoln has been doing in this process—move to Abraham Lincoln. He made no public statements following his election. He stayed in Springfield. Just as during the campaign he hadn't made statements, after the election he did not make statements. He and Seward at first believed, as we said earlier, that Unionist sentiment in the Lower South would be greater than it was and that Unionists would step forward to help end the crisis. The North could simply wait out the South, they thought. If they could just drag the process out for long enough, these Unionists—who were timid, perhaps unwilling to go against some of their neighbors who were secessionists— give them enough time and they will step forward. Once they know that it's a true crisis for the Union, they'll do the right thing, is what Lincoln and Seward and others believed.

They also believed, Lincoln certainly did, that the Upper South and the border states, those eight slave states still in the Union, all of which, the key ones in the Upper South anyway, had voted for Bell and the Constitutional Union Party, those key states would never join the Deep South states in secession. They believed that Unionist sentiment clearly in those states was too strong. Lincoln had a lot of friends from those states, old Whig friends and others, that he believed would clearly be the leaders of the Upper South and the border states. We've only lost seven slave states. The eight that are still in the Union, believed many Republicans, will not join the Confederacy, and if we just can wait a while, the whole thing might be worked out to our advantage.

In fact, before the firing on Fort Sumter, all the states of the Upper South and the border had either voted against secession in state conventions or had refused even to consider the question of secession in a state convention. So there's some reason for Lincoln to believe what he believed. It seems that there's not great support for secession in the states that had not left.

The dark cloud in this for Lincoln and the Republicans and the North, however, is that these same states had made it absolutely clear that they would not countenance an overt application of force on the part of the federal government to make the seven states that had left the Union come back. We're not ready to secede, they said, in effect, but don't try to force them to come back. They had the right to go. You're going to have to leave them alone. These states, they said, would remain loyal to the Union only so long as the Lincoln administration would do two things: guarantee slavery where it existed, that is, guarantee it within their borders, and refrain from moving against the states that had already seceded.

So Lincoln is waiting, Seward is waiting, and they're watching; they're corresponding with people in the South. They're trying to get an accurate reading of what's going on in the South, but their belief is very strong that there's Unionist sentiment that simply hasn't showed itself yet.

The crisis came to focus on Fort Sumter, and let's move to Sumter, a federal fort as yet unfinished, nearly finished but not quite finished, sitting in Charleston Harbor—a substantial piece of military engineering, garrisoned by Major Robert Anderson, a Kentuckian, and a small contingent of United States soldiers.

In his inaugural address, Lincoln very adeptly and, in his usual brilliant, I think, use of language, sought to place responsibility for the start of hostilities on the Confederacy. He said that the federal government will hold, occupy, and possess its property in the South—hold, occupy, and possess its property in the South—and collect duties and imports. He also said, there will be no invasion, no using of force beyond what may be necessary for these objects: "In your hands, my dissatisfied fellow countrymen, and not in mine, is the momentous issue of civil war. The government will not assail you. You can have no conflict without being yourselves the aggressors."

It was a brilliant speech that left deliberately vague just what "occupy and posses" might mean, how Lincoln meant to collect the customs duties, and so forth. How could he do all that without using force? Just exactly what did he mean? Well, he didn't specify exactly what he meant, but he in effect lobbed the ball into the Confederacy's court to see what they would do with it. Again, he's mainly hoping to buy time to let Unionism work in the Deep South and the Upper South. But time ran out.

James Buchanan had faced a crisis at Sumter earlier back in January because he had found out that supplies were low in the fort, and he sent an unarmed ship with reinforcements. That ship, the *Star of the West*, had been fired upon by batteries in Charleston Harbor. Remember, only two states were out of the Union at that point. This is early in January, January 9, 1861. Only South Carolina and Mississippi had yet left the Union. There's no Confederacy yet when the *Star of the West* approaches Fort Sumter.

The vessel's fired upon. Tensions escalate, but no general fighting resulted from that. Both sides postured, but war didn't come. After that incident at Sumter, it became a tremendously important symbol, a growing symbol, to both the North and the South. Much of the North was saying, it's ours, it's federal property, we need to take it. In the South, white Southerners were saying, it's in Charleston Harbor. It's part of South Carolina. It should belong to the Confederacy. We can't let the United States government continue to hold that. It was enormously important psychologically. Most Republicans were adamantly against giving up Fort Sumter. Confederates were just as adamant that it was theirs and they should have it.

Word came from Major Anderson on March 5, 1861, just after Abraham Lincoln was in office, that he had to have supplies or he couldn't hold out. Convinced that Northern public opinion wouldn't tolerate giving up the fort, Lincoln decided to send an unarmed ship with provisions. I'm not sending soldiers; I'm not sending ammunition. I'm only sending provisions to the garrison at Fort Sumter.

Now, he acted against the advice of a number of his advisors in this decision. Secretary of State William Henry Seward said, it's not worth the risk. Don't do this, Mr. President. Winfield Scott, the General-in-Chief of the United States Army and the greatest soldier in the United States at this point, in fact, one of the greatest soldiers in United States history, also recommended against doing this.

But Lincoln said, I'm not going to abandon the fort, and he understood better than Scott, I think, and better than Seward just how important Sumter had become as a symbol to people in the North and especially to Republicans in the North. He knew that if he let it go it might cause enormous difficulties for him and for the potential success of holding the Union together or putting it back together, so he decided to reprovision it.

A full-scale effort to supply and reinforce the fort, Lincoln knew, would brand the North as an aggressor. Here's the North coming in with troops and ammunition to Fort Sumter, and that would almost certainly send at least the Upper South out of the Union, Lincoln thought. But an unarmed supply ship, he thought, was a different thing. If that were fired on by the Confederates, the Confederates would be the aggressors. All we're doing is sending food. If they won't allow us to send food to our garrison, that would be a warlike act on their part rather than on our part.

We, the North, reasoned Lincoln, would be in the role of the assaulted party. The secessionists, the Confederates, would be in the role of the aggressive party in that instance. Perhaps the Upper South would understand that, he thought. Perhaps that wouldn't be enough to send them out of the Union.

Lincoln told the governor of South Carolina, Francis Pickens, what was going to happen. He said, this vessel is coming, this is what it's carrying, this is what it's not carrying. I just want you to know. I don't want there to be any misunderstanding about this. We will not fire, said Lincoln, unless fired upon.

Well, Jefferson Davis and the Confederate cabinet faced a tremendous dilemma now because they didn't want to be labeled as the aggressors either. No one wanted to fire the first shot. Everyone wanted to be able to have the high ground, but Davis was under intense political pressure, public pressure, not to give up Fort Sumter. What he and his advisors decided to do was to ask for the surrender of the fort before the Union vessel arrived with the supplies.

They did. Robert Anderson refused to give up the fort, and on April 12, 1861, Southern batteries ringing the fort in Charleston Harbor opened fire on

Fort Sumter. Hoards of people watched. They got on rooftops and watched. They found the good vantage points around the harbor and watched this spectacular display—36 hours of bombardment. At the end of that 36 hours, the United States garrison surrendered Fort Sumter. The next day, on April 15, 1861, Abraham Lincoln issued a call for 75,000 volunteers to put down the rebellion.

And we have reached the great trigger of the war. War was not inevitable to that point. As I said last time, we shouldn't ever fall into the trap of seeing it as inevitable, but once Lincoln called for 75,000 volunteers, events moved very rapidly. Let's move to our last section here, which is what the effect of all these events at Fort Sumter and Lincoln's call had on the Upper South, four states of the Upper South.

War fever swept across the North and South, both sides, uniting, I think, public opinion in both sections to a degree that it certainly had not been united before. Northerners were angry that a United States installation had been fired upon. Confederates were angry that Lincoln had called for volunteers to suppress the rebellion. Theoretically, that meant that troops from all those other slave states that were still in the Union might be used against their Deep South brethren, and that was something that the Upper South simply was not willing to countenance.

The North was in no mood after this to think about placating the South anymore. The North had a great sense of union. Untold Northerners, reared on the rhetoric of Daniel Webster and others, and Lincoln certainly falls into this pattern, saw the North as a democratic beacon in a world that had not yet embraced democracy.

They believed that the sundering of the Union not only had implications for the future of the United States but also had implications for the future of democracy in the world. If this democratic beacon were snuffed out, and they believed secession would do that in the long term, it would lead perhaps to an endless division of the United States and redivision. If it were ever snuffed out, there was no guarantee that it would be lighted again anywhere. So more was at stake in the minds of many white Northerners than just the Union. There was also the democratic example for the world.

The Upper South states of Virginia and Tennessee and North Carolina and Arkansas decided that the call for volunteers was the last straw, and one by one they left. Virginia left in April, North Carolina in May, and Tennessee in June—three key states. Arkansas also left. It's not nearly as important that Arkansas left because Arkansas isn't exactly central to what goes on in our story from here to the end of the Civil War, but these other three states are absolutely central because they're the three most populous states to join the Confederacy. Virginia is number one, Tennessee number is two, and North Carolina is number three.

As a set, as a trio, they have more than half of all the manufacturing capacity of the Confederacy. An inordinate percentage of the top military leaders are going to come from these three states, beginning with Robert E. Lee, Stonewall Jackson, and moving on down through many of the key commanders who served in both the Eastern and the Western Theaters. These three states produce more than half of all the food crops of all the Confederate states. They contain nearly half its mules and horses, which are crucial in waging mid-nineteenth century warfare.

In other words, these states, these three states of the Upper South that left after Lincoln called for volunteers, are going to be absolutely central to the Confederate war effort. Without them on the side of the Confederacy, it's very difficult to imagine the war lasting four years or being as destructive of physical and human resources as it was. It's absolutely unthinkable that the seven Deep South states by themselves could have mounted the kind of resistance that the Confederacy would mount over the next four years.

In recognition of Virginia's centrality, the capital of the Confederacy was moved from Montgomery to Richmond. It made sense on a number of levels. It would cement Virginia's loyalty. It's the biggest city, the most important city in the biggest and most important state that was in the Confederacy, and it also had an enormous array of manufacturing. Richmond by itself had roughly 40 percent of the manufacturing capacity in the Confederacy, including the famous Tredager Iron Works that were the most important iron works in the Confederacy.

So it was a huge change in the picture of how the war might go when these three states joined the Confederacy. And there's irony here, too, especially in Virginia's case, but also in the Upper South states, because, during the secession debate, it seemed that there might be a shift in power within these states, the western areas of the states, the states settled later, the states that had fewer slaves in the old eastern parts of the state. The sections of the states that had always looked somewhat askance at politicians from the eastern parts of the states who were in control had seemed to be making progress toward achieving a realignment of political power in much of the Upper South during the secession crisis.

Lincoln's call ended that. Once the call for volunteers went out, support for secession solidified in these three states, the three key states of Virginia and Tennessee and North Carolina, and that process of realignment that had seemed to be in place simply ended.

Now, again, this isn't to say that there's unanimity in these states, in the four Upper South states that went, especially the three key ones, because there clearly wasn't, as we'll see. Not too far down the road in our discussion of the war, we'll see that a huge part of Virginia was disaffected enough so that it would break away and form a new state, the new state of Western Virginia. That's because of the Unionist sentiment there, the unhappiness there with secessionists and the road that Virginia was going down.

But enough support, ample support, in all of these states coalesced behind secession in response to Lincoln's call for volunteers, and it changed the picture absolutely dramatically. Now we have 11 states in the Confederacy. Now we have a Confederacy that's much larger and poses a much more intimidating potential foe to the United States. It has far more resources and far more people. It's just going to be a far more difficult task for Abraham Lincoln and the United States government to deal with this.

Not only have these states gone out of the Union but shots have been fired now. There's actually been shooting. So the notion that somehow we're going to navigate among all these perilous difficulties and find a peaceful solution to this great crisis is no longer reasonable. That is not going to happen. The war is imminent at this point. It's imminent, and there's no way to get around it in the view of most quite reasonable people on both sides. The question is just how long it will be before serious fighting starts.

We will leave the political side of our discussion here at this point: eleven Confederate states, war imminent. Next time we will turn to a consideration of the relative strength and weaknesses of the two contestants. Is one side almost certain to win, or is this really a contest that could go either way?

The Opposing Sides, I
Lecture 5

Now we'll turn our attention to a consideration of the strengths and weaknesses of each side as military action approached in the spring and early summer of 1861. In this lecture, we'll examine areas in which one side or the other seemed to have a clear advantage.

At first glance, it might seem that the North had such decisive advantages in almost every measurable category as to guarantee victory. Much of the literature of the "Lost Cause," which flourished in the South in the late nineteenth century and continues to influence writing about the conflict, argued that the Confederacy waged a gallant but doomed struggle for independence. In reality, important factors favored each side as fighting began. We will take a close look at these factors to underscore the importance of the fact that the outcome of the war was not predetermined. Either side could have won, and the Confederacy more than once came close to persuading the Northern people that the contest was too costly in lives and treasure. The first of the two lectures on this subject will focus on areas in which one side or the other possessed a significant edge; the next lecture will address elements of the balance sheet that favored neither of the combatants.

Courtesy National Archives.

One advantage of the North over the South was its 22,000-mile railroad network.

The North had an edge of about five to two in manpower; its population of approximately 22.5 million far outstripped that of the South, which had 9.1 million—of which 3.5 million were blacks, including only 130,000 free blacks. The North drew on its much larger population, as well as a significant portion of the Confederacy's white and black male populations that never supported the Southern cause. But the presence of slave labor allowed the Confederacy to muster a higher percentage of its military-age white males (about 75 to 80 percent, as opposed to about 50 percent in the North). A total of between 2.1 and 2.2 million men served in the military in the Civil War; between 750,000 and 850,000 served in the Confederate Army.

The Northern economy, boasting approximately 110,000 businesses involving 1.3 million workers, dwarfed that of the Confederacy (with 18,000 business employing 110,000 workers). The North had as many manufacturing establishments as the Confederacy had factory workers. The Northern railroad network was more extensive and modern, with 22,000 miles of track, compared to only 9,000 in the Confederacy. And the Northern production of iron, ships, textiles, weapons, draft animals, and other crucial items far outstripped that in the South.

Overall, geography favored the Confederacy ... as did the size of the South, the coastline, and the nature of the transportation infrastructure. Only the rivers might be reckoned at least a partial Union advantage.

The North began the war with a professional army and navy, although this advantage was less important than might be assumed. The United States Army was only 15,000 strong and was spread across the continent; most units were west of the Mississippi. The United States Navy had only 42 vessels in commission, and most of these were patrolling far from the South. It was a deep-water cruising navy not skilled in coastal or riverine warfare.

However, the Confederacy also possessed significant advantages. War aims favored the Confederacy, which only had to defend itself to win independence. The American Revolution offered an example of a weaker power winning over a stronger power: The Confederacy could win just by demoralizing the Northern people.

Defending home ground conveyed advantages to the Confederacy. The side defending its homes often exhibits greater motivation than an invader. Geography often favored the Confederacy as well. The sheer size of the Confederacy (more than 750,000 square miles with 3,500 miles of coastline) posed a daunting obstacle to the North. And Confederates generally knew the terrain and roads better than Northerners. Access for commerce was provided by more than 200 mouths of rivers and bays. The Appalachian Mountains presented an obstacle, and the Shenandoah Valley provided a protected corridor for military action against the North. Rivers were a mixed bag—they sometimes served as avenues of advance for the Federals (as in the Western Theater along the Tennessee and Cumberland Rivers) and at other times posed barriers to Northern armies (as in Virginia).

The poor Southern transportation network would also complicate Northern logistics. The Vicksburg campaign of 1863 is one example, and the infamous "mud march" in Virginia (January 1863) is another. ■

Essential Reading

Hattaway and Jones, *How the North Won: A Military History of the Civil War*, chapters 1–2.

McPherson, *Battle Cry of Freedom: The Civil War Era*, chapter 10.

Supplementary Reading

Nevins, *The War for the Union: The Improvised War, 1861–1862*, chapters 4–5.

Questions to Consider

1. Considering the factors covered in this lecture, how would you assess each side's chances for victory?

2. Is it possible to gauge accurately the possible impact of intangibles, such as fighting to defend home and hearth?

The Opposing Sides, I
Lecture 5—Transcript

In our last lecture, we saw the dramatic movement toward armed conflict in the wake of the attack on Fort Sumter and Abraham Lincoln's call for 75,000 volunteers to suppress the rebellion. Now we'll turn our attention to a consideration of the strengths and weaknesses of each side as military action approached in the spring and early summer of 1861. In this lecture, we'll examine areas in which one side or the other seemed to have a clear advantage. Next time, in a follow-up lecture, we'll look at categories in which neither side really seemed to have an advantage concerning factors that would play a role in how the war would be resolved.

But let's start with areas where one side or the other did have an advantage. At first glance it would seem that the North had overwhelming advantages in most of the crucial categories and, in fact, that the North almost certainly would win the conflict. The myth of the Lost Cause, the writers, in which began to publish their work in the 1870s and then published it throughout the rest of the century, did in fact argue that the North had overwhelming advantages and that the Confederacy never really had a chance to win the war. But the Lost Cause writers said that the admirable thing about the Confederate effort was that they fought so long and so hard against such overwhelming odds and that they were so gallant and pulled together as a people to such an extent that they held off this massive tide of Northern superiority for four long years.

You can find many echoes of that argument today. Shelby Foote, for example, has a famous statement where he says that the North fought the war with one hand behind its back and that, if things had become more grim for the North, the North would have just pulled that other hand from behind its back and prosecuted the war to victory. Foote says that, in effect, the Confederacy never had a chance to win that war. Well, that's not the case. The Confederacy did have a chance to win the war, and, in fact, I think it came close to doing so on more than one occasion.

What we'll do now is assess some of the factors that would contribute toward one side's winning or losing the war. As I said earlier, we'll begin by looking at categories in which one side had a distinct advantage over the other. We'll look first at the North and then at the Confederacy, and we'll start with population as a crucial Northern advantage.

Here there is no question about it—the United States, the North, had a clear edge when it came to manpower. The 1860 census put the U.S. population at about 31 and a half million people. Of those, the 11 states of the Confederacy had about 9.1 million people, and, of those 9.1, about five and a half million people were white, three and a half million were African American slaves, and another 130,000 or so were free black people living in the Confederate states. About 600,000 white people in states remaining loyal to the Union cast their lot with the Confederacy, bringing the total white population in support of the Confederacy to about six million. These numbers are all very rough, and historians have debated them, so I'm not pretending that we can be precise here, but roughly six million white people supported the Confederacy.

The North's population was about 22 and a half million, less the 600,000 sympathizers, for a total of about 21.8 million people that the North could draw on. There were significant numbers of Northern sympathizers in western Virginia, however, and in eastern Tennessee and western North Carolina and the uplands of Alabama and the hill country of Texas and Arkansas. Every state in the Confederacy had sections, sometimes significant pockets, in fact, of pro-Unionist, anti-Confederate sentiment. They're often in the mountainous or hill country sections of these states. And beyond those white Southerners who never really supported the Confederacy, you have to factor in the 150,000 black men residing in the Confederacy who fought in the Union army in the United States Colored Troops, as they were called in the course of the war.

Slaves did not carry arms for the South, but that fact was offset by their doing the kinds of labor that freed a disproportionate percentage of the white, military-age population of the South to go into the Confederate army. The Confederacy achieved a quite astonishing level of mobilization because white men were able to go fight in the army while the economy continued to run behind the lines using a huge reservoir of black labor.

When we take into account all the factors, all the pluses and minuses, the Unionists canceling the pro-Confederate people in the North and so forth, you come down to a North that had about a five to two advantage in manpower over the Confederacy. A two and a half to one, if you want to put it another way, advantage over the Confederacy. During the course of the war, between 2.1 and 2.2 million men served in the United States military, just about half of the military-age population of the North. One in two Northern men, in other words, of military age went into the service.

The Confederacy mustered between 750,000 and 850,000 of its roughly one million military-age white males. The Confederate figures are much less reliable than the figures for the North, but it's an astonishing rate of mobilization. As I said before, they put roughly 80 percent of their military-age white males into the army. That's a very impressive feat made possible only by the presence of slave laborers behind the lines. But in the area of population, potential soldiers, the North has a huge advantage. There's no way around it—two and a half to one.

What about economic strength? Here again the North is overwhelming more powerful. By almost any yardstick, the North enjoyed a huge advantage in this area, and there are any number of ways you can get at this using different kinds of figures. I don't want to overwhelm you with numbers, but let me just throw a few out for your consideration. There were 110,000 manufacturing establishments in the North that employed about 1.3 million workers. In the Confederacy, there were 18,000 manufacturing establishments that employed about 110,000 workers. The easiest way to think about it is that there were as many manufacturing establishments in the North as there were factory workers in the South. It's an enormous edge to the North.

Northern railroads were far more extensive, at nearly 22,000 miles to only a shade more than 9,000 miles in the Confederacy, and the Northern roads tended to be better. Beyond that, the North had the capacity to replace worn-out rails and to add new rolling stock. The Confederacy did not. So, as the war goes along, Northern railroads get stronger; Confederate railroads become more and more decrepit.

According to the 1860 census, the North was at an enormous advantage in key categories. The North had 11 times as many vessels as the Confederacy had. It had 15 times as much iron production, 17 times as many textile goods, 24 times as many locomotives, more than 30 times as many firearms, and on and on and on. Northern manufacturing was colossal compared to the rather modest level of manufacturing in the Confederacy.

There were roughly 800,000 draft animals in the North; about 300,000 in the South. Again, we have to remember that mid-nineteenth century armies moved by horse and mule power. That's how you hauled the supplies, that's how you pulled the cannons, that's how you moved the cavalry, and the North has a huge advantage in this area. Overall, the North had enormous strength.

Even in food production, the North far exceeds the South, but here we have to remember that the North is feeding far more people. If you factor that in, the food production on each side turns out to be roughly equal. Each side can certainly feed itself, but in terms of manufacturing, the North has a huge advantage. So in population and in manufacturing, the North is almost off the scale compared to the South.

There's another advantage the North has, a clear advantage, and that is in the presence, on the Northern side of the balance sheet, of the United States Army and the United States Navy. The North starts the war with a regular army and a regular navy. The Confederacy starts the war with neither. It has to build from scratch. We have to count this as a plus for the North, but I think it's not as large a plus as it might seem to be because the United States Army was tiny in 1861, between 15,000 and 16,000 men. And, in the spring of 1861, after many Southerners had left, the U.S. Army was down to around 14,000. More than that, it was spread out across a continent, much of it on duty in the far West. So there isn't a United States Army present in one place and able to march against the Confederacy. It's a very small organization, and it's scattered across a gigantic landscape, much of it west of the Mississippi River.

The North also did something else that prevented best use of the United States regular army early in the war, and I'll talk a little bit more about this later, but for now I'll just say that the United States decided to keep its regular army together and not to parcel out this pool of trained soldiers to help instruct the hordes of volunteers who would be coming into the army. They kept the United States Army together, and that denied all of that knowledge and expertise to volunteers who had no expertise and didn't really know the first thing about being soldiers. So that's the army.

What about the navy? The U.S. Navy only had 90 vessels in 1861, 42 of which were in commission, and most of those 42 were patrolling waters far from the coastal areas and rivers of the South where they would be needed during the Civil War. So it's a small navy, and it is a very widely dispersed navy. Indeed, in the spring of 1861, only three ships were available for immediate service against the Confederate states—three ships. That's not enough to make much of a difference.

Moreover, the United States Navy was a deepwater navy with little expertise in the type of coastal and inshore operations that would characterize the Civil War. This is, for the most part, going to be a naval war fought along the coastlines and on the Mississippi River and other great rivers that lead into the Confederacy. The United States Navy of 1861 is not a navy constructed to wage that kind of war. So place the U.S. Army and the U.S. Navy on the side of Union strengths at the outset of the war, but put a little asterisk beside them because it's not as important a strength, I guess it would be fair to say, as it might at first appear to be.

All right, those are Northern advantages, clear categories in which the North has an advantage. What about the Confederacy? It also has clear advantages, although they don't seem as obvious in some ways as the Northern ones. Perhaps the greatest Confederate plus lay in the area of war aims or conditions for victory. The South had only to defend itself to achieve independence. In fact, it could do nothing, and, if the United States didn't do anything, the Confederacy would win by default. The North, in contrast, had to invade the South and destroy its war making capacity or at least the will to win or to resist on the part of the Southern people. It would take a protracted, major effort for the United States to accomplish that. It was a much different goal for the North than the goal for the Confederacy going into the war to achieve their respective objects.

If the South could just prolong the war long enough to convince a majority of the Northern people that it was too expensive of lives, or too expensive of treasure to continue, they would win the war. A tie was as good as a win for the Confederacy. If they could just hold off the North until the North said, that's enough, the Confederacy would win. The North did not have that luxury. The Confederacy, in other words, didn't have to send its armies into the North. It didn't have to try to capture Northern cities. It didn't have to try to destroy the war making capacity of the United States in order to win. The North did have to do all of those things to defeat the Confederacy.

There was a tremendous example readily at hand to bolster Confederate expectations and will. They had to look no further than the experience of the colonies during the American Revolution to see a weaker party that had won in a war against a much stronger party by dragging the war out and convincing the more powerful party that its interests lay elsewhere and that it was simply too expensive to continue that war. That's how the United States had achieved independence, and people in both the North and the South were well aware of that.

Now, closely tied to the fact that the Confederacy enjoyed an edge in this respect, in what it had to do to win, was the fact that a defending force almost always enjoys an advantage over an invading force, an advantage in morale. Men tend to fight harder to defend their homes than they do to try to impose their will on others who are defending their homes. Observers on both sides were again well aware of this, that the defender often enjoys higher morale.

Soldiers on both sides commented about this phenomenon during the war. Confederate soldiers in Maryland and Pennsylvania during Lee's invasions of 1862 and 1863 said that they noticed a different attitude within their ranks about carrying the war to the enemy as opposed to defending home and hearth. And Northern soldiers defending Southern Pennsylvania talked about how it seemed more important all of a sudden to do well because they were defending their homes rather than carrying the war to the Confederates. So it is an advantage to be defending hearth and home.

It's also an advantage to be fighting the war on your home ground for a number of reasons. One is that you're likely to have a better understanding of the topography: how the rivers flow, where the roads are, where the gaps in the mountains are. And, if you don't know those things, the likelihood is high that a friendly population will tell you those things when they will not tell the invading army those things.

There are innumerable examples of civilians helping out a Confederate army in this regard during the course of the war. An obvious one is at the Battle of Chancellorsville in early May 1863, when, on the night of May 1, Lee and Stonewall Jackson were trying to figure out a way to get around Joseph Hooker's right flank without being detected, and local people came forward and said, we know back roads that will take you around to the position you want to be. During the night, those guides showed staff officers how to get there, and the next day Jackson made his famous flanking march. That showed the advantage of being on your home ground and having friendly people show you how to get to where you want to go to achieve your military ends.

By fighting on the defensive on their home ground, the Confederates also, in many instances, enjoyed the advantage of what were called "interior lines" in military parlance. That meant simply that they were often with their different forces closer to one another and better able to reinforce one another than the advancing Federals were, who might be coming at them on a more widely dispersed line of advance. There's a perfect example of that very early in the war during the campaign of First Manassas or Bull Run, when each side has two armies. Each side has an army near Washington, and each side has an army in the lower Shenandoah Valley, that is, the Northern end of the Shenandoah Valley.

The Confederates have a railroad that links their two forces. They have the advantage of interior lines there that the Union does not enjoy, and they use those interior lines to reinforce their army near Washington with their army in the lower Shenandoah Valley and to win a victory in July of 1861. So this is another plus that has to be placed on the side of the Confederacy.

One of the largest factors favoring the Confederacy involved geography. This one really, I think, cannot be overstated. The geography of the South constituted an overall military advantage that greatly impressed people at the time, trained military men on both sides as well as civilians who had at least a rough grasp of what it would take for one side or the other to win. The Confederate States of America was a huge nation, more than three quarters of a million square miles. It was equal in size to modern France, West Germany, Italy, Spain, and other pieces of Western Europe.

I'll quote a couple of Confederate observers on this. George Wythe Randolph, who became a brigadier general in the Confederacy and also served as Secretary of War for a time, declared at the beginning of the war, "The enemy may overrun our frontier states and plunder our coast, but as for conquering us, the thing is an impossibility. There is no instance in history of a people as numerous as we are, inhabiting a country so extensive as ours, being subjected if true to themselves." In other words, Randolph was saying, if we fight hard in this enormous country of ours with the inherent advantages of the defenders, we should win this war. There shouldn't be any two ways about it.

Pierre Gustave Toutant Beauregard, who went by simply Gustave Toutant Beauregard during the war and who was one of the leading Confederate generals, similarly remarked about the conflict that "No people ever warred for independence with more relative advantages than the Confederates." Among those advantages he listed the enormous size of the Confederacy and the geographic obstacles that the North would have to try to overcome. If, as a military question, said Beauregard, the Confederate people are true to themselves, much as Randolph had said, they would succeed in this war. These are both men who had a very good understanding of the role geography would play, and I think that we should pay attention to them and to others who realized the intimidating nature of trying to enforce the North's will on the Confederacy.

Let's just look at some of the geographic features beyond the sheer size of the Confederacy that we need to keep in mind. Start with the coastline. The Confederate coastline ran for approximately 3,500 miles. It's enormous. And in that 3,500 miles were nearly 200 mouths of rivers, inlets, bays, and other places where vessels could move in and out, vessels to bring goods into the Confederacy and vessels to take goods out of the Confederacy. It would be very difficult for the North to blockade that huge coastline, and, of course, blockade it is what they sought to do from the very beginning of the war. They never succeeded in really sealing off the Confederate coast, although they became much, much better at it as the war went on—the Union navy did as the navy grew.

The Appalachian Mountains were a daunting barrier that frustrated the Federals from shifting effectively strength from east to west or from west to east, at least until William Tecumseh Sherman moved into Georgia in 1864. The Shenandoah Valley of Virginia, the famous Valley of Virginia, formed a protected corridor that Confederate forces used repeatedly. Confederate troops could move across the Blue Ridge into the Shenandoah Valley and march northward down the valley, cross the Potomac River, sheltering themselves in the gaps of the Blue Ridge to their east, and find themselves across the Potomac to the right rear of Washington, in a position to menace the United States capital.

In contrast, Northern forces marching into the Shenandoah Valley and marching up the valley found themselves getting farther and farther away from the Confederate capital of Richmond and from key military points in the eastern part of the state. So the Shenandoah Valley worked very nicely for the Confederates as a military avenue of advance.

Rivers would play a key role in the war because rivers were a wonderful way to move men and material, especially in a country, the South—and I'll talk move about this in a minute—that didn't have a really well-developed network of roads or a railroad network that would hold up during the war. So the rivers were important. Which way did they go? Would they form barriers, or would they form avenues of advance? Here the geographic plus goes partly to the North and partly to the South.

Kentucky made a huge difference here. Had Kentucky become a Confederate state, the Confederacy would have enjoyed the enormous advantage of having the Ohio River as a barrier. They could have arrayed their forces south of the Ohio River and disputed Northern crossings of that tremendous artery. But Kentucky didn't go with the Confederacy, and the North retained access to two absolutely critical rivers, the Cumberland River and the Tennessee River, which both flow into the Ohio River. They're within about a dozen miles of one another, and they lead directly into the heartland of the Confederacy, both of them.

The Tennessee River plunges through middle Tennessee, dips down into northern Alabama, and then makes its way over to Chattanooga. The Cumberland River flows again into the heart of middle Tennessee into the Tennessee capital of Nashville. Both were very important axes of advance for United States military forces in the Western Theater. It was very difficult to defend against those kinds of advances. Those rivers were a definite plus for the North, as was the Mississippi, of course, which plunged all the way through the Confederacy. It really cut the Confederacy in two and offered enormous opportunities for the North to employ its naval and army strength in joint operations along the Mississippi River. So in the west the rivers favor the North.

In Virginia it's more problematical. There the rivers flow generally west to east or northwest to southeast. The four major rivers in Virginia, of course, include the Potomac, which is the frontier early in the war. Then you drop down to the Rappahannock, which flows through Fredericksburg, and then there is the York and finally the James, which comes from western Virginia through Richmond and then flows on down to the southeast. Each of those could be used as a barrier to Northern advances if the Northern advances were coming overland as they often did during the war, and Lee made use, and other Confederate commanders did as well, of each of those rivers.

But the rivers in Virginia could also be a weakness for the Confederacy if the United States decided to use them as waterborne avenues of advance against the Confederacy to turn Confederate units who were positioned north of any of the rivers. For example, after the Battle of First Manassas, when the main Confederate force was north of the Rappahannock and south of the Potomac, a Union advance to the Rappahannock River would have gotten in the rear of those Confederate forces and forced a retreat.

George B. McClellan used the rivers brilliantly. In the spring and early summer of 1862, he moved his massive Army of the Potomac down the Potomac River to the mouth of the York and the James Rivers and used the York and James as axes of advance against Richmond from the southeast.

It was a very efficient use of the Virginia rivers against the Confederate defenders. So in Virginia the rivers can go either way. They are perhaps a plus and perhaps a minus for the Confederacy. In the west the rivers are a decided advantage for the North—the one area of geography that really did favor the North.

The North faced an incredible problem once it got away from the rivers when it moved into the hinterlands of the Confederacy because it came up against the fact that there was a very poor network of roads and railroads in the Confederacy, and the logistical demands were almost insurmountable in some cases. The rough yardstick is that, for a Civil War army, a United States Army campaigning during the Civil War, 100,000 men required at least 600 tons of supplies a day to maintain itself. That's an enormous flow of supplies.

Carried in wagons drawn by draft animals, if you don't have well-developed roads, it is a nightmare to maintain an army of that size in the hinterlands of the Confederacy. It's much easier to supply them using rivers, but the North ran out of rivers in the Western Theater, for example, and had to strike into the hinterlands, and then the obstacles became such that they often frustrated campaigns.

I'll use Ulysses S. Grant's campaign against Vicksburg in 1863 as an example. Grant commanded almost 100,000 men during that operation, but as his supply lines lengthened, as he moved deeper and deeper into the Confederacy, it took more and more men to guard the rear areas. He had to deploy troops all the way along this long line of supply to keep the materials coming to his army. In the end he had fewer than a third of his troops at the point of contact with the Confederates, roughly two-thirds of them strung out along these enormous lines of advance. It showed just how much of an effect the size of the Confederacy and the poor nature of its transportation infrastructure could have on an advancing Union army.

The North solved this problem later in the war when they decided simply to live off the countryside when they struck into the Confederacy. Sherman did it in Georgia in 1864. Sheridan did it in the Shenandoah Valley, and other Federal commanders did it in other places as well. But we should never forget the importance of the Union troops trying to come to grips with a poor transportation network in an enormous country, a factor made all the worse when bad weather combined with the poor nature of the roads.

There were only a handful of roads in the Confederacy as good as the Valley Pike in the Shenandoah Valley, for example, which was an all-weather road, macadamized, that is, crushed stone graded with bar pits on each side so that it would drain, to a degree. It could stand rain and still have heavy use. Most of the roads of the South could not. They became muddy tracks very quickly and almost impassable in poor weather. There's a document in the official records of the War of the Rebellion from a Union officer with a sense of humor. He put in a request through channels. He was taking part in a winter campaign. He said that he would like 50 men, 25 feet tall, to work in mud 18 feet deep. That's the nature of Southern roads.

Ambrose Burnside's frustrating "mud march" in January of 1863 was an excellent example of bad roads and the weather conspiring to stop a Northern offensive. So keep this in mind when you try to judge just how daunting were the obstacles facing the North. Overall, geography favored the Confederacy, just to summarize this part of the lecture, as did the size of the South, the coastline, and the nature of the transportation infrastructure. Only the rivers might be reckoned at least a partial Union advantage.

So let's leave this part of our reckoning of pluses and minuses on each side with the firm understanding that both sides enjoyed the advantage in some categories. It's not just the case of the overwhelmingly more powerful North getting ready to work its will on the Confederacy. Each side had some advantages. Next time, in our follow-up lecture, we'll look at categories of strengths and weakness where neither side really had an advantage and where it was essentially a standoff.

The Opposing Sides, II
Lecture 6

This lecture continues the discussion begun with our last lecture. The analysis shifts to the topics of pools of trained officers available to each side, political leadership, and the wild card of foreign intervention. Although it remains a common idea that the Confederacy had better generals, we will see that each side drew from a pool that essentially mirrored the other's. Officers trained at West Point held the top positions in both armies.

In terms of political leadership, I will argue that Jefferson Davis provided capable direction to the Confederate war effort, although his performance inevitably suffers in comparison to Lincoln's deft leadership. Unknown at the time hostilities began—and a subject of intense Union and Confederate interest for at least two years thereafter—were the attitudes abroad. England and France represented a potentially significant element in any reckoning of strengths and weaknesses. Should the Confederacy win the kind of support the colonies received from France during the Revolution, the entire balance sheet of the war would be upset. Absent major intervention from abroad, the victory would go to the side that mustered its resources and exploited its advantages most effectively to maintain national morale and purpose while convincing the opposing population that the war was not worth the cost.

Southern schools like the Military College of South Carolina (a.k.a. the Citadel) supplied the Confederacy with many trained officers.

Prints and Photographs Division, Library of Congress.

There were 824 officers on the active list at the outbreak of the war. Of this total, 640 stayed with the North and only 184 went with the Confederacy. Of the approximately 900 professional officers then in private life, 114 served the North while 99 served the South. Several factors largely offset the fact that roughly three-quarters of all West Pointers and other pre-war professional officers fought for the North. Larger Union armies required more officers. Professional officers were kept in Regular United States units rather than being spread out among volunteer regiments for the first part of the war.

Southern state schools, such as the Virginia Military Institute (VMI) and the Citadel (Charleston, South Carolina), sent a large number of trained officers into the Confederacy's armies. A total of 2,000 men had trained at VMI, and about 1,700 served in the Confederate States Army (CSA), especially in the Army of Northern Virginia.

The North had some very considerable advantages, but the South was by no means facing a hopeless struggle for independence.

Professional officers on both sides shared a common heritage. Drawn from this pool of professionals, there were 583 general officers in the Union Army during the war and 425 general officers in the CSA. These officers learned from the same professors at West Point, and they learned the same lessons during the Mexican War under Generals Scott and Taylor. The officers tended to subscribe to the same strategic and tactical ideas concerning the power of rifled muskets and cannons in giving advantages to the defender; the need to avoid frontal assaults; the desirability of trying to turn an enemy's flank, if possible; and the advantage of exploiting interior lines of movement, both strategically and tactically. The officers also had similar ideas about communication, supply, and the use of field fortifications as a defensive tactical measure.

Political realities forced both sides to use politicians as generals. Lincoln appointed these "political generals" based on party affiliation and nationality. There were many famous, albeit not overly capable, political generals during the Civil War.

However, Lincoln and Davis both did well as war leaders. Lincoln began the conflict with little military knowledge (he was a company grade officer during the Black Hawk War in the 1830s), but he learned quickly. He grasped strategic ideas well, listened to his military advisers, and read about strategy. He was willing to grant wide authority to generals if necessary to win, and he was willing to grow and change his ideas about what kind of war needed to be fought.

Davis, on the other hand, had considerable military experience, and he put it to good use. He was a West Point graduate (class of 1828), he had been a colonel in the Mexican War, and he had been secretary of war under President Franklin Pierce. But he never found a second able army commander to do in the Western Theater what Lee did in the Eastern Theater. Davis sometimes was reluctant to step aside and allow Lee to have wider authority.

The possibility of foreign intervention constituted a wild card. The eventual decisions of England and France were crucial; the example of the American Revolution impressed both sides. Military events would largely determine the decisions of European powers. ■

Essential Reading

Hattaway and Jones, *How the North Won: A Military History of the Civil War*, chapters 1–2.

McPherson, *Battle Cry of Freedom: The Civil War Era*, chapter 10.

Supplementary Reading

Boritt, ed., *Why the Confederacy Lost*, Essays One and Three (by James M. McPherson and Gary W. Gallagher, respectively).

Questions to Consider

1. Which factors favoring one side or the other likely would change as the war developed? Which would remain relatively constant?

2. Do you think human or material factors loomed larger in the balance sheet of strengths and weaknesses?

The Opposing Sides, II
Lecture 6—Transcript

We spent our last lecture examining factors that favored either the North or the Confederacy as the two sides moved toward war. Population, the economy, and professional military forces we saw as advantages for the North, and war aims, conditions for victory, and geography we saw as advantages for the Confederacy.

Now we'll shift to an analysis of categories in which neither side had a clear edge. We'll start by looking at resources of military command, and then we'll move on to assess the performances of the two presidents, Lincoln and Davis, as war leaders. We'll finish up by examining in brief detail the possibility that either England or France would intervene on the side of the Confederacy and thus change the overall balance of the war.

Let's start with resources of command. One of the most persistent, durable myths about the Civil War is that the Confederacy had better military leadership but lost the war because they were simply overwhelmed by Northern might, by the number of sheer regiments that the North could deploy against the Confederacy, by the amount of material that the North could lavish on its war effort. These spectacularly gifted Confederate generals, especially Lee and Stonewall Jackson, runs a common argument, would have won a war in which the two sides had had even remotely equal resources of men and material.

That's a basic of the Lost Cause interpretation of how the war played out and why the Confederacy lost—that these better Confederate generals were eventually overwhelmed. But it simply isn't true. The Confederacy didn't have better generals overall. It's easy to decide that they did if you only look at the Eastern Theater, and that is often the case because the Virginia, Maryland, Pennsylvania Theater often looms as most important in much of what's been written about the war.

If you just look at the east and see Lee and Jackson and James Longstreet and Jeb Stuart arrayed on one side against John Pope and Ambrose Burnside and Joseph Hooker and a group of other less talented Union generals on the other side, it's possible to conclude that indeed the Confederacy did have better generals and that they must have lost because they didn't have enough of anything else. But if you shift your lens of focus to the Western Theater, if you move beyond the Appalachian Mountains toward the Mississippi River Valley, you have the absolutely opposite situation in place.

You have Grant and William Tecumseh Sherman and George H. Thomas and John Schofield and other very successful Union commanders fighting a group of Confederates that included Braxton Bragg and Leonidas Polk and others who were obviously not as talented as their Northern competitors. The North achieved great success in the west just as Lee and his lieutenants achieved great success in the east.

So if we're assessing the resources of command, looking at the entire landscape of the war, you end up with approximately equal numbers of very able officers—great officers—which is small on both sides. You have Lee and Jackson for the Confederacy. You have Grant and Sherman and perhaps Thomas and Sheridan for the North. Then you drop to a big mid-range where there are many competent officers but not brilliant on both sides. And then drop again to a rung where you have many officers on both sides in significant levels of command who are not very talented at all and who really aren't up to their jobs. My point is that the whole picture shows approximately equal pools of command from which each side drew.

The North did have a significant advantage in the number of West Pointers who fought for the North, and West Pointers will occupy most of the key posts during the war. Virtually all of the army commanders were trained at West Point. Most of the corps commanders were trained at West Point, the corps being the next level of command down. Just below the corps command were divisions. Divisions made up corps; corps made up armies. Most of the division commanders, the most successful ones, were also West Pointers. You drop down below the division level to brigades and below brigades to regiments. Even at those levels many West Pointers held commands at some point during their Civil War career.

So West Point is a crucial contributing institution to the high commands of both sides, and in sheer numbers the North had far more West Pointers.

There were 824 West Point graduates on the active list at the outbreak of war, of whom 184 became Confederate officers and 640 became Union officers, a very large advantage to the North there. Of approximately 900 graduates of West Point who were in private life at the time of the bombardment of Fort Sumter, 99 went into the Confederate service and 114 went into the Northern service. Add those two sets of numbers together, and you have the total number of West Pointers in the Southern army as 283 and the total in the Northern army as 754.

Of all United States Army officers in service at the beginning of the war, that is West Pointers and men who were not trained at West Point, 313 resigned to go with the South, and 767 remained loyal to the United States. Again, a decisive edge goes to the North.

But three factors helped offset this preponderance in terms of numbers of Northern West Pointers and men with previous military experience. In fact, these three factors may have given the Confederate Army of Northern Virginia a slight edge over its Federal opponent in the early stage of the war. It's not so true in the western armies of the Confederacy, but it is true with the army in northern Virginia. It had an initial edge both in terms of company officers, that is, lieutenants and captains, and field grade officers, that is, majors and lieutenant colonels and colonels, and these three factors break down like this:

The first is that the larger Northern armies needed far more officers, so the fact that the North has more in an absolute sense is necessary so that they can staff their armies at the same level that the Confederacy could. A second factor was the decision that I mentioned in our last lecture made early in the war on the part of the North to keep the cadre of professional soldiers together rather than to take those officers who were in the United States Army at the beginning of the war and spread them out among all the volunteer units that were pouring in to Union service. So you denied those many thousands of volunteers the benefit of the experience and training of the professional officers who were in the United States Army. The North changed that policy later in the war, but initially it denied the volunteers the services of these men.

The third factor that offset the Northern advantage in numbers here was the fact that Southern military schools sent many hundreds of officers into Confederate service. The two most prominent of these schools were the Virginia Military Institute in Lexington, Virginia, and the Military College of South Carolina, more popularly known as the Citadel, in Charleston, South Carolina. There were also military schools in all of the other Confederate states. Far more men were trained in all of these Southern institutions than were trained in comparable institutions in the North.

The Virginia Military Institute was the most important of all of them, and we can use it as an example. Nearly 2,000 men had gone to the Virginia Military Institute from the time of its founding in the late 1830s down through the end of the Civil War, more than 1,700 of whom served in the Confederate army, and virtually all of whom served in the Army of Northern Virginia and brought a tremendous amount of expertise and training into the army as captains, lieutenants, regimental commanders, and men who held even higher positions than that.

The vast majority of the Citadel's graduates also served in the Confederate army and a disproportionate number of them also served in the Eastern Theater with the Army of Northern Virginia. The presence of all of these men with military training amidst the thousands of volunteers provided a tremendous boost to Confederate efforts to build what would pass for a professional army during the Civil War.

Richard McMurray, an excellent scholar of military affairs during the Civil War, has written a book called *Two Great Rebel Armies* that specifically looks at the impact on the structure and performance of the Army of Northern Virginia of all of these men trained at the Citadel and at VMI and elsewhere. McMurray concludes, and I think correctly, that the presence of these men, top to bottom, made the Army of Northern Virginia the most efficient and effective military force early in the war.

Now, the North caught up as the war went on and men trained on the job, as it were—they went into positions where they could make their talent felt on the battlefield and in camp. By the midpoint of the war or later, there was a great evening out and, I think, rough parity among most of the forces, North and South, in terms of their officer material, but there is a slight advantage, I think, at least early on, to the Army of Northern Virginia because of these men trained in state schools, the major factor that helped offset the Northern advantage in numbers of men who'd gone to West Point or served in the United States Army before the war without having gone to West Point.

The quality of general officers, as I've already suggested, was about the same for the North and the South. We can give a few numbers here as well. There were eventually 583 men who became United States generals, Union generals, during the war. Four hundred twenty-five became Confederate generals. Of those Union generals, 264, or 47 percent, were either West Pointers or had significant military experience before the war. On the Confederate side, 194, or 45 percent, were either West Pointers or had significant military experience before the war. So it's almost exactly the same proportion.

Again, both sides are drawing on pools of potential commanders that look very much like each other, although there were instances where men with no military training achieved high command and in some cases did very well. Wade Hampton of South Carolina, Nathan Bedford Forest of Tennessee, and John Brown Gordon of Georgia are the three most conspicuous Confederate examples, I think, of men with no military training who achieved high command. Daniel Sickles, a politician from New York, is a man who achieved corps command in the Union Army without benefit of significant military background. But those men are clear exceptions to the rule that high commands, posts of great responsibility, went to West Pointers and other regularly trained men on both sides.

In terms of army commanders, it is a West Point club. Because it was a West Point club, it's very important to remember that these men shared essentially the same experience as cadets at West Point. They took the same courses from the same professors. They read the same books. They absorbed the same body of doctrine, to use a modern term that they wouldn't have used, during the course of their studies there. Beyond that, they shared, in a wider sense, a common military heritage. Many of them had served together in Mexico, where again they had learned the same lessons, whether as a soldier in Winfield Scott's army that made the famous campaign from

Vera Cruz to Mexico City, or whether they served in northern Mexico with Zachary Taylor.

They watched Scott, and they watched Taylor, and many of them tried to emulate one or another or in some instances both of those officers during their Civil War careers. For example, Ulysses S. Grant, I think, was much influenced both by service under Zachary Taylor and Zachary Taylor's example and by Winfield Scott on the campaign from Vera Cruz to Mexico City. These are men whose training and experience all came from one common group of sources, and, because of that, they tended to subscribe to the same ideas about strategy and tactics.

Now, for our purposes, we can define tactics as that branch of warfare involving the actual combat between attackers and defenders. Strategy for us is the branch of warfare involving the movement of armies to a particular point to bring about combat with an enemy under favorable circumstances or to force the retreat of the enemy. It's possible to divide this into more levels than that. You can call what I've just described strategy, operational strategy, and then move to a higher level called national strategy or grand strategy, which would involve the overall war aims of each side.

For our discussion today, let's use the simpler definition of tactics and of strategy. Most of these men who held high positions of command on both sides subscribed to basically the same ideas about what you should try to do. The most important of these tactical and strategic beliefs can be quickly summarized. One was that men on both sides realized that the defense was more powerful than the offense because of recent developments in weapons.

The key development that we would be talking about there is the development of the rifle musket as opposed to the old smoothbore musket, which had been in use for many decades before the Civil War. The advent of the rifle musket brought great changes to battlefield tactics. Before the Civil War, when both sides were armed with smoothbores, frontal assaults had a much better chance of being successful because the range of the smoothbore weapons, the effective range, was really only about 100 yards. Therefore, it was possible for an attacking force to be on top of the defenders before the defenders could get off many shots against them.

It was possible for cavalry to attack infantry because the cavalry could be on top of them very quickly. It was possible to bring artillery up close to infantry because, if they stayed just 200 or 300 yards out of range of the smoothbore-armed infantry, the artillery could fire at the infantry without fear of taking heavy losses.

In fact, a good way to think of how effective, how active you could be as a defender with a smoothbore musket—active in pushing back an attack, that is—think about one person at one goal line of a football field and another person at the other goal line of a football field. Armed with a smoothbore musket, chances are that one person 100 yards away from another one only had about an even-even chance of hitting the person at the other end of the football field. That's not a very long range, and it gives attackers very wide latitude.

Rifle muskets, which came into general use in the mid-1850s and which became the most dominant shoulder weapon, certainly by the midpoint of the Civil War, had a much longer range. They had an extreme range of upwards of 1,000 yards but an effective range of at least 300 yards, which means that the amount of ground that an attacker would have to cover under fire, under effective fire from defenders, was three times as far as it had been in the days of smoothbores. That meant that attacking formations could be broken up much more effectively.

It meant that cavalry was useless as an attacking arm against infantry during the Civil War because veteran infantry armed with rifle muskets could render any cavalry formation completely chaotic long before it reached the defending position because they could shoot down so many horses. It also meant that artillery could no longer be run up close to defending infantry because, again, the rifle muskets allowed the infantrymen to shoot down artillery horses and pick off gunners who came too close to the defensive positions. So the rifle musket made an enormous difference in that regard.

This change was made possible by the advent of what we now call the Minié ball, and it worked very simply. There had been rifles for many, many years before the Civil War. You've heard of Pennsylvania rifles and other rifles used in the eighteenth century and early nineteenth century. The problem with them was that you had a ball that was very closely fitted and very difficult to get down the barrel of one of the early rifles. The black powder was a very dirty propellant, so it fouled the rifling and the barrel quickly. You could not fire these early rifles rapidly, and you also had to clean them quite frequently.

The development of the Minié ball solved this. The Minié ball was slightly smaller than the caliber of the weapon. It had a hollow base. It's a lead projectile with a hollow base. When you fired it the base expanded. It engaged the grooves in the rifling and gave you all that extra distance from your shoulder weapon. It was a major step forward. Although the rifle muskets to our eyes outwardly look no more modern than a smoothbore musket, in fact they brought great changes to Civil War battlefields.

At the same time you had a change in artillery weapons as well with the advent of rifle tubes in cannons at the same time that you're getting rifling in the shoulder weapons. One other factor also increased the power of the defenders on Civil War battlefields, and that was the advent of field fortifications. If you put a soldier armed with a rifled weapon behind field works, it made him that much stronger. As the attackers came toward him, he not only had all the range that the rifle musket gave him but he also had protection of the field fortifications.

It was a good rule of thumb recognized by soldiers on both sides in the war that a defender armed with a rifle musket behind fieldworks was worth at least three attackers in terms of power and effectiveness on the battlefield. Officers on both sides were aware of this, and one of the key pieces of tactical doctrine that they shared was that it was very difficult to come to grips in an advantageous situation with defenders armed with these rifle muskets. The defense had the advantage over the offense.

The next thing they shared flowed naturally from this, and that was that you should avoid frontal assaults if at all possible. If defenders are so much stronger, and especially if defenders behind field fortifications are so much stronger, then you shouldn't try to attack them head-on. It's better to try to get at them some other way. They had seen in Mexico—many of these soldiers under Winfield Scott's leadership—how effective turning movements could be. That is, instead of attacking directly your opponent, try to get around either the right or left flank of your opponent. Bring the mass of your troops to bear on the weak end points of the enemy's line. Flank the enemy; don't attack him head-on. Soldiers on both sides agreed that that would be a better way to try to achieve tactical success on a battlefield.

A third widely held belief was that to achieve strategic success, an army should operate on interior lines, and that, in fact, even tactically interior lines would pay off. I used the example in the last lecture of the interior lines strategically that helped the Confederates in the campaign of First Manassas, where they hurried reinforcements from the lower Shenandoah Valley to the Battlefield at Manassas along a direct rail route that the Union could not match.

In a tactical sense, interior lines showed very effectively at Gettysburg for the Union Army under George Gordon Meade. The famous Union fishhook was about two and a half miles from one end to the other. The Confederates were arrayed on a much larger fishhook outside the Union fishhook, which meant that Meade could shift troops from his right flank on Culps Hill to positions on his left flank, the wheat field, for example, on the second day much more rapidly than Lee could match that by shifting troops from his left or right to the other flank. So interior lines tactically were good; interior lines strategically were good. Soldiers on both sides agreed.

The fact that they all accepted these basic things, the strength of the defense, the problematical nature of frontal assaults, the usefulness of interior lines, doesn't mean that they all could execute them equally well. That's where the ability of generals comes in. Some are simply better than others, and although most of the soldiers on both sides recognized these things were ideals to strive for, some proved to be much more adept at achieving them than did others. But a pretty much equal body of learning and experience underlay the thinking on both sides. Again, it was a very similar situation, North and South.

One more factor of command is worth mentioning, and that is the role of political generals on both sides. We should always remember that this is a case of two democratic societies at war, and it is imperative for the political leaders of those two societies to take into account public opinion and certain key constituencies. That was the case on both sides.

Abraham Lincoln appointed a number of German generals because the German element was so important in the North in keeping the war effort going. There were Irish generals. There were Democratic generals from Democratic areas. There were Republican generals from Republican areas. Jefferson Davis did the same thing. He had to take care of some powerful political constituencies within the Confederacy as well.

There were many famous political officers on both sides. Not many talented ones, not many successful ones, but many famous ones: Benjamin Butler for the North; Nathaniel P. Banks for the North; Carl Shirtz, one of the German generals from the North; and Frantz Sigel, another German general from the North. On the Southern side you have such politicians as the two Georgians, Robert Toombs and Hal Cobb. My point is that these men were selected not because they were great officers but because they served a particular constituency and it was important to keep those constituencies tied to the war effort. Overall—and I may have belabored this too much, but I think it's important because the notion that the Confederacy had better generals is so widely held—the bottom line here is that both sides drew from quite comparable pools of potential military leadership.

Let's move on to our second topic here, and that is the relative success of Jefferson Davis and Abraham Lincoln as war leaders. Now, it would seem at the outset that Lincoln would be much the less effective of the two. He had virtually no military experience. He'd been a company grade officer very briefly in the Black Hawk War back in the 1830s. But Lincoln was a very bright man. He applied himself diligently to gaining a better grasp of military affairs. He listened to his military advisors: Winfield Scott, George B. McClellan, and others. He read what they told him to read, and he very early on developed, I think, a quite sound strategic grasp of what it would take for Northern victory.

He understood that it was imperative to apply pressure across the board against the Confederacy so it would be difficult for the Confederates to match all these Union advances with the smaller pool of Confederate resources. He understood, did Lincoln, that it was important to target enemy armies rather than cities because, if you defeated the armies, if you smashed the armies or bled the armies sufficiently, the Confederate resistance would wither.

It was more important, Lincoln understood early in the war, to come to grips with Lee's Army of Northern Virginia and hurt it as much as possible. It was more important to do that than to try to get into Richmond without inflicting the greatest possible damage on the Army of Northern Virginia. A great strength of Lincoln's was that he saw these two key strategic imperatives for the North.

He also was a man who could put his own ego aside in dealing with officers in the hope that they would give him victories. That's one of his great strengths. He put up with a great deal from George B. McClellan, hoping that McClellan would give him victories, and when he finally found Grant and knew that he had a very effective General-in-Chief in Grant, he gave Grant extremely wide latitude. He did not try to micromanage Grant. He still certainly took an active role, Lincoln did, in what was going on, but he let his good generals have quite a free rein to win successes on the battlefield.

And Lincoln was willing to change his view of what kind of war it would take to win. He was willing to go from a rather limited vision of what it would take to a vision that encompassed striking at the Confederate home front, hitting civilian property, freeing Confederate slaves, doing whatever it took to give the Union an edge. So Lincoln grew tremendously during the war and turned into a very good war leader.

Jefferson Davis, I think, was a good war leader as well. He brought great military experience to his position as Confederate president. He'd been a West Pointer. He commanded a regiment in the war with Mexico very effectively; he became a hero in that war. He was Secretary of War under Franklin Pierce in the 1850s and a very effective Secretary of War. I think that he did a very sound job, although he's often criticized as a Confederate war leader. He initially, I think, tried to protect too much Confederate territory, but he eventually embraced what has been called the offensive-defensive strategy, or defensive-offensive, which had the Confederacy stand on a broadly defensive posture and launch limited counteroffensives where it seemed that they might be successful.

I think he had a good strategic grasp. I think one of his failings was that he was unwilling to give as much latitude to his generals, even to Robert E. Lee, as Lincoln was willing to give to his good generals. I think Davis fancied himself a sort of General-in-Chief as well as president of the Confederacy and, therefore, it was very late in the war and only at the Confederate Congress's insistence that Lee was made General-in-Chief. On the whole, however, I think Jefferson Davis had a good grasp of strategy and military theory in practice. Davis will always suffer in comparative estimates of the presidential leadership on both sides, but in the area of war leader—not political but military leader—I think Jefferson Davis did very well, as did Abraham Lincoln. I wouldn't give a large edge to either one of them.

This brings us to our last variable, the great unknown as the war got underway: What would Europe do? Would either of the great European powers, would either England or France, decide that it was to their advantage to come into the war on the side of the Confederacy, to extend recognition to the Confederacy, to make it difficult for the Northern blockade to try to strangle the Confederacy? If the Royal Navy decided that it was going to clear the way for commerce between the Confederacy and Great Britain, that would be an enormous headache for the United States Navy.

Now, again, in the minds of everybody, North and South, who was in a position of authority and had anything at all to do with foreign affairs, the example of the American Revolution loomed extremely large because, in our fight for independence, the intervention of the French had been crucial. It is almost inconceivable that the colonies would have thrown off the yoke, as they saw it, of British tyranny without the help of the French after the Battle of Saratoga. The French sent a fleet. They sent thousands of troops. They gave major loans. French help was absolutely crucial to the success of the colonists in the American Revolution, and both Union and Confederate planners were extremely well aware of this during the Civil War.

In fact, both foreign policies, as we'll talk about later in the course, were tailored to a significant extent to try, on the Confederate side, to achieve recognition from Europe and maybe even material help and, on the Union side, to prevent European recognition of the Confederacy. No one knew what would happen at this stage of the war. I think everyone knew that Europe potentially could be a crucial player in how the war would be resolved.

So, if we look overall—both at what we've talked about in this lecture and in the last one—at the balance sheet, so to speak, North and South, the conclusions, I think, are obvious. The North had some very considerable advantages, but the South was by no means facing a hopeless struggle for independence. Other countries had won at longer odds. In the end, it would come down to a question of which side would muster its resources and use its advantages in such a way as to gain enough of an edge over the opponent to convince that opponent's population that it was useless to continue the struggle.

We'll leave that now with our balance sheet in mind, and we will shift next time to consider the men who were going to be the critical actors in one sense in what would happen in the war—the common soldiers who, by the hundreds of thousands and, in the end, by the millions, went into the armies and would be the men who fought the battles that in large measure determined the outcome of the war.

The Common Soldier
Lecture 7

Now we're going to shift our focus to the most important resource that each side had at hand, and that was the men who would fight the war.

This lecture examines several elements of the common soldier's experience. Approximately 3 million men served in the Union and Confederate military forces, and they mirrored their respective societies in terms of occupation, class, and other demographic categories. They served in units with strong regional identification—often in companies raised from the same town or area and regiments from the same part of a state—and frequently shared tents with relatives or friends. Approximately 2.1 million served in the North (roughly 50 percent of the military-age pool). A total of 750,000 to 850,000 served in the Confederacy (roughly 75 to 85 percent of the white military-age pool).

About the Soldiers

- The "average" soldier was a native-born, white, Protestant farmer between the ages of 18 and 29.

- About 25 percent of the North's soldiers were foreign born, with Germans and Irish predominating (more than 30 percent of the military-age white males in the North were foreign born).

- About 9 to 10 percent of the Confederate soldiers were foreign born (7.5 percent of the military-age white males were foreign born).

- A few Native Americans fought on each side (more fought for the Confederacy).

- Approximately 180,000 blacks served in the United States Army; some blacks served in the CSA but in noncombatant roles.

- African American soldiers, who made up almost 10 percent of the Union army, will be discussed in a later lecture.

Soldiers left a mass of letters, diaries, and other evidence that enables us to reconstruct their lives in the army and gain at least some understanding of their motivations and attitudes. A number of factors prompted them to enlist and remain in the ranks; ideology and patriotism ranked highest among men who volunteered in 1861 and 1862. Quite understandably, men who enlisted because they feared being conscripted and those drafted directly into the army often exhibited less enthusiasm and willingness to fight hard and make sacrifices than the early volunteers did.

The breakdown of soldiers by class reflected that in society at large:

- Farmers were the largest group in each army.

- Skilled laborers were the next largest group.

- Professional men and white-collar workers combined were slightly underrepresented in the armies.

It was not a "rich man's war but a poor man's fight."

Various factors motivated soldiers to enlist and remain in the ranks. Those who volunteered in 1861–62 were more likely to be motivated by ideology and patriotism (Professor James McPherson is a leading advocate of this assertion). Other factors included peer or community pressure, a search for adventure, masculine identity, the desire to be a hero, hatred of the enemy, and the lure of money (e.g., enlistment bounties in the North). This was the general view of the pioneering Civil War historian Bell Wiley.

How did slavery factor in? Slavery was a part of Southern society, even though most soldiers did not own slaves. On the Union side, probably only a very small percentage of soldiers fought for emancipation. The key reason for fighting for the most part was to restore the Union. Most soldiers probably combined several of these factors in their decisions to serve.

Soldiers spent most of their time in camp. They contended with a number of problems and unpleasant duties in this environment:

- Boredom was a common phenomenon.

- They drilled frequently.

- They resisted strict military discipline.

- They suffered from homesickness.

Soldiers engaged in various amusements to dispel camp boredom:

- They gambled and played cards.

- They read and wrote letters.

- They played a variety of games (chess, checkers, and so on).

- They sang and played music (sentimental songs were the favorites).

- They chased animals.

- They engaged in enormous snowball fights.

Soldiers complained most often about the food:

- Confederates often lacked enough to eat.

- Hardtack (Union), cornbread (Confederate), and problematical meat were staples.

- Fresh vegetables and fruit were often in short supply.

Soldiers suffered terribly from disease and poor medical care. Disease killed two soldiers for each man killed or mortally wounded in battle. Childhood diseases, such as measles, chickenpox, and mumps, were great problems (especially among rural men and early in the war). Also, poor food and contaminated water complicated health issues. Latrines were often poorly situated, and soldiers drank from rivers, creeks, and ponds. Dysentery, diarrhea, and malaria were scourges. Yet another difficulty soldiers faced was inadequate clothing, which caused poor health in winter.

Medicine could not treat many battlefield injuries effectively. Physicians were most successful in treating wounds to the limbs through amputation but could not do much for torso wounds. Soldiers often waited many hours (or even days) to receive treatment for wounds.

Although desertion plagued both armies (rates were nearly the same on each side—12 to 14 percent), most soldiers served competently in camp and in battle. ■

Essential Reading

McPherson and Cooper (eds.), *Writing the Civil War: The Quest to Understand*, Mitchell essay.

Supplementary Reading

McPherson, *For Cause and Comrades: Why Men Fought in the Civil War*.

Mitchell, *Civil War Soldiers*.

Wiley, *The Life of Billy Yank: The Common Soldier of the Union*.

———, *The Life of Johnny Reb: The Common Soldier of the Confederacy*.

1. To what extent did Union and Confederate soldiers share a common experience? To what extent did their wartime service differ?

2. What do you think it would take to motivate modern Americans to undertake the type of service rendered by Civil War soldiers?

The Common Soldier
Lecture 7—Transcript

In our last two lectures we assessed the relative strengths and weaknesses of the two sides as they moved toward war in 1861, looking at the resources on which each side could draw. Now we're going to shift our focus to the most important resource that each side had at hand and that was the men who would fight the war.

We'll look at the ways in which approximately three million soldiers mirrored the two societies from which they came. We'll consider some of the factors that motivated men to enlist and to remain in the ranks. We'll discuss the routine of camp life. We'll assess the ravages of disease and wounds on the ranks of the men in both armies, and we'll finish with a brief examination of just how resolute the soldiers on both sides proved to be in the face of the many difficult circumstances associated with being a soldier.

Let's start by looking at who these men were. Who were the Civil War soldiers? How well did they reflect their societies? The number overall is about three million who served on one side or the other. As we've said before, there were about 2.2 million in the Northern military and between 750,000 and 850,000 on the Confederate side. They went into the army often surrounded by their neighbors or their relatives—their cousins, brothers, sometimes even their fathers or uncles—because the principal component of Civil War armies, the major building block, the company, was often raised from a single town or from a single county, especially early in the war. Often whole regiments were sent into the service the same way.

On paper a company had 100 men, and on paper a regiment had 10 companies, so a regiment would have 1,000 men. There'd be two or more regiments in a brigade, often four or more, and then two or more brigades in a division. Two or more divisions in a corps and then two or more corps would make up an army. By the midpoint of the war, a veteran regiment, which on paper should have had a 1,000 men in it, might have 400 men or might even have fewer than 400 men because of losses to disease, to battle wounds, to desertion, to straggling, or whatever. When Lee's Army of Northern Virginia reached the battlefield at Antietam in mid-September

1862, the average strength of his regiments on that field was fewer than 180 men. On paper it should have been 1,000. So the war took a tremendous toll on these units.

But early on, when the men went into the service they went with people they knew. They went from communities. There's a very strong community component to Civil War units. You would be serving alongside men who likely would be writing home about what you were doing, or they could be anyway. So there was not a feeling that once you got off into the army, you'd be far away from everyone who knew you and no one would know what was going on. There were lots of ties to the people back home, to the circle of people with whom you had grown up, and a good sense that there would be a communitywide perception of how your unit was doing, how individual members of the unit were doing. There was just a tremendous bond tying the home front to the battlefield in this instance.

The men who went into the army were diverse, very diverse, in terms of what kinds of backgrounds they had. More than 100 occupations, for example, existed among Southern troops. We've identified more than 100. A typical unit was the 19th Virginia: of the 749 original members who went into the 19th Virginia, 302 were farmers, 80 were laborers, 56 were machinists, 24 were students, 14 were teachers, 10 were lawyers, 3 were blacksmiths, and 2 were artists. There was also one distiller, probably much prized once he got into the army, a well digger, a dentist, and four men who classified themselves simply as gentlemen. That is a snapshot of what kinds of people were in this one Confederate regiment.

The average Northern regiment was even more diverse, although, as in the South, approximately half of all men in Northern service were farmers or agricultural laborers. Over 300 occupations can be found on Federal muster rolls, an even wider array, a much wider array, that I think suggests the degree to which the North had developed a more sophisticated economy than the Confederacy had.

The typical soldier from both North and South was white, a native-born farmer, Protestant, single, and falling in the range between 18 and 29 years old. That would be your average soldier if you can have such a thing as an average soldier. Eighteen was the minimum age of enlistment for much of the war, but there's evidence of children, really—ages nine or ten or eleven—who served in the armies as drummer boys or musicians or ambulance drivers. They also fought and died, as did many men in their sixties, and some men even in their seventies volunteered. There are a handful of men, eighty years old, who volunteered for service during the Civil War. They weren't put in units that actively campaigned and made prodigious marches, but my point is that there's an astonishingly wide range of ages represented in the Northern and Southern military forces during the Civil War.

Most were Protestants, as I said. Most were native born, but immigrants also played a key role, many of whom were Catholics, both German Catholics and Irish Catholics, especially in the Northern forces. Immigration rates in antebellum America were unusually high. In 1860, roughly 30 percent of all the men in the North had been born somewhere else—just about 30 percent. In the United States Army during the war, one out of four soldiers was either a first- or second-generation immigrant. The most numerous category in this case was the Germans, followed closely by the Irish, but there were also many other nationalities represented: Norwegians and Swedes and many others in the Union army.

The Confederate armies had a much lower proportion of foreign-born men, about 9 percent, which was actually much higher than the proportion of foreign-born men in the Confederacy itself, which was about between 5 and 6 percent. Slightly less than 10 percent in the Confederate army and slightly more than 25 percent in the Union army were foreign born or second-generation immigrants.

Native Americans fought on both sides in the war. Three brigades of Cherokees, Choctaws, Chickasaws, and Seminoles went into the Confederate army. One brigade, mostly of Creeks, fought for the Union. The Native American soldiers on both sides, I must add, were very poorly treated by the respective governments. They did not receive the same kind of treatment that most white troops did in the two armies.

The Union put approximately 180,000 black men in uniform as United States Colored Troops, as they were called, during the war. They made up just about 9 percent of all the men who wore the blue uniform of the United States during the war. There's been a good deal of discussion and publication lately about black men serving in the Confederate army, and you can read in some places estimates as high as 50,000 black soldiers in the Confederate army. Well, there were many black men accompanying Confederate armies, many slaves with any Confederate army, but they were not serving as soldiers. They were serving in many noncombatant roles. I suspect the vast majority of them would have preferred to be somewhere else rather than with the army.

The notion that there were thousands of black men actually enrolled in the Confederate army and carrying muskets simply isn't so. That notion has come up, and it's proved quite persistent, but it's simply inaccurate. It didn't happen, although there were black faces in both armies serving in noncombatant roles early in the war on the Northern side and then eventually as soldiers, and slaves performing these noncombatant activities in the Confederate army.

There's been a great debate as well among Civil War historians about just why men went into service during the Civil War and why they stayed there as the war dragged on and conditions became more and more difficult in many circumstances. It's very common to find in parts of the literature an argument that goes something like this: Most Civil War soldiers were not well attuned to the great ideological currents of their time. They weren't especially well attuned to the political debates that went on before the war and during the war. They didn't care about those kinds of things. What their primary allegiance was to was their fellow soldiers in their unit. Their small unit cohesion was the key. That's what kept them in the service; that's what they gave primary loyalty to. William Faulkner, for example, in one of his novels, has a Confederate veteran character respond, when he's asked why he fought in the Civil War, "Damned if I ever did know why I fought in the Civil War."

There was a study of United States soldiers in World War II that came out shortly after World War II that argued that men in the United States forces during World War II were not especially concerned with the great political issues of the time. As I said earlier, they were loyal to their peers. Well, some

Civil War historians have taken that study of American soldiers in World War II and have, in essence, applied it to soldiers during the Civil War and have concluded that there wasn't that much political discussion or political thinking that went into why Civil War soldiers decided to fight.

Bell Wiley, one of the pioneering historians of the common soldier, certainly takes that view in much of his work. He doesn't find that the men were much concerned at all with ideological issues. He says that they joined for a number of reasons. They might have wanted adventure, a desire for camaraderie with other men, the chance to earn glory in battle—any number of reasons apart from an ideological reason. A war against slavery, a war to defend freedoms, a war to advance the legacy of the founding generation—Wiley would have said those things were not very important. He would have said peer pressure could be important. If all your friends were going into the service, then you'd probably go too if you didn't want to be held up as someone who was not patriotic.

There's another current in the literature, however, that argues just the opposite, and one of the leading practitioners of this is James M. McPherson. His book *For Cause and Comrades* is an excellent example of a work that presents these arguments. This strain in the literature says that, yes, there was a strong ideological component in why men decided to fight on one side or the other. Historians make the argument that soldiers read a lot. Most of them are 24 years old or so—that's sort of the average age of enlistees. They're from a literate society. They read newspapers. They read other books. They like to go to political speeches. They are attuned to the politics of their time. They do care about ideology.

They would say that they fought for liberty or Republican ideals from the Revolution. They would say on both sides that they were the inheritors of the revolutionary tradition. This strain in the literature, this group of scholars, says just the opposite, that, unlike American soldiers in World War II, if it's true that our World War II soldiers didn't much care about ideology, Civil War soldiers—both sides, in contrast—did care about those things and cared passionately, especially the soldiers who enlisted freely before the draft in either side, before the Confederate draft in the spring of 1862, before the United States draft the following spring. The soldiers who went by the hundreds of thousands into the armies in 1861 and early 1862, those men especially, cared about the great issues, the great ideological issues of the time.

There's also been an argument about whether idealism, if it was present in the beginning, survived. Some scholars have said, no, that the process of fighting and marching and the humdrum of camp life and seeing your friends blown apart and so forth eroded that idealism and soon men did end up basically with loyalty to their comrades and to their units. Others again have argued that the ideology remained right to the end, especially among those men who enlisted freely, which would be the majority of the soldiers in the first year of the war.

What about slavery and emancipation? How did those figure as motivations? Did Southern soldiers go into the army to protect slavery? We know that the vast majority of Southern soldiers didn't own slaves just as the vast majority of white Southerners as a whole did not. So was slavery the primary motivational factor for them? They certainly didn't write about it in their letters home, but they probably wouldn't because it was such a given of their society—of course slavery's part of their society.

I think that, without doubt, the overwhelming majority of Confederate soldiers would have considered their slave-based society the right kind of society. They would have approved of slavery in that society. But that doesn't mean that most of them went to war just to protect slavery. They had ideas about personal liberty and freedom that were not necessarily just centered on slavery. They didn't want someone else telling them how they should order their society and run their lives, and I think many of them believed that's why they were fighting.

On the Union side, how many white soldiers were fighting for emancipation? I think a very small percentage would have said emancipation was the key reason that they were taking up arms to fight the South. The overwhelming majority of Northern soldiers, I think, would say they were fighting for union, to preserve the Union, to put the Union back together. Some from the very beginning would have said emancipation was the key, but I suspect not more than 10 percent. As the war went on, most Union soldiers embraced emancipation as a goal that would help bring union if nothing else, but, even at the end of the war, I think by far more Union soldiers would have said the key goal in terms of their service to the United States was to restore the Union. If emancipation also came that would be fine, but I don't think they would have listed emancipation as their primary reason for being in the army and staying in the army.

There's been some interesting work lately about a gender dimension of why men fought during the Civil War. It emphasizes masculinity and how important concepts of masculinity were in leading men to go into the army and to believe that they couldn't really be seen as men if they didn't do their duty, their military duty, because conceptions of masculinity were very much tied to fighting being part of a man's—a strong man's—responsibility to his society and to his family. Some scholars have argued, in fact, that masculine identity was probably more important even than ideology in propelling a lot of men into the army.

Well, I think all of these factors played a role. In fact, individuals probably were prompted by any number of these things. You could be passionate about the Union but also give in to peer pressure or at least feel peer pressure to go in. You could want to get at the enemy. There could be revenge as a motive. All kinds of things could come together in individual soldiers to get them into the army and then keep them in the ranks. I don't think there's any way really to rank these different factors in order, but I think on any list you'd have to have ideology. Certainly at least 50 percent of the men, again that first great wave that went in, would have had ideology as an important component.

You can call it different things, whether it's love of Union or of the Southern way of life, or of liberty, freedom, or patriotism; whatever you call it, ideology certainly would play an important part. Others, peer pressure, community pressure—if all your friends from your little township have gone and there are only two or three men who haven't gone, there will be tremendous pressure to go. There are instances of women wrapping up articles of feminine clothing, petticoats and such, and sending them to men who hadn't volunteered with a little note that said, enlist or start to wear these. In effect, if you're going to be a real man, enlist. If not, perhaps you'd like to try petticoats as an article of attire in the future.

Some men were simply bored—bored on the farm, bored being a clerk. They saw military service as a chance for adventure. Some thought glory in battle would be nice. They'd seen woodcuts from Napoleonic wars or from the war with Mexico, and they wanted to go be a hero, come home as a hero, impress a girlfriend or a spouse as a military hero. Hatred certainly played a role with some men, either hatred of Yankees or hatred of traders, if you're looking at it from the Northern point of view.

Slavery, either to defend it, or emancipation to kill it, certainly played a role. Money—some poor Northern men, especially many poor immigrants, went into the army because they would get a regular paycheck, they'd have clothing, they'd be fed regularly. This was a way to make your economic way in the world early on. That is not a factor in the Confederacy because Confederates don't offer bounties and they don't pay enough to their soldiers even really to keep body and soul together.

All of these things would go into a mix that helps to explain why the soldiers went into service and then why they stayed in the service. Different men would be primarily guided by different parts of that list as they were in the army. Once they are in the army they underwent an experience, and we'll turn now to camp life and how men spent the great majority of their time.

Most of their time wasn't spent in battle. You have an occasional battle for most of the war, and then you're not fighting or marching for a good deal of the time. You're in camp. Most winters you're in camp for protracted periods. How did men deal with what was going on in camp? They faced a different set of challenges in camp than they did in battle. They had to contend with boredom as soldiers throughout history have, and they had to contend with what they viewed as an unpleasant set of duties and experiences in camp.

One of those unpleasant experiences was drill. Soldiers drilled incessantly during the Civil War. They had to so that on a battlefield they would perform effectively as a unit. They had to do it without thinking about it, to just respond to their officers' commands. So they were drilled and drilled and drilled. They were drilled by companies. They were drilled by regiments. In some instances, they were drilled by brigades. And the men grew very tired of it. They didn't like it at all. They didn't like discipline. These are men who are used to not having much discipline exercised in their lives. American society was democratic with a small "d," and these men weren't used to having people order them around and hem them in with all kinds of rules. Many of them responded by arching their backs and saying they didn't like that and resisting that discipline. They complained about it tremendously.

They also complained about the homesickness, the being gone from home for such long periods of time, and missing their families and missing their friends and missing the familiar scenes of home. So drill and discipline and homesickness—all of these figured in as experiences that soldiers dealt with and experiences that they did not particularly like.

They came up with innumerable ways to pass the time in camp. They read letters. They wrote letters. They read other things. They read the Bible, many of them did. It was a much more religious time than we live in now, and religion figured very prominently in the lives of many of these soldiers. But it didn't figure prominently in the lives of all of them, and some of the more devout soldiers often complained. I'll quote for just a couple of them here.

One Virginian wrote from his camp, "There's some of the orneriest men here that I ever did see and the most swearing and card playing and fighting and drunkenness that I ever saw in one place." A Northern soldier similarly wrote that, "In our camps, wickedness prevails to an almost unlimited extent. Gambling, card playing, profanity, Sabbath breaking—all these are among the vices practiced by our soldiers."

Some generals tried to prohibit profanity in their camps, and you can imagine how effective that was—an order from your colonel or your brigadier general saying there will be no more profanity in this camp. It was not very effective, especially when some of the generals and colonels were notorious for the imaginative strings of oaths that they would string together. So there is definitely a devout element in the service, and then there's an element that is much at odds with that devout element.

Men engaged in all kinds of nongambling games. They played chess and they played checkers, all of the things that you can imagine. They loved to sing and play music. Sentimental songs were by far the most popular. "Home Sweet Home" was the single most popular, I think without much doubt, song from the Civil War, and both sides sang it. Both sides tended to sing many of the same songs, sometimes with different lyrics. The most popular ones were sentimental songs.

In the summertime, soldiers chased animals. They chased rabbits, squirrels, and deer sometimes. They had races between lice. They would put lice on a hot pan and bet on which one would get across the pan faster. In the wintertime, they had enormous snowball battles sometimes. This was a special novelty for soldiers from the Deep South, and some of these involved literally thousands of men, thousands and thousands of men, with many casualties, including broken limbs and some fatalities even, in the largest of these battles.

As all soldiers have, the men complained a great deal, and they complained most often about the food. They complained about beef that seemed ancient. It was moldy. They complained about hardtack in the Northern armies that seemed to have been prepared for the Mexican War rather than the Civil War. The Confederate soldiers got cornmeal. That was their staple. Sometimes it was so coarsely ground that they said it made their gums bleed and made their teeth chip.

Civil War troops were hungry a good bit of the time, especially Confederates. As a general rule, you can say that Northern soldiers were better fed, much better fed. You don't see any really heavy Confederate soldiers in pictures from the Civil War. They're much lighter than many reenactors today, for example, who play Confederate soldiers. We're a better fed group of reenactors than the Confederates were as soldiers. A ration in Lee's army in the winter of 1863-64, for example, consisted of a quarter of a pound of meat a day and pint of cornmeal. That is not very much of an intake of calories to sustain a soldier in the field.

So, although both sides could be hungry, the Confederates tended to be less well fed than their Federal opposite numbers. Often fresh vegetables were hard to come by, and scurvy was a problem in both armies but especially in the Confederate army. There were tremendous complaints about food.

There were also complaints about medical care, and it was a very unhappy conjunction of two trends on the medical side that put Civil War soldiers in a difficult position. On the one hand, the war is fought at a time when the killing power has been made much more effective by rifled weapons. At the same time that the killing power has been made worse, medicine has not made some of the great discoveries that would come later in the nineteenth century. Battlefield tactics and wounds were way ahead of medical care, and what we would consider very common diseases also took a terrible toll. Civil War soldiers were the losers because of this situation in the mid-nineteenth century.

The bottom line was that two-thirds of all the men who died during the war on both sides died of disease—two-thirds. One-third died from battlefield wounds or were killed outright on the battlefield; two-thirds on each side died of disease. Some of the greatest killers were what we would call childhood diseases now: mumps and measles. In *Gone With the Wind*, when Scarlett marries her first husband, Charles Hamilton, he dies of measles in camp. Well, that was a very common situation, especially early in the war when men were first going into the service, especially among rural boys who hadn't been exposed to many of these diseases where they grew up. The city boys actually fared better in this regard. Many of them had developed immunities to some of the things that struck down the country boys.

But mumps, measles, and so forth took a tremendous toll, as did things like dysentery and chronic diarrhea. These were tremendous killers during the war and were things that medicine did not deal very effectively with. Dysentery, malaria, and diarrhea again and again and again appear in the letters that soldiers write home: My friend died of this; all of us are suffering from this. Partly it was the terrible regimen of food that they had. Part of it was that they lived in filthy camps, many of them. They wouldn't dig latrines in the right places. They wouldn't observe what we would consider the most basic hygiene. And medicine in many instances didn't help them out by telling them what to do.

Men wounded in battle suffered miserably, many times lying on the battlefield for hours or even a day or more before they had any medical attention at all. And when they did get it, the best that the surgeons could do for the most part was deal with wounds to the extremities. You could amputate an arm or a leg that had been shattered by a Minié ball, but if it was a wound anywhere in the torso, the conventional wisdom was, it's untreatable, put that person aside. He'll either live or he'll die, but there's nothing that we as physicians can do about it. We can cut off an arm or a leg—and there were untold numbers of amputations during the war—but we can't deal with that kind of a wound and the infection and the shocks that come from it.

Some men had horrible diseases. Some had horrible wounds and lived, but they lived in spite of the medical care that they got in many instances rather than because of it. In fact, many soldiers would write home in their letters and put in their diaries that they would rather remain in their tents and try to battle out a terrible bout of this or that disease or try to recover from one of their wounds on their own than put themselves into the hands of the surgeons and go into the hospitals where they thought they would probably not have as good a chance of surviving as they did on their own. Unfortunately, there was more than a little bit of truth in that.

The bottom line is that we wouldn't want to be either sick or wounded if we were Civil War soldiers because of the care. This is no reflection on the surgeons and physicians involved. They represented the best of their craft at the time. It's just that their craft had not advanced to the point where it could deal with much of what was happening to these soldiers.

If we step back and look at Civil War soldiers and try to assess how well they did in the face of the long marches and the horrible battles and the boredom of camp and the diseases that swept through their ranks, especially early in the war (veteran armies suffered less from disease than the armies early in the war, you'd winnow out the weak soldiers early on and, as the war went on, you got down to really a core of quite tough men who didn't suffer nearly as much from the debilitating medical things that hit the armies so hard early in the war)—how did they deal with the battles and with the marches and with the boredom and with the disease, the terror of going into a fight, the agony of the wounds that they received? I think that the vast majority served honorably. They served well. Desertion rates were between 12 and 14 percent for both armies. Between 12 and 14 percent of the men on each side deserted.

Overall the soldiers forged a record that did credit to them and I think underscored the degree to which many of them, North and South, saw the conflict as one waged over very important issues and principles, important enough to keep them in the ranks, important enough to make them put up with a great deal of discomfort, sometimes discomfort beyond what any of them could even imagine. Overall they were a quite stalwart set of men, I think, although I don't want to romanticize them. There were plenty of slackers and plenty of cowards and plenty of deserters, but on the whole I think the record was quite strong on the part of both Confederates and Federals.

So those are the men who are going to fight, who did fight the battles. Next time we will move to our first great battle of the war. We'll look at First Manassas or Bull Run.

First Manassas or Bull Run
Lecture 8

This lecture will examine Union planning in the late spring and early summer of 1861. We will then move on to consider the background and the conduct and the consequences of the Battle of First Manassas or Bull Run, the first major military engagement of the war.

After the Upper South's secession and the transfer of the Confederate seat of government from Montgomery, Alabama, to Richmond, Virginia, both sides sought to mobilize men and resources and plot military strategies. The North had to mount an active campaign to force the Confederate states back into the Union; the Confederacy had the easier task of countering the North's moves. If the Lincoln government did nothing, the Confederacy would win by default.

The crucial figure in the North was General Winfield Scott. Scott was a distinguished military man whose career went all the way back to the War of 1812 and included brilliant service in the Mexican War. Old and infirm by the time of the Civil War, he still had a good strategic grasp. This brilliant soldier formulated a long-range strategy that came to be called the "Anaconda Plan," which called for blockading the Confederate coast; seizing control of the Mississippi River; and if necessary, invading the South with a large army.

Scott argued for pressure on the coasts, along the Mississippi River, and possibly against the Confederate hinterlands. He argued that the North would have to be patient while the military built and trained a large force, perhaps as large as 300,000 men. But the Northern public clamored for an immediate march against Richmond, the Confederate capital, which is the first example of how important politics and public opinion would be in shaping Civil War military affairs. Lincoln believed that a battle could be won immediately, and he prodded General Irvin McDowell into action. To avoid any confusion, I should mention that the battle has two names because the North named battles after terrain features—Bull Run Creek—while the South used the nearest town or railroad junction—Manassas Junction.

The disposition of forces is important to understand. Confederate commander Joseph E. Johnston (with 12,000 men) faced Union General Robert Patterson (with 18,000 men) in the lower (northern) end of the Shenandoah Valley. Confederate General P. G. T. Beauregard (with 20,000 men) faced Union General Irvin McDowell (with 35,000 men) near Washington, D.C.

Union success depended on keeping the Confederate forces divided. A railroad connection gave the Confederates the advantage of interior lines. Patterson's goal was to tie Johnston down in the valley while McDowell struck Beauregard. McDowell wanted to avoid a direct assault and planned to turn the Confederate flank. McDowell marched from Washington, D.C., on 16 July 1861. By 20 July, the Confederates had concentrated near Manassas Junction.

The result was the campaign of First Manassas or Bull Run, which climaxed on July 21, 1861, in the war's first major clash. The Confederates won the battle, a fumbling affair that saw commanders on each side trying to apply lessons they had learned about flank attacks and interior lines. Although relatively modest by the standards of later battles of the war, First Manassas had a major impact on civilian morale and persuaded people on both sides that the war would not

Winfield Scott, general-in-chief of the U.S. armies.

Prints and Photographs Division, Library of Congress.

be won or lost in a matter of a few months. The Battle of First Manassas or Bull Run on 21 July 1861 yielded a major Confederate triumph.

The initial Union moves promised victory. But a strong Confederate defense under General Thomas J. Jackson on Henry House Hill bought time. Also, Johnston's troops eluded Patterson and joined Beauregard's force in time to turn the tide of battle.

The battle demonstrated the similarity between generalship on both sides. McDowell and Beauregard both planned to strike the other's flank rather than mount direct attacks. Both sides were well aware of the Confederacy's interior lines. The Federal retreat turned into a rout hampered by civilians who had come out to watch the battle; however, the Federal army showed resiliency after the initial rout, a pattern that would be repeated (e.g., after Chancellorsville and Chickamauga).

> **So 2,000 were lost on the Confederate side; 2,700 were lost on the Federal side. Later in the war, as I said, this would be considered a midsize battle or even a modest size battle, but here in July of 1861 it's an enormous battle, the biggest battle in United States history.**

The battle may have had long-term influence on expectations of success in the Union and Confederate armies in Virginia. As the largest battle in American history to that point, it made people on both sides think in terms of a bloodier contest. The North suffered 2,700 casualties; the South, about 2,000 (casualties included men killed, wounded, missing, and captured). The Northern public suffered a major disappointment and no longer expected a quick resolution to the war. The Confederate public took heart and expected to win independence. ∎

Essential Reading

Hattaway and Jones, *How the North Won: A Military History of the Civil War*, chapter 2.

McPherson, *Battle Cry of Freedom: The Civil War Era*, chapters 10–11.

Supplementary Reading

Adams, *Our Masters the Rebels*, chapter 4.

Davis, *Battle at Bull Run*.

1. What lessons should each side have learned from the First Manassas campaign?

2. What factors are crucial to a proper evaluation of the importance of a military campaign?

First Manassas or Bull Run
Lecture 8—Transcript

Following the Upper South's secession and the transfer of the seat of the Confederate government from Montgomery, Alabama, to Richmond, Virginia, both sides sought to mobilize men and resources and to plot their military strategies. This lecture will examine Union planning in the late spring and early summer of 1861. We will then move on to consider the background and the conduct and the consequences of the Battle of First Manassas or Bull Run, the first major military engagement of the war.

Let's start by looking at the task that the North faced in trying to come up with a strategy that would force the wayward states back into the Union. The key actor in the early consideration of this question will be Winfield Scott. Winfield Scott was in Washington, D.C. He was presiding as General-in-Chief of the United States armies, over the initial Union attempt to come up with a strategy to mobilize resources. In the process he also was advising Abraham Lincoln, trying to bring the new president along, a president who had virtually no military experience and hadn't read much about the military. Scott was trying to run things in a military sense on the one hand and to bring the new president along, bring him up to speed militarily, on the other hand.

Both sides, both Richmond and Washington, were concerned about maintaining the safety of the capital cities at this point. Jefferson Davis and his advisors were thinking about that in Richmond, and in Washington there was great concern about the safety of the capital. That started a pattern that would continue throughout the war. Congress always was worried about the safety of Washington, D.C. It paid an inordinate amount of attention to it, really, and Lincoln of course had to be concerned about it as well. So that's going on. There's worry about the respective capitals and planning.

In terms of overall strategy, I'll reiterate a point that I've made earlier, and that is the Confederacy had an easier task at this point. All it had to do was respond to whatever the North did. If the North, the United States, chose not to do anything, if it didn't invade the Confederacy, the Confederacy would achieve its independence by default. It wouldn't have to fight for it at all. But the North, if it were going to reunite the Union, had to come up with a plan that would allow Union forces to strike into the South, defeat Confederate armies, and force the 11 seceding states to come back into the Union. It had to bring the Richmond government to its knees, in other words.

In the vortex of this planning in the North is Lieutenant General Winfield Scott. Scott is one of the great military figures in United States history, although he's not often thought of in those terms by students of the Civil War because, by the time of the war, he was a very old man. He was in his mid-seventies, and he's often seen in caricature as someone who was well past his prime. That really isn't accurate. He had been in the army a long time. Winfield Scott's service went all the way back to before the War of 1812. He'd been one of the great United States heroes in the War of 1812, an officer who'd been innovative, who'd been a good leader in combat, and who had forged an exceptional record.

He had towered over the military landscape of the Mexican War. He had conducted a campaign from Vera Cruz to Mexico City and captured the Mexican capital in what ranks as one of the most brilliant campaigns in United States military history. The Duke of Wellington followed Scott's campaign very closely in Mexico and pronounced Scott to be the greatest soldier of the age.

Scott also had had political ambitions. He was a Whig. He'd run as the Whig candidate for president in 1852, so he had been at the center of national affairs for many, many decades. And now he found himself, as I said before, the only soldier holding the rank that the sainted George Washington had held. He found himself presiding over the early Union effort to begin this war successfully.

In his mid-seventies, as I said, he was an imposing man in his youth. He was six feet five inches tall and affected very showy uniforms. He impressed people tremendously who saw him in his prime. Among those who saw him was a young Ulysses S. Grant, who reminisced after the war about a time when Winfield Scott visited the cadets at West Point. Grant wrote this about Scott. He said, "With his commanding figure and his quite colossal size and showy uniform, I thought him the finest specimen of manhood my eyes had ever beheld." "He was the man," said Grant, "the most to be envied."

Well, he didn't look like that anymore in 1861. He weighed about 350 pounds. He had to literally be winched up into the air; his poor horse would be led underneath him. Scott would be eased down onto his horse and then he would ride—I hope not very far, for the animal's sake—and then he would be lifted off, and then he would do his job. But that somewhat decrepit physical appearance—he suffered from dropsy, among many other ailments—that physical picture of Scott should not obscure the fact that his mind still worked extremely well.

And what Winfield Scott did in April and early May of 1861 was apply his powerful intellect to the problem of how to defeat the Confederacy. He came up with a long-range plan to win the war that in effect anticipated almost exactly how the war would be fought. This is what Scott said the North needed to do: He envisioned first a powerful move down the Mississippi River. He wanted to gain control of the river and divide the Confederacy into two pieces. He envisioned doing this by having a naval flotilla work together with army forces on the Mississippi River and having them move down supporting one another, taking one position after another if the Confederates chose to resist until finally the Mississippi would be in Union control and the Confederacy would be divided.

At the same time that this movement down the Mississippi was taking place, Scott called for a blockade of the Confederate coastline. He wanted to seal the Confederate coast, deny the Confederacy war material that they would need to import from abroad, and prevent the Confederacy from shipping its goods, especially its cotton, out to foreign markets and getting the money that that cotton would yield, that the Confederacy could then apply to its war effort.

So strike down the Mississippi, divide the Confederacy, seal off the coastline. These elements of the plan, because they called for constricting the Confederacy, came to be called the "Anaconda Plan." That's what the Northern newspapers called it. The plans were printed in all the Northern newspapers. The Confederates read them too. As Scott was formulating his strategy, the Confederates were reading about it in the newspapers. They knew what the North might be doing, but it didn't really matter. The proof would come in the execution.

Scott had one more element to his plan. If striking down the river and sealing the coast was not enough to defeat the Confederacy, he said it would take a major invasion into the heartland of the Confederacy to finish off the South. He thought that invasion might take two to three years and as many as 300,000 men. So he's thinking on a very broad scale. Most people at the time were not. Scott understands that it's going to be a long war and that it might take hundreds of thousands of men. Remember, this is at a time when the United States Army is about 15,000 strong. So Scott understands the magnitude of the task ahead of the North, and his Anaconda Plan shows that.

Except by underestimating by about half how many men it would actually take in the end—it took many more hundreds of thousands—and how many years it would take, Scott had formulated a plan that anticipated pretty much how the war would be played out. Scott understood that time was going to be a necessary ingredient. It was going to take a long time to bring all these volunteers into the army, to train them, to prepare the fleets, to get everything ready to move down the Mississippi River.

He worried that Northern public opinion would not tolerate too much time going by. He understood how public opinion worked. The citizens behind the lines in the North, once the Confederate capital had been moved to Richmond, looked at the map and said, well, it's only 100 miles away from Washington. Why don't we just go take it? If we take Richmond we'll end the war. A drumbeat began behind the lines in the North of, let's move against Richmond, let's move on to Richmond. Get our forces in the field. Take the Confederate capital. Let's end this war.

Scott told Lincoln, and other military figures did as well, it's going to take longer than that. We can't rush our troops into the field. We have to take our time and build real armies. Scott's greatest worry was that political considerations, pressure from the civilian sector, would force the Lincoln government to move before the military was really in a good position to move. But we have this call for an "on to Richmond" campaign that really would remain for the rest of the war. Much of the North would, throughout the war, look at that little piece of ground between Virginia and Washington and just think that our forces should be able to move down and take the Rebel capital.

There would be constant pressure for the United States government to do that. It began a preoccupation on the part of the Northern people with Virginia and Richmond and the Eastern Theater that will continue for the rest of the war, and it would, of course, help make Virginia the bloodiest battleground of the war. More of the great battles of the conflict would be fought in that strip of ground between the Potomac River and the James River than anywhere else.

Well, at this point in the war, Lincoln was ready to try to satisfy the demands of the Northern public. He would be much more sophisticated about these things very quickly, but early on, Lincoln thought that it was probably possible to just move south and capture Richmond as well. He knew that the Union forces were green, but he knew that they were larger than the Confederate forces, which were also green. He reasoned that since we have more green troops than the enemy has, why don't we let our larger number of green troops defeat their smaller number of green troops? If we can win a victory early in the war, thought Lincoln, we might be able to discourage the South. We might even be able to persuade them that their experiment in rebellion is going to fail.

So Lincoln did not listen to Scott's advice here. He thought that it was possible to move more quickly than his principal military advisors did. Another soldier who agreed with Scott was a brigadier general named Irvin McDowell. Irvin McDowell commanded the largest United States force in the field. It was near Washington. He's the field commander. Scott is the overall General-in-Chief at this point. McDowell agreed with Scott that his troops were not ready to engage in a campaign, that it would take more time to get them ready, but he, like Scott, was not going to be successful in these arguments.

The upshot was he was pushed into what became the campaign of First Manassas or Bull Run. It's a battle with two names, and there are a number of those during the Civil War. We might as well touch on that now, the pattern in naming battles. If a battle has two names, almost invariably the North would have named it after some terrain feature in the vicinity and the South would have named it after a railroad crossroads or a town.

In this instance, Manassas Junction is the railroad junction. There's not a town there, but the railroads come together there. That's the Confederate name. Bull Run is a local creek, and so the Federals used the terrain feature. Other examples of this are Antietam, the Union name for the battle in Western Maryland, named after the creek. Sharpsburg is the Confederate name for that battle, named after the little local village. In Tennessee there's the Battle of Murfreesboro or Stone's River. Murfreesboro is the Confederate name; Stone's River is the Union name. There are many other examples.

This is the first one, Manassas or Bull Run, and let's turn now to that campaign, the first large military campaign of the war. It pitted four forces against one another in Virginia: two Confederate, two Union. The strategic picture was this: The largest Union army under Irvin McDowell was just a few miles outside Washington, about 35,000 men. McDowell had never commanded troops in the field. He was a former staff officer. He has no field experience, and here he is commanding the largest army in United States history. No one had ever commanded an army, no one else, as large as the one that Irvin McDowell was commanding.

He'd taught tactics at West Point. He was a friend of Secretary of the Treasury Salmon P. Chase, which certainly didn't hurt him in his search for a command early in the war. It was nice to have friends in powerful places. He wasn't known for much, but he was known as a man who could certainly hold his own at the table. There's one famous anecdote of a staff officer bringing in a watermelon, sort of triumphantly bringing it into camp and putting it down on the table and the officers gathering around hoping to get a piece. McDowell sat down, pulled out a knife, and ate the entire melon, including the seeds and rind, in front of his somewhat astonished staffers. He's known somewhat as an eater; he's not really known as an officer who might bring great success in the field. So he's the largest Union army in this theater.

The second Union force consisted of about 18,000 men in the lower Shenandoah Valley, commanded by another veteran of the War of 1812 named Robert Patterson. Twenty miles from McDowell, near Manassas Junction, was Gustave Toutant Beauregard, whom we have seen before. He commanded the principal Southern force of about 20,000 men. Beauregard was also a former staff officer. He very briefly had been superintendent at West Point on the eve of the war—very, very briefly. His tenure lasted less than a week. And here he was commanding the largest Confederate force in the field.

He was a Louisiana Creole, not a Cajun but a Creole. He had something of a Napoleonic complex. A very vain man, he dyed his hair. In his early war pictures, his hair is nice and dark. The chemicals he used to do that ceased to come in through the blockade later in the war, and his hair turned its natural color, which was gray at that point. He's not a brilliant general, but on the whole he's a very capable one.

The other Confederate on the board was Joseph Eggleston Johnston, who had about 12,000 Confederates opposite Patterson in the lower valley. So you have McDowell and Beauregard facing each other, and you have Patterson and Joseph Johnston. Johnston was a Virginian, a classmate of Lee's at West Point and a man we will see again and again in the course of our study of the Civil War.

He has quite a substantial reputation as a Civil War commander, one that I think is probably not deserved, as will become clear as we go through the course. I don't have a very high opinion of Johnston as a soldier. He had had a distinguished career in the old army, that is, the prewar army. He had fought well and gallantly in Mexico and had been wounded there.

Beauregard and Johnston have a great advantage over their Federal opponents here because they have a rail link. I've mentioned this before—the Manassas Gap Railroad connects their two forces. So the Confederates enjoy interior strategic lines here that will allow them to reinforce one another more easily than their Federal opponents.

McDowell's plan was a good one, although it was probably too complicated for his largely untrained army, his troops and officers, men used to dealing with much smaller bodies of men. He wanted to keep Patterson to the task of looking after Johnston in the valley. He told Patterson, you hold Johnston in the valley, and I will deal with the force under Beauregard. So don't let Johnston leave the Shenandoah Valley.

He planned to avoid a direct attack. We've seen that most people knew this was the case. His plan was to march against Beauregard and not attack him directly but march against him and turn the southern left flank. So as he faces Beauregard he will hold his attention in front and then try a flanking maneuver against the Confederate left. Interestingly, Beauregard had the same plan. He planned, when coming in contact with the Federals, to hold in front and try to turn McDowell's left. Both officers were essentially hoping to do the same thing.

There's no surprise involved here. McDowell's army left Washington on July 16 and moved very slowly to the west. Confederates knew immediately what was going on. They had lots of intelligence coming in from local people friendly to them and so forth.

The key breakdown on the Union side came early when General Patterson failed to engage Johnston and hold him in the valley and Johnston began to shift his army by rail to Manassas Junction to link up with Beauregard. Also some smaller units elsewhere in Virginia began to march toward Beauregard. By July 20, the Confederates had utilized their interior lines to bring together a formidable force near Manassas Junction.

While the Confederates concentrated there, McDowell moved forward very sedately again. Remember, it's going to take him several days to get from Washington to Manassas Junction. It's a matter of just a few more than 20 miles. On July 21, 1861, McDowell was in position to implement his plan for a turning movement against the southern left, and let's pick up the battle itself now here.

It's July 21, 1861. Early that morning 12,000 Federals crossed Bull Run, and they swung up around the Confederate left flank, moving to get into position to launch a significant blow. Joe Johnston was in command on the Confederate side by this point because his command predated. He was the same rank as Beauregard, but his date of command was earlier than Beauregard's, so Johnston is in overall command.

They realize that the Federals are applying pressure in their front, and they're aware also that there are some Federals moving around to their left. Before the Confederates could inaugurate their own flanking movement against the Union army, the Federals were in position and launched their attacks against the Confederate left flank. The attacks went well in the beginning. They pushed the Confederates back to the south and confronted the Confederates with a crisis.

Johnston and Beauregard responded by utilizing their tactical interior lines and shifting strength from their right flank to their left flank to try to meet the threat mounted by the Federals in that direction, and the battle came to center on a high knob called Henry House Hill. The Confederates held it. It's right near the Warrenton Turnpike. The Federals were attacking it, and the battle swayed back and forth.

A key stand was made on Henry House Hill by a Virginia brigade commanded by Thomas Jonathan Jackson, a former teacher at the Virginia Military Institute, a very dour man. We'll talk more about him later, but Jackson and his Virginians made a stand on Henry House Hill. A South Carolina officer named Barnard Bee at one point pointed to the Virginians and urged his men to do as they were doing. He said, "There stands Jackson like a stone wall. Rally on the Virginians."

Later there was some dispute about what Bee actually meant by that. Some said that he was being derisive in saying, "There stands Jackson like a stone wall." He thought Jackson should have been moving, not standing like a stone wall. We can't be certain what he meant, but the point was, Jackson was making a stand. It was a nickname that would stick to him. He would be "Stonewall" Jackson ever after, and everybody interpreted it as a positive nickname, whether that's how Barnard Bee meant it or not. Bee would be dead very shortly, so no one could interview him about what he had meant precisely.

But Jackson did hold, he and his troops. For more than two hours the fighting raged on Henry House Hill. There was a widow named Judith Carter Henry who lived on that hill, on the top of it in her house. She fell victim to a cannonball that crashed into her bedroom. It sent splinters into her face and stomach and nearly severed one of her feet. She held on in great pain until late in the afternoon when she finally died of her multiple wounds. Outside her house her son hugged the ground, worried about his mother, raising himself up occasionally to cry out, "They have killed my mother!"

About 4:00 p.m., Southern reinforcements, the last of Joseph Johnston's troops from the valley, marched onto the field, marched into the critical sector of the field, and turned the tide. It's late in the day. These troops were the crucial component in setting in motion a major Union retreat. The Confederates raised the Rebel yell for one of the first times, if not the first time in the war. It's an interesting aspect of the war that Union and Confederate soldiers seem to yell differently.

Union soldiers yelled in a more disciplined way. They tended to chant in a sort of low voice, "huzzah" as they went into battle. It sounds odd, but that's what they did. The Confederates, in contrast, had a much more freeform way of yelling. They would just sort of whoop and holler in a loud, high cry that some people likened to a foxhunter's cry. I think that says something about the respective civilizations. I'm not sure what, but it must say something. At any rate, the Rebel yell floated across the battlefield for one of the first times of the war, and the Confederates slowly gained momentum until they had the Union soldiers in full retreat.

It was hot on that July 21st. The troops on both sides were hungry, and they were thirsty, and they were green. Once their momentum had been stopped and then reversed, the Federal soldiers very rapidly made their way away from the battlefield. Orderly retreats are even a problem with veteran troops. With green troops they very quickly disintegrate into a rout, and that's what happened here. As the Union troops made their way away from the battlefield, they ran into a large number of civilians.

Civilians had come out from Washington to watch what they thought was going to be the one great battle of the war. They thought they'd come out and see the conflict resolved at Manassas. Whichever side would win, would win the war. They'd spread out picnic lunches. They had blankets spread out and hampers with food and carriages with parasols. Young children were scampering around the hills near the battlefield.

And now in the afternoon, this group of civilians saw this mass, this disorganized mass of Union soldiers, coming toward them, and the whole group became intermingled and made their way back to Washington. There was a congressman from New York, a man named Alfred Ely, who'd come out to watch the battle. He was captured by the Confederates in the course of the retreat, roughly handled by some South Carolinians, and soon on his way to a prison in Richmond.

The Federal army reached the Washington defenses late that night, having covered in a few hours the same distance it had taken them several days to cover going the other way. By the end of the next day order had been restored to much of McDowell's force, and Washington really wasn't in danger. If there was any moment when the Confederates really could have exploited this victory, it was on the afternoon of July 21, but the Confederate army was just about as disorganized in victory as the Union army was in defeat.

Jefferson Davis had ridden out to the field late in the day, president of the Confederacy. He had urged a pursuit. Stonewall Jackson had hoped to be able to pursue, but Joseph Johnston said, no, darkness is coming. We are very much confused. Our units are intermingled with one another. We'll have to wait and reassess the situation tomorrow. Whether or not there was a real opportunity is up in the air. The point is Johnston did not try to push it, and the Federal army escaped and gathered itself in Washington and was something like an effective force by the next day. Whatever opportunity there had been was gone.

Let's look at the battle as representative of other Civil War battles. Of the many battles in the war, this one showed several things that we'll see again and again. One is the attempt to avoid a frontal assault. As we've said, both sides tried to get around the other side's flank. It showed the side with interior lines making good use of that feature both strategically on the Confederate side and then tactically on the Confederate side as well, reinforcing one part of their line from another. We will see those again and again.

We'll see as well that when an army or a piece of an army was driven from the field, it often had the resiliency to gather itself and put up a stand and not be utterly destroyed. The Union army showed this at Manassas, and we'll see it again and again during the war. At Chancellorsville, for example, Stonewall Jackson's flank attack utterly routed one entire Union corps, but the rest of the army simply pulled itself into a position, the rest of the Union army, to resist Jackson's attack. At Chickamauga, a third of the entire Federal army was driven from the field in a rout, but the rest managed to pull itself together and stave off a terrible defeat. So these are things that are anticipated at Manassas that we'll see again and again in the war.

Let's talk just a minute in closing here about the results of the battle. First, the casualties by later Civil War standards were not high. They were really quite modest. It would be a midsize battle later in the war. About 18,000 men on each side actually got into the fight. The Federals lost 1,500 killed and wounded and another 1,200 missing. Most of those missing were captured, although some may have been mortally wounded and just crawled off and died or something, but most were captured.

The South lost about 2,000 men. So 2,000 were lost on the Confederate side; 2,700 were lost on the Federal side. Later in the war, as I said, this would be considered a midsize battle or even a modest size battle, but here in July of 1861 it's an enormous battle, the biggest battle in United States history, with far more casualties than any other battle had had. It seemed like a ghastly bloodletting to the people at the time.

The South, of course, took heart from the Battle of First Manassas. They thought they were well on their way to winning the war. Morale in the North, civilian morale, was depressed. It seemed that the war now was going to drag on, and it actually made most people in the North more resolute, determined to make whatever sacrifices would be necessary to win the war. For many Confederates it seemed that the notion that one Southerner could whip two or three Yankees or however many Yankees might be true. They didn't pay attention to the fine details that they'd actually been losing the battle until late in the contest when the tide turned.

There has been some speculation by scholars that this early defeat at Manassas actually had a tremendous long-term psychological impact on the Union army in the east—that the Union army for many, many months or even years after this expected to be defeated when they went up against the Confederates, that there really was a sort of First Manassas syndrome in the Northern army. That's very hard either to prove or disprove, but I offer it to you as something that some scholars have thought existed after this battle. Whether or not that's true, it was clear to everyone in the North that stamping out the rebellion was not going to be a one-battle affair, which is what many people had thought before the Battle of First Manassas.

There were not going to be any more big battles in Virginia in 1861. This was going to be the biggest one, the only big one for the whole year in Virginia, so the effects of Manassas lingered. The impressions from the battle held on for a long time, that is, impressions of Confederate success and of Union failure would hold on for a long time after the last soldiers had left what were called "the rolling plains of Manassas" at the time.

We're going to leave the battlefield with this lecture, and we're going to move briefly to a consideration of the great border in our next lecture and see how Lincoln's administration coped with a political rather than a military problem.

Contending for the Border States
Lecture 9

> At the time that [the 1861] battle was fought ... both sides wondered
> how the four slaveholding border states would react to events both on
> the battlefield and to political events during this period. Would they
> decide to cast their lot with the Confederacy—all four of them or some
> of them—or would they remain loyal to the Union?

We know now that the four slaveholding border states (Kentucky,
Maryland, Missouri, and Delaware) remained in the Union, but
in the summer and autumn of 1861, no one could predict this
with certainty. As we've already seen, the firing on Fort Sumter had sent the
four Upper South states into the Confederacy. Both the Lincoln and Davis
Administrations devoted considerable attention to the border states, all of
which witnessed internal debates of varying intensity about the question of
secession. Rich in manpower and material resources, the border states stood
as prizes of enormous strategic value. The loss to the Union of Missouri
and Kentucky would dramatically alter the strategic situation west of the
Appalachians; the loss of Maryland would place Washington, D.C., inside
Confederate territory.

A key Northern goal was to keep the four border states loyal to the Union,
so they would not follow the four states of the Upper South into the
Confederacy. Kentucky suffered severe internal strife before electing to
remain in the Union. It had strong economic and social ties with both the
North and the South, and it was the birthplace of both Abraham Lincoln and
Jefferson Davis. It did permit slavery, and it had a history of working for
compromise during sectional crises. It was, after all, the home state of the
"Great Compromiser" Henry Clay and of John J. Crittenden.

Kentucky sought to maintain a neutral stance for the first months of the war.
It sent soldiers into both side's armies and traded with both the North and
the South. This was especially hard on Kentucky, and its statesmen over
the years had worked to achieve compromise. But Confederate military
incursions under Leonidas Polk in September 1861 decided the issue in favor

of the North. Kentuckian pro-secessionists created a shadow Confederate government and sent representatives to the Confederate Congress.

Missouri, meanwhile, experienced some of the worst violence of the war. Antebellum "border war" strife carried over into the Civil War. Military clashes between pro-Union and pro-Confederate Missourians marked the first months of the conflict.

A captain named Nathaniel Lyon, a very aggressive anti-Southern man, led Unionist troops against pro-Southern militia men at Camp Jackson near St. Louis and compelled them to surrender. As the prisoners were being marched through the city, a pro-Southern mob gathered and harassed the column, and shots were exchanged. By the end of the day more than 25 people had been killed.

Lyon's actions sent many conditional Unionists over to the Confederacy: People who'd been on the fence didn't like what Lyon had done, and they decided perhaps they'd better support the Confederacy. Military events came to a head in Missouri on August 10 in the Battle of Wilson's Creek. It's the second big battle of the Civil War. Confederates under Sterling Price won a victory there. Brigadier General Lyons (Union) was killed in this battle, and John C. Frémont was sent to take overall command of the Union forces.

John C. Frémont, who took command of Union forces in 1861.

In addition to the 90,000 men Missouri sent into the Union forces and the 30,000 it sent into the Confederate army, the state had about 3,000 or so more Missourians who fought as guerrillas in what was the most vicious guerrilla war of the entire conflict.

Maryland posed a special problem to Lincoln because of its location. Baltimore and parts of eastern Maryland favored the Confederacy; the Union 6th Massachusetts Regiment was attacked in Baltimore in April, and pro-Confederates isolated Washington by destroying bridges and cutting telegraph wires. Lincoln acted decisively after the Maryland state legislature voted to recognize the Confederacy. He sent troops to Baltimore, suspended the *writ of habeas corpus* in part of the state, watched as Federals arrested pro-Confederate Marylanders, and took strong measures to ensure a Unionist victory in the 1861 governor's race. Maryland remained in the Union but sent troops to both side's armies, 40,000 to the North and 20,000 to the South.

Meanwhile, Delaware's loyalty to the Union was never in doubt. There were very few slaveholders in the state, and its economic orientation was toward the North. Only a handful of Delaware men joined the Confederate army. Western Virginia counties broke with the rest of the state and formed West Virginia. This part of the state had few slaves and strong economic ties to the North.

Trans-Allegheny counties met in convention following Virginia's secession on 17 April 1861. Union military successes in the area during June and July strengthened their hand. The delegates declared themselves the legitimate government of Virginia on 2 August 1861. They drew boundaries of the proposed new state of Kanawah. They set up a mechanism for approving their work that left pro-Confederates unrepresented. The new state of West Virginia was created in May 1862 and accepted by Congress in 1863.

Retention of the border states proved invaluable to the Union. The North controlled strategic access to important rivers, such as the Tennessee, the Cumberland, and the Mississippi itself. The Confederacy was denied control of vital military resources, such as animals, minerals, food, and manpower. Retention of the border states was a key strategic victory for the North.

In the end, a combination of effective Northern policy (including heavy-handed interference with Maryland's internal political affairs), Southern blunders, and strong Unionist sentiment prevented any of the border states from embracing the Confederacy. Union military success and a strong internal movement to break away from Virginia and the Confederacy created, in effect, a fifth border state when West Virginia was formed. ■

Essential Reading

McPherson, *Battle Cry of Freedom: The Civil War Era*, chapter 9.

Nevins, *The War for the Union: The Improvised War, 1861–1862*, chapters 6–7.

Supplementary Reading

Fellman, *Inside War: The Guerrilla Conflict in Missouri during the American Civil War*.

Questions to Consider

1. How important was it for the Lincoln Administration to keep the border states in the Union?

2. Why did the border states react differently to Fort Sumter and Lincoln's call for 75,000 troops than the four states of the Upper South?

Contending for the Border States
Lecture 9—Transcript

In our last lecture we discussed the first great battle of the war at Manassas or Bull Run in Virginia. At the time that battle was fought in July 1861, both sides wondered how the four slaveholding border states would react to events both on the battlefield and to political events during this period. Would they decide to cast their lot with the Confederacy—all four of them or some of them—or would they remain loyal to the Union?

That is the subject that we will turn to now with this lecture. We'll look at these four border states in turn and see the process by which all four made the decision to remain in the Union. We'll look first at Kentucky, then at Missouri, Maryland, and Delaware. We'll finish this lecture by considering the events that led a piece of the state of Virginia, most of the trans-Allegheny region of Virginia, to split from the state and form a new state called West Virginia, which in effect became a fifth border state.

The first eight months of the war were full of activity as both sides, as we've seen, pulled their thousands of men into uniform, tried to train them after a fashion, and tried to come up with strategies to apply against the enemy. In the largest sense of the broad Northern military strategy, a very key goal, in fact, the most important goal in many ways for Abraham Lincoln, was to maintain the loyalty of the four slaveholding states that remained in the Union. They possessed large populations, important resources, and key geographical positions, and Lincoln desperately wanted to keep all of them in the Union.

It's important to remember that no one knew at the time what these states would do. We all know now that they remained loyal to the United States. But no one at the time knew, and the stakes seemed very high on this issue of what these four states would do. So that is an immediate concern for Abraham Lincoln, and it continues from the spring of 1861 all through the summer and even into the fall of that year, the uncertainty of what these states will do, the necessity of keeping them in the Union.

As we've already seen, the firing on Fort Sumter had sent the four Upper South states into the Confederacy. Let me just give you the votes and dates on those now, which I didn't give earlier. Virginia left on April 17, and the vote in the Virginia convention was 88 to 55. Arkansas was next on May 6, the vote 69 to 1, but that vote doesn't really reflect the degree to which Arkansas was divided over secession. North Carolina was next on May 20. The vote was unanimous, but, again, the convention just decided to make the vote unanimous. There had been significant debate in North Carolina about whether the state should secede or not.

Finally, Tennessee went out on June 8. Tennessee didn't have a secession convention. It had actually put the question to a popular referendum in the state, and that popular vote had been 105,000 in favor of secession, 47,000 against secession. Tennesseans had voted directly. Among the Lower South states, only Texas had held a comparable popular referendum to see if the people agreed with the decision of the state secession convention.

After those four states were gone, that left the four. Four out of the 15 slave states are still with the Union. Now let's look at those in turn, and we will start with Kentucky.

Perhaps more than any other border state, Kentucky was torn between allegiances to the North and South. It was the birthplace of both Abraham Lincoln and Jefferson Davis. They were born a relatively short distance apart and at almost the same time early in the century. Kentucky had profound ties to the South through the institution of slavery, through family connections, and through various economic ties that looked southward and tied the state to other slaveholding states. But it also had connections with the Lower North because of its long Ohio River border. There was a good deal of economic activity that went north from Kentucky and tied at least thousands of people in Kentucky, not all of them but thousands at least, to the Northern economy.

Kentucky had always been a state that worked hard to achieve compromise between the sections. We've touched on that before as well. It's in a difficult position, right on the great border area between the North and the South, and when sectional controversy would heat up, Kentucky felt it especially hard in many ways, and its statesmen over the years had worked to achieve compromise. It had voted, the state had, for John Bell and the Union in 1860. Henry Clay, who so often pushed for compromise over many decades, the Missouri Compromise, the Compromise of 1850, and so forth, and John J. Crittenden, who had tried to find a compromise in late 1860 and early 1861—Clay and Crittenden, I think, represent the compromising spirit of the state of Kentucky when it came to sectional tensions and sectional problems.

The description of the war as a brother's war had real meaning in Kentucky. Three of Henry Clay's grandsons fought for the Union; four fought for the Confederacy. In John J. Crittenden's family, one of his sons became a United States general during the war; one of his sons became a Confederate general during the war. So these families in Kentucky are literally divided by this great conflict.

Kentucky at first hoped to remain neutral. It's sort of pathetic to think about it, really, that the state thought that, amid this enormous cataclysm, they could be an island of neutrality, the citizens of Kentucky could. But that's what they tried to do at first. They sent no troops in response to Lincoln's call for 75,000 volunteers, and they declined to meet a similar request from Jefferson Davis.

The governor of the state, a man named Beriah Magoffin, was pro-Southern. He issued a proclamation of neutrality. We will stand aloof from what's going on in this nation, in effect is what he said. Well, that condition lasted from May until September 1861. During this time Lincoln made no move to coerce Kentucky. He didn't want to push Kentucky and neither did Davis. They hoped that Kentucky would come their way, each of the presidents did, and they wanted to avoid some overt act that would alienate the state and its people.

Well, while this uneasy time was passing, individual Kentuckians were making their choice. Some went into the United States Army, some went into the Confederate army, some went into pro-Confederate militia units, and some went into pro-Union militia units in the state. There was a thriving trade in military supplies that went on between Kentucky and the Confederacy.

In the end, Lincoln's hands-off policy paid off. In special elections for Congress in June and for the state legislature in August, Unionists won convincingly in Kentucky. On September 3, 1861, the crucial moment arrived because, on that date, Confederate General Leonidas Polk ordered Southern troops to occupy Columbus, Kentucky, a strong point on the Mississippi River, a key position that overlooked the river and would allow the Confederates to place artillery there and try to frustrate Northern attempts to penetrate the Confederacy via the Mississippi River.

It might have been a wise military move. In a strictly military sense, it was. It gave the Confederates this great spot from which to contest Union naval advances. But politically it was a disaster, and the political side was more important than the military because the Unionist legislature in Kentucky condemned what they called these Confederate invaders. They asked the federal government to help drive the Confederates out, and they created a military force to oppose Confederates in the state.

Kentucky had made its choice. It had chosen to remain in the Union, an official part of the United States. That didn't mean that sentiment came together, however. Sentiment remained divided in Kentucky. There were still many thousands of pro-Confederate people in Kentucky. The secessionist minority, in fact, called a convention of its own in November 1861 and voted to join the Confederacy. In fact, there's a star in the Confederate flag for Kentucky. There are only 11 Confederate states. The Confederate flag has 13 stars. One of those is for Kentucky. Kentucky didn't really leave the Union, but this minority pretended they did, and the Confederacy pretended that it was all on the level.

Kentucky sent nearly 75,000 men into the Union armies—50,000 of them white, the rest black men—and 35,000 Kentuckians fought with the Confederate army. Kentucky voted against Abraham Lincoln in the 1864 presidential election, and the state suffered from a particularly vicious form of guerrilla warfare during the conflict. A lot of really nasty bushwhacking and that kind of activity was carried out in the state during the war. Ironically, after the war Kentucky became really the most Confederate state. It hadn't been a Confederate state during the war officially, but it seemed that everybody in Kentucky was pro-Confederate after the war. That was amusing to many people in states that had actually joined the Confederacy.

So Kentucky, Lincoln and Davis's home state, is in the Union column by the fall of 1861. Let's move to Missouri. Missouri had had a head start on the Civil War, really, because it had been embroiled ever since the mid-1850s in that nasty border war along the Kansas-Missouri border. When the fights had taken place over whether Kansas would be free territory or slave territory, Missouri had been involved in that for many years by the time the war came. It had been used to that sort of low-level violence on the border.

In 1861, the governor of Missouri was a man named Clayburn Jackson, a pro-Southern veteran of the border fighting of the 1850s and a man who did everything he could to take Missouri into the Confederacy. Jackson worked very hard to make Missouri a Confederate state. He persuaded the legislature to call a secession convention, but he was unhappy when most of the men elected to the convention were strong Unionists. Missouri Unionists and secessionists organized and armed themselves in April and sort of eyed each other warily in the state.

On May 10, violence broke out when a captain named Nathaniel Lyon, a firebrand, really—sort of the Northern equivalent of a fire-eater in the South, a very aggressive anti-Southern man—led Unionist troops against pro-Southern militia men at Camp Jackson near St. Louis and compelled them to surrender. As the prisoners were being marched through the city, a pro-Southern mob gathered and harassed the column, and shots were exchanged. By the end of the day more than 25 people had been killed—a very ugly incident in St. Louis.

Well, Lyon's actions sent many conditional Unionists over to the Confederacy. People who'd sort of been on the fence didn't like what Lyon had done, and they decided, perhaps we'd better support the Confederacy. One of these was a man named Sterling Price, a former governor of the state, who was given command of pro-Southern troops in Missouri. Lyon, meanwhile, was made a brigadier general. He was a hero to many strong Unionists in Missouri and to many people in the North who thought that he had treated these Rebel militiamen as they should have been treated in St. Louis. He's a brigadier general put in charge of about 10,000 troops.

In June, Lyon took this force, not a well-trained force—this is a green army, just as green as the armies had been at First Manassas—and he pushed in to the southwest corner of the state. Meanwhile, the Unionist state convention, which had adjourned in March without voting in favor of secession, reconvened to function as the state legislature in Missouri. So you have a very strong Unionist group functioning as the state legislature. It declared the governorship vacant. Clayburn Jackson was wildly out of step with what this legislature wanted. It declared the governorship vacant and named a Unionist governor.

Well, military events came to a head in Missouri on August 10 in the Battle of Wilson's Creek. It's the second big battle of the Civil War. It takes place in southwest Missouri when Nathaniel Lyon and about 6,000 men attack Sterling Price, who commanded a motley force about twice that large. Lyon boldly divided his army, if you can call it an army. He divided his 6,000-man force and tried to hit the Southerners in the front and rear simultaneously—a very nice idea if you can pull it off. He achieved some early success, but he was eventually driven back, and he lost his life in the process. He became a great martyr to the Union cause at the Battle of Wilson's Creek.

Each side suffered more than 1,200 casualties at Wilson's Creek, and Sterling Price followed up the victory by marching north to the Missouri River. John C. Frémont enters the picture for us here, the Republican nominee for the presidency in 1856, the famous pathfinder from the antebellum years who had explored so much of the Western territory. He was very well connected in Missouri. John C. Frémont had been sent to Missouri in late July to take overall command of the Federal troops. He now mounted a counteroffensive that slowly pushed Sterling Price's forces back toward Arkansas.

By November the military situation in Missouri was stable, and Missouri was firmly in the Union. Like Kentucky, however, it remained a very much divided state. Clayburn Jackson and the pro-South portion of the deposed legislature met and said that they were seceding from the Union. So, just as in Kentucky, you have this rump part of the state meeting and declaring that they will cast their lot with the Confederacy. The Confederacy added a star to their flag for Missouri. There's the thirteenth star in the Confederate flag, although it's the same process. Missouri doesn't really leave the Union, but these pro-Southern people in the state pretend it did, as did the Confederate government.

Missouri sent nearly 90,000 soldiers into the Union army, about 10 percent of whom were black. They sent at least 30,000 into the Confederate army, and about 3,000 or so more Missourians fought as guerrillas in what was the most vicious guerilla war of the entire conflict. Missouri was absolutely pulled apart by guerrilla fighting during the course of the Civil War. It was incredibly vicious.

William Quantrill, Bloody Bill Anderson, Jesse and Frank James, the Younger brothers—all of these men and many others were Confederate guerrillas in Missouri. Their opposite numbers, just as vicious as they were, were the Jayhawkers from Kansas, the Redlegs. It was just a kind of war with essentially no rules. Civilians got caught up in it; whole counties were de-populated. Many of the things we associate with twentieth century wars and think didn't happen in the Civil War actually did happen in Missouri. It was a very, very bitter situation there. But the state remains in the Union. It is safe for Lincoln.

Maryland—let's go to Maryland. Maryland demanded special attention because the United States would have a real problem if Maryland left the Union. The United States capital would be in the Confederacy if Maryland left the Union. It was very important not to let that happen. Washington was full of Southern sympathizers. It was sort of a Southern city at this point and remained so even after the war in many ways. But there were lots of rumors in Washington early in the war about what was going on in Maryland and how Maryland was going to join the Confederacy.

The state, actually a majority of it, was opposed to secession and opposed to the Confederacy, but Baltimore was a hotbed of pro-Confederate sympathy. That was apparent from a very early point, and it troubled the Lincoln administration. On April 19, a mob in Baltimore attacked the 6th Massachusetts Infantry Regiment as it marched through town. The soldiers returned the fire. Four soldiers and 12 residents of Baltimore were killed in this riot, as it was called. Outraged pro-Confederate Marylanders then proceeded to burn railroad bridges and cut telegraph wires leading into Washington, D.C., and cut Washington off from the rest of the North for a significant period.

Not until the 7th New York Infantry and other Northern troops began reaching Washington on April 25 was the city considered safe. This is a very problematical time in the capital of the United States. The Maryland legislature met in April, and although it made no move toward secession, it did vote to recognize the Confederate States of America as a nation, and it implored Abraham Lincoln to let the seceding states go in peace. Let them go, said the Maryland legislature. They're gone; they're a nation. We just need to come to terms with that.

Well, of course, Lincoln was not going to do that. Lincoln decided that he was going to have to act decisively to keep Maryland in the Union, to make sure that it remained loyal. So he did a number of things. He sent troops to Baltimore and other key points just to show the flag and have the presence of United States power in those places. He suspended the *writ of habeas corpus* in part of the state, which, of course, meant that citizens didn't have to be told why they were being held. You could be arrested and not told why you were being arrested.

Many Marylanders were arrested for pro-Confederate activities, even for saying things in favor of the Confederacy. I don't mean for blowing up bridges or cutting telegraph wires or sniping at Union troops but just for saying, "Hurrah for Jeff Davis" or "Long live the Confederacy." You could be arrested for doing those kinds of things in Maryland.

One of the men so arrested was named John Merriman, and he appealed for his release under a *writ of habeas corpus*. Chief Justice Roger B. Taney heard the case while he was sitting as a circuit judge and ruled that only Congress had the power to suspend the writ of habeas corpus. Lincoln said, that's very interesting, but I think I have the power to do that, and, since Lincoln commanded the army, Lincoln's view won out.

I'll give you just a couple of details about the Merriman case. Merriman was a lieutenant in a secessionist drill company in Maryland. He was arrested by authority of a general named Cad Walader in late May 1861. Taney issued his opinion a little bit later in May. Shortly after Taney issued his opinion, Merriman was released from military confinement. He'd been held at Fort McHenry, as many of the people arrested in Maryland were. He was transferred to civil authority. An indictment for treason was filed against him in the U.S. Circuit Court in Baltimore, and he was set free on $20,000 bail. That's a huge bail, a huge sum in the mid-nineteenth century, and he was scheduled to appear in court on November 12, 1861.

Well, the case went no further. After a continuance, it was dropped, and that was very common in these kinds of cases. These people would be arrested, they'd be held for a while, and, in the end, they would just be released. It was a way to get potential problems off the street, so to speak, and to send a message that pro-Southern, pro-Confederate activity would not be countenanced in the state of Maryland.

During the fall of 1861, Maryland had a gubernatorial election. Lincoln thought it was vital that a Unionist be elected governor of Maryland, and so he took extraordinary steps to see that that happened. He did things such as arresting 19 members of the Maryland legislature, arbitrarily. Some literally were hauled out of the statehouse in arrest. Maryland soldiers in the Union army who were known to be Unionists were given three-day furloughs to go home and vote, and Federal troops—this is the most direct and, I suspect, effective thing that they did—Union troops were sent to the polling places, where they discouraged anti-Unionist voters from casting ballots and encouraged Unionist voters to cast their ballots.

Well, it should come as no surprise that the Unionist candidate won in Maryland, a man named Augustus Bradford. In fact, he won handily. Lincoln's firm response to secessionist sentiment in Maryland kept the state in the Union. However, many Maryland residents deeply resented some of the measures used to keep Maryland in the Union, and many people in the Confederacy read about what was going on in Maryland and assumed that the state was literally being held in the Union at the point of a bayonet. They didn't understand that most Marylanders were actually loyal to the Union.

We'll talk more about the impact of that notion on the Confederate side when we talk about the Antietam campaign.

But some Marylanders did feel that they, in effect, were living under military occupation—the ones who were pro-Confederate. The state remained divided in loyalty. It sent not quite 40,000 men to the Union army, 9,000 of them black, and about 20,000 to the Confederate army.

Delaware is our fourth border state. Delaware was never really in doubt. It was overwhelmingly loyal to the Union. There were only about 20,000 black people in Delaware; only 2,000 of them were slaves. Delaware's commerce was tied to the North, to Pennsylvania, rather than to the South. Southern sympathizers were a tiny minority in the state. There was really no chance that Delaware was not going to remain loyal to the Union, and, in fact, it did. It sent about 11,000 men into the Union army, 1,000 of them black, and it sent a handful of men to the Confederate army, perhaps about 1,000.

Those are the four official border states. Now let's move to the case of West Virginia, a border state that was created in 1861 from the counties of western Virginia. Western Virginia didn't have very many slaves. It had strong economic and cultural ties to Pennsylvania and Ohio. That spike of West Virginia, what was then Virginia, goes way north. It goes almost up to Pittsburgh. So it had strong ties to Pennsylvania and Ohio and very little in common with the eastern parts of the state of Virginia. Political power, however, had traditionally been concentrated in the east, and there were long-standing grievances on the part of many people in western Virginia against the eastern part of the state. They believed in the west that they were underrepresented and overtaxed, and, when Virginia voted to secede on April 17, 1861, the delegates to that secession convention from west of the Alleghenies decided to secede from Virginia, or from the Confederacy— however you want to look at it.

Voters in the area supported that position, and, in June and July, Union armies won a series of small victories in West Virginia—at Philippi, at Cheat Mountain, at Corrick's Ford, and elsewhere—that effectively removed any major Confederate military presence from the area and opened the way for Union control. Two conventions representing 34 trans-Allegheny counties were held at Wheeling, the second of which voted on August 2, 1861, to set itself up as the legitimate government of the entire state of Virginia. The convention next called for a constitutional convention to meet in November for the purpose of creating a new state to be called Kanawha after a major river in the area. It was later decided to change the name to West Virginia, but initially it was going to be called Kanawha. The boundaries of the new state-to-be were drawn arbitrarily to include 48 counties. That's more counties than were represented in these meetings at Wheeling, but those were the boundaries that the group in Wheeling drew—48 counties.

It's significant that fully half the potential population of this proposed state was entirely unrepresented at Wheeling. A popular referendum, in which only those who took a loyalty oath to the Union could vote, ratified the work of the convention. In May 1862, a Unionist legislature that theoretically represented all of the state of Virginia but, in fact, represented only part of the trans-Allegheny region approved the creation of a new state. This technically satisfied the clause in the U.S. Constitution that's in Article IV, Section 3 that says no state can be formed within the boundaries of an existing state without the consent of the existing state's legislature. So that takes care of that, at least in theory here.

The United States Congress admitted West Virginia to the Union in 1863, and the new state consisted of 50 counties, not the 34 originally, not the 48 of the expanded view, but 50. Two more were added so that the Baltimore and Ohio Railroad, which dipped down into Virginia just a little bit—those two counties where the B&O dipped down were added to West Virginia so that the B&O would now be entirely in loyal United States territory. Those counties even today, a lot of the people in them, wish they were still in Virginia rather than in West Virginia. Probably about half of the people in this new state were actually pro-Confederacy and would have preferred to stay in the Confederacy. West Virginia sent 25,000 men to the Union army. It sent 15,000 to the Confederate army. The most important among those 15,000 was Stonewall Jackson, who was born in what is now West Virginia.

Through very different processes, then, the border states were kept out of the Confederacy, and, while there remained tensions and, in Kentucky and Missouri, at least, open guerrilla warfare after the decisions were made to stay in the Union, there was no realistic chance after the autumn of 1861 that any of these border states would cast their lot officially with the Confederacy. By retaining these states, the Union achieved an enormous amount. It held strategic access, as we've said before, to the major rivers in the west—we'll talk more about this later—to the Cumberland and the Tennessee and the Mississippi. That would be very important.

They also controlled, the United States and its people, military resources greater than those of the Upper South states that had seceded after Lincoln's call for 75,000 volunteers: draft animals, areas of iron production, salt production, food production, and so forth—enormous resources in those areas in the border states. Overall, retention of the border states must be counted a major Union strategic success that far overshadowed results on battlefields such as First Manassas or Wilson's Creek or the other smaller engagements in 1861. Lincoln's government had achieved this victory, this strategic victory, that would dramatically enhance Northern efforts to defeat the Confederacy.

The first striking military success along the North's road to eventual victory would come in the Western Theater, and that will be the subject of our next lecture.

Early Union Triumphs in the West
Lecture 10

We return to the military front with this lecture, training our lens on events west of the Appalachian Mountains in 1861 and 1862. We'll look at the shakeup in the Union high command in the autumn of 1861 that saw Winfield Scott step aside and George B. McClellan take his place. We'll then examine four more topics.

The battle of First Manassas captured the imagination of citizens in both the United States and the Confederacy, and most people almost certainly still looked to Virginia as the critical military arena. But a number of generals on both sides believed that the war would be decided in the vast Trans-Appalachian Theater, a view Abraham Lincoln quickly came to share. The first important battles of 1862 would be fought in the West, and the Union would develop a group of officers there who would eventually win the war.

Ulysses S. Grant, who commanded Union forces in the West in autumn 1961 with marked success.

The next two lectures will address the Western Theater between the autumn of 1861 and the summer of 1862, describing a remarkable series of Union victories and introducing major military figures, such as Henry W. Halleck, Ulysses S. Grant, Albert Sidney Johnston, and Don Carlos Buell.

The Union shuffled its high command in the autumn of 1861. Thirty-four-year old George B. McClellan replaced the aged Winfield Scott as general-in-chief. McClellan also took field command of the Army of the Potomac. Generals Henry W. Halleck and Don Carlos Buell took command in the West. Halleck (known as "Old Brains") was to pacify Missouri and seize control of the upper Mississippi west of the Cumberland River. Buell, in command east of the Cumberland, was to liberate eastern Tennessee and sever rail connections between Virginia and Tennessee.

The Confederacy faced a difficult situation in the West. Albert Sidney Johnston held overall command of a vast theater that stretched from the Appalachians to the Mississippi River. He had been trained at West Point and had served in the United States Army. He had also fought in the Texas Revolution and had risen to be the commander-in-chief of the Army of the Republic of Texas. He was the ranking field general of the Confederacy. Johnston's theater was vulnerable along four avenues of advance available to the Union:

- The Mississippi River flowed through the Confederate heartland.

- The Tennessee River sliced through Tennessee into northern Mississippi.

- The Cumberland River flowed to Nashville.

- The Louisville and Nashville Railroad ran through Kentucky and Tennessee to Nashville.

Johnston placed his forces to cover all four lines of advance. Troops stationed at Columbus, Kentucky, under General (and Episcopal bishop) Leonidas Polk blocked the upper Mississippi on Johnston's left. Troops at Bowling Green, Kentucky, blocked the L&N Railroad and anchored Johnston's right. Weaker positions in the center were at Fort Henry (blocking the Tennessee River) and Fort Donelson (blocking the Cumberland River). Other smaller forces were also available to Johnston in the theater.

Each side held two advantages in the Western Theater: Johnston had interior lines with a good rail connection from Memphis, Tennessee, to Bowling Green, Kentucky, and a unified command. Halleck and Buell had superior numbers and four good avenues of advance.

The North mounted a generally effective offensive in early 1862 to attack Johnston where he was the weakest, in the center. Buell achieved mixed success. Some of his troops under George Thomas won the Battle of Mill Springs (or Logan's Crossroads) in January 1862 and compelled the Confederate forces to abandon eastern Kentucky. However, Buell proved unable to liberate eastern Tennessee. Halleck's forces, on the other hand, achieved excellent results. All major Confederate influence in Missouri was eliminated. In February, General Ulysses S. Grant captured Fort Henry (on the Tennessee River). He cooperated successfully with Flag Officer Foote and his gunboat flotilla. Grant then broke the Confederates' railroad connection and attacked Fort Donelson on the Cumberland River. General Floyd, the Confederate commanding officer, was not competent to defend against a concerted attack. In fact, he and his second-in-command, General Pillow, fled the fort, and command devolved on S. B. Buckner, who surrendered the fort unconditionally to Grant. During this campaign, the Confederates abandoned Columbus and Bowling Green. Nashville and much of middle Tennessee fell to the Union. Johnston's entire line was gone, and he lost over one-quarter of his forces. ■

Essential Reading

Hattaway and Jones, *How the North Won: A Military History of the Civil War*, chapter 3.

McPherson, *Battle Cry of Freedom: The Civil War Era*, chapter 13.

Supplementary Reading

Connelly, *Army of the Heartland: The Army of Tennessee, 1861–1862*, chapters 1–7.

Cooling, *Forts Henry and Donelson: The Key to the Confederate Heartland.*

1. What does campaigning in the Western Theater in early 1862 tell us about communications and logistics during the Civil War?

2. Could the Confederates have mounted a more effective defense of the region or were numbers and terrain too strongly against them?

Early Union Triumphs in the West
Lecture 10—Transcript

We return to the military front with this lecture, training our lens on events west of the Appalachian Mountains in 1861 and 1862. We'll look at the shakeup in the Union high command in the autumn of 1861 that saw Winfield Scott step aside and George B. McClellan take his place. We'll then examine four more topics.

We'll start with Union commanders and strategy in the west in 1861 and early 1862 and move to Confederate leadership and strategy in the west during that same period. Then we'll look at the military advantages and disadvantages of each side in the west and finish by looking at the opening Northern offensive in the Kentucky-Tennessee Theater, an offensive that brought Union success at Fort Henry and Fort Donelson.

The battle of First Manassas or Bull Run had captured the imagination of citizens North and South, as we've seen. As the first great battle of the war, it had been one that garnered many, many headlines. Most people in both nations, I think, still looked to the area between the two national capitals as the cockpit of the war. That's where the war would be decided, most people thought.

But many professional soldiers looked instead to the west, to that great area between the Appalachian Mountains and the Mississippi River, as the most decisive arena of the war. There the South had much more territory to cover. There the North had excellent avenues of advance, and there, many generals and Jefferson Davis and, very quickly, Abraham Lincoln all agreed, the decisive campaigns most likely would be waged.

Let's begin by looking at the shuffling of the Union high command in 1861 and the command structure of the North in the west. General-in-Chief Winfield Scott, who had done so much in the way of early planning from the North, stepped aside in November 1861. He had been troubled with health problems, but he'd also been troubled by the attitude of George B. McClellan, a bright young major general who criticized Scott, thought he knew better than Scott, and, I think, in the end helped to push Scott off the center stage.

Scott left, a man in his mid-seventies. He was replaced as General-in-Chief by George B. McClellan, a 34-year-old officer of enormous ambition and talent but also a man with enormous flaws, as we'll see. McClellan would not only be General-in-Chief of all the Union armies, he would also take field command as the commander of the biggest army in the Eastern Theater, the Army of the Potomac.

In the west, two men were given important commands. Henry Wager Halleck controlled the area from the Cumberland River west, including Missouri. Halleck was 46 years old. He'd been a brilliant student at West Point, absolutely brilliant, and before the war had written a number of books on military topics, on law, and on engineering. He'd been a professor at West Point, and he had turned down a full professorship at Harvard. He resigned from the army in the mid-1850s, went into business, and did very well. He was an able man who did well at everything he tried before the Civil War. He, in fact, amassed a fortune as a businessman.

He was not an imposing individual. He didn't look like a soldier. He had a potbelly. He was balding. He had an unsettling habit of staring at people without blinking. He'd sort of drop his head and just look at the person who was talking to him without blinking. As one witness said, "He looked at me with eyes wide open, staring, dull, fishy." There's a great photograph of Halleck with his hands folded in front of him, with his head just like that. He's looking at the camera just the way that people described him in person. Great things were expected of Henry W. Halleck. His nickname before the war had been, quite appropriately, "Old Brains." People thought that in Halleck they had a winner in the west.

The other major commander in the west was named Don Carlos Buell. He commanded from the Cumberland River east, including most of Kentucky, and would have responsibility for eastern Tennessee as well. Much of that area was quite Unionist in sentiment. Buell was also a professional soldier, and, like McDowell, he had been a staff officer. He wasn't brilliant. He was methodical, careful, and in some ways competent, but, as we'll see, very loath to do anything very active in the way of campaigning. He was a hard man to move.

Halleck had two goals. First, pacify Missouri and bring it under complete Federal control. Second, concentrate on the Mississippi River for a push southward into the Confederacy, either along the Mississippi or along one of the other rivers. Buell also had two main goals, one of which was political. The soundest military move in Buell's arena would be to march down the Louisville and Nashville Railroad, which, interestingly enough, ran from Louisville straight to Nashville. It was a great line of advance for a Union army into middle Tennessee. You could supply the army using that railroad as your logistical line of advance.

But Lincoln was concerned about the Unionists in east Tennessee, and he wanted Buell to liberate that region, as he put it. So this was a political goal. Rather than moving on Nashville, which was the obvious move, Lincoln wanted Buell to move into eastern Tennessee and liberate the Unionists there. The second goal for Buell was to cut the railroad connections between Virginia and Tennessee. This would deny the Confederacy the strategic interior lines in that part of the military landscape.

At this stage of the war, Lincoln was obsessed with interior lines. That's one of the lessons he'd learned from talking to his generals: Interior lines are important. He could look at a map and see these interior lines. He and his generals agreed that it would be good to cut those lines. So the plans for Buell reflected a mixture of political and military objectives, and that's very common in the Civil War. We have to remember always that the armies don't operate in a military vacuum. They're subject to all kinds of pressures from the civilian sector, and here's the civilian sector, via Lincoln, making the liberation of Unionist east Tennessee one of Buell's goals.

All right, that's the Union side. Let's move on and look at the Confederate situation in the Western Theater. What is the command situation for them?

They face a very difficult problem in the Western Theater, the Confederates do, because it is such an enormous expanse of territory that they need to defend, all of that territory between the Appalachians and the Mississippi

River. The commander on the scene was Albert Sidney Johnston, and he had complete charge of this enormous department on the Confederate side, this department that stretched all those hundreds of miles from the Appalachians clear across the river into Arkansas at the western end of his theater. His theater included all of Tennessee and all of Kentucky, an enormous chunk of territory.

He was 58 years old. He was tall, well built—very impressive. Unlike Halleck, he looked like a soldier, Albert Sidney Johnston did. He came to the Confederacy with a reputation as perhaps the best soldier they had. He had been a West Pointer, two classes ahead of Jefferson Davis. He served eight years in the United States Army and then resigned to go fight in the Texas Revolution. He eventually became commanding general of the Republic of Texas's forces. He was also Texas Secretary of War.

He came back to the U.S. Army when Texas joined the Union as a state in 1845, and, in the late antebellum years, he was a full colonel commanding one of the cavalry regiments, the new cavalry regiments that had been created in the 1850s. He is the senior field commander in the Confederacy. The ranking general of all the Confederate generals was a bureaucrat named Samuel Cooper who pushed paper in Richmond for the whole war, but the ranking officer who actually took the field was Albert Sidney Johnston. His commission predated those of the other senior officers. Robert E. Lee was next and then Beauregard and then Joseph Johnston.

Jefferson Davis remarked on one occasion that, "If Sidney Johnston is not a general, we have no general." He especially expected great things from Albert Sidney Johnston. Davis clearly considered him the best soldier in the Confederacy. As with Halleck then, there are high expectations for Albert Sidney Johnston, and the fact that he was given this enormous command suggests the degree to which he was trusted by those in power in the Confederacy. He has the most important command on the Confederate side at this stage of the war.

Johnston's department, as we've mentioned before, was vulnerable along four main routes: the Mississippi River, the Tennessee River, the Cumberland River, and the Louisville and Nashville Railroad. These were all very nice avenues of advance for the Federals. To meet these threats, Johnston spread his strength across a great arc—sort of an inverted arc with the big flat "U," if you like, as an image—trying to protect the heartland of Tennessee with his flanks anchored in Kentucky.

This is how the line was laid out. The left flank was anchored at Columbus, Kentucky. Twelve thousand Confederates were there on that high strong point on the Mississippi River. In command was Episcopal Bishop of the Southwest Leonidas Polk. Polk was a West Pointer but a man of very limited military ability. As one discerning Confederate officer put it, "God may have made a bishop in Leonidis Polk, but he did not make a general." I think that's a very accurate thumbnail sketch of Polk.

Columbus, a very strong position, was heavily fortified. The Confederates gave a lot of attention to it because they thought it would block one part of Scott's Anaconda strategy, that is, movement down the Mississippi. That's the left flank for Johnston. The right flank was anchored on the Louisville and Nashville Railroad at Bowling Green, Kentucky. About 25,000 men were there. Those are the anchors.

In between were two weaker positions, a pair of forts guarding the Cumberland and Tennessee Rivers. On the Tennessee River was Fort Henry and on the Cumberland River Fort Donelson up near the Kentucky-Tennessee border. Donelson was considerably stronger than Henry, but Albert Sidney Johnston didn't give much attention to either one of them, focusing instead on his flanks at Columbus and Bowling Green.

Two final components of the Confederate forces in the west were a small army under General Earl Van Dorn that was operating in Arkansas but might be expected to move to the eastern side of the Mississippi River at some point and an even smaller one near Cumberland Gap, commanded by an officer named Felix Zollicoffer. So that is the defensive posture of Albert Sidney Johnston: a vast area and a huge line to defend it.

Let's look very quickly at the advantages that each side enjoyed, and this will just be very quick. Let's start with the Confederates. The Confederates had an excellent railroad that moved behind a good deal of their line, which would give them a good opportunity to shift strength back and forth. There was a line that ran from Memphis past Forts Henry and Donelson to Bowling Green, Kentucky. It gave them interior lines and would have allowed them to shift strength from Bowling Green to either of the forts or to points farther west along their line.

The Confederates also benefited from the fact that Johnston was in overall command. He didn't have to consult with someone else. He didn't have to try to make sure that whatever he did conformed to what someone else was doing. He was in command. He could decide what the strategy was. He could move units around as he wanted to move them. He could make decisions. He could act decisively. Potentially he could do those things, so that is another strength for the Confederates: unified command.

The Federals had the advantages of numbers. There were far more Federal soldiers in this theater than there were Confederate soldiers. Between Halleck and Buell they commanded far more men than Johnston did. And, of course, they had the advantage of those wonderful avenues of advance. I keep hammering on that as a strength, but it really cannot be overstated because rivers were so crucial as avenues of advance, and the Louisville and Nashville Railroad was a splendid one as well. So those must be reckoned major Union advantages: numbers and the four avenues of advance.

Now let's shift to the first great Union offensive in the Western Theater, and it would turn out to be the first successful major Union military operation during the war. Halleck and Buell looked at the map, looked at the situation, and they both understood that the weakest point in Albert Sidney Johnston's long line was in the middle where the line dipped down and ran through Fort Donelson on the Cumberland and Fort Henry on the Tennessee River.

These were both in Halleck's department, so he formulated a plan to take these forts and have the force that succeeded in capturing the forts drop south and cut that railroad that ran from Memphis to Bowling Green. So not only would he get the forts, but he would deny the Confederacy those interior lines that they had. That would, reasoned Halleck, split Albert Sidney Johnston's defending forces into two pieces, the piece over on the Bowling Green end of the line and the piece on the Columbus, Kentucky, end of the line. It would allow the Federals then to concentrate on either one of those and to defeat them in detail.

Nashville would be one of Halleck's key targets—Nashville was the most important city in Tennessee at that point in Tennessee's history. A rail center, a manufacturing center, and a supply center, Nashville would be a key target. It sat on the Cumberland River, and success against Fort Donelson likely would yield success against the city of Nashville. If he captured Nashville, reasoned Halleck, with a major Union force positioned in middle Tennessee well to the south of the Confederates at Bowling Green and at Columbus, Johnston would have to abandon those forward positions and bring his whole force deep into Tennessee.

So that's Halleck's overall plan. Just before he got the major part of his plan going, Buell sent a small force under an officer named George H. Thomas— we'll see a lot more about Thomas later in the war. He was a Virginian who stayed loyal to the Union and would become one of the four great Union war heroes. He would come after Grant and Sherman and Philip Sheridan, I think, in the Northern pantheon. Those three would be at the top. George Thomas would be next. At this stage of the war Thomas is serving under Don Carlos Buell, and, on January 19, 1862, Thomas defeated Felix Zollicoffer's small Southern force at the Battle of Mill Springs or Logan's Crossroads, a position on the Cumberland River. Old Senator Crittenden's son, George B. Crittenden, was also involved in this battle.

This defeat compelled the Confederates to withdraw from eastern Kentucky and marked the first crack in Albert Sidney Johnston's western line. It also gave the South an early war hero because General Zollicoffer was killed in the battle. There are a number of engravings from the time, heroic engravings, depicting Felix Zollicoffer in this battle. In fact, it wasn't a very gallant end for him. He was riding around on the battlefield in an old white rubber raincoat. He got ahead of his troops in a difficult position. He was very nearsighted. He mistook a Federal officer for a Confederate, and he paid for it with his life.

At any rate, this early Union victory is the first sign of trouble for Albert Sidney Johnston's defense of his huge theater. But the significant fighting would come at Fort Henry and at Fort Donelson on the crucial rivers. Halleck selected Ulysses S. Grant as the man who would command this part of the Union advance. We're going to talk more about Grant in our next lecture, but, for now, he is going to be the person who executes Halleck's strategy in this part of the war.

This is what Halleck's strategy called for. He was to clean up Missouri, remember, and make it safe for the Union. That's where most of his troops were. But then he was to begin the movement into the Confederacy either along the Mississippi River or along one of the other two key rivers. So he kept most of his strength in Missouri, and he did a very good job of sort of mopping up there, but he selected Grant and gave him a small force, about 15,000 men, and gave Grant instructions to begin movement up the Tennessee River toward Fort Henry. That's going to be the first major action in this theater.

Grant began his march at the very end of January, on January 30, with his 15,000 troops and orders to take Fort Henry and then march southward and break the railroad that ran from Memphis to Bowling Green. It was called the Memphis and Ohio. Once you accomplish that, said Halleck, turn your attention to Fort Donelson. So there are three targets for Grant here. He's to move rapidly against Henry, reduce it, break the railroad, and then shift his attention eastward to Fort Donelson on the Cumberland River.

That is exactly what Grant would do. He used the Tennessee River as his route, of course. He had a flotilla of gunboats that accompanied him, so this is a combined operation of Union naval and military strength. The man in charge of the little flotilla was Flag Officer Andrew Foote. The Federal navy, in fact, is going to be the key component of the approach against Fort Henry. The gunboats come along the river, and they surround the fort—the Federals do. The Federal soldiers surround the fort on the land side while Foote bombards the installation from the river.

Fort Henry was a very poorly designed installation. The Confederate commander knew that he couldn't hold it. He sent most of his garrison away before the Federals even arrived. He had a 2,500-man garrison. Most of them went off toward Fort Donelson before the Battle of Fort Henry even started.

The man in charge knew that he didn't really have a prayer. He put up the best fight he could, but it was really a quixotic effort because the fort was badly located. It was too near the river, and it was badly constructed.

The river was high at this point in the season. Early in the spring part of the fort actually flooded. Water came in to part of the fort at one stage in the battle. In fact, a little naval boat, one of the Union naval boats, floated into the fort. The fort was not a very defensible place. Many of the Southern guns couldn't even be used. Defense was hopeless, as I said, and the fort fell on February 6.

On February 6, 1862, Fort Henry's gone, the Tennessee River is open, and the way deeper into the middle Tennessee heartland is there in front of Grant. Grant did his next stage very efficiently. He went south, cut the railroad, and then turned his attention to Fort Donelson. The best way to get at Donelson with a joint force involved steaming back down the Tennessee River, going up the Ohio River just a few miles, and then steaming up the Cumberland River. That's what the Federals did.

Fort Donelson would be a much tougher nut to crack. It was a much stronger fort, better constructed, and with far more troops there, but it was still vulnerable to the same kind of approach that Grant had used at Fort Henry. If Grant could get there with a sizable army and establish contact above and below the fort on the river, if he could have his troops with their left downriver from the fort and with their right upriver from the fort, it would seal the Confederates inside the fort and the Union navy could control the river. The fort was very vulnerable, just as Fort Henry had been, even though it was a much stronger place.

Halleck gave Grant an extra 8,000 troops for the march against Fort Donelson, bringing his army up to about 23,000. Albert Sidney Johnston at this point began to make a series of serious mistakes. First he withdrew from Bowling Green. He abandoned Bowling Green even before there was a resolution at Fort Donelson, even before Nashville was really in jeopardy. He split the garrison that had been there, pulling some back to Nashville but sending thousands of them to Fort Donelson to bolster the garrison that was already stationed there.

He was concentrating infantry at Fort Donelson, in other words, where they would be in a precarious position if a major Union force approached, and they would be useless against Foote's gunboats. There is no Confederate navy on the rivers in the west—none. The Union navy is unopposed in these early campaigns in the west. So that's one mistake, abandoning Bowling Green and sending so many thousands of troops to Donelson.

He then put a thoroughly incompetent man in command at Fort Donelson, an officer named John B. Floyd, a Virginian who had been governor of Virginia. He had been a member of James Buchanan's cabinet. He had absolutely no military ability, and he's going to be in charge of the most important place in Albert Sidney Johnston's arena of operations.

Grant reached Donelson within a week of taking Fort Henry, and the inept Floyd allowed him to make contact above and below the fort very quickly after he arrived on the scene, thus cutting Floyd's communication with Albert Sidney Johnston. The Federal gunboats were on the river bearing down on the fort, and, as they approached the fort, they found out very quickly that this was a very different kind of place than Fort Henry.

Confederate batteries at Fort Donelson drove the Union fleet back, the flotilla back. In fact, a number of Union officers were wounded, and significant damage was done to a number of the Union vessels. This was not going to be an instance of the Union navy deciding the issue. Fort Donelson, which was a large earthen fort proper and then surrounded by a ring of smaller earthworks, was going to be a much more difficult place for Grant to capture.

John B. Floyd realized, after Grant had surrounded his installation, that he was in trouble, and he roused himself in consultation with his principal subordinates, a man named Gideon Pillow, a political general from Tennessee, and another man named Simon Bolivar Buckner, a professional soldier, a West Pointer. The three of them consulted, decided to break out of this encircling Union ring, and managed to accomplish that.

They launched an assault. They broke out of the surrounding Union forces, but then they stopped. They had the way open to extricate the soldiers. They then pulled back, went back into their works, and Grant reestablished his line. That was the last chance for the Confederates, really.

Floyd had been Secretary of War under Buchanan, and he feared that he would be hanged as a traitor if captured by Grant, so he decided to leave the fort. He could still escape across the river because the Union gunboats had been held at bay, so he turned command over to Gideon Pillow. Well, Gideon Pillow didn't want to be captured, so he decided that he would leave with Floyd. He turned command over to Simon Bolivar Buckner.

Well, Buckner was enough of a soldier to know that you just couldn't keep doing this. Someone had to take responsibility for what was going on at Fort Donelson, and Buckner did. Floyd and Pillow and about 3,000 men—they were Floyd's men—took all the boats that were available and escaped across the river, leaving Buckner and somewhere in the vicinity of 12,000 or 13,000 men, probably—we don't know exactly how many—inside the fort.

After Floyd and Pillow fled, Buckner realized he was in a hopeless situation, and he sent a message to Grant asking what Grant's terms would be. Buckner and Grant were old friends. They'd known each other in the old army. In fact, Buckner had loaned money to Grant when Grant was down and out at one stage. Grant's response to Buckner was, the only terms that he would offer were unconditional surrender. Buckner didn't like that. He said it was ungentlemanly and ungenerous and ungallant of Grant to offer those terms, but those were the terms, so Buckner accepted them. He had no choice.

Fort Donelson had fallen. An entire Confederate army, really, had been lost, and it was enormously good news in the North. Grant became a hero in the North, and the unconditional surrender business worked extremely well because Grant's initials were U. S. Grant. He became known as "Unconditional Surrender" Grant now in the North and was lauded as a great war hero.

Well, with Henry and Donelson gone, Nashville also had to be abandoned as Grant could move straight up the Cumberland River against it, and that is what happened. The Confederates abandoned it. Buell came down the Louisville and Nashville Railroad toward Nashville. There are no more

Confederates at Bowling Green, remember. When Nashville fell it was an enormous loss to the Confederacy. It was the most important city in the western Confederacy except for New Orleans. New Orleans was the most important, but Nashville was the second most important. It was strategically located, as I said earlier, a hub of transportation and communications and the site of a major powder and rifle works. Its loss was a devastating blow.

Columbus, Kentucky, was similarly abandoned in late February and early March. The withdrawal took a number of days. A Federal column under John Polk threatened Island Number Ten and New Madrid, Missouri, which were downriver from Columbus, Kentucky, and thus flanked the Confederate position there. That abandonment of Columbus completed the complete collapse of Albert Sidney Johnston's entire line. Bowling Green was gone, Columbus was gone, Henry and Donelson were gone, and Mill Springs had been a disaster even farther to the east. The entire line was gone.

And there was still more bad news for the Confederates to come because, on March 7 and 8, Earl Van Dorn—remember, he had the Confederate army off in Arkansas—suffered a defeat at the Battle of Pea Ridge or Elkhorn Tavern in northwestern Arkansas. That victory not only made Missouri safer for the Union but also allowed the Federals to control part of northern Arkansas. So it's a complete story of disaster for the Confederates in this theater.

Albert Sidney Johnston had not lived up to his reputation. He had not used his interior lines along the railroads and rivers to concentrate his forces in an effective way. He had waited for the attacks with his troops dispersed, and his forces were now scattered, divided by Federal armies under Grant and Buell. Beauregard would be sent west to serve as second in command to Johnston, and his presence would help, but 25 percent of all of Albert Sidney Johnston's troops were gone, and his entire defensive position was in a shambles.

The first three months of 1862 scarcely could have yielded more good news for the Union in the Western Theater. The question was, would United States forces add even more triumphs to this roster of success in this area? That's the question we'll turn to in our next lecture.

Shiloh and Corinth
Lecture 11

[In this lecture, we'll] look at the follow-up Northern successes at New Orleans and Corinth, Mississippi, and Memphis after Shiloh. We'll finish by offering a summary of the effects of five months of hard campaigning in the West during the first half of 1862.

Union and Confederate planning set the stage for a major confrontation at Shiloh (Tennessee). Union forces under Grant and Buell were ordered by Halleck to unite on the Tennessee River, just north of the Mississippi border. But before describing the campaign, we should look at Ulysses S. ("Sam") Grant, the person and the general.

Up to the start of the war, Grant had an unremarkable record at West Point, in Mexico, and in the regular army. He left the army in 1854 after a posting to the West Coast (Fort Humboldt in northern California). He was successful in a variety of civilian jobs. His early successes in the Civil War earned him advancements.

Southern leaders orchestrated an impressive concentration of troops drawn from many parts of the Confederacy at the vital railroad junction of Corinth. The use of railroads and interior lines helped this concentration. The Confederate plan was to strike Grant before he united with Buell's forces.

Each side had ambitious goals. Halleck hoped to push the Confederates entirely out of Tennessee and into central Mississippi. The Confederates hoped to defeat Grant's force at Pittsburg Landing, then turn against Buell's army approaching from Nashville.

Shiloh (or Pittsburg Landing) unfolded as a chaotic battle that set a new standard for slaughter and ended in Union victory. The Confederate advance from Corinth was slow and poorly masked, and the timetable for the attack was too optimistic, so General Beauregard counseled Johnston to call off the attack.

Grant's army was surprised by the Confederate attacks on April 6, 1862. The Confederates drove Grant's army back to the banks of the Tennessee River in the morning fighting. The fighting was savage; the center of the Union line managed to hold out in a spot that came to be known as "the Hornet's Nest." The delay in the Confederate advance enabled Buell to come up to supporting distance across the Tennessee. Thousands of green soldiers on each side failed to fight well.

Grant, William Tecumseh Sherman, A. S. Johnston, and other senior officers also made a number of mistakes: Grant and Sherman were sloppy in taking precautions against a Confederate attack. Johnston mismanaged the Confederate attacks on April 6 and failed to seize Pittsburg Landing.

Confederate general Albert Sidney Johnston died in the Battle of Shiloh.

Johnston was wounded while on the Confederate right and died at about 2:30 p.m. Command devolved on Beauregard, who called off the attacks in the evening.

Grant's resolve and Buell's reinforcements eventually won the day for the Union. On 7 April, Beauregard, unsupported and with no reinforcements from General Van Dorn, was unable to stop Union counterattacks. Grant's forces regained the ground lost the day before, and Beauregard abandoned the field. Casualties at Shiloh exceeded those suffered by Americans in all previous wars combined. Confederate casualties numbered 11,000, and Union casualties, 13,000. This carnage shocked people in both the North and the South.

The momentum of Union success in the West continued after Shiloh. New Orleans fell to Admiral Farragut on 25 April 1862. Corinth capitulated to Halleck in late May, giving Halleck a good base for operations. And Memphis fell after a naval battle in early June.

Five months of campaigning had witnessed substantial Union progress in the West and fulfilled part of the Anaconda Plan. The North held the upper and lower reaches of the Mississippi. Four important Southern cities were in Union hands:

- New Orleans—the largest city and biggest port.

- Nashville—a center of communications and industry.

- Memphis—a major port on the Mississippi.

- Corinth—a major rail center.

Additionally, large parts of Tennessee were in Union hands, and 100,000 Federals at Corinth stood ready for further movements. ■

Essential Reading

Hattaway and Jones, *How the North Won: A Military History of the Civil War*, chapter 7.

McPherson, *Battle Cry of Freedom: The Civil War Era*, chapter 13.

Supplementary Reading

Connelly, *Army of the Heartland: The Army of Tennessee, 1861–1862*, chapters 8–9.

Daniel, *Shiloh: The Battle That Changed the Civil War*.

1. As a Confederate leader, would you worry more about the civilian or military repercussions of events in Tennessee during the first six months of 1862?

2. What does the Confederacy's ability to maintain a defense after the loss of such crucial cities as New Orleans, Nashville, and Memphis suggest about the magnitude of the North's problem in subduing the rebellion?

Shiloh and Corinth
Lecture 11—Transcript

Our last lecture closed with Union forces triumphant at Forts Henry and Donelson and their Confederate opponents in retreat in Tennessee. We'll continue our examination of events in the Western Theater in this lecture, looking at several topics. We will look at the strategic planning on both sides in late March and early April 1862. We'll then move on to a consideration of the pivotal campaign and battle of Shiloh, the first really massive battle of the war. We'll then look at the follow-up Northern successes at New Orleans and Corinth, Mississippi, and Memphis after Shiloh. We'll finish by offering a summary of the effects of five months of hard campaigning in the west during the first half of 1862.

Let's start with Union and Confederate planning that set up the major confrontation at Shiloh. We saw what Henry Halleck had planned in the campaign that moved up the Tennessee and Cumberland Rivers and resulted in the capture of Forts Henry and Donelson and the loss of Nashville. He had done just what he hoped to do in that campaign. He'd ended up in control of Nashville with a good chunk of Tennessee in his hands and the Confederate defense in the west in almost complete disarray.

In reward for this, Halleck was given supreme command of the United States forces in the Western Theater. Buell was now under his command. They had been equal in rank before and equal in responsibility, really. Now Henry W. Halleck is the principal Union commander in the west. So he's promoted—in terms of position, anyway. Ulysses S. Grant is also promoted, as are Don Carlos Buell and others. Success begat advancement in the Union high command in the west, and all of these men are moving up.

Halleck was not satisfied, however, with what he had accomplished. He meant to do more damage to the Rebels, and soon he had Grant press up the Tennessee River into southwestern Tennessee toward the Mississippi border. Buell, in the meantime, was moving from Nashville overland to join forces with Grant on the Tennessee River. Once those two armies had united, there would be a very powerful Union presence deep in the western Confederacy.

Halleck wanted them at that point to push Albert Sidney Johnston on into central Mississippi and take control of the crucial city of Corinth, which, as I've mentioned before, was a railroad center. Two major railroads crossed at Corinth, one north-south route and one east-west route, and it would benefit the Union cause enormously to take control of that railroad center. U.S. Grant was going to be the key in this phase of the campaigning, and I think it is worthwhile to stop and take a quick look at just who Ulysses S. Grant was and what kind of promise he had at the beginning of the war.

We all know that he ended up as the premier military hero of the North by the time of Appomattox in 1865. He's the man who, more than any other man but Abraham Lincoln, saved the Union. No one would have expected that from Grant in 1861. He was 39 years old at the beginning of the war, and his life to that point had not been a story rich with success.

He had gone to West Point. He'd been undistinguished there, really. He'd been distinguished for one thing. He'd been the best horseman at the academy, according to many accounts. He loved animals. He was wonderful with horses. But he'd not distinguished himself in the classroom, not graduating anywhere near the top of his class. He'd gone off to the war with Mexico, where he had served competently as a junior officer but hadn't really forged a great record there. He hadn't come to people's attention as some other men his age had. Stonewall Jackson, for example, had done much better in Mexico than Grant had.

He'd been sent off to the Pacific Coast in the period after the Mexican War. He'd been sent off by himself; he couldn't take his family with him. Grant was, in the truest sense of the word, a family man. He depended on his wife Julia. He depended on his children. He really drew strength and sustenance from them, and it was very hard for Grant to be separated from them when he was sent off to the Pacific Coast. He languished out there. He tried various means to make a little extra money, and those failed. He became lonelier and lonelier, very bored, and disenchanted with army life. He began to drink too much on the West Coast, and in the end he left the army in 1854.

Charges of alcoholism would dog Grant for a good part of his life and continue to do so right down to the present. I don't think we know whether

Grant was an alcoholic or not. We do know that sometimes he did drink too much. We also know that at no point during the entire Civil War did drinking get in his way as a commander. Not a single time did consumption of alcohol compromise Grant's performance on the battlefield.

But he's out of the army in 1854. He then tried a string of professions or ways to make a living. He tried farming for a while and didn't really succeed at that. He tried shopkeeping; he tried speculating in land. All of these things really came to very little, and he ended up essentially working as a clerk very late in the antebellum years. He was not a successful man financially. He did have some connections, however. He had a relationship with a congressman from Illinois who helped him get an appointment as a brigadier general in 1861.

And he had fought an aggressive little battle at a place called Belmont, Missouri, which is right across the Mississippi River from Columbus, Kentucky. He fought that in November 1861. He didn't win the battle, but he impressed Abraham Lincoln and others because he'd been aggressive in this battle. He had tried to make something happen, which not too many Union commanders were doing at that point. So Lincoln made a note to watch Grant.

Halleck gave him his first break with the campaign that ended in the capture of Fort Henry and Donelson and the fall of Nashville, and now Halleck was going to give Grant the opportunity to build on that success by continuing his advance deeper into Tennessee. Grant, as I said, will be the principal Union person for us to watch in the campaign of Shiloh.

Let's turn to the Confederates for a minute. What are they thinking in the wake of all of this awful news that came in the Western Theater in early 1862? They realized the extent of their defeats, of course. They could read a map just as well as anyone else. Jefferson Davis was bombarded with complaints, pleas for help, and suggestions that he needed to do something to retrieve Tennessee and the like. He and his generals tried to find a way to restore Confederate fortunes in the Western Theater. How can we turn this around? How can we try to regain part of this valuable Tennessee territory?

How can we deal a blow to the Federals who have done so much good out in that theater?

What they decided to do was concentrate forces at Corinth. They would pull forces from many places in the Confederacy to give Albert Sidney Johnston and G. T. Beauregard—who, as you'll recall, had come east to serve as second in command to Johnston—an army that was large enough to confront Grant's army. They would use railroads in the interior of the south to effect this concentration. In addition to uniting major forces under Johnston and Polk, some of the troops who'd retreated from Columbus, Kentucky, and from Bowling Green, Kentucky, they would bring 5,000 men from New Orleans. They would bring troops from as far away as the Gulf Coast and from Charleston, South Carolina.

So it's a really impressive example of using railroads, which are new in war, really, to bring troops from all across this sprawling Confederacy to Corinth, Mississippi, so they would have a major army. Earl Van Dorn's little army in Arkansas also was ordered to join the rest of the Confederates at Corinth. It's a most impressive instance of using the railroad to bring troops together. Once the men were there the plan was to move north from Corinth and to strike Ulysses S. Grant's army before it could be reinforced by Don Carlos Buell's men coming overland from Nashville.

Johnston and Beauregard together had about 40,000 men, not counting Earl Van Dorn's troops, which were not present yet. Grant had 42,000, and Buell had another 20,000, but Grant and Buell, of course, had not yet united.

What the Confederates wanted to do was hit Grant before Buell got there and then turn their attention to Buell. They wanted to strike the Federals in detail, so speed was absolutely important. They had to get at Grant before the Federals came together. Beauregard drew up a plan that called for a march from Corinth to Pittsburgh Landing on April 3, 1862. He wanted to launch his attack against Grant's army on the 4th, so he envisioned a march that would consume all of the 3rd and part of the 4th, the attack is coming on the 4th.

He wanted a frontal attack rather than a turning movement against Grant. He knew Grant was up against the Tennessee River at Pittsburgh Landing; therefore, it would be hard to get around either one of his flanks. The river guarded his flanks. He thought that a frontal attack would work because the element of surprise was on the Confederate side. Beauregard thought that Grant would not be expecting a counteroffensive from the Confederates, and he thought that they would be able to use surprise to overcome the usual problems that faced anyone launching a frontal attack. So the Confederates would have to march rapidly to the point of attack and then attack effectively and with surprise on their side to achieve success.

They moved north on two roads, the Confederates did. The plan was to muster the troops just outside Pittsburgh Landing in four long lines and assault straight on against the Union forces. Now, there were problems with this plan, the most important of which was that the Confederate troops— many, many thousands of them—were absolutely green. They had no experience whatsoever as soldiers. This was going to be their very first practical experience. Many of them literally had never fired their muskets. Many of them had not really drilled at all. They were being thrown into a campaign without being prepared for that kind of campaigning in the field.

So that's one problem. There were a lot of green Union troops on the other side as well. This is an instance of a major battle that's going to be fought with a very large proportion of the men on both sides having no idea what was going on and being thrown together in this enormous contest.

A second problem was the timetable. It was too optimistic. The march, in fact, took all of the 3rd, all of the 4th, and part of the 5th. It took more than a full day longer than they had envisioned. It was late afternoon on April 5 before the Confederates were in place to begin the attack the next day. Beauregard thought they were too late. He suggested that they call off the attack, that it couldn't possibly succeed, but Albert Sidney Johnston overruled him. Albert Sidney Johnston insisted that they should attack at daylight on April 6. He announced, "I would fight them if they were a million." It was sort of a silly thing to say, but, nonetheless, that's what he said.

Now, there weren't a million Federals, but the delay in the Confederate advance had allowed Buell to come up to within easy supporting distance of Grant. He hadn't joined Grant, but he was very close to Grant because of the extra time the Confederate march took. Confederate attack on April 6 should not have been a surprise. There is no way that the Federals should not have known by that point that a major army was approaching. Grant's men had ample opportunity to discover the Confederate presence because the Confederate advance was not a quiet advance.

Many of these untrained troops did really silly things. On more than one occasion, large numbers in regiments would stop and fire volleys at deer that had run across the road. Some units practiced their Rebel yells on the way to the battlefield so they'd have their yelling just right in case they needed to use it. This is not the way that a veteran army, of course, would have approached something like this.

But, unbelievably, the Federals were surprised on the morning of April 6, and there is enough culpability to go around on the Union side. Grant was partly culpable. William Tecumseh Sherman, who commanded one of the Federal divisions at Shiloh, nearest the approaching Confederates, was culpable. The Federals hadn't expected the Confederates to come, and they had not taken proper precautions to protect against any advance from the direction of Corinth.

The Southern attack began at daylight on April 6, and it routed a number of Federal units. Men were caught cooking their breakfast; some were caught stumbling out of their tents only partly clothed. It was a wild success for the Confederates catching Union troops totally unaware of the danger approaching in a position where they couldn't really defend themselves, and the Confederates drove back a significant part of Grant's army. They drove it back toward the Tennessee River.

Just as the attack began, Albert Sidney Johnston turned to his staff and said, "Gentlemen, tonight we water our horses in the Tennessee River." He meant by that, most people thought, that they were going to drive the Union army into the river and win a great Confederate success. He could have meant, and this would have actually made more sense, that they were going to slice in between Grant's army and the river, push Grant into the wilderness of that part of Tennessee, and hold the key ground at Pittsburgh Landing. It would cut Grant off from Buell's army, which was approaching. He might have meant that. Whatever he meant, he anticipated a success on April 6.

Savage fighting very quickly developed as wave after wave of Southern soldiers were fed in to these assaults against the Federals. Confederates made some progress on their left; they made progress on their right early on. But quite soon in the battle a pocket of very resolute defense formed in the middle of the Union line in a place that came to be called the Hornet's Nest eventually.

Some recent scholarship has suggested that the Hornet's Nest may not have been as important a position at Shiloh as everybody thought it was for many, many years. The soldiers at the time seemed to think it was an important position, and I think we should give a good deal of weight to what they thought. The point was this one part of the Union line did rally, and, as the day went on, the Confederate focus shifted toward that point of strongest resistance on the Union line. More and more Confederate units were fed toward the middle, and the most promising avenue of advance really languished.

The most promising avenue of advance was on the Confederate right flank against the Union left. It was there that the Confederates might have been able to push along the banks or near the Tennessee River and push Grant's army away from the river into a very rough piece of ground that would have been difficult for the Federals to defend successfully. That would have given the Confederates control of Pittsburgh Landing on the river, which was vital because that would have made it very difficult for Don Carlos Buell to play any role in the battle whatsoever. He wouldn't have had a place to ferry his troops over to support the Federals commanded by Grant.

But the Confederates did not push that way. Their attention instead went toward the Hornet's Nest. Attack after attack by Confederate brigade after Confederate brigade went against the Hornet's Nest, and the rest of the battle seemed to be suspended, in a way. In the end, the Confederates massed artillery and succeeded in carrying the Hornet's Nest. They captured a couple of thousand Union soldiers there, drove the rest out, and then pushed on toward a new line that Grant had established closer to Pittsburgh Landing. But it took many hours. It wasn't until about five o'clock in the afternoon that the Hornet's Nest finally fell.

Now, by that time, Albert Sidney Johnston was dead. He had been shot over on the Confederate right in the area where a great deal of good might have been done. He was hit behind in the back of one of his legs, just about at boot level. He had a surgeon quite near by, but the bullet cut an artery, and Albert Sidney Johnston bled to death very quickly. A simple tourniquet probably would have saved his life, but it didn't happen, so the ranking Confederate field commander is dead about 2:30 on the afternoon of April 6.

Command devolved on Gustave Toutant Beauregard, who was on a different part of the field, and there was, of course, a lull on the Confederate side while this new command arrangement kicked in. It was hard for Beauregard to come up to speed. It took a while to get news to him, so there's a sort of lull in the fighting, and then the Confederate pressure begins again, and the Hornet's Nest falls. Beauregard thought toward the end of the day that he would stop the attacks, wait until the morning, and then finish off the Federals. He thought that Earl Van Dorn was going to reinforce him before the fighting began the next day. He also thought that Don Carlos Buell would not reach Grant in time to take part in the fighting the next day. Those were his assumptions: I'll be stronger; Grant will be weaker. I'll finish it tomorrow.

At the end of the day, the Federal army was in considerable disarray. Thousands of Union soldiers had fled panic-stricken from the zones of fighting, and they had cowered along the banks of the Tennessee River, literally hugging the banks of the river for protection against the artillery and musketry. A good part of Grant's army simply disappeared during the fighting on April 6, but Grant's great qualities as a general showed through on the 6th. He at no point panicked. That is one of the very great virtues he had as a general. As William Tecumseh Sherman said one time, "The enemy didn't scare Grant." "They scare me," said Sherman, "scare me like hell sometimes, but they don't scare Grant."

That's the way Grant was here. He was absolutely imperturbable in battle, and he oversaw the construction of a successful defensive line, buttressed by strong artillery close to Pittsburgh Landing, and that enabled the Federals to hold on, to hold the Landing. That night Buell linked up with Grant. Don Carlos Buell reached the field. He ferried his 20,000 men across the river before daylight on the 7th of April. No reinforcements came to the Confederates, in contrast. Earl Van Dorn didn't show up. So, as daylight came on April 7, Beauregard found himself in the position of having a quite fought-out army on his hands and facing an opponent with 20,000 fresh troops, and the course of the battle on the 7th is quite predictable.

It's the reverse of what had happened on the 6th. Grant mounted counterattacks, and slowly the Federals pushed the Confederates back, regaining the ground that they had lost, the Federals had lost, on April 6. Beauregard's lines were much confused from the fighting on the previous day, and he seemed helpless to stem this Union advance. He kept one eye sort of over his shoulder in the course of the fighting on the 7th, hoping that Van Dorn was going to show up. At one point a report came that a group of soldiers in white jackets were approaching the field. Well, Van Dorn was a colorful fellow in a number of ways, but he had a reputation for a flamboyant side to his personality, and they thought, well, if these are Van Dorn's men, maybe they would have white jackets on.

It turned out not to be the case, however. These were some New Orleans troops who were coming to the field. They'd had blue coats on, and, as they marched to the field, a Confederate unit had mistaken them for Yankee troops and had fired on them. The New Orleans troops knew that these were Confederates firing on them, but they fired back. They talked eventually about it, and one of the troops who had fired on the New Orleans men said, "If you knew we were Confederates, why did you shoot at us?" The New Orleans guy said, "Well, whenever somebody fires on us we fire back."

Anyway, they took their coats off, and they turned them inside out so that the linings were showing. That's why they'd had what appeared to be white jackets on. The bottom line was they weren't Earl Van Dorn's troops. It was clear major reinforcements were not going to arrive, and Beauregard decided to abandon the field. The two-day battle ended with Grant in possession of the field and this Confederate army that had been put together with such effort and care completely defeated.

The scale of the Battle of Shiloh dwarfed anything that had happened previously in United States history, in American history, I should say, because that encompasses colonial times as well. There'd been nearly 11,000 Confederate casualties in the two days, about 10,7000, and 13,000 Union casualties in the two days. There were more casualties at Shiloh, in those smoking woods at Shiloh, in two days than in all other battles in American history put together down to that point. If you add up all the killed and wounded from the colonial wars, all the killed and wounded from the Revolution, the War of 1812, the Mexican War, all of them put together, not as many as at Shiloh in two days.

That sent a shock to people in both North and South. This war is going to be something far beyond what we imagined, they knew now. If casualties like this can come in two days, this tells us that we're in for something that nothing in our previous experience has prepared us to deal with.

Now, this could have been a disaster for Grant and Sherman. It was a close thing in some ways, but they held together, held their army together, and they came out with their reputations generally enhanced. This might have been a very difficult day for Grant. It turned out not to be on the 7th. This well-planned Confederate concentration, as I said, came to nothing. The Confederates were soon back at Corinth, and Henry W. Halleck would soon arrive on the scene to coordinate a major advance against Corinth, an advance by an army that eventually would grow to 100,000 men and push against this major railroad center in northern Mississippi. The Confederacy's hope for a victory that would win back some of Tennessee was dashed. Never again in the entire war was there a real chance that the Confederacy would reclaim on a permanent basis any of this crucial Tennessee territory lost in the first few months of 1862.

So Shiloh was an enormously important battle for a number of reasons because it showed the way the war was going to go in terms of scale, it frustrated this major Confederate counteroffensive, and it set Grant up for even greater things.

Now let's move on to the momentum of Union success in the west after Shiloh and just look briefly at some of the other successes the Union had. Before the end of April, another piece of wonderful news reached the North; terrible news for the Confederacy. On April 25, the Union flotilla under David Glasgow Farragut captured the city of New Orleans. At 160,000 citizens, this was by far the largest city in the Confederacy, the most important port, and, in terms of its symbolic value, an enormously consequential place.

Three days after Farragut had had his success, Benjamin F. Butler's Union army occupied the city. The Federals controlled New Orleans. They would control it for the rest of the war. The South's largest city, the South's largest port, the gateway to the Mississippi Valley, is gone for the Confederacy. In late May, forces under Halleck captured Corinth and placed a Union army in position to move deeper into the Confederate hinterlands. Early in June another Union naval force won a battle outside Memphis, and control of that important river city passed to the Union. So the North continues its unbroken string of successes in the west with the capture of these three important cities: New Orleans and Corinth and finally Memphis.

So what had these five months of campaigning in the west really done in terms of altering the landscape of the war? Let's look at that briefly. First, the North had gained control of both the upper and the lower reaches of the Mississippi River. It controlled the Mississippi all the way to Memphis, and it controlled New Orleans. The river is no longer a viable waterway for the Confederacy in terms of moving goods out to be shipped abroad or in terms of moving goods internally. The river is on its way to becoming a Union river. The Anaconda Plan is well underway, with the upper and northern parts of the river held by the North.

A number of very important Southern cities are in Union hands. We've already talked about all of them but just to tick them off again, New Orleans— just finished talking about that— Corinth, Memphis, and Nashville. Again, do not overlook the importance of Nashville in all the things that it offered, potentially offered, to the Confederacy. As a group, these cities constituted major ports, communication centers, supply centers, industrial centers, and psychological points of great value to the Confederacy. They are all gone. Huge parts of Tennessee, a logistical area of great bounty, are now in

Union hands. The Confederate losses in Tennessee in early 1862 represent the single greatest logistical disaster that the Confederacy suffered in the entire war.

There would be other very bad ones. As Sherman struck across Georgia, as Philip Sheridan cleaned out part of the Shenandoah Valley in 1864, those hurt the logistical capacity of the Confederacy as well, but none was as great a blow as the loss of these big pieces of middle Tennessee and west Tennessee in early 1862. And, of course, we have a major Union army poised at Corinth for the next phase of whatever the North decided to do. It seemed that an enormous section of the Confederacy was vulnerable now to penetration by this Union army, and no one knew where Halleck might strike next.

All the Confederacy knew is that there had been no good news—absolutely no good news—from the Western Theater in this entire five-month period, and they had lost the one man most of them had looked to as the principal rallying point in the Western Theater. Albert Sidney Johnston was dead. P. G. T. Beauregard had removed himself from command on account of illness, he said, during the Corinth operations and permanently alienated himself from Jefferson Davis by doing so. He did so without permission to do it. So the second most famous officer in the west was gone, too. Not only had there been disaster for the Confederates in the west, but there seemed no one in place to turn this tide around.

We'll leave Halleck and Grant now as the victors in the Western Theater, poised to do more—they and all of their soldiers in Corinth—because great events were also taking place in the east during this same period, where George B. McClellan was first building an army and then advancing against Richmond with that army. In our next lecture we'll see if "Little Mac," as McClellan was called both by his soldiers and by the people behind the lines, could match the success of his subordinates in the Western Theater.

The Peninsula Campaign
Lecture 12

In this lecture we're going to continue our look at the military side of the war in 1861 and 1862, but we're going to leave the Western Theater behind us and change our focus to the Eastern Theater.

The advent of George B. McClellan was a major development in the war. He was general-in-chief—he was commanding all of the Union armies across the entire strategic map of the war. But most people think of him in terms of what went on in the Eastern Theater because not only was he general-in-chief, he was also the commander in the field of the Army of the Potomac. It was the events associated with the Army of the Potomac that made or broke his reputation, as we will see.

General McClellan wielded immense influence over the conduct of the war in late 1861 and early 1862. He became general-in-chief because of his victories in 1861 and his reputation as a gifted soldier. He was a West Pointer (class of 1846) who had fought in the Mexican War and traveled to Europe as a military observer. He had effective command presence and charisma. He came to think of himself as more knowledgeable than either Scott or Lincoln and essentially forced Scott into retirement in November of 1861.

General McClellan was a master organizer, and by the end of September 1861, he'd built the Army of the Potomac into a formidable force of more than 100,000 well-equipped and well-trained men. He motivated his men and made them feel like soldiers; for this, he was the best-loved Union commander in the war, inspiring his men with the kind of devotion that the Army of Northern Virginia gave to General Robert E. Lee. But he was not quick to move them into battle.

McClellan and Lincoln clashed repeatedly over the army's inaction. Lincoln wanted an offensive in 1861 and the early spring of 1862. However, McClellan refused to move against Joseph E. Johnston's forces in northern Virginia. He exaggerated the Confederate strength and asked for reinforcements. He showed contempt for Lincoln's military views, often ignoring him completely. He also expressed disdain for Republicans who sought to add emancipation to the cause of restoring the Union as a war aim of the North.

The Battle of Ball's Bluff (21 October 1861) underscored the political nature of the war. A small Federal force suffered a humiliating defeat near Leesburg, Virginia, near Washington, D.C. Lincoln's friend Colonel Edward D. Baker (a U.S. Senator from Oregon) was killed in the battle, and nearly 1,000 Union soldiers were casualties. Republicans blamed Baker's superior, Charles P. Stone (a Democrat), for the defeat.

Republicans in Congress created the Joint Committee on the Conduct of the War. Congress began a pattern of examining Federal officers in the wake of military campaigns, often targeting Democrats, such as George B. McClellan and, later, George G. Meade. This sensitized senior officers to the possibility that they might be removed from command for political reasons. General Stone was kept in prison for six months without any charges being brought and without being sent to a court-martial. His career and reputation were ruined.

Confederate general Robert E. Lee would later assume command of all Southern armies.

In April–May of 1862, the Federals mounted a major threat in Virginia. McClellan moved his army to the peninsula between the James and York Rivers after extensive delays. He was secretive with Lincoln about his plans. Lincoln finally ordered him to move but still got no immediate action. He removed McClellan as general-in-chief but left him in command of the Army of the Potomac. Joseph Johnston fell back from northern Virginia to protect Richmond, negating McClellan's initial plan for an attack via the Rappahannock. Irvin McDowell commanded another substantial Union force at Fredericksburg, and there were smaller forces under Generals John C. Frémont and Banks in the Shenandoah Valley and western Virginia.

The Confederates responded on two fronts to Union movements in Virginia, using their advantage of interior lines. Johnston withdrew to the peninsula from Fredericksburg and joined other forces already there. Stonewall Jackson launched his Shenandoah Valley campaign with a very small force. General Robert E. Lee (chief military adviser to President Jefferson Davis) gave Jackson broad instructions and goals, and Jackson conducted a brilliant campaign that tied down Banks and Frémont and inspired the Confederate people. Jackson took the initiative, moved fast, struck hard, and effectively tied down superior Union forces. By early April, McClellan had 70,000 men before Yorktown, Virginia, against only 20,000 Confederates under John B. Magruder. Magruder bluffed McClellan into thinking that he had a much larger force. McClellan laid siege to Yorktown for a month. The Confederates finally abandoned their positions and fell back toward Richmond; McClellan followed them up the peninsula. ■

Essential Reading

Hattaway and Jones, *How the North Won: A Military History of the Civil War*, chapter 7.

McPherson, *Battle Cry of Freedom: The Civil War Era*, chapters 13, 15.

Supplementary Reading

Catton, *Mr. Lincoln's Army*, parts 2–3.

Freeman, *Lee's Lieutenants*, vol. 1, chapters 10–16, 21–29.

Sears, *To the Gates of Richmond: The Peninsula Campaign*, chapters 1–5.

Tanner, *Stonewall in the Valley: Thomas J. "Stonewall" Jackson's Shenandoah Valley Campaign of 1862*.

Tap, *Over Lincoln's Shoulder: The Committee on the Conduct of the War*, chapter 2.

1. Should the Republicans have allowed McClellan to plan and execute his strategy without interference?

2. Is it possible to achieve true balance between military and political imperatives in a war waged by a democratic people?

The Peninsula Campaign
Lecture 12—Transcript

In this lecture we're going to continue our look at the military side of the war in 1861 and 1862, but we're going to leave the Western Theater behind us and change our focus to the Eastern Theater. We're going to trace the events that brought George B. McClellan to command in the east, watch him build the Army of the Potomac into a great army, and then look on as he begins the first major campaign against the Confederate capital of Richmond.

The advent of George B. McClellan was a major development in the war. He was General-in-Chief—he was commanding all of the Union armies across the entire strategic map of the war. But most people think of him in terms of what went on in the Eastern Theater because, not only was he General-in-Chief, he was also the commander in the field of the Army of the Potomac. It was the events associated with the Army of the Potomac that made or broke his reputation, as we will see. He's going to be a crucial factor in the war for more than a year, the major Union player on the military side in many ways.

Following the disaster at First Manassas in July of 1861, Lincoln knew that Irvin McDowell was not the long-term solution to the Northern problem of defeating the rebellion. McDowell had to be replaced, and he was replaced with George B. McClellan. McClellan was given command of that Union army outside Washington, D.C. McDowell was demoted to a division commander. Old Robert Patterson out in the Shenandoah Valley was eased aside completely. He left the service and retired. So you have a major shake-up in the east of the command structure.

McClellan had won some little victories in western Virginia early in the war. It might be more accurate to say his subordinates had won some little victories in western Virginia, but he got the credit for them, and his reputation rose accordingly. He seemed to be a good choice to command the Union armies in the east. He was a West Pointer, of course, a very bright cadet at West Point. He'd been sent to Europe as a military observer in the 1850s to study European military theory and practices. He'd fought with distinction in the Mexican War. He was a man who thought about military questions as well as participated in military affairs in the real world.

But he didn't make enough money in the army, or the army wasn't enough of a challenge for him, and he got out of the army in the 1850s and became a railroad executive. He was very successful at that and made a handsome living in the Midwest.

He was of medium height. You often read that he was short. He wasn't really short. He was about average height for the time. He had a very barrel-like chest, stood up very straight, and sort of threw his chest out even farther. He was broad-shouldered and had deep-set eyes, a nice thick head of hair, and an aura of command about him. He had what we would call today charisma, I think. People spoke about George B. McClellan. He'd walk into the room, and people would naturally gravitate toward him. He's one of those individuals who simply can impose his will on other people or at least get the attention of people that he's around.

He would prove to be, without a doubt, the most popular commander of any Union army during the war. His men were absolutely devoted to him. There's no question about that. In fact, he's the only Union general who came close to inspiring the kind of blind devotion among his men that the soldiers in the Army of Northern Virginia expressed toward Robert E. Lee for much of the war.

The Northern press hailed McClellan as the man who would save the Union, and before long that kind of praise went to his head. He came to consider himself not Lincoln's subordinate, not Winfield Scott's subordinate, but their superior—the man who knew better than they, his civilian and military betters, so to speak, what was necessary to win the war. "I'm leaving nothing undone to increase our force," he wrote to his wife in the early fall of 1861, "but the old general always comes in the way." He meant Scott. As for Lincoln, McClellan said simply, "The president is an idiot."

Winfield Scott had had enough of this by late October, as I said—his physical ailments, his aggravation with McClellan—and in early November he very gracefully stepped aside. McClellan took his place as General-in-Chief. Lincoln was willing—this is one of Lincoln's strengths we talked about earlier—he was willing to put up with the obnoxious qualities in McClellan's personality because he thought McClellan would give him victories. He was willing to do that, Lincoln was—put aside his own ego, let this young egomaniac have his rein, and, if he wins, the Union will be preserved.

Lincoln did warn McClellan that he was taking on two huge jobs here: You are General-in-Chief of all the armies, and you're the field commander of our largest United States army. McClellan shrugged that off. He said, I can do it all. He was a master organizer, and, by the end of September 1861, he'd built the Army of the Potomac into a formidable force of more than 100,000 well-equipped and well-trained men.

But he began to show a pattern that would be with him the rest of the war. He chronically overestimated Confederate strength in his front. He thought there were 150,000 Confederates facing his 100,000 Union soldiers; then he thought there were 200,000. He kept telling Lincoln, I need more men; I need more equipment before I can move. Well, he overestimated by two or three times how many Confederates were really opposite him, but this is something we'll see with McClellan again and again. He always inflated Confederate numbers. He always seemed to find an excuse not to move rapidly and not to force the issue militarily.

I think the bottom line is that McClellan lacked what they would have called, in the nineteenth century, the moral courage to commit this wonderful instrument he had created, the Army of the Potomac, to a decisive contest with the Rebel opponents. He played it safe. He sought perfection, and, as a result, he can never be counted among the great generals of the war.

Let's look just for a minute at Lincoln and McClellan's relationship. They clashed repeatedly, Lincoln pushing McClellan to do something and receiving in return nothing but silence. McClellan would ignore him. He wouldn't share his plans with his Commander-in-Chief. He had a constant stream of excuses for not moving against the Confederates.

McClellan was a Democrat. He was anti-emancipation. He had a set of political beliefs almost completely at odds with the dominant Republican Party, and that proved to be a problem. Most of the officers in the United States Army were Democrats. The army was a conservative institution then as it usually has been in American history, and many of these officers didn't agree with the vision for the United States that many of the Republicans, especially the radical Republicans in Congress, had, but they even departed tremendously from Lincoln.

As a result, there was a growing gulf between a number of these Democratic soldiers and the Republicans in the government in Washington. Many of the radical Republicans, in fact, whispered that McClellan wasn't even loyal to the United States. They said, he doesn't really want to beat the Rebels. He loves society as it was with slavery. And they were right on that regard. What McClellan wanted to do was put Humpty Dumpty back together again. He wanted to restore the Union to what it had been. He was very happy with that Union. And that was not going to be possible during the war once it had gone past a certain point.

He let it be known that he had contempt for Lincoln. He called him the "original gorilla" in public. Lincoln knew this. Lincoln was willing to overlook it. The depth of this contempt for Lincoln came out one night when Lincoln and Secretary of State Seward went to visit McClellan. They went to visit McClellan rather than telling him to come to the White House. McClellan wasn't home. Lincoln and Seward went off into a sitting room. McClellan came home and was told that the president and secretary of state were there. He went on upstairs and 20 minutes later told his butler or one of his servants to go down and tell the president that he wasn't going to come down and talk to them but they were free to come back some other time if they wanted to talk to him.

Well, that's astonishing. Lincoln never went back to McClellan's house, but he was willing to put aside this behavior on McClellan's part, still hoping that McClellan would give him victories.

McClellan was very clear about what kind of war he wanted. He wanted to beat the Rebels just enough to persuade them to come back. He didn't want to slaughter their armies. He didn't want to overturn their civilization, and he wanted to keep emancipation out of the picture. As he wrote to one influential Northern Democratic friend, and I'll quote him here, "Help me to dodge the nigger. I'm fighting to preserve the integrity of the Union." That's McClellan's take on the war.

Now, at that stage of the war, Lincoln was also emphasizing union. He didn't want to emphasize emancipation because he thought it would alienate the border states, and he wanted to make sure that they stayed in line. Lincoln didn't think the North was ready for emancipation, but McClellan never changed his attitude.

The bigger problem, as far as Lincoln was concerned, was that he wouldn't move against Joseph Johnston's army in northern Virginia, and he kept his plans secret. He sat and he sat, and, in the end, the fall campaigning season of 1861 passed with no major movement on the part of McClellan.

Campaigning was seasonal in the Civil War for the most part because the roads were impassable. The weather was a problem in the winter, so you'd have a spring season of campaigning. You'd campaign through the summer and on into the fall, and then that was it. Well, McClellan had let the summer go by, and he'd let the fall go by, so now it meant it would be the spring of 1862 before anything happened in Virginia.

One more clash of note did take place in Virginia, however, and let's move to that briefly. That's the Battle of Ball's Bluff, which took place on October 21 near Leesburg, Virginia, right on the bluffs overlooking the Potomac River there. Militarily it was a minor affair. McClellan ordered General Charles P. Stone to send part of his division on a reconnaissance across the Potomac River and see what the Rebels were up to on the Virginia side.

Stone selected Colonel Edward D. Baker, a senator from Oregon and a friend of Abraham Lincoln's, to head the mission. Baker's force was, in effect, ambushed by Confederates on the other side. Baker was inept as a military leader. The Federals were driven back toward the river and pushed down the bluff at Ball's Bluff. Many of them were shot in the back as they went down the hill, and a number of them drowned in the Potomac River. Edward Baker himself was killed. There were nearly 1,000 Union casualties at Ball's Bluff.

The political repercussions of this little battle were enormous. Congress created a joint committee to investigate the conduct of the war. It focused initially on Ball's Bluff. It later looked at a range of things. It looked at graft in procurement and it looked at a number of things related to the Union war effort, but it was especially interested in examining, under a microscope, the activities of Democratic generals. If a Democratic general hadn't done well, they would pull him in to testify. They did it with George Gordon Meade later. They did it with a number of Democrats. They wanted the war run their way. The committee was dominated by Republicans, and they held the Democratic generals' feet to the fire.

Stone was the committee's first target. He was a Democrat. He was a friend of McClellan's. He was blamed for the failure of the operation led by Baker at Ball's Bluff. It was Baker's fault, but Stone is the scapegoat. In the course of their investigation, the committee found that Stone had ordered slaves who had escaped into his lines to be returned to their masters. They found as well—they didn't actually find; they listened to rumors, I should say—that Stone had been in contact with Rebel officers in Virginia.

Ugly questions were raised. Was Stone disloyal? Had he deliberately sent Edward Baker into a trap at Ball's Bluff? There were all kinds of innuendo and not much solid evidence, but the committee brought Stone in. They bullied him during the examination. They refused to tell him what charges he faced when he came before them. I think that Stone's loyalty cannot be questioned. His crime was that he was a Democrat, he had pro-slavery opinions, and he had been in the wrong place at the wrong time. The price he paid was six months in prison without ever having a trial or even a military inquiry. Later he was restored to minor commands, but his career was ruined.

The Ball's Bluff episode and subsequent treatment of Stone by the committee on the conduct of the war showed that there was a struggle going on in the North over just what kind of war this was going to be. Is this going to be a war that eventually will strike at the social system of the Confederacy and try to overturn this slave-based social system, or is it going to be the kind of a war that McClellan would prefer and Stone would prefer: a more gentlemanly war where the armies fight but you don't really strike at the broader fabric of either side's society?

Well, powerful congressional Republican forces were determined that they were going to shape what kind of war it was, and Ball's Bluff gave them the opportunity to create this committee that would do a great deal of work toward that end in the course of the war.

Let's move on to what's come to be called the Peninsula campaign, a sprawling military operation that has enormous significance in the greater sweep of the war. The word "peninsula" comes from the finger of land in between the York River and the James River in Virginia. That's the Virginia Peninsula. There are other peninsulas in the state, too. There's one between the York River and the Rappahannock, for example, and one between the Rappahannock and the Potomac. The farthest north is the Northern Neck. The one between the James and the York is the Peninsula and that's the piece of land that gives its name to this campaign.

By the end of 1861, McClellan actually had a plan to capture Richmond. It was a turning movement. He proposed taking his troops down the Potomac River and then moving them along the Rappahannock River to come in behind Joseph Johnston's forces in northern Virginia. He would then force Johnston to either try to get around him and flee to the south or turn and attack McClellan's army, which would give McClellan's army the advantage. If Johnston did nothing, McClellan would be closer to Richmond than Johnston was, and he would simply march against the Confederate capital.

It was a good plan. McClellan actually shared his plan with Lincoln, and Lincoln said, good, execute it, put it into motion. But McClellan did not. An exasperated Lincoln finally ordered McClellan to advance. Very unusual. On January 27, 1862, he ordered McClellan to advance directly against Joseph Johnston's army. He said, I want this advance to begin on February 22, George Washington's birthday. Advance against the Rebels.

Lincoln's preemptory order for an advance jolted McClellan into a momentary sense of reality in terms of his relationship with civilian authorities. He explained his plan in detail now. He said, we're going to go by water, and we're going to get behind the Rebels, and these are all the good things that can come from that. But he still managed to procrastinate. February 22 came and went, and, in March, an exasperated Lincoln ordered him again to advance. Finally Lincoln lost patience with McClellan, and he said, look, I'm going to leave you in the command of the Army of the

Potomac, but you're not going to be General-in-Chief anymore. You're in command of your army, but you're not in overall command.

Well, while all this is going on Joseph Johnston drops back to the Rappahannock River from his position up near Washington, so the notion of McClellan's coming to the Rappahannock won't work anymore because Johnston is already there. What McClellan decided on was a wider turning movement by water. This time he would go clear down to the Peninsula, and he would land troops on the Peninsula, and he would use the Union navy to secure his supply lines, and he would advance against Richmond up the Peninsula.

In late March, 70,000 Federal troops got on vessels and headed for Fort Monroe, a Federal installation right at the tip of the Virginia Peninsula, a piece of ground that the United States had held onto. Another 35,000 troops under Irvin McDowell shifted down to Fredericksburg, Virginia, 50 miles north of Richmond. So there are going to be two threats coming against Richmond. There were also about 25,000 men in the Shenandoah Valley under Nathaniel P. Banks, a former governor of Massachusetts, one of the political generals that Lincoln named and successor to old Robert Patterson, who'd been pushed off to the side. Finally, John C. Frémont, who had been shifted to the Eastern Theater after his sojourn in Missouri early in the war, commanded a few less than 10,000 men in western Virginia, out in the Allegheny region.

So you have all these Federals mustering and getting into position in Virginia, on the Peninsula at Fredericksburg, in the Shenandoah Valley, and in the Allegheny Mountains. Now let's look at what the Confederates decided to do to react to this looming threat against their capital.

The Confederates enjoyed interior lines between Johnston's army and the Peninsula, and what they did was use those interior lines to shift Joseph Johnston's forces down to reinforce Confederate troops on the Peninsula who would be blocking McClellan's main advance, the advance of that big Union army that had landed at Fort Monroe. Johnston pulled back from Fredericksburg. McDowell would follow him after he pulled out, and Johnston joined two smaller forces already on the Peninsula.

In the Shenandoah Valley a very small force, about 5,000 men commanded by Stonewall Jackson, moved against a Union force in their front. Jackson fought a small battle in March, the Battle of First Kernstown, as it was called, just south of Winchester, Virginia. It was a defeat for Jackson, a tactical defeat. He made contact with the Federals, they fought, and Jackson retreated. But he accomplished his goal. What he had hoped to do with this battle was gain the attention of the Federals and make them commit to leaving troops in that part of the valley so those troops wouldn't be shifted to reinforce those approaching Richmond.

Jackson succeeded in that when he attacked a piece of Banks's army in the Battle of First Kernstown. There aren't going to be troops shifted now to McClellan from that arena. It was just what Jackson and his superiors in Richmond hoped he would accomplish.

By early April, McClellan had 70,000 troops, or a few more, perhaps, in position at Yorktown on the old revolutionary battleground at Yorktown. There were about 20,000 Confederates opposing him. He had at least a three-to-one advantage. Thirty thousand more Federals would soon arrive to reinforce McClellan. But the man opposite McClellan here, an officer named John Bankhead Magruder, did a very good job of bluffing his Federal opponent. Now, he has the perfect foil in this sense because McClellan loves to be bluffed. He already thinks there are more Confederates than there ever are. There are three behind every tree and two behind every rock, and God knows where else they are.

John Bankhead Magruder used a number of devices to convince the Federals that he had more men than he had, and McClellan decided to wait and to take his time. So he decided to lay siege to Yorktown. He brought up huge siege mortars, and he wasted a month at Yorktown getting everything just right for his attempt to reduce this Confederate stronghold, all the time sending complaining messages to Washington. Let McDowell come and reinforce me, he said. I need McDowell's troops. No, we want McDowell where he is. But I need McDowell's troops. Well, there may be other Confederate threats somewhere else.

McClellan was working himself into quite a state at Yorktown and eating up time in the process as day after day after day passed. Two hundred thousand seemed to be the figure he'd settled on as to how many Confederates there were in his front. It was fantasy, actually. Confederates had far fewer than half that many, even after some reinforcements came.

Slowly the Confederates fell back. There was no firing at Yorktown. They spent about a month there, and then the Confederates just left, and McClellan started to follow them very slowly toward Richmond. April was gone. The month of May came and went as the armies, amid quite heavy rains for much of the month, very deliberately made their way toward Richmond: Joseph Johnston in command on the Confederate side retreating, retreating, retreating, and George B. McClellan on the Union side following very cautiously, gaining ground but following very cautiously.

All the while Confederates are calling in reinforcements from the South Atlantic Coast and from elsewhere. This army eventually outside Richmond, as we'll see a little bit later, would become the largest army the Confederate States ever fielded. Well, those reinforcements are coming in as McClellan's moving slowly forward and Joseph Johnston is retreating.

The Confederates would respond in another way. One way they responded to McClellan's campaign was by shifting this strength to the Peninsula. The other way they responded was by giving Stonewall Jackson more troops in the Shenandoah Valley and asking him to tie down a number of Federals. This is really the first aggressive response. Johnston's response is a defensive one, in a sense. He's falling back toward Richmond. Jackson is going to take the offensive.

General Lee, who is operating as Jefferson Davis's chief military advisor, is the real architect of the strategy that was going to be put in place now. Lee told Jackson that what he wanted him to do was use these reinforcements he'd get and tie down all the troops of Nathaniel P. Banks and John C. Frémont. Make enough of a commotion in the valley so that all of those troops will be held in the valley and won't be used to reinforce the forces that are coming against Richmond. Those were the marching orders that Stonewall Jackson got.

How he accomplished that would be left up to him, and he would show his true brilliance as an independent field commander now in what has come to be called the 1862 Shenandoah Valley campaign or more typically just Jackson's Valley campaign. Jackson was reinforced to a level of about 17,000 troops. He looked at the strategic board, knew what his instructions were, and then put together a campaign that remains a model for what an officer using interior lines, the lay of the land, and the geography to his advantage; using fast movements; and having a willingness to fight could accomplish in a difficult strategic situation.

He had a brilliant cartographer who was with him through the whole campaign, a New Yorker named Jedediah Hotchkiss, who'd gone south in the 1840s and then cast his lot with the Confederacy. Hotchkiss helped Jackson immensely in the Shenandoah Valley by helping him understand the geography and providing wonderful maps for him.

Jackson is the opposite kind of personality from the cautious McClellan. The two really couldn't be more different. Born in western Virginia, as we've seen, he was secretive with his subordinates, but his strongest characteristics as an officer were an aggressiveness, a willingness to take risks, and a sense that you had to inflict the greatest possible damage on your enemy. Just hit them and hit them and hit them and don't give them a chance to get up if it's possible for you to do that. He believed that war was a very hard thing, and that's how he would conduct it.

He's one of the great bizarre characters from the Civil War, just a bundle of oddities and eccentricities as a person. He was a hypochondriac. He had all kinds of worries about his body. He would often hold his right hand up in the air—not because he was praying. He was extremely religious, but he didn't hold his hand up because he was praying, as some people thought, but because he thought he didn't have an equilibrium of blood in his body and if he held his right hand up, then the blood would flow down and reestablish equilibrium, as he put it. An interesting notion.

He wouldn't eat pepper because he thought it weakened his left leg—not his right leg, just his left leg—if he ate pepper. He wouldn't let his back touch the back of a chair because he said it jumbled his organs and it was important to sit upright so that your organs were naturally atop one another. He's a very odd fellow.

He's in his late thirties early in the war and about to embark on a campaign that will make him the most famous Confederate military leader. He's decisive, with a killer instinct. He began his campaign on May 8 at the little Battle of McDowell, west of Staunton, Virginia, where he pushed back the advance guard of part of John C. Frémont's army. He then marched rapidly back into the Shenandoah Valley proper.

The valley is divided in one 50-mile stretch by the Massanutten Mountain range. There's the valley proper to the west and then the Page Valley or the Luray Valley to the right. Jackson marched into the valley proper, crossed over to the Luray Valley, and swept against Front Royal, marching rapidly down the valley. He won a little battle there on the 23rd of May. Two days later Jackson won the Battle of First Winchester against Nathaniel P. Banks and went all the way to the banks of the Potomac River.

Many in the North were panicked by this. Lincoln saw it as an opportunity to trap Jackson's army in the lower valley, and he tried to get Frémont to come out of the Alleghenies and some troops from McDowell to come from the direction of Fredericksburg and cut Jackson off in the valley, and then Banks would push against him from the North, and they would destroy him.

But Jackson simply pushed his men harder than the Federals did. He marched them back southward, up the valley, escaped the trap that the Federals were trying to set for him, and marched all the way to the southern terminus of the Massanutten Range. Federals followed, both in the Page Valley or Luray Valley and in the valley proper, and Jackson turned against them on June 8 and 9. He defeated Frémont's troops, who'd been coming along the valley proper, in the Battle of Cross Keys on the 8th and defeated Federals who'd been in the Luray Valley on the 9th of June at the Battle of Port Republic.

He had accomplished everything that he'd been asked to do. He tied down those Federal troops. Not only had they stayed where they were, but McDowell's were kept at Fredericksburg as well because no one was sure what Jackson was going to do. So upwards of 60,000 Union troops are not defeated by Jackson, but they're kept in place, which is what Lee's goal had been all along.

Jackson had marched 350 miles. He'd captured an enormous amount of material. He had done everything that he'd been asked to do, and, at the end of this campaign, he marched out of the valley to reinforce the Confederate troops defending Richmond while all those thousands of Federal troops remained in place.

It was an absolutely brilliant campaign militarily but also very important in terms of morale for the Confederate people. The Confederates had been starved for good news from the battlefield. All that bad news from the west, a Union army almost in Richmond, and now, finally—as if after a very long drought you finally get some rain—here comes good news from the valley, from McDowell and Front Royal and Cross Keys and Port Republic and First Winchester. These are small battles, but they made a great impact in the Confederacy because the people were so desperate for good news from the battlefield. They responded by making Jackson their great military idol.

And this is where we'll leave the Confederates right now in the East: Jackson successful but the larger picture still dark because McClellan's approaching Richmond with 100,000 men. McDowell is still up there at Fredericksburg. Banks and Frémont could still come back into the picture. No one knew what they would do. And Joseph Johnston seemed unable to do anything but retreat.

That situation would change dramatically over the next month in the rest of June and early July, as the war in Virginia went through one of the great turning points of the conflict, and that's what we'll look at next time.

The Seven Days' Battles
Lecture 13

[In this lecture, we are] going to examine the Battle of Seven Pines or Fair Oaks, which took place on May 31 and June 1, 1862, and had far-reaching consequences. We'll then look at the elevation of Robert E. Lee to command the Confederate army defending Richmond, and then we'll look at the Confederate offensive in the Seven Days' Battles in late June and early July.

The Battle of Fair Oaks or Seven Pines (31 May–1 June 1862) set the stage for the Seven Days' Battles. General Joseph Johnston ended a pattern of Confederate retreat up the peninsula with a poorly executed attack against McClellan's divided forces on May 31. The battle ended as a tactical draw but had long-range consequences:

- McClellan was upset by the scale of the carnage and became more timid.

- Johnston was wounded during the battle and was replaced by Robert E. Lee.

Lee took command under difficult circumstances. Robert E. Lee was the scion of one of the greatest families in Virginia—indeed, in the United States. He attended West Point and graduated with distinction in 1829, and he had a dazzling record in the Mexican War, with three brevet promotions. He served as Superintendent of West Point from 1852 to 1855. He was offered command of the Union army in 1861, but he cast his lot with Virginia and the Confederacy. Lee's early military experience serving the South was not too successful.

When Lee assumed command, Confederate civilian morale was at a low point because of defeats in the West and McClellan's proximity to Richmond. The Confederate army required considerable reorganization before it would be ready to assume the offensive, which was Lee's preferred mode of fighting. Reinforcements had to be integrated into the army, which grew to 100,000 men, the largest Confederate army ever fielded. Lee had to coordinate with Jackson's troops that would be marching toward Richmond from the Shenandoah Valley in mid-June.

The Seven Days' Battles reversed the strategic picture in Virginia by placing McClellan on the defensive. Lee was never comfortable reacting to an enemy, and he believed he could counter the North's greater numbers by seizing and holding the initiative.

The United States Military Academy at West Point.

The Seven Days' Battles consisted of five significant engagements in which the Confederates were the aggressors. McClellan's forces were still divided by the Chickahominy River, and Lee chose to hit his exposed right flank under Fitz John Porter. Following are brief descriptions of these five engagements:

- Mechanicsville (June 26)—Jackson's failure to arrive on time upset the Confederate plan.

- Gaines's Mill (June 27)—the largest battle of the Seven Days. Again Jackson was late to deploy. Lee launched 50,000 men in the largest single attack of the war against Porter's position.

- Savage Station (June 29)—Porter was reunited with McClellan's main body south of the Chickahominy, and McClellan changed his base of operations.

- Glendale or Frayser's Farm (June 30)—marked by uncoordinated attacks by Lee's forces.

- Malvern Hill (July 1)—McClellan occupied an easily defensible position. Lee's attack was poorly coordinated. Frontal assaults took a high toll on the Confederates. McClellan failed to take the opportunity to counterattack against Lee.

The Seven Days had enormous consequences. War arrived in the Eastern Theater on a much bloodier scale than ever before, with 20,000 Confederate and 16,000 Union casualties. The strategic initiative passed to Lee and his army. Confederate morale rebounded after a dark period of reversals in the West. European nations interpreted the Seven Days as evidence that the South was winning the war. Lee's replacement of Joseph Johnston placed in command the soldier who would do the most to drive the Confederacy toward independence over the next three years. ■

Essential Reading

Hattaway and Jones, *How the North Won: A Military History of the Civil War*, chapter 7.

McPherson, *Battle Cry of Freedom: The Civil War Era*, chapter 15.

Supplementary Reading

Catton, *Mr. Lincoln's Army*, part 3.

Dowdey, *The Seven Days: The Emergence of Lee*.

Freeman, *Lee's Lieutenants: A Study in Command*, vol. 1, chapters 30–43.

Sears, *To the Gates of Richmond: The Peninsula Campaign*, chapters 6–13.

1. Contingency often looms large in warfare. Speculate about how the conflict might have been different if Joseph E. Johnston had not been wounded at Seven Pines and replaced by Robert E. Lee.

2. Should the Seven Days' Battles be interpreted as a major missed opportunity for McClellan?

The Seven Days' Battles
Lecture 13—Transcript

At the end of our last lecture, George B. McClellan and his Army of the Potomac stood poised in May 1862 to make a major attempt to capture Richmond. Between the end of May and mid-July, enormously important military events transpired on that front, a sequence of action that will be the topic of this lecture.

We're going to examine the Battle of Seven Pines or Fair Oaks, which took place on May 31 and June 1, 1862, and had far-reaching consequences. We'll then look at the elevation of Robert E. Lee to command the Confederate army defending Richmond, and then we'll look at the Confederate offensive in the Seven Days' Battles in late June and early July. We'll finish by examining the enormous short- and long-range impact of the 1862 Richmond campaign on the broader framework of the war.

Let's start with the Battle of Fair Oaks or Seven Pines at the end of May 1862. It set the stage for the Seven Days' Battles, the larger and more famous Seven Days' Battles that would come just about a month later. We talked last time about Stonewall Jackson's Shenandoah Valley campaign. While Jackson was operating in the valley in May, winning his victories at McDowell and at Front Royal and at First Winchester, there wasn't significant action on the front where the armies of McClellan and Joseph E. Johnston were arrayed outside Richmond.

But Johnston had reached a point, as the end of May drew near, where he really had no more room to retreat. This was often the case during the Civil War. When one side was on the strategic defensive, they would find themselves at some point where they either had to take the offensive against their opponent or find themselves in a siege situation. All the major sieges of the war ended in the same way—with the surrender of a Confederate army. We've already seen that at Fort Donelson. It would happen at Vicksburg; it would happen, in effect, at Petersburg with Robert E. Lee's army later in the war. It also happened in Atlanta.

Well, here Johnston had run out of retreating room. He had to find some way to get at McClellan's army, or he would be inside Richmond, and it would look very dark indeed for the Confederacy. He thought he saw an opportunity late in May when McClellan placed his army in a position with about one-third of it south of the Chickahominy River and two-thirds of it north of the Chickahominy River. It being hard to move reinforcements back and forth across a river, Johnston decided to hit the one-third of the army that was south of the Chickahominy River.

He put together a plan. It was not a great plan, but the plan, such as it was, was not executed well by the Confederates on May 31, and you ended up with a sort of bumbling battle at Fair Oaks or Seven Pines. Neither side won a decisive tactical victory—there were about 5,000 casualties on each side. In that sense it's not a very important battle. But it is an important battle in terms of its impact on later events, and there are two ways especially where it's important.

The first and less important of the two concerns McClellan. I've already talked about how McClellan was reluctant, really, to commit himself to battle, to risk losing a big part of his precious Army of the Potomac. Well, that part of his personality was reinforced after the Battle of Seven Pines or Fair Oaks because, as he rode over the battlefield and saw the wreckage of his troops who had fought there, he shrank from that vision. He admitted to someone that he was upset by "the mangled corpses," as he put it, and he added that "victory has no charms for me when purchased at such cost."

Well, that's an admirable attitude in one sense. He didn't like to see bodies that had been torn apart in combat, but in another sense it spelled trouble for the North because it meant that McClellan was going to be even more reluctant to commit his army to a major battle. It was a fatal flaw in him as a commander because, as much as he loved his army, and as much as his troops loved him, he had to be willing at some point to risk them, and McClellan was simply not very willing to do that. So that's one outcome of this battle.

By far the more important one was on the Confederate side, and that was that Joseph Johnston was wounded on May 31, hit in the chest by a shell fragment from an artillery round. The Union solider who pulled the lanyard on that artillery piece fired the worst shot of the war for the North because that round that wounded Joseph Johnston opened the way for Jefferson Davis to put Robert E. Lee in command of the army defending Richmond, the army that Lee would call the Army of Northern Virginia.

This brought to the fore the man who would become the greatest by far of the Confederate generals and a man who, well before the war was over, would be the most important figure, political or civilian, in the Confederacy and who would become the great rallying point for most Confederates.

Lee was born into one of the oldest and most respected families in Virginia, or the United States, for that matter. He had two ancestors who signed the Declaration of Independence. His father had been a major military figure during the War for Independence and had led cavalry very effectively. "Light Horse Harry" Lee had been governor of Virginia after the American Revolution. He's the man who gave the famous eulogy for George Washington where he called him "First in war, first in peace, and first in the hearts of his countrymen."

Lee could not have been better connected, both through his father and through his mother, who was tied in to the great Carter clan in Virginia. But, although he had this tremendous family tree to look back on, he didn't grow up in privileged circumstances because his father was a terrible manager of money. He took great risks, involved himself in all kinds of speculations, and, in fact, spent time in debtors' prison when Lee was a little boy.

Harry Lee fled the United States when Lee was a little boy as well. He'd been disfigured in a riot in Baltimore, Maryland. He was a Federalist, and a Republican mob had disfigured his face. One of the people tried to cut off his nose, and they poured hot candle wax in his eyes to see if he was still alive. So a really beaten, disfigured, and in many ways discredited Light Horse Harry Lee left the United States and left his son Robert to be reared by his mother, who was essentially an invalid.

Lee grew up in some ways as the man of the house. That's how his mother spoke of him and thought of him. He went off to West Point, which was a free education, after all. He did very well there; he graduated second in his class. He served in a number of engineering posts very well, very effectively, in the 1830s and 1840s. He compiled a dazzling record as a staff officer during the war with Mexico. He convinced Winfield Scott by his exploits that he was perhaps the best officer in the United States Army. That's how Scott described Lee after the war with Mexico. He had served on Scott's staff there.

Later on he was superintendent at West Point in the 1850s and then was a lieutenant colonel in one of the cavalry regiments created in the 1850s. In short, he had a very impressive résumé as a result of his work at West Point in the Mexican War and in the post-Mexican War army.

You often read that Lee was antislavery. Well, he wasn't antislavery. He was a man of very conventional views for one of his class and time. He thought it would be well if slavery ended at some point, but he said that was in God's hands, not in man's hands, and Lee thought that, for the moment anyway, slavery was the best condition for black people to be in. So the notion that he was antislavery simply isn't right.

In 1861, Winfield Scott recommended that Lee be given command of the main Union army outside Washington, the one that McDowell ended up commanding. Lincoln agreed with him; the offer was made to Lee. But Lee, when he knew that Virginia was going to secede in mid-April, decided that he could not take that command, and in the end he cast his lot first with his state and eventually with the Confederacy when Virginia joined the Confederacy.

His early wartime career was not really distinguished. He helped muster Virginia forces very early in the war, but when he went into Confederate service his first two assignments did not prove to be particularly successful for him. He went off to western Virginia and presided over a dismal campaign in the fall of 1861 that added absolutely nothing to his reputation, and, in fact, tarnished it considerably. Then in the winter of 1861-1862 and on into the early spring, he commanded along the South Atlantic coast, where he helped put in place a good defensive system but gained a reputation as a man who was more interested in entrenching and building fortifications than in taking the war to the enemy and smiting the enemy.

What the Confederate people wanted early in the war and pretty much straight through to the end was military leadership that gave evidence of forward movement, of trying to smite the enemy, of taking the war to the enemy and not just waiting for the enemy to come to you. Lee did not show any of that in this phase of the war, and his reputation, which had been very high initially because of Winfield Scott's lavish praise, dropped precipitately in late 1861 and early 1862 so that, by the time he was named as Joseph E. Johnston's replacement by Jefferson Davis, many of the Confederate people were very unhappy with the choice of Lee.

This is hard for most people to understand now because Lee became such a towering figure, but in June of 1862, June 1 when he took command of the army, many people had tremendous doubts about whether Lee was the right man. One of Lee's staff officers recalled that, at the time he took command, some of the newspapers pitched into him with extraordinary virulence. These papers claimed that now our army will never be allowed to fight.

A North Carolina slaveholding woman named Catherine Edmondston, who kept a wonderful diary—one of the best published accounts by anybody on either side of the war—wrote in her diary at the time that Lee took command, "I'm afraid he's too timid. He believes too much in masterful inactivity. He finds his strength too much in sitting still. His nickname last summer was 'old-stick-in-the-mud.'" She underlined that in her journal. "There's mud enough now in and about our lines. Pray God he may not fulfill the whole of his name."

Kate Edmondston became an almost slavish admirer of Lee's as the war went on, but, at this point in the conflict, she, like many other Confederates, thought he was the wrong man for the job because they thought he was timid. He wasn't aggressive; he wasn't audacious. This is an example of why it's so important to read contemporary accounts to understand what's going on during the Civil War or any other historical event rather than what people wrote later to explain what was going on. Later most people would not write that Lee had been problematical in June of 1862, but, in fact, he really was.

There was no hint, believed many Confederates, that Lee would be the kind of daring, risk-taking general who could save Richmond and turn the war around in Virginia. They did know that he was a man in his mid-fifties. He was 55 years old. He looked absolutely like a soldier. He had a very erect bearing. He was not quite six feet tall and was very well proportioned. He looked good on the ground; he looked good on a horse. He was a very modest man, a very religious man, and someone who had most of the characteristics that are considered admirable in people, but he didn't have what was most important in this instance, and that was a reputation at this stage of the war as someone who was going to be a really aggressive commander—a different Lee than the people would come to know later.

He faced a tremendously difficult situation when he took command. In many ways the most intimidating part of this situation lay not in the military sphere but in the civilian sphere, and it's something we talked about last time. Confederate morale was in a terrible state in early June 1962 because so many bad things had been happening to their armies seemingly everywhere: in the west, along the Mississippi River, in Tennessee, in northern Mississippi, and now in Virginia with McClellan coming so close to the Confederate capital.

Only Jackson's little valley campaign had broken that dark spell for the Confederate people, but that was not nearly enough to offset all of this other news. The Confederate people needed victories, and they especially needed a victory in Richmond. Lee also had to spend time reorganizing the army outside Richmond and putting into its ranks units that were coming in from different parts of the South. So he faces an organizational problem as well when he first comes into command.

He also had to coordinate with Stonewall Jackson's troops in the valley— what exactly should be done with those troops. In the end, the decision was made to bring them to Richmond. That's what he spends most of June doing, getting his army in shape, an army that would grow to 90,000 men—as I said last time, the largest army the Confederacy ever fielded—and figuring out what to do with Stonewall Jackson's army once it got to Richmond. What Lee decided to do with it, what he decided to do overall, would become apparent in the Seven Days campaign, and let's turn to that.

Lee had no doubt about what he wanted to do. The people who doubted his audacity completely misread him. There couldn't be a more extreme example of misunderstanding the character of a soldier because Lee immediately decided that he should go on the offensive, and that's what he did throughout his career as a Confederate soldier. His inclination always was to take the offensive, always was to deny the enemy the ability to dictate the action. Lee was never comfortable reacting to what the enemy did. He always wanted to be in the position of dictating the action. Sometimes it led him to take risks that were too great and placed his army in great peril, but that was his military personality. He was not comfortable on the defensive.

He believed it was important to maintain the initiative if you were the Confederates because the Union had so much more of everything. If you simply sat down and waited for them to come to you, he reasoned, they had the resources eventually to pin you down and overwhelm you. So the way to counteract that and the way to lift morale across the Confederacy was to counterpunch and try to defeat the Federals in the field, and that is what he set about planning for.

McClellan's army was still divided by the Chickahominy River, only now the proportions were reversed. At Fair Oaks or Seven Pines, a third of it had been south of the river and two-thirds north. Now roughly two-thirds lay south of the river and one-third north. That one third was commanded by an officer named Fitz John Porter. Lee decided that the best way to get at the enemy once Jackson arrived from the Shenandoah Valley was to strike at the exposed right flank, that third of the Union army that was north of the Chickahominy River.

McClellan had between 100,000 and 110,000 soldiers outside Richmond. Lee had 90,000. You often read that the Federals were overwhelmingly more powerful during the Seven Days campaign, that Lee had a small army fending off this Union juggernaut. That's not the case. This is one of the few times in the war when the armies were relatively equally matched in terms of numbers, Lee at only a modest disadvantage in this instance.

So Lee planned to hit McClellan's right flank. He would have a force to demonstrate in front of the bulk of the Army of the Potomac, and John Bankhead Magruder would play a key role there and do a good job while the bulk of the Confederate army would strike Fitz John Porter's troops north of the Chickahominy.

Jackson would be crucial in this plan. He was to come in on the enemy's flank, and Lee hoped that the valley army of Stonewall Jackson would play a key role once the fighting began in the battles that came to be called the Sevens Days. Those battles began on June 25 when Lee repulsed a strong Union reconnaissance. It was not a major battle that day, but it's really the opening of the Seven Days' Battles. There are really six days of battles and really only five significant battles, but it's called the Seven Days, so there we are—it's the Seven Days.

After June 25, Lee always held the initiative, and the first significant battle came on June 26 at Mechanicsville, called Beaver Dam Creek by the Federals in many of their accounts. At Mechanicsville, Jackson was to come in on the Federal flank and fight in concert with several other Confederate divisions, but Jackson never showed up. The hours ticked by. The morning went by. Noon came and went. One o'clock, two o'clock, still no Jackson.

The other Confederates on the ground, especially A. P. Hill, who commanded the biggest division in Lee's army, simply couldn't restrain himself anymore, and he attacked without Jackson there. The attacks were quite easily repulsed by the Federals at Mechanicsville. After the fighting, Fitz John Porter simply withdrew to another position at a place called Gaines's Mill, and there the second and by far the biggest battle of the Seven Days took place, the Battle of Gaines's Mill, on June 27, 1862.

Once again, Jackson was slow to advance. He eventually got in position, and by the afternoon Lee had his army in place, and he launched the largest set of Confederate assaults of the entire war. More than 50,000 Confederates participated in the attacks at Gaines's Mill on the afternoon of June 27. Very late in the day on the Union left flank near a house called the Watt House, the Confederates finally achieved a breakthrough, Texas troops commanded by John Bell Hood playing a conspicuous role and beginning their record as the most famous and really the most effective brigade in the Army of Northern Virginia.

Fitz John Porter was driven back about dusk, but the Confederates were not in a position to follow up this victory. Their breakthrough came too late. Fitz John Porter very effectively withdrew and managed to get his corps, his third of the army, roughly, back across the Chickahominy River without further damage. Gaines's Mill was a very large battle, but, due largely to ineffective staff work and failure of coordination, the Confederate attacks had gotten started late and the Confederate troops had not been in a position to deliver a more decisive blow against the Federals.

Most often Jackson's poor behavior—and it was poor again at Gaines's Mill—has been attributed to his sheer exhaustion. He'd been up for most of those preceding several days, and I think there's no doubt he was exhausted. Others were exhausted as well. John Bankhead Magruder got three hours of sleep over a three-day period during the Seven Days, and I think men—soldiers or generals, it doesn't make any difference—who've been up that long for a protracted period of time—Magruder was in his fifties, Jackson in his later thirties—their performances are bound to suffer. You simply can't focus as effectively if you haven't been getting very much sleep.

So I think it's probably true that Jackson was exhausted, but his exhaustion, the other soldiers' exhaustion, and poor staff work all had helped contribute to Lee's failure to achieve more while McClellan's army was divided. Well, over the next four days, McClellan withdrew southward across the Peninsula. He changed his base from the York River to the James River. He knew he had powerful Federal naval forces on the James River—he would be safe down there. So he withdrew his enormous army southward.

And Lee tried over the next four days to deliver a heavy blow against the retreating Federals. There was skirmishing on June 28—not a major battle. But then on the twenty-ninth, the Battle of Savage Station and on the thirtieth, the Battle of Fraser's Farm or Glendale saw Lee's army fumbling to get into a position to hit the Federals effectively and failing in both instances. Magruder had a very bad day at Savage Station, and Lee essentially wrote him off as a useless subordinate.

At Glendale there were heavy Confederate attacks. Time and again they attacked, but the attacks again were not delivered in concert, and

McClellan's army held off the Confederates and retreated finally to a very strong position at Malvern Hill. Malvern Hill was an almost perfect military position. It was a gentle slope. Along the crest the Federals packed infantry, they packed artillery, and then they had a spectacular vision in front of them, a very gentle slope up which the Confederate infantry would have to come if they were going to attack. It was the kind of position that generals dream of. McClellan put his army there, and they were in a splendid spot if they were going to have to fight off another series of Confederate attacks.

Lee was frustrated by this point in the campaign. He had hoped to accomplish a great deal more. He'd seen his plans fail to be executed time and again. He'd seen lieutenants fail him. Part of the problem was that he was trying to do too much with an army that was still finding its way. It was a new army. Many of his subordinates didn't really have a record that suggested they could perform very well, and he didn't have a staff that was adequate to try to coordinate some of the complex things he was trying to put in motion.

But never mind all of that. The most important thing is, in my view, that Lee was frustrated. He thought that he'd missed opportunities, especially at Savage Station and elsewhere, and he meant to retrieve those at Malvern Hill and to rely on his infantry to do so. He decided to launch assaults against this strong Union position, and that's what he did on the afternoon of July 1 in the Battle of Malvern Hill.

Again there was poor coordination. Troops taking the wrong roads, taking a long time to get into position, delayed the assaults until about mid-afternoon. The Confederate artillery proved largely ineffective against the Union artillery at Malvern Hill, and in the end the Confederate infantry attacked up the hill unit after unit after unit, and they were easily driven back. They never really threatened the Union position at Malvern Hill.

Daniel Harvey Hill, one of the Confederate division commanders and a soldier with an absolutely impeccable reputation as a tough combat officer, after the war quite aptly, I think, wrote this of Malvern Hill. He said, "It was not war; it was murder, just sending the infantry up and watching them be slaughtered."

Many Northern officers recommended a quick counterattack after the failure of these Confederate assaults, but McClellan, who had spent the battle well to the rear, really not even in touch with what was going on, overruled that. He said, no, we're not going to do that. He was a thoroughly beaten man mentally, I believe. Others would disagree with that. But here he was in a splendid position, his army still very much intact and having suffered far fewer casualties than they had inflicted, and he didn't have even a moment's thought of aggressive counterpunching. He was content to hunker down under the safe view of the Union navy on the James River.

Upon hearing of the order to retreat after Malvern Hill, McClellan decided he would drop down the James River a little bit farther to an even safer position at a place called Harrison's Landing. When he heard that the army was to retreat, a Union general named Philip Carney is said to have remarked with disgust, "We ought instead of retreating to follow up the enemy and take Richmond. I say to all of you, such an order can only be prompted by cowardice or treason." That is Carney's view of what McClellan was doing, retreating from this great position at Malvern Hill.

That was the end of the Seven Days. Malvern Hill was a terrible decision on Lee's part. It would rank with the decision to assault Cemetery Ridge at Gettysburg on the third day as one of Lee's worst. But McClellan retreated anyway.

Let's move on now to talk for a just a few minutes about the consequences of the Seven Days' Battles and the 1862 Richmond campaign overall. The Seven Days' Battles were the eastern equivalent of Shiloh in that they brought the new scale of fighting to both home fronts. There were even more casualties here than there had been at Shiloh: 20,000 Confederate casualties during the Seven Days; 16,000 Union casualties during the Seven Days.

A woman in Richmond named Sally Putnam, who left us one of the best accounts of life in Richmond during the war, described the horrors of the aftermath of the battle as thousands of wounded men poured into Richmond. She wrote, "We lived in one immense hospital and breathed the vapors of the charnel house." The weather was excessively hot. It was mid-summer.

Gangrene and erysipelas attacked the wounded, and those who might have been cured of their wounds were cut down by disease.

The diaries from Richmond are very graphic in what it meant to be close to the scene of a great Civil War battlefield. That's what had happened at the Seven Days. There were enormous casualties that showed that the war was going in a very different direction.

In a strategic sense, the initiative passed from McClellan to Lee. Lee had taken it from McClellan. The whole story in Richmond down to the Seven Days' Battles had been, here come the Federals. They're coming at us up the Peninsula. They're coming at us or at least menacing us from the direction of Fredericksburg. But now Lee has changed that dynamic. Now it's McClellan who's retreating away from Richmond, down the James River, and hunkering down along the river at Harrison's Landing.

Lee is now in charge, in that regard. Confederate morale rebounded remarkably after the Seven Days. It's really quite astonishing how quickly it happened. It was almost as if all those bad things in the West hadn't happened. Lee's own reputation did the same thing. All those doubts about him seemed to be swept away by the Seven Days campaign. One of the Richmond papers that had been very hard on Lee when he first took command of the army, wondering whether he'd fight, wondering whether all he'd want to do is dig in, commented on this just a few days after Malvern Hill.

It said that it couldn't remember another instance when the reputation of a general changed so dramatically. And the paper went on to say that—I'll paraphrase it—we just didn't understand what kind of general Lee was. Now we know, and now we have faith in him. We've seen that he will be aggressive.

The European observers decided that the war was going the Confederacy's way after the Seven Days. That really is quite an astounding fact because it's as if they had blinders on for anything that happened west of the Appalachian Mountains. How could they cancel all of that good Union activity out west and decide the Union's losing the war just because of the Seven Days? But many in the North took the same view.

It frustrated Lincoln immensely. He poured out that frustration—to the degree that he would pour things out—in a letter, writing to a French diplomat. He said, he couldn't understand how all the good work of six months of clearing 100,000 square miles of territory in the west should count for so little when a "single half defeat," as Lincoln put it—that's how he termed the Seven Days—should count for so much. But the fact was it did.

I think the most important outgrowth of this campaign was the emergence of Lee. It placed him in a position from which, over the next year, he would forge a record with his army that inspirited the Confederate people tremendously and made them resolutely look toward victory. They expected victory as long as Lee and his army were in the field. Lee and his army became almost exactly the equivalent of George Washington and the Continental Army during the American Revolution, and they would be the key factor in driving the Confederacy toward independence, in the view of the Confederates.

The next military phase of the conflict would see a major strategic offensive on the part of the Confederates, both in the Western Theater and the East. In our next lecture we will look at the western component of that great counteroffensive.

The Kentucky Campaign of 1862
Lecture 14

Let's begin by looking at the strategic situation that the Confederates saw in front of them in the wake of the Seven Days and the fall of Corinth, Mississippi—two key events. Corinth is gone. The Confederates are going to have to deal with that and decide what to do in the West.

The Confederacy faced a difficult strategic situation in July 1862. Union armies posed threats against several crucial parts of the Confederacy. McClellan's 100,000-man Army of the Potomac remained just a few miles southeast of Richmond. John Pope's new Army of Virginia (comprised of Frémont's, Banks's, and McDowell's old commands) was prepared to move along the Orange and Alexandria Railroad into central Virginia. Union forces menaced Chattanooga and the railroad that connected it to Atlanta and the interior of Georgia. Henry W. Halleck had been made general-in-chief of the Union armies on 11 July (replacing McClellan in this role) and would henceforth coordinate all Northern efforts.

Bragg's and Kirby Smith's retreat from Kentucky ended the western dimension of this great Confederate counteroffensive in the late summer and fall of 1862.

Nonmilitary factors also loomed large as these campaigns began. England and France were watching closely to see how the next round of campaigns unfolded, following the Confederate success in the Seven Days' Battles. Meanwhile, Abraham Lincoln was looking for a battlefield victory that would permit him to announce his Emancipation Proclamation. The Confederacy responded to these threats by invading Kentucky and Maryland.

Two Confederate armies marched into Kentucky in August and September. Braxton Bragg commanded the larger of the two forces. Bragg was a West Pointer and a decorated artillerist in the Mexican War. Loyal to Jefferson Davis, he rose rapidly from brigadier to full general after Shiloh. Bragg replaced Beauregard in command of the Army of Mississippi (later the Army of Tennessee) after the fall of Corinth and trained his army near Tupelo, Mississippi. A strict disciplinarian, Bragg had a number of physical ailments. He was argumentative and often short-tempered. His plan called for taking half the army to Chattanooga for a movement northward and leaving the other half under Earl Van Dorn and Sterling Price to defend Mississippi. Bragg was helped when Don Carlos Buell abandoned plans to strike at Chattanooga, because Confederate cavalry disrupted Federal supply lines.

Edmund Kirby Smith commanded the smaller of the Confederate armies and would lead the march into Kentucky. The Confederates hoped to accomplish several things by this campaign:

- Gather food and fodder in Kentucky.

- Recruit among Kentuckians assumed to be friendly to the South.

- Remove Federal forces from parts of Tennessee.

- Create problems for the Republicans during the elections of the fall of 1862.

The campaign began on a successful note for the Confederates. Smith marched into Kentucky in August and captured a Federal garrison at Richmond, Kentucky, on August 30. He then moved deeper into the bluegrass region. Bragg followed Smith northward and also enjoyed success; he captured a Federal force at Munfordville on September 17.

Smith drew Buell out of Nashville, but the campaign unraveled in late September and early October. Bragg marched into the bluegrass region after waiting at Munfordville for Buell to attack him. Buell moved on to Louisville. He hoped that Van Dorn and Price would march north from Mississippi and capture Nashville (vacated by Buell). The Confederates took time to inaugurate a Confederate governor of Kentucky at Frankfort on 2 October. This move was designed to give legitimacy to Kentucky's place in the Confederacy. The Confederates also hoped to boost enlistment in Kentucky.

Van Dorn and Price were defeated at the Battle of Corinth (Mississippi) on October 3–4, ending hope that Nashville would be liberated. The campaign climaxed at Perryville, in Kentucky's largest Civil War battle. A reinforced Buell moved lethargically from Louisville toward Bragg starting on 1 October. The armies made contact about 35 miles southeast of Louisville on October 7, engaged in combat into the night, and fought a major battle the next day. Neither army commander understood what was happening or had a clear picture of the other force's strength. Each side enjoyed some tactical success before night ended the fighting on October 8, with the Confederates gaining momentum.

Confederate General Braxton Bragg.

Bragg decided to abandon the field, reunite with Smith, and abandon Kentucky. He failed to achieve any of his goals for this campaign, including the recapture of Nashville and the liberation of Tennessee. Possible explanations for his decision include the following:

- He lacked a good grasp of how the Battle of Perryville had actually gone.

- The Confederates lacked a safe supply line.

- Kentuckians had failed to flock to the Confederate colors.

- The campaign did not affect the Northern elections as hoped. ∎

Essential Reading

Hattaway and Jones, *How the North Won: A Military History of the Civil War*, chapter 8.

McPherson, *Battle Cry of Freedom: The Civil War Era*, chapter 17.

Supplementary Reading

Connelly, *Army of the Heartland: The Army of Tennessee, 1861–1862*, chapters 10–14.

Cozzens, *The Darkest Days of the War: The Battles of Iuka and Corinth*.

McDonough, *War in Kentucky: From Shiloh to Perryville*.

Questions to Consider

1. Do you think better military leadership would have yielded a more positive result for the Confederates in Kentucky? Or was the negative result a failure of political leadership in misreading the state of public opinion in Kentucky and supporting an invasion in the first place?

2. Did the fact that Bragg's army withdrew only into Tennessee after the Battle of Perryville justify a sense of some Confederate accomplishment?

The Kentucky Campaign of 1862
Lecture 14—Transcript

We completed our last lecture with an assessment of the impact of the Seven Days campaign. Part of that assessment emphasized the fact that George B. McClellan had relinquished the strategic offensive in Virginia to Robert E. Lee. The next move would be up to Lee there. In fact, the Confederates would take the strategic offensive across most of the strategic map in the summer and fall of 1862.

What we're going to do in this lecture is begin our look at a major Confederate counteroffensive that stretched from late summer well into the autumn of 1862 and saw Confederate armies move into Northern territory in both Maryland and Kentucky. We'll begin by setting up the strategic situation in July 1862 and the problems that faced the Confederacy in mounting these offensives, and then we'll move on to describe the movement of Confederate armies into Kentucky in August and September. We'll look at the initial successes that those armies achieved, and then we'll look at the climactic Battle of Perryville, the biggest battle fought in Kentucky during the war, and the ultimate failure of the Southern campaign in Kentucky.

Let's begin by looking at the strategic situation that the Confederates saw in front of them in the wake of the Seven Days and the fall of Corinth, Mississippi, two key events. Corinth is gone. The Confederates are going to have to deal with that and decide what to do in the west. After the Seven Days, the question is, McClellan has been pushed back along the James River—he's hunkered down at Harrison's Landing—but now what? It was still a very problematical board of war facing the Confederates. What are we going to do?

These are the components that were most important. First is McClellan. He's still there with more than 100,000 men. He'd only retreated a few miles. He wasn't doing anything aggressive, but his mere presence below Richmond posed a great threat to the Confederates. Also in Virginia was a new Union commander, a man named John Pope who had won some successes out West. He had been brought east and placed in command of a new army, christened the Army of Virginia, that was really made up of the old commands of John C. Frémont and Nathaniel C. Banks and Irvin McDowell.

Pope was placed in northern Virginia, north central Virginia, and seemed to be about to menace the railroads in that part of the state of Virginia. So there were two major threats in Virginia. Union forces also seemed poised to strike against Chattanooga, Tennessee. Chattanooga was a major rail center for the Confederacy, an east-west rail line that went through Chattanooga and then on up to Virginia. There was also a major rail line from Chattanooga down to Atlanta, Georgia. Atlanta was a very important city.

Federal forces seemed ready to move against Chattanooga. If they did so successfully and then moved on to Atlanta, that would open up the great heartland of Georgia to Union military operations. So here's another threat the Confederates are going to have to deal with. All of those Union commands were in a menacing position, and, as the Confederates looked at this strategic situation, there was a change of command in the North. On July 11, Abraham Lincoln promoted Henry W. Halleck to be General-in-Chief of the United States armies.

It was a position Halleck richly deserved. He had orchestrated the wonderful series of Union successes out in the Kentucky/Tennessee/northern Mississippi Theater, so Halleck was an obvious person. He'd proved himself to be an excellent administrator and strategist in the west. This was his reward. His goal—the goal put before him by Lincoln—was to orchestrate Union forces across the entire map and try to apply pressure to Confederates at so many points that the Confederates, with their smaller pool of resources, would not be able to respond adequately to what the Federals were doing.

There were other, nonmilitary factors that were also in play at this stage of the war. One was that Lincoln had decided by mid-July that he was going to issue a proclamation of emancipation, but he needed a Union victory. He didn't want to issue it in the wake of a defeat such as the Seven Days. So that is there. It's a major factor. It's just offstage, so to speak. Lincoln wants to do it, but he has to wait to see what happens militarily before he can do it.

There were also potentially great things that might happen on the diplomatic front. We mentioned earlier that the Seven Days, Lee's victory at the Seven Days, persuaded many observers in France and Great Britain that the Confederacy was winning the war. Were more success to follow in Virginia, it seemed likely to observers both in the North and the South that either London or Paris might make some decisive move to assist the Confederacy—extend recognition to the Confederacy or perhaps even send some type of material aid to the Confederacy.

So all of these things are sort of percolating in July of 1862, and what the Confederates in the end decide to do is mount these twin offensives, one in the Western Theater that will move troops from Mississippi up through Tennessee and into Kentucky, and, in the Eastern Theater, one in which Robert E. Lee and the Army of Northern Virginia will go out of Virginia across the Potomac River into western Maryland.

What we'll do first is look at events in the Western Theater. We'll look at the two Confederates armies that marched into Kentucky in August and September of 1862. After Beauregard had evacuated Corinth, Mississippi, at the end of May 1862 and Halleck had followed him in with his huge army of 100,000 men—after those events had transpired—Jefferson Davis replaced Beauregard with Braxton Bragg.

I spoke earlier about how Beauregard, in effect, went on sick leave without telling anybody what he was going to do. He alienated Jefferson Davis tremendously by doing that. He would remain in Davis's doghouse for the rest of the war. His replacement was Braxton Bragg, a man who would be a staunch ally of Davis's through the war. He was a man Davis trusted and liked, a man who was always loyal to Davis, and that was very important to Jefferson Davis.

Bragg is going to loom very large in the military story of the war in the Western Theater for a good long while. We're going to see a great deal of Braxton Bragg. He is an excellent example of how someone who's not successful can nonetheless be a very important figure in a conflict. He's going to be one of the most important military figures in the Civil War even though he's going to have virtually no success as a military commander on the Confederate side.

Braxton Bragg was a North Carolinian. He'd graduated from West Point. He'd served conspicuously in the Mexican War. He was a hero in the Mexican War, in fact. He'd been an artillerist there, and he was one of the bright young officers in the war, in the view of the American people after that conflict. He had done very well. He'd resigned from the army in the mid-1850s and had become a sugar planter in Tennessee. He had become quite a prominent sugar planter, in fact.

When war came, he came back into Confederate service. He was made a brigadier general, and then he was advanced through the ranks until he became a full general, a four-star general. He's just after that first group of full Confederate generals that we talked about earlier: Albert Sidney Johnston, Robert E. Lee, Beauregard, and Joseph Johnston. Those are the first four; Braxton Bragg is next.

He fought at Shiloh in April of 1962, and he was promoted to full general shortly after that, and now he is commander of the Army of Mississippi, as it's called. It would later be the Army of Tennessee, and it, together with the Army of Northern Virginia, are the two principal field commands in Confederate military service.

But here he is in command of the Army of Mississippi. Bragg in many ways was an able man. He had a high intellect. He was a very stern taskmaster. He wanted troops to toe the line. He really did have a West Pointer's view of how soldiers should behave. He was capable of prodigious amounts of work. He also suffered from a range of ailments. He had migraine headaches, he seemed to be nervous all the time, he suffered from rheumatism, and he had problems with his stomach. It may have been an ulcer—we don't know.

He seemed to be in pain a good deal of the time, and I think that colored his personality. He had a very prickly personality. He was quick to snap at people, quick to take offense, and very argumentative. In the mid-nineteenth century there weren't all the remedies that we have at hand to deal with ailments like that. I think many people were in what we would call chronic pain, and I think those who suffered most from that almost certainly showed it in their personalities. I think Braxton Bragg is one of those people.

He loved to argue. He was a hairsplitter. There's a wonderful story from the old army that U.S. Grant related in his memoirs and others related as well. It may be apocryphal, but I think it gets at the essence of Braxton Bragg, at one part of his personality. As the story goes, Bragg was out at a small post commanding a company in the west, and, because there was a shortage of officers there, he was also acting as temporary post quartermaster in commissary.

Well, as company commander he made a request of the quartermaster for something. In other words, he wrote it out, and, as quartermaster, he denied it. As company commander he gave a fuller explanation of why he needed it, gave it to the quartermaster, and, as quartermaster, he denied it again and passed it on up to the post commander. Well, the post commander looked at it, really couldn't believe it, and said, "My God, Mr. Bragg. You've quarreled with every other officer in the army and now you're quarreling with yourself."

Now, this may not have ever happened, but a number of soldiers related the anecdote, and it makes the point that Bragg was an argumentative fellow. He was not popular among his troops. Never during the war was he popular among his troops. He was seen as a martinet. He could be aggressive on the battlefield, but he's an officer whose aggression on the battlefield never seemed to yield substantial results. So that is Braxton Bragg, a person we'll see a good deal of as we go through the course.

Before Henry Halleck journeyed east to take up his duties as General-in-Chief, he had planned a movement against Chattanooga, Tennessee, and then against the railroad that ran from there to Atlanta. Don Carlos Buell was to carry out this move, but in a scenario that would be replayed many times in the Western Theater, Confederate cavalry and guerrillas so disrupted Buell's supply lines that this campaign never really came to anything.

The Federals were not successful in taking Chattanooga, and they learned, as they would learn time and time again, that it was a prodigiously difficult task to move a substantial body of troops through country such as that in east Tennessee and keep them supplied if there were Confederate cavalry and guerrillas operating in their rear. So the Union threat to Chattanooga was not going to come to anything.

Bragg cast his eye toward Chattanooga. He had been retraining and refitting his army near Tupelo, Mississippi, and this is what he planned to do. He planned to leave about half of his army under Earl Van Dorn and Sterling Price. Sterling Price we last saw in Missouri. He's now come to northern Mississippi, and he and Van Dorn will share command of about half of Bragg's force. The other half, roughly 35,000 men, would first go to Chattanooga, there to unite with about 10,000 Confederates under a general named Edmund Kirby Smith, and then the joint Confederate force would mount an invasion first into Tennessee and then on into Kentucky.

Bragg had a range of things that he hoped to achieve. He hoped to cut Don Carlos Buell's supply line back to Louisville. Buell is in Nashville. He hoped to cut that supply line—cut Buell off from Kentucky. He thought he could compel Buell to abandon Tennessee if he did that, that he could make Buell come out of Nashville and head back toward Kentucky. He thought he could make Buell fight his way back toward Louisville, and Bragg's force would have the advantage of being in between Buell and Louisville and in a strong defensive position potentially. So that's one thing he hoped to do.

He also hoped that, by marching into Kentucky, he would rally the citizens of Kentucky to come to the Confederate banner. He and many other Confederates believed that Kentuckians were really Confederates at heart and that they were being held in the Union against their will by Union military might. If we can just take an army into Kentucky, he thought, they will flock to our banners.

He also thought that perhaps if he could remain in Kentucky through the fall—and he hoped to maneuver for a good long while there—he would be in a position to menace Union forces in Kentucky at the time of the Northern off-year elections in November of 1862, and he hoped that his presence would hurt the Republicans and help the Democrats. Confederates believed that if the Democrats were in control they'd have a better chance of negotiating some kind of peace with independence for the Confederacy. So there were many things that Bragg hoped he might accomplish.

Let's move on to look at the beginning part of the campaign. It went splendidly for the Confederates initially. Kirby Smith moved first. He marched quickly northward. He bypassed Cumberland Gap on his way north and struck deep into Kentucky, where on August 30 he defeated and captured most of a 6,000-man Union garrison at Richmond, Kentucky. Bragg followed shortly thereafter. They didn't move on the same track. Bragg was actually moving on a line of march about 100 miles west of Kirby Smith's, but Bragg followed through Tennessee and eventually entered Kentucky.

With two Rebel armies in Kentucky, Don Carlos Buell did what Bragg had hoped he would do. He left a garrison at Nashville and set out with the bulk of his army after Bragg. On September 17, Bragg captured a small Federal force at Munfordville, Kentucky. That was a town on the Louisville and Nashville Railroad. He thought that he was in precisely the position that he wanted to be in. He was going to force Don Carlos Buell now, whose line of communications to Louisville had been cut, to come after him.

There had been an almost farcical episode at Munfordville when the Confederates surrounded the place. The Union commander was a man named Wilder who was not a professional soldier and was really quite beside himself as to what he should do. The Confederates came up in manifestly more strength than Wilder had, and they said, "We want you to surrender." Wilder, under a flag of truce, parlayed with the Confederates, in effect, and said, "Well, I'm not sure whether I should surrender. I'm not sure what the circumstances are," and he, in effect, asked the Confederates if he should surrender.

The Confederates responded—in this case it was Simon Bolivar Buckner— "Well, I don't know how many men you have. I don't know what your position looks like. I can't tell you whether you should surrender." And Wilder said, "Well, this is how many men I have, and this is what my position is. Now do you think I should surrender?" And they said, "Yes," and so he did, and Munfordville fell.

And there is Braxton Bragg controlling this position on the Louisville and Nashville Railroad. He expected Buell to come and attack him. He underestimated Buell's capacity for lethargy. The thing that Buell was best at, really, was not doing anything, and that's what he did here. He sat and he waited. And Bragg waited and Buell waited.

People came up to reinforce Buell from the south. He eventually had nearly 50,000 men. Bragg became impatient. He ran out of food in the area, and he left. He left the line of the L&N and drew his army eastward into the lush Bluegrass region, where food and fodder were plentiful to feed his men and his animals. Buell then simply moved on to Louisville.

So Bragg had done what he wanted to do, but then he hadn't waited and forced the issue. He'd moved out of the way. Buell had gone on to Louisville. Now that Buell had committed himself to Kentucky, however, Bragg hoped that the troops he left behind under Earl Van Dorn and Sterling Price would be able to march out of northern Mississippi and recapture Nashville. Bragg thought, I've drawn the major Union force with me. They're out of the way. Now maybe my compatriots back in northern Mississippi will be able to liberate Nashville and parts of middle Tennessee.

A political dimension entered the campaign at this point in early October. On the second day of the month, Bragg decided to go to Frankfurt, the capital of Kentucky, which Kirby Smith had captured and where the Confederates planned to inaugurate a Secessionist governor. They're continuing this charade that Kentucky's really a Confederate state: There's a star in the Confederate flag for Kentucky; let's go over and officially inaugurate a Confederate governor in the capital of the state. So he heads over to do that.

Meanwhile, back in Mississippi there's a battle at Corinth, another battle at Corinth, on the third and fourth of October. Earl Van Dorn and Sterling Price fight a bloody contest there against a Federal force that they cannot defeat. It's a Union victory in the Battle of Corinth, which means that Braxton Bragg's hope that something would happen at Nashville is not going to come to fruition. That part of the campaign is over. Those Confederate troops are going to remain far away from the scene of principal action in that campaign.

Still, if we look at the Confederate campaign into Kentucky, down to that point, down to the point of the Battle of Corinth, it would have to be reckoned a success. Bragg and Kirby Smith had captured 8,000 Federals, they had drawn another 50,000 out of Tennessee, and they were menacing Louisville and perhaps even Cincinnati. No one knew where they were going to go. They were getting close to the Ohio River, and they could have moved in any one of a number of directions.

The inauguration of a Confederate governor was intended to give legitimacy to the presence of these Confederate soldiers in the state and also, as I said earlier, to send the message that it was not just a sham, that Kentucky was counted as one of the states of the Confederacy. Both Bragg and Kirby Smith also hoped that, by inaugurating this governor, it would encourage more Kentuckians to come in. Bragg had gone north with more than 15,000 extra muskets, which he hoped to distribute to the Kentuckians he hoped would come to his army. The men hadn't been coming to his army. Those muskets remained in the wagons they'd been in all the way into Kentucky. He hoped that this inaugural ceremony would encourage more Kentuckians, embolden them, if you like, to come forward and cast their lot with the Confederacy.

Buell, meanwhile, was sitting in Louisville, and he was coming under increasing criticism for doing that. The Northern people and Buell's superiors wanted him to move more decisively. Earlier in the war, George B. McClellan, when he was General-in-Chief, had learned that Buell could be very obstinate, very reluctant to move. Buell was even less willing to move than McClellan had been. Well, that pattern is holding true here as well. He's made his way back to Louisville, but he's almost acting as if there aren't two Confederate armies in Kentucky.

There he is with by far the largest army in the state, and he's allowing Bragg and Kirby Smith essentially to roam at will without trying to do violence to them. The Federals shifted some reinforcements from Ulysses S. Grant's army in Mississippi up toward Buell so that Buell eventually had more than 60,000 men. There are 60,000 men sitting in Louisville, and there is a feeling that he should be doing something with them. On October 1 he finally departed from Louisville and made his way very slowly toward the region of the state where he knew that Bragg and Kirby Smith were lurking.

Let's move on now and look at the climactic Battle of Perryville. Buell's troops marched in four columns as they went eastward. They were spread out because it had been an extremely dry season in Kentucky that year and they were looking for water. They needed water. Armies, animals, and men needed water. They were hoping to find water as they moved eastward.

Bragg was reported to be about 30 to 40 miles southeast of Louisville. His troops were also thirsty. They also were suffering for water. Some of them were sort of feeling their way westward at the same time that Buell was coming toward them from Louisville. On October 7, one of the columns— one of the Federal columns—found water and also found Confederates at a place called Doctor's Creek, which was a tributary of the Salt River near Perryville.

The two pieces of these armies simply bumbled into one another there, and they fought for possession of the pools of water in that creek on October 7, the fighting continuing well past dark. The soldiers fought under moonlight on the night of October 7 around those pools of water. Parts of the armies, as I said, had thus made contact. It wasn't a deliberate thing. It wasn't orchestrated by Buell or by Bragg; it just happened. Neither Bragg nor Buell knew exactly what was going on.

The Battle of Perryville would take place the next day on October 8. As I said earlier, it was the largest contest that the state of Kentucky would see. It was a strange fight. Neither commander really knew what was going on at Perryville. Buell thought that he faced all of Bragg's and Kirby Smith's forces while Bragg thought he was up against just a fragment of Buell's army. Actually, more nearly the reverse was true. There were about 16,000 Confederates who would become engaged at Perryville; more than twice that many Federals would get into the battle.

A strange feature of the topography at Perryville made it difficult to hear battle noises behind the lines. This is clear from testimony on both sides. Units that were really quite close to one another could hear almost nothing of what was going on, and officers of some units were entirely unaware that a battle was going on at all. Among those who were unaware that a battle was going on was Don Carlos Buell. He didn't know really what was happening with his army. He didn't know the general engagement was taking place until quite late in the afternoon.

The fight seesawed back and forth. A series of disjointed Federal attacks failed early on, and then a general Confederate attack that was launched about mid-afternoon began to gain ground, driving the Union slowly backward. Nightfall came without a really decisive result on the battlefield, but many of the Confederate soldiers who had finished the day with momentum on their side believed that not only had they had the better of the fighting on October 8, but they really believed that they would be launching further assaults on the ninth and that they would perhaps win a more decisive victory when the next day's fighting began. They didn't reckon with Braxton Bragg's attitude about what had gone on.

Bragg decided that the day had not gone well for his soldiers and began to worry about his exposed position deep in Kentucky. He began to worry about how many Federals might be nearby, and he worried as well about his supply lines. He didn't think that they were safe. He ruminated about these things on the night of the eighth, and he decided to retreat from the battlefield, to withdraw and reunite with Kirby Smith, which he did. Shortly thereafter, the Confederates withdrew from Kentucky.

As I said earlier, Perryville was the largest battle fought in Kentucky during the war. There were about 4,200 Union casualties and about 3,400 Confederate casualties. In a strictly tactical sense, it would have to be called a stalemate. Neither army drove the other from the field. They pretty much fought each other to a standstill on October 8, but because Bragg abandoned the field and began his retreat first to rejoin Kirby Smith and then from Kentucky, I think that it has to be reckoned a Union victory.

This is typical of a pattern in Braxton Bragg's generalship. He'd actually had the better of the fighting on October 8, but he let whatever advantage he had won that day slip away from him. We'll see this happen again and again. He's a general, as I said earlier, who can show an aggressive spirit, who will try to take the battle to his opponent, and who, in some cases, even wins quite striking tactical success, but then he never seems to know quite what to do with it.

Perryville is a preview of what would happen with Braxton Bragg later. We'll see it again in the Battle of Murfreesboro when he retreats from a battlefield that by any measure would have to be called a draw. We'll see it again at Chickamauga when his troops win a striking tactical success during the fighting at that battle and then Bragg seems to be frozen in indecision following the battle.

Well, he does make a decision here. His decision is to leave Kentucky, and so the Confederates withdraw. Along with them go those wagons still filled with the muskets that they had hoped to put in the hands of Kentuckians. Bragg had not accomplished any of his long-range goals that he had set for himself in Kentucky. First is the matter of the guns in the wagons. The Kentuckians had not flocked to the Confederate's colors. This came as a surprise to many in the South. Many in the South now couldn't look at Kentucky as a captive state anymore. They'd had their chance. Confederate armies had been there, Confederates willing to fight for the Kentuckians. The Kentuckians had not seemed willing to fight for themselves.

Bragg also was not able to remain north long enough to influence the Northern elections as he had hoped to do. He'd operated into about the middle part of October, but he was in retreat long before voters would go to the polls in the North in the November elections. He also didn't cause a reorientation of the strategic situation in Tennessee, really. He retreated into Tennessee. He didn't retreat all the way back down into Mississippi, but he hadn't seen the recapture of Nashville by the Confederates. It remained in Union hands, and more Federals troops would move back to Nashville very shortly. So Tennessee had not been liberated either. Moreover, to many Confederates, Bragg seemed to have relinquished the offensive too quickly after Perryville and then abandoned the Bluegrass state too precipitately. Overall, the operation did absolutely nothing to enhance Braxton Bragg's reputation. It's his first real field command, and he didn't do that well.

Bragg's and Kirby Smith's retreat from Kentucky ended the western dimension of this great Confederate counteroffensive in the late summer and fall of 1862. What we'll do in our next lecture is turn to the eastern component of that counteroffensive and see what Robert E. Lee and the Army of Northern Virginia did in Maryland.

Antietam
Lecture 15

In August and September 1862, while Braxton Bragg and Kirby Smith marched their armies into Kentucky, major military events also were transpiring in Virginia and Maryland. This lecture will assess the movements and battles in the Eastern Theater during the late summer and early autumn of 1862.

This lecture shifts the spotlight from Kentucky to Virginia to complete our consideration of the great Confederate counteroffensive in the autumn of 1862. However important the campaign in Kentucky might have been militarily, the Virginia theater continued to command greater attention. This gave special urgency to the events that followed McClellan's retreat from Richmond after the Seven Days.

The initial confrontation pitted Lee against John Pope. Pope was born into an important family and was related by marriage to Mary Todd Lincoln. He was a graduate of West Point and had enjoyed some success in the Western Theater under Halleck. Pope held center stage in Virginia after the Seven Days; he was also arrogant and a braggart. As a Republican, he was attuned to congressional feelings.

Pope brought a harsher type of war to Virginia. He threatened to execute guerrillas, arrest citizens who harbored irregulars, and drive from their homes civilians in Union lines who refused to take the oath of allegiance. He also vowed to take whatever his army needed from civilians, thus earning the enmity of white Southerners in Virginia. Pope planned a campaign toward the rail junction at Gordonsville that would sever Lee's rail connections to the Shenandoah Valley via the Orange and Alexandria and the Virginia Central Railroads.

Lee reacted to Pope's movements by first reorganizing his army, then dividing and then reuniting it. Longstreet's wing kept an eye on McClellan below Richmond. Jackson's wing marched to meet Pope along the Rappahannock.

Jackson defeated part of Pope's army (under Banks's command) at Cedar Mountain on August 9, 1862. He probed along the Rappahannock after Pope's troops withdrew. Lee and Longstreet joined Jackson along the Rappahannock after McClellan was recalled to Washington.

The reunited Army of Northern Virginia defeated Pope's army at Second Manassas (August 28–30). Jackson's wing flanked the Federals, destroyed their main supply base at Manassas Junction, and engaged them on the old Manassas (Bull Run) battlefield. Longstreet's wing arrived on the battlefield opposite Pope's left flank. Pope didn't realize that these CSA forces had arrived to face him. The Confederates delivered a decisive attack on August 30 that drove the Federals from the field. The Union troops withdrew in good order back to the defenses of Washington, D.C. This battle resulted in approximately 9,000 Confederate and 16,000 Union casualties. Pope was removed from command and posted to Minnesota to fight the Sioux; McClellan was reinstated by Lincoln as the field commander.

Lee retained the strategic initiative by moving across the Potomac into Maryland. He had a range of goals:

- He wanted to dictate the action and not react to Northern moves.

- He planned to gather food and fodder in Maryland and perhaps Pennsylvania.

- This move would give northern Virginia a respite from the presence of the armies and allow farmers to get their crops in.

- Lee hoped to recruit Marylanders to the Confederate cause.

- He wanted to influence the North's fall elections (cf., Bragg's objective in Kentucky in this same general time frame).

- He thought that success would perhaps gain foreign support for the Confederacy.

Lee counted on a slow response from McClellan, so Lee divided his forces by dispatching Jackson with more than half of the army to capture the Union garrison at Harpers Ferry, a key strategic point. However, the campaign quickly turned against Lee. His army suffered from large-scale straggling and desertion after crossing the Potomac because many of the men were reluctant to leave their homes in Virginia. Furthermore, many were sick and all were tired from the heavy campaigning. A copy of his Special Orders 191 for the campaign fell into McClellan's hands on 13 September. He moved more rapidly than anticipated and took control of the gaps in South Mountain on September 14. Jackson took longer than expected to capture Harpers Ferry, which finally fell on 15 September.

Prints and Photographs Division, Library of Congress.

The Battle of Second Bull Run (or Second Manassas), August 28–30, 1862.

The campaign reached a climax at Antietam on September 17. Lee recalled Jackson and concentrated his nearly 35,000-man army near Sharpsburg, Maryland (along Antietam Creek, a tributary of the Potomac River). One division (A. P. Hill's) remained in Harpers Ferry to guard the 12,000 Union prisoners. McClellan, with nearly 70,000 men, launched heavy assaults in three sectors of the battlefield. His goal was to grind Lee down and cut him off from the Potomac River, his line of retreat. The Union assaults were not coordinated, however. A. P. Hill's Light Division made a forced march from Harpers Ferry and arrived in time to turn the tide of the battle.

Lee barely held his position on the 17th but remained on the field for another day before retreating across the Potomac. The battle resulted in over 23,000 casualties (10,500 Confederate and 12,500 Union), making this the bloodiest single day in U.S. history. Photographs from the battlefield caused a sensation.

If the Confederacy lost the war, they would lose slavery, and their whole social system would be turned topsy-turvy.

Few campaigns matched the impact of Antietam. The military consequences of this tactical draw were mixed. Lee retreated but held his ground just south of the Potomac for some time. McClellan elected not to press the retreating Confederate forces and was removed from command the day after the fall 1862 elections. England and France decided to await further military results before attempting some type of intervention in the American war.

Lincoln used the battle as a pretext to issue his preliminary Emancipation Proclamation. This move forestalled foreign intervention. The proclamation also marked a change in Northern war aims. The war for the Union had become a war for union and freedom because, wherever Union forces marched now, they would be taking the possibility of freedom with them. The stakes were much higher now: The whole social fabric of the South was on the table. If the Confederacy lost the war, they would lose slavery, and their whole social system would be turned topsy-turvy. ■

Essential Reading

Hattaway and Jones, *How the North Won: A Military History of the Civil War*, chapters 8–9.

McPherson, *Battle Cry of Freedom: The Civil War Era*, chapter 17.

Supplementary Reading

Catton, *Mr. Lincoln's Army*, parts 4–6.

Freeman, *Lee's Lieutenants: A Study in Command*, vol. 2., chapters 1–15.

Gallagher, ed., *The Antietam Campaign*.

Hennessy, *Return to Bull Run: The Campaign and Battle of Second Manassas*.

Jones, *Union in Peril: The Crisis over British Intervention in the Civil War*.

Sears, *Landscape Turned Red: The Battle of Antietam*.

Questions to Consider

1. Was Lee too aggressive in invading Maryland and remaining north of the Potomac after September 14?

2. How would you handicap the Confederacy's chances for independence in the aftermath of the Maryland campaign?

Antietam

Lecture 15—Transcript

In August and September 1862, while Braxton Bragg and Kirby Smith marched their armies into Kentucky, major military events also were transpiring in Virginia and Maryland. This lecture will assess the movements and battles in the Eastern Theater during the late summer and early autumn of 1862.

We'll look at the arrival in Virginia and activities of Union general John Pope. We'll look at the campaign and Battle of Second Manassas or Bull Run, which took place in late August. We'll assess Lee's decision to strike north across the Potomac after the Battle of Second Manassas. Then we'll look at the Antietam campaign and the Battle of Antietam. We'll finish by assessing the impact of the 1862 Maryland campaign on the broader framework of the war.

Let's start with John Pope and his arrival in Virginia. Although important military events were unfolding in the west, as usual, the Northern public and foreign observers—and, I would think, a majority of the Confederate people—focused most on Virginia. They wondered what was going to happen in Virginia. That was a situation, as we've noted earlier, that bothered Lincoln tremendously. Lincoln wished that people would focus more on the west because that's where all the good news had been happening for the North. I mentioned the letter he wrote to the French diplomat after the Seven Days, complaining about the fact that things in Virginia seemed to overshadow events everywhere else. Nonetheless, that's the way it was.

So there'd be a great deal of attention paid to what happened with John Pope and his army in Virginia. In mid-July 1862, Pope moved this army, again made up of the old commands of Frémont and Banks and McDowell—and about 50,000 strong—toward Gordonsville in central Virginia. There he would be able to menace key railroads in Virginia, the Orange and Alexandria Railroad and the Virginia Central Railroad. The Virginia Central ran over into the Shenandoah Valley and was a principal artery bringing supplies to the Confederate army defending Richmond. He'd be able to perhaps interrupt the movement of those supplies if he could gain control of the Virginia Central.

He also hoped to get into a position where he would menace Robert E. Lee's western flank. Lee was still watching McClellan below Richmond. Pope would be out menacing his western and northwestern flank.

Pope was a West Pointer. He'd been born into a prominent family in Kentucky and then had gone to West Point. He was a collateral descendent of George Washington. Perhaps more important for his military career during the early part of the Civil War, he was also connected by marriage to the family of Mary Todd Lincoln, a connection that certainly didn't hurt his early rise to prominence.

He had served effectively in the Mexican War, and he was commissioned a brigadier general soon after the firing on Fort Sumter. His early war service was in the west under Halleck, and he had won some successes in campaigning along the Mississippi River. He was part of that group of western officers who advanced as Halleck advanced in the wake of all those Union successes out there. He was brought east to try to see if he could change the strategic balance in the state. McClellan wasn't getting the job done. Perhaps John Pope, a man who'd been successful in the west, would be able to do so.

Soon after he arrived in Virginia he began to make statements that revealed him to be, in the eyes of many, even in his own army, a very arrogant man and a braggart. He announced to his new troops that he came from the west, where, he said, "we have always seen the backs of our enemies," a calculated snub to the eastern troops who had retreated on more than one occasion. He said he didn't care about defensive lines or avenues of retreat because it was going to be the Rebels who would be retreating, not the Federals. He said, let them worry about those kinds of things.

More important than these statements he made was the fact that Pope brought a tougher kind of war to Virginia. He anticipated the direction the war was going to go in a broader sense. He was a Republican, unlike most of the generals in the east. He was attuned, well attuned, to what the Republicans in Congress wanted to do. He promised to confiscate all Rebel property. He said, I'm going to execute guerrillas. I'm going to arrest citizens who aid guerrillas. I'm going to drive out of Union lines all citizens who aren't loyal to the United States.

He was going to bring the kind of war that tough radical Republicans and others in the North wanted to see taken to the South—make the Rebels feel the pain of their decision to be traitors to the Union. Now, he didn't, in fact, hang guerrillas or drive civilians off their land, but nonetheless, his arrival and his statements set a different tone, and he did lay a heavier hand on northern and north central Virginia than previous commanders had.

Property was destroyed at a much greater rate. Fence rails were consumed by Northern soldiers who used them for their fires. Barns were torn down to repair bridges, livestock and food stuffs were impressed, and homes were pillaged. White Southerners came to hate John Pope. He became a great villain. Robert E. Lee even seemed to take what Pope was doing quite personally. Lee was usually very careful about what he said about his opponents, but he wrote, "This miscreant Pope must be suppressed." So Pope has cut a wide swath.

Let's see how the Confederates reacted to John Pope. For Lee and Jefferson Davis, the next campaign would be centered on logistics. They wanted to secure the railroad communications between the Shenandoah Valley and eastern Virginia to protect that line of supply and communications. Just before the campaign opened, Lee reorganized his army. He gave half of it, in effect, to Stonewall Jackson and half of it to James Longstreet—two wings of the army, as he called them. Each of those subordinates would be his key subordinates now for a number of months and would command half the army.

Lee and Longstreet kept an eye on McClellan below Richmond. Lee divided his army, a quite daring move, and sent Stonewall Jackson to deal with the threat of John Pope. In early August, on the ninth, Jackson's force met the advance guard of Pope's army under Banks's command in the Battle of Cedar Mountain near Culpepper in central Virginia. The Federals fell back after that battle.

Lee waited a while longer and soon perceived that McClellan was being recalled to the Washington area. Lincoln had had it with McClellan and had decided to bring McClellan's army back to Washington to reinforce Pope because McClellan wasn't making anything happen below Richmond. Scholars have debated whether that was a good or a bad thing because McClellan did pose a real threat just by being where he was below Richmond. At any rate, the Army of the Potomac was recalled to Washington. Once Lee was certain that that was happening, he took the rest of his force, Longstreet's wing, and reunited the army near the Rappahannock River frontier.

He had to decide what to do next, and what he did next was divide his army again. He had just reunited it, but he decided to divide it again and commence a series of movements that would result in the Battle of Second Manassas or Bull Run. Lee sent Jackson's corps on a wide turning movement around John Pope's right flank and rear. Jackson went all the way around Pope, came in from Pope's rear, and captured an enormous Union supply depot at Manassas Junction. He carried off everything that he could and burned the rest.

Jackson thought that that would get Pope's attention and have him come back to deal with Jackson, which is precisely what happened. Pope turned around. Jackson dug in on ground on the old Manassas battlefield and, on August 29, the Federals opened the Battle of Second Manassas with a series of attacks that almost broke Jackson's line. Those attacks would continue all through the twenty-ninth and into the thirtieth.

On the twenty-ninth, Lee and Longstreet arrived on the battlefield and went into position. Pope didn't realize that they were there. He didn't realize it even the next morning, although a number of officers had warned him that they thought Longstreet was on the field. Pope continued the attacks against Jackson on the thirtieth, again pushing Jackson's troops right to the edge of their endurance. But in the afternoon, after careful preparation, James Longstreet launched a massive assault against Pope's left flank, shattered a number of Pope's units, and drove a good part of the Federal army from the field.

The Union army didn't panic and sprint back to Washington, but it did retreat from the battlefield. It retreated in a quite orderly way back to the capital city. It was the second major victory on the ground at Manassas for the Confederates. Lee had suffered about 9,000 casualties. Pope's army, which had done most of the attacking, suffered 16,000 casualties.

Lee had used quick marching. He had used his interior lines. Initially, when McClellan was below Richmond and Pope was operating up in central Virginia, it was harder for those Union armies to reinforce each other or to move from one point to another than for Lee's army to move from near Richmond over to near Culpepper. So he'd used those interior lines. He had taken great risks in dividing his army twice, and he had won a great victory.

Pope was removed from command. He only got one chance in Virginia. He was unpopular with a lot of people. Off he went to Minnesota, which is about as far as you could be sent as a Union commander, to deal with the Sioux Indians who had taken advantage of the "big fight" between the white Northerners and the white Southerners to rise up in Minnesota and try to reestablish their control over their ancient lands. So off goes Pope to Minnesota.

Lincoln had to have another commander to take Pope's place, and he reluctantly turned to George B. McClellan. McClellan comes back to be in command of all the troops now in Washington, all the units from the Army of the Potomac and all the units from Pope's Army of Virginia. Now, the immediate question is, why would Lincoln do this? He was so fed up with McClellan and McClellan's behavior over a long period of time, why bring him back?

The answer is really quite simple. There's no one else available with any experience commanding an army, and more than that, McClellan had more than once showed his genius at organization, and he had this wonderful bond with his soldiers. They would feel better having McClellan back. He could bring order out of chaos. He was the obvious man for the job even though he and Lincoln had this history of difficult relations. McClellan came back in command and did just what Lincoln had hoped he would do. He did re-inspirit the army, and that set up a confrontation between Lee and McClellan, another confrontation.

Let's move now to Lee's decision to continue the momentum generated in his victories at the Seven Days and Second Manassas by carrying the war across the Potomac frontier. Lee lost very little time after Second Manassas in preparing for a movement into Maryland. A number of factors went into his decision to do so. As always, he wanted to maintain the initiative. As I've said before, he was never comfortable being in the position of merely reacting to what his opponent was doing. He wanted to be the one who was dictating, and the way to do that was to continue his momentum here, to carry the war into the enemy's territory. Otherwise, he would simply be sitting still and awaiting McClellan's next move. So that's part of what's going on.

There was also a huge logistical component to what Lee wanted to accomplish. Northern and north central Virginia had been ravaged because of the presence of the armies maneuvering back and forth across their territory. You didn't have to have wanton destruction to have significant logistical losses. If an army merely camped for one day in the vicinity of a farmer's land, it would be catastrophic for that farmer. The fences would disappear; the livestock would likely disappear. They'd drink the farmer's well dry. They would trample the crops, or, if they were capable of being harvested and used for forage, they'd probably be taken for that.

It would absolutely be a disaster, a one-day visit from an army, and these armies had been operating in northern/north central Virginia for a good while. Lee wanted to pull the war out of that part of Virginia and give the farmers, those whose crops hadn't been ruined, a chance to get the fall crops in, which would then be used by the armies.

Lee thought that if he went north of the Potomac he could live off the land there. He could gather food and fodder from the Maryland countryside and eventually move into Pennsylvania, into the Cumberland Valley, and do it there. So there's a two-sided potential advantage logistically: give a respite to northern Virginia and take supplies from Maryland and perhaps from Pennsylvania.

He also thought he could harass the Federals from a position west of Washington. They wouldn't like him up there. He knew they would follow him if he went. They'd have to. He thought that if he could remain north long enough—this is much like Braxton Bragg—he could perhaps have some influence on voting in the elections in November. He also, like Bragg, thought that he would have Marylanders, as Bragg thought he'd have Kentuckians, flock to his army. The Confederates really did believe Maryland was being held in the Union at the point of bayonets. They thought that the presence of a Confederate army would make a huge difference.

What they didn't quite understand is that western Maryland was strongly Unionist. If they'd marched through Baltimore, a lot of men would have come forward. Eastern Maryland was much more Confederate. They're going to be in the wrong part of Maryland.

Lee also hoped that if he could stay north long enough he might be able to prevent the Federals from mounting another campaign. If he could stay north until late into the fall, the winter would be on them, and Virginia would be safe from another campaign until the following spring. He probably knew as well that if he did well in Maryland or Pennsylvania, the European powers would take note of that and it might work to the Confederacy's advantage in the diplomatic sphere. But his main goals, I think, are to maintain the strategic initiative and to take care of the serious logistical problems that were facing the Confederacy in Virginia.

Early September, on the fourth, the Army of Northern Virginia crossed the Potomac River at White's Ferry, White's Ford. Across they went into Maryland and made their way to Frederick. While he was in Frederick, Lee decided on his plan for the campaign. He was going to need a supply line going back into Virginia. He couldn't get everything he needed in Maryland. He would need to be able to get ordnance, medicine, and other supplies that he couldn't get from the Marylanders, so he had to have a supply line. He decided the obvious line would run through the Shenandoah Valley and then on into Maryland.

Harper's Ferry was a critical point. It was in Union hands. He couldn't allow it to remain in Union hands because it would be a sort of dagger in his back while he campaigned in Maryland. There were 12,000 Federals at Harper's Ferry. So, while he was at Frederick, he decided to divide his army yet again. He would send several pieces of it, three key pieces of it, against Harper's

Ferry under the overall command of Stonewall Jackson. The other two pieces would move deeper into Maryland toward Hagerstown. They would move across the South Mountain range toward Hagerstown.

This was his plan. It was called Special Orders 191, and he put it into operation, and all the Confederates marched away from Frederick in different directions. But the campaign quickly began to unravel after that. Part of the problem was that Lee's army was suffering enormously from straggling and desertion. About 55,000 Confederates crossed the Potomac at White's Ford. By Lee's own estimate, a third to a half of his army fell out of the ranks in the course of the campaigning in Maryland. A third to a half is an enormous rate of attrition. It would never plague his army again, but it did during the Maryland campaign.

Part of these men didn't want to fight outside Confederate soil. Many of them didn't have adequate shoes. They hadn't been eating well either. Many of them were living on green applies, green corn—a terrible diet. Chronic diarrhea was rampant in the army. The dehydration that came with that was striking down many men. Many just physically couldn't keep up. Many were reluctant to go across the river. Others, I think, had simply had enough hard campaigning and fighting. The Seven Days and Second Manassas had been incredibly bloody, and some just simply deserted. The bottom line was that a huge part of Lee's army dropped out of the ranks as the army moved into Maryland.

Lee also noted very quickly that McClellan seemed to be pursuing more quickly than he thought he would. One reason Lee was willing to divide his army into so many pieces was because he thought McClellan would move slowly, but McClellan was moving more quickly, and the reason was that, through an incredible series of lucky circumstances, McClellan came into possession of Lee's blueprint for the whole invasion, the Special Orders 191.

When the Confederates marched out of Frederick, the Union army marched in behind them, and some Federal soldiers who were sort of kicking through the debris in one of the Confederate camps saw some papers wrapped around three cigars. They sort of leaned down, picked them up, parceled the cigars out, and glanced at the papers in front of them, and the papers were Special

Orders 191, an extra set that had been dropped, an extra set that had gone to D. H. Hill, as a matter of fact.

These made their way up to the Union high command, and there was George B. McClellan holding Lee's blueprint for the entire campaign. He held that paper up in the air and announced to one of his subordinates, "Here is a paper with which, if I cannot whip Bobby Lee, I will be willing to go home."

So he moved a little faster than he would have otherwise, but he didn't move fast. We have to make that distinction. He let the rest of September 13 go by. That was the day he got this. But, on the fourteenth, he pressed against the part of Lee's army that had moved toward Hagerstown, and there was fighting in the gaps of the South Mountain range on the fourteenth, at Fox's Gap and Turner's Gap and Crampton's Gap.

McClellan's troops pushed the Confederates out of those gaps and found themselves on the same side, the western side of the South Mountain range, as the Confederate army. Lee was in a very delicate position. He had expected Harper's Ferry to fall quickly. It still hadn't fallen on the fourteenth. Lee thought for awhile about abandoning his campaign and retreating from Maryland, but he received word on the fifteenth that Harper's Ferry had fallen, and he decided instead to concentrate his army on some high ground near Sharpsburg, Maryland, to bring Stonewall Jackson's troops up from Harper's Ferry and make a stand.

He sent out the orders for that, and, on the fifteenth and sixteenth, the Confederate army gathered at Sharpsburg. By the morning of September 17, Lee had probably between 30,000 and 35,000 troops in place. One division was back at Harper's Ferry overseeing the parole of the 12,000 Federals who'd surrendered there and also looking after all the supplies that had been captured. Thirty to 35,000 Confederates were in place. McClellan had let precious time slip by on the fifteenth and sixteenth. He had not hit Lee then when Lee was really quite vulnerable.

But that brings us now to the Battle of Antietam on September 17, 1862. McClellan had more than 70,000 troops in position at Antietam on the morning of the seventeenth, at least a two-to-one advantage over Lee, probably more. His plan was this, as he explained it later: apply pressure to both Confederate flanks, hope to weaken the center, and then punch through the center and cut Lee off from the Potomac River, which was just a few miles away. There was only one ford across the Potomac. If anything really serious had happened to Lee's army at Sharpsburg, it would have been an utter disaster. That's what McClellan hoped to do, but he didn't manage to apply simultaneous pressure against the line.

The Battle of Antietam broke down into three very separate battles as the day went along. It began on the northern end of the field with very heavy Union attacks that were held off by the slimmest of margins on the Confederate side. Then it shifted to the center part of the field. Again, there were heavy attacks. McClellan actually broke through in the center. The officers in command of his troops there begged for reinforcements to exploit the break.

This is what McClellan later said he'd wanted to do, but McClellan decided not to commit his reserves. He said it would have been too dangerous to do that—what if something bad had happened with all his reserves committed? So the fighting died out in the center part of the field, and it shifted to the left in the afternoon, the southern end of the field. There the Federals literally pushed the Confederates to within a few dozen yards of the key road that led to the fords over the Potomac River. If they had captured that road, Lee would have been in awful shape.

But just at the moment they seemed to be about to win, that last division from Harper's Ferry, which had been marching hard all day, a 17-mile march, came onto the battlefield, immediately deployed and plowed into the Union left flank, and stopped the final attacks. The battle sputtered to a halt late in the afternoon of the seventeenth.

It had been a series of near disasters for Lee and his army. Lee had been very active, moving back and forth along the line from heavy fighting in a cornfield on the northern end of the field, watching the fighting at what was called the Sunken Road or the Bloody Lane in the middle of the field, and watching anxiously in the afternoon as his right flank seemed about to crumble. Time and again he had plugged in troops at just the last moment to stave off disaster. Good luck and effective management had allowed him to keep his army intact.

As for McClellan, fully a quarter of his army didn't fire a shot during the Battle of Antietam. Lee mustered every man he had. McClellan didn't use a good part of his army, and, in the end, Lee was able to hold on, just barely, just barely.

It was the bloodiest day in American history. Ten thousand, five hundred Confederates, a third of Lee's army, were shot down at Antietam in one day, as were 12,500 Federals, a total of more than 23,000. As many men were shot down in this one day at Antietam as in both days of the Battle of Shiloh—a nice comparison. Not any other day in United States history was as bloody.

It seemed endless to those who were fighting it. One soldier in the Confederate army said the sun seemed almost to go backward during the day. In a cornfield on the Confederate left, the musketry was so heavy that, after the battle—and, remember, it's September, this corn was taller than the men when the battle started; it was almost ready to be harvested—one officer said, "Every stalk of corn in the greater part of the field was cut as closely as with a knife, and the slain lay in rows precisely as they had stood in their ranks a few minutes before."

There were more than 8,000 casualties in this cornfield. It was about a 23-acre cornfield. Eight thousand men were shot down there. One Confederate regiment, the First Texas, suffered more than 80 percent casualties in about 10 minutes, fighting in the cornfield. It was just a maelstrom. In a small country lane in the center of the battlefield, the sunken lane later called Bloody Lane, Confederate bodies lay so thickly packed that a Union officer said that he walked for more than 100 yards without ever touching the ground in this lane, just going from body to body to body.

A Pennsylvania solider put it quite simply. He said, "No tongue can tell, no mind conceive, no pen portray the horrible sights I witnessed." Photographers got to the battlefield in time to take pictures of the corpses of the dead Confederates. The Union dead had been buried. These pictures caused a sensation in the North. No one had seen what a battlefield really looked like before. They'd seen heroic woodcuts and so forth. Here was the true human debris of a battlefield, and it caused a sensation. Long lines of people would wait outside the photographic galleries to see these pictures. It was quite something.

Lee remained on the field through most of September 18. Incredibly, McClellan did not press him anymore. I think it was a very risky move on Lee's part, but he got away with it because McClellan chose not to renew the attacks. Lee withdrew that night toward the fords over the Potomac. McClellan let him go. That was the end of the military side of the campaign.

Let's look at the consequences and the impact of this campaign, which were immense. The military consequences were mixed. The battle itself was a tactical standoff. Neither side drove the other from the field. It was very bloody, but there was no real decisive decision on the battlefield. It was not interpreted as a great defeat in the Confederacy at the time. It was seen as essentially a drawn battle.

Lee didn't retreat that far. He didn't retreat until a full day later, and then he took up a position along the Potomac River, and the military frontier essentially remained where it had been at the time following the Battle of Second Manassas. McClellan elected not to pursue Lee. Days went by. Lincoln grew frustrated. He visited McClellan and the army. He could not get McClellan to move. The rest of September passed by. October passed by. Eventually, in early November, the day after the elections in the North, Lincoln removed McClellan. He finally had had it with George B. McClellan.

So militarily it's a little bit of a murky picture, certainly tactically. But the fact that Lee did retreat and he lost the momentum that he had generated with the Seven Days and Second Manassas means that it must be seen in that light as a Union victory. But the real consequences were not the military consequences.

On the diplomatic front, Great Britain had been edging toward some kind of intervention in the war. In fact, the day of the battle, key British leaders had said, if Lee wins another victory we should try to mediate an end to this war. When they found out that Lee had retreated, they pulled back from that idea and said, let's wait. Let's wait and see what the Confederates do in the next campaign. So they edged back from what seemed like a likely intervention. It would be much harder for them to intervene because of another thing that happened right after Antietam, and that was Lincoln's issuance of the preliminary Proclamation of Emancipation.

Here was enough of a victory for Lincoln to issue his proclamation. This was far more important than just the diplomatic side of what had happened. Once the proclamation had been issued, of course, it made it more difficult for France and Great Britain to come in on the side of the Confederacy because they had ended slavery, both of them already, and it would be hard for them to support an overtly slaveholding republic in its contest against a nation that was at least partly on record against the institution of slavery.

The preliminary proclamation meant that Northern war aims had changed. The war for the Union had become a war for union and freedom because, wherever Union forces marched now, they would be taking the possibility of freedom with them. The stakes were much higher in the war. The whole social fabric of the South was now on the table. If the Confederacy lost the war, they would lose slavery, and their whole social system would be turned topsy-turvy.

So there is a great deal more at risk. For the white South there would be no more status quo antebellum after the Emancipation Proclamation. It changed the whole nature of the war. What we will do next time in our next lecture is look at the process that brought the North to the Emancipation Proclamation.

The Background to Emancipation
Lecture 16

In this lecture, we will look at the Democratic Party's very negative view of emancipation. We'll look at the idea of black colonization and why it appealed to Abraham Lincoln and many other white people in the North.

This lecture will examine the debate over emancipation from the beginning of the war through the spring of 1862. Slavery was at the heart of sectional tensions that eventually brought on the Civil War. The South seceded in large measure to protect its slave-based society from a perceived threat posed by the Republican Party, but for at least the first year of the conflict, the issues of slavery and emancipation remained in the background.

The North actually went to war to preserve the Union rather than to destroy slavery. The Republican platform of 1860 explicitly stated that slavery would be protected where it already existed, and this position was repeated in Lincoln's First Inaugural Address. Lincoln reiterated the position in his July 4th message to Congress. A Congressional Resolution offered by John Crittenden reaffirmed the position in 1861. This effort was made to help maintain the border states in the Union. It was passed almost unanimously.

> I think that whatever the merits of the different historians' arguments, there's absolutely no doubt that runaway slaves weakened slavery in the Confederacy.

Lincoln also declined to call for emancipation. He stated that the Constitution protected slavery and that only the states controlled it. He worried about the loyalty of the border states and feared antislavery rhetoric might lead them to join the Confederacy. He knew the North was divided about emancipation and knew he would alienate Democrats if he called for emancipation.

The Republican Party was divided over how best to address emancipation. The conservatives wanted slavery to end but insisted on a gradual process controlled by the states and supported colonization of freed slaves. The moderates (including Lincoln) sought an earlier end to slavery, accepted a cautious approach in the beginning, and supported colonization but moved closer to the radicals as the war grew increasingly bitter and costly.

The radicals favored outright emancipation as a war aim from the outset. They pointed to the "war powers" clause of the Constitution as giving the North the right to free slaves, arguing that the Southern states did not enjoy constitutional protection while in secession. The radicals were a minority of the party but held disproportionate power in Congress. Such senators as Charles Sumner (MA—Foreign Affairs), Henry Wilson (MA—Military Affairs), John P. Hall (NH—Naval), Benjamin Wade (OH—Territories and the Committee on the Conduct of the War), Zacharia Chandler (MI), and others held key committee posts. Members of the House of Representatives, such as arch-radicals Galusha Grove and Thaddeus Stevens, both of Pennsylvania, also had great influence in their chamber. The radicals used the Joint Committee on the Conduct of the War to press their agenda of punishing slaveholders. They gradually persuaded many moderates to support their views.

Prints and Photographs Division, Library of Congress.

Abolitionist Frederick Douglass.

Most Democrats supported a war for the Union but violently opposed emancipation. They feared black competition for jobs and the specter of racial intermarriage. Many Union soldiers held similar views. The idea of black colonization appealed to many Northerners. This idea went back to the early part of the nineteenth century; proponents said it would avoid a race war and would protect white laborers from black competition.

Lincoln met with a group of free black men in 1862 to urge them to support colonization. He argued that they would never be equal in the United States. They refused to support the idea. Lincoln supported a trial expedition to an island off the coast of Haiti; conditions proved to be terrible, and the expedition failed miserably.

Slaves furthered the process of emancipation by escaping to Union lines. Historians have argued about the impact of this phenomenon. Those who support the concept of self-emancipation insist that slaves were the crucial actors in bringing about emancipation. Others insist that the Union Army, Congress, and Lincoln played greater roles. Whatever the merits of the different historians' arguments, there is no doubt that runaway slaves weakened slavery in the Confederacy and forced Union military and political leaders to consider their status. ■

Essential Reading

Berlin et al., eds., *Free at Last: A Documentary History of Slavery, Freedom, and the Civil War*, chapter 1.

Supplementary Reading

Cox, *Lincoln and Black Freedom: A Study in Presidential Leadership*, chapter 1.

McPherson, ed., *The Negro's Civil War: How American Negroes Felt and Acted during the War for the Union*, chapters 1–2.

McPherson and Cooper, eds., *Writing the Civil War: The Quest to Understand*, Gallagher essay.

Questions to Consider

1. If slavery lay at the heart of sectional tensions, why did the North choose not to pursue emancipation from the beginning of the war?

2. Would the Confederacy have benefited from stronger efforts to place emancipation on the North's political agenda before the summer of 1862?

The Background to Emancipation
Lecture 16—Transcript

In our summary of the impact of Antietam in our last lecture, we emphasized that the battle gave Abraham Lincoln an opportunity to issue his preliminary Proclamation of Emancipation. In this lecture we'll examine the background of emancipation. We'll look at the place of emancipation among early Union war aims. We'll look at the divisions within the Republican Party as to how best to pursue the question of emancipation.

We'll look at the Democratic Party's very negative view of emancipation. We'll look at the idea of black colonization and why it appealed to Abraham Lincoln and many other white people in the North. We'll finish by looking at the topic of whether or not slaves themselves were as responsible for emancipation as any of the politicians or generals or others in the North who were involved with finally bringing the North to a point where emancipation was on its agenda.

Let's look first at where emancipation figured in the war goals of the North early in the war. Slavery was the taproot of the sectional tensions that eventually brought the war. We've talked about this many times earlier in this course. The secession of the South was largely a reaction to a perceived threat that the victorious Republican Party would not only prevent slavery from expanding into the Federal territories but also would strike at slavery where it existed in the Southern states.

Yet, for the first year and a half of the war, the issue of slavery was in the background in terms of Northern war aims. The North went to war to save the Union, and, as long as this was the war aim, there was remarkable unity in the North. But soon there was a growing debate about what kind of Union should follow a Northern victory: a Union with slavery, as Northern Democrats favored and even some conservative Republicans were willing to consider, or a Union without slavery, as black and white abolitionists and the radical Republicans insisted should be the case?

On the resolution of this debate hinged the question of whether it would be an all-out war fought for total victory, after which the South would be remade in the North's image, or whether it would be a rather limited war aimed at bringing the South to a conference table where the two sides could hammer out their differences and arrive at a more peaceful solution through compromise.

There's no doubt, as I said, that it was a war for union in the beginning. Overwhelmingly, had we been able to poll people in the spring and early summer of 1861—polled the white North, asked them what the war was about, what they hoped to accomplish—they would have said, this is a war about whether or not we will maintain our Federal Union or if the South will be able to destroy it.

The Republican platform of 1860 explicitly said there'd be no interference with slavery where it already existed. Lincoln reaffirmed this on many occasions, including in his inaugural address in March 1861 and a July 4, 1861, message to Congress. In a resolution offered by Senator Crittenden of Kentucky in July 1861, Congress stated that the war was not being prosecuted with the intention of overthrowing the established institutions of the Southern states. Read "slavery" there. This isn't a war to kill slavery in the South.

This resolution sought to reassure the border states who had remained loyal to the North and keep them on the side of the Union as the war progressed. The resolution passed almost unanimously in Congress. Not only did Democrats support it but many Republicans supported it as well.

Now, Abraham Lincoln personally hated slavery. There's no question about that. He would have been happiest if slavery would end immediately. But he also understood that he was president of all the people in the North and he had to be careful as to how he navigated among the different constituencies of the North regarding the questions of emancipation or pursuing a war without emancipation as a key goal.

He knew, as did everyone in the North, that the Constitution protected the legality of slavery. Everyone had known that. The North fought the war on the theory, at least in many quarters, that the South really couldn't secede, that secession was illegal. The states did not have the right to secede. Lincoln often put this forward. He would change his interpretation according to the circumstances, but he often said, these states can't secede; they're really still in the Union. They're only temporarily under the sway of these evil men who've gotten them to do this. They're really still in the Union.

If they were still in the Union, then the Constitution still applied and slavery was still protected. He didn't have the power to kill slavery if it was protected by the Constitution. The Constitution left control of what it called "domestic institutions" to the states. Everyone agreed that slavery was a domestic institution, and, by that reasoning, only the states could get rid of slavery. It's not something the president could just do. A majority in both the North and the South accepted this concept in 1861.

The loyalty of the border states was also critical for Lincoln, as we've seen. He cared a very great deal about whether especially Missouri and Kentucky and Maryland stayed in the Union. He had to have them in the Union, he believed, and, if he moved quickly against slavery, he believed that he would alienate all of those border slave states, and he was almost certainly correct. Congress also wanted to avoid alienating the border states.

Finally, Lincoln was very conscious of the fact that the white North was deeply divided over the question of emancipation. Many white Northerners—I would say virtually all the Democrats in the North—were perfectly happy with slavery. They didn't have any reason at all to get rid of slavery, and many conservative Republicans also were not that concerned with emancipation. Nearly half of the free state voters had voted against Lincoln in 1860. He certainly remembered that, and he wanted to keep as much of the North as possible united in the effort to defeat the South and restore the Union.

He believed that, by insinuating emancipation into the mix of issues in play, he might alienate a significant part of the North. So, although he wanted to kill slavery personally, he knew that he should move slowly on this issue if he were to keep any kind of consensus in the North. Northern Democrats and even some Republicans feared Lincoln might fall away from the war effort if he moved too swiftly.

Let's look at the Republican Party itself. How did the Republicans divide on this issue? There are a number of viewpoints within the Republican Party. It's far too complex for us to really flesh it out here, but, for our purposes, there are three main divisions within the Republican Party, and we'll start with the conservatives.

Conservatives, most of them, wanted the ultimate end of slavery. They thought it was a bad institution. But they were clearly gradualists who generally believed in action by the individual states, and they mostly wanted to link emancipation to colonization of the freed slaves abroad. So, do it slowly, let the states oversee it, and then ship those people out of the country once they're freed. That would be the general view of most of the conservative Republicans.

The largest group of Republicans were the moderates, and Lincoln is in this group. He's the foremost member of this group of moderates. The moderates wanted to end slavery sooner than did the conservatives, but most of them feared what they thought might be wrenching social upheaval if you did it immediately. If you just step in and say, all of the slaves are free and let the chips fall where they would, they were afraid that there might be some kind of race war or certainly tremendous racial tension between white people and black people in areas where slavery had been prominent.

Early in the war most of the moderates agreed with the conservatives in their party in urging a very careful course on this issue. Don't move too quickly, they said. Take your time, and make sure you handle this correctly. Many of the moderates also believed in colonization, and Lincoln is one of them. Lincoln thought colonization of freed slaves was a good idea, and we'll talk more about that in a minute. As the war progressed, however, and increased in cost both human and material, many of the moderates began to drift toward the radical position on emancipation. They moved further away from the conservatives and moved toward the radicals.

Let's look at the radicals now. They're the third faction in the party. The radicals are the outright antislavery members of the party. They want slavery killed now. They want that to be part of Northern policy immediately. Let's make freedom a war aim. Let's put it right alongside union, the radicals said from the beginning. This is what this war is about; it's about freedom as well as union. They said, never mind these constitutional niceties about this being a domestic institution and let the states take care of it. They said, there's a way around that. There's a way that we can finesse that.

The war power clause of the Constitution, they said, gave the Federal government the power to strike at slavery. They said, the South lost its constitutional guarantees when it seceded. Let's don't pretend they're still part of our country. Let's don't pretend they're still entitled to our constitutional guarantees. They're out of the country. Let's use the war powers clause of the Constitution to get at them.

Now, the radicals were always a minority in the party, but they were aggressive; they wielded great influence. They had a clear vision of what they wanted to do, which is always an advantage, of course. And they held key posts in Congress, all out of proportion to their numbers. Let's look in the Senate and just run down some of the key radicals in the Senate.

I'll start with Charles Sumner of Massachusetts, a very striking figure. Remember him from the late antebellum period when he'd been caned on the floor of the Senate by Preston Brooks of South Carolina after he gave his speech, "The Crime Against Kansas."

He was a tall man, very handsome, immensely learned, a really brilliant orator, and also absolutely and obnoxiously self-assured. Charles Sumner believed he was smarter than everybody else, and he *was* smarter than almost everybody else, probably. But he also took pains to let everyone else know that he thought he was smarter than they were.

He was a Harvard-trained lawyer and a veteran of many reform crusades, especially antislavery. He called for immediate emancipation as soon as the war began and argued that the South had forfeited all of its constitutional rights and should be made over in the North's image. The South should look like us. We're the future of the United States, not the slaveholding South. So he is one of the senators from Massachusetts.

The other's Henry Wilson, another radical. He was not as commanding or famous a person as Sumner but still a formidable person. Sumner chaired the Committee on Foreign Affairs, which is a very important committee in the Senate. Wilson chaired the Committee on Military Affairs in the midst of a war, also a very important committee. Senator John P. Hale of New Hampshire, another radical, chaired the Committee on Naval Affairs in the Senate, and Zachariah Chandler of Michigan, another radical, chaired the Committee on Commerce, which brings us to Benjamin Franklin Wade of Ohio.

Ben Wade of Ohio was a true radical and not just on the issue of emancipation. He was for women's rights, he was for labor reform—he was for a galaxy of reform movements in the mid-nineteenth century. He'd grown up poor. He was one of the founders of the Republican Party. He, unlike many abolitionists and radicals, was willing to defend his ideas with his fists by fighting. He didn't shrink from confrontations. He sought out confrontations with slaveholders. He had a very quick temper and tongue. He was for immediate emancipation as soon as the war started and a no-holds-barred prosecution of the war.

Benjamin Wade also—this is one of the ironies, and this indicates why it's always important to separate feelings about slavery and emancipation on the one hand and racial attitudes on the other—was an intense racist. He had very racist attitudes toward black people yet insisted on immediate emancipation. Ben Wade chaired the Committee on Territories in the Senate, which was very important because of the question of slavery in the territories, and he chaired the immensely important Joint Committee on the Conduct of the War.

In the House of Representatives, a pair of radicals stood out, both from Pennsylvania. Galusha Grow was Speaker of the House, and the fearsome Thaddeus Stevens, my favorite radical of all of them—he's an incredibly interesting and compelling figure in many ways—chaired the Committee on Ways and Means.

Let me talk just a minute about Thaddeus Stevens. He was the most revolutionary of all the Republicans. That would come out during

Reconstruction even more than it did during the war. He suffered from a clubfoot. He'd been jeered at and taunted as a boy, he'd grown up poor, and throughout his life he championed the weak. He championed black people and championed other groups who seemed not to be able to fight equally for their place in American society.

He made a considerable fortune, and he gave lavishly to charities. He hated, with a white-hot hatred, what he called the bloated aristocrats of the South, the slaveholding elite of the South. He wanted the pre-war South destroyed, literally pulled apart. He wanted slaveholders reduced to absolute poverty. If he had had his way, that's what would have happened. He was for the immediate emancipation of all slaves, and he wanted to punish slaveholders: confiscate all their land, take all their money, and leave them without anything. That's what Stevens thought would be just.

He had a grim sense of humor and a very sharp tongue in debate. As he was coming out of the chamber one time, a woman asked him for a lock of his hair, which was a mid-nineteenth century custom. You'd collect locks of hair from famous people. Well, Stevens was completely bald. He wore a wig, a sort of shoulder-length wig, not quite to his shoulders but long hair. When this woman asked if she could have a lock of his hair, he pulled his wig off and said, "Madam, have them all." So he also wasn't hung up on appearances, I would say.

In debate one time he was making a point. He saw one of his opponents coming into the floor of the chamber, and he said, "I'm going to pause while the gentleman from [whatever state he was from] slinks across the floor of this chamber and adheres to his seat by his own slime." That's a great line. We don't get lines like that very often anymore in the United States Congress.

Most of these men that I've been talking about had been born and reared in New England, the home of true Republican and antislavery radicalism. Indeed, of 22 committees in the Senate, men from or born and reared in New England controlled 16 of them. So there's enormous power in the hands of the radical Republicans, and they would not remain content to fight a war for union. They consistently pushed for faster action on the issue of freedom.

Before the midpoint of the war, many of the moderates, as I said earlier, were gravitating toward the radical point of view. As the war went on and it seemed necessary to punish the Confederacy more, hurt them more to win, many of the moderates moved toward them. Even some of the conservatives did.

Well, what about the Democrats? Democrats almost universally opposed emancipation in the North. They were willing to fight to preserve the Union. They were not willing to fight to free the slaves. Let me quote from a typical Democratic statement. This is from a senator, and I'm going to quote it directly. The language is offensive to us now, but I think it's important that we understand just how many people in the white North felt about this. This senator said, and I quote, "We mean that the United States shall be the white man's home and that the nigger shall never be his equal." That is a Democratic senator saying that during the war.

The Irish and other immigrants—residents of the lower tier of counties in the Midwest that were called the Butternut Counties and had a lot of ties across the Ohio River with slaveholding Kentucky—these people were violently antiblack, as were many laborers who feared competition from black labor. Virtually all the black people lived in the South at this time. I mean virtually all of them, and it was feared that free black men and women would flood into the North if they were emancipated and would compete for jobs.

There was a lot of talk about miscegenation. One shrill newspaper prophesied that, "Two or three million semi-savages will inundate the North after emancipation to mix with the sons and daughters of white working men." A Republican congressman from Indiana sadly reported that, "Our people hate the Negro with a perfect if not supreme hatred." So there's a very strong strain of racism in the North, and most Democrats wanted anything but emancipation.

Those attitudes extended to soldiers in the army. Most soldiers in the army did not enlist to free slaves. Now, some did, probably as many as 10 percent did, but the vast majority of the Northern soldiers were in the army to save the Union, not to free slaves. Most of them eventually accepted emancipation as a necessary tool to defeat the South, but they didn't go into the army to end slavery.

The dual specters of economic competition and racial mixing brought out the worst in the white North and created a great deal of antipathy toward black people.

Let's move on to the topic of black colonization. The colonization of freed slaves was a solution that attracted many Northerners, including Lincoln, for a long while. It's an idea that goes back early in the nineteenth century to a number of fairly prominent people then, including political leaders Thomas Jefferson, Henry Clay, and others, all advocates of the notion of colonization, which would have seen freed slaves shipped somewhere out of the United States to avoid the problem of having to try to integrate them into American society.

Some people supported this, the idea of colonization, because they hated black people. Others, and I would put Lincoln in this category, supported it from a mixture of self-interest and concern for the plight of freed blacks in a racist American society. The colonizationists argued that this would avoid a postemancipation race war. They said it would avoid competition between freed black laborers and white laborers in the North and in the South. They said that, overall, it would simply make the process of emancipation work much more smoothly, that it would be a much less wrenching social experience for the nation than if you allowed the freed slaves to remain in the United States.

Lincoln met with a group of free black men at the White House in August 1862, the first time a president had met with or had invited black people to the White House. He met with them in August 1862 to try to get them to support colonization. He said, slavery's the greatest wrong ever inflicted on any people. We all know that. You know it and I know it. But, he said, emancipation will not get rid of radical differences between you, the black people in the United States, and us, the white people.

He said, you have virtually no chance for equality in the United States. Most white Americans simply won't accept it. He said, I do not mean to discuss this but to propose it as a fact with which we have to deal. I cannot alter it if I would. It's better for us both, therefore, to be separated. And he asked these leaders to try to get volunteers to go in a first wave of colonists to show that colonization might be practical.

Well, these men who went to the White House as well as virtually all other black leaders in the country said, no, we don't want to leave the United States. We live here, too. We've been here for many generations, in most instances. This is our country as well as yours.

Robert Purvis, a wealthy and influential black Philadelphia abolitionist, summed up feeling in his community on the subject in an open letter to Lincoln. He said, "It is in vain you talk to me of two races and their mutual antagonism. In the matter of rights there is but one race and that is the human race. Sir, this is our country as much as it is yours, and we will not leave it." The great black abolitionist Frederick Douglass was more direct. He was very upset at reports of this meeting with Lincoln. He said that it showed all of Lincoln's inconsistencies, his pride of race and blood, his contempt for Negroes, and his canting hypocrisy.

White abolitionists also opposed colonization, but Lincoln held to it for a surprisingly long time. In fact, there was one expedition mounted during the war to see if this would be practical. It was a group of about 500 freed slaves who were sent to an island named Il au Vache (Cow Island) off Haiti. A speculator had come to the government and said, I'll do this for X number of dollars for each person. I'll supply schools and a hospital, and they'll be given agriculture tools and so forth that they will need to make a living. You give me this much money, and we'll ship them down there.

Five hundred went. They arrived in Haiti. There were no schools, no roads, no hospital, no anything. They were dumped off on Cow Island, pretty much left to fend for themselves, and it was a disaster. A disease swept through their ranks. Very quickly reports came back to Lincoln that things were going wrong there. The expedition had been mounted in April of 1863. Before a year had passed, it was clear that it was not going to work, so a United States vessel was sent to bring these people back. They returned in February of 1864. There were 368 survivors. That was the end of the notion of colonization. Lincoln abandoned it. It really wasn't brought up seriously again, but it persisted through much of the war.

Let's finish up this lecture by looking at the question of self-emancipation. There's been a great deal of discussion of this among historians over the last few years, the question of who should get credit for emancipation. Who really freed the slaves?

Now, the old view, the view represented in Thomas Ball's statue in Washington, D.C., is that Lincoln did. Lincoln stands in that statute. He's reaching down, and a black man is rising up from slavery, as Lincoln obviously has freed him. That was the view for a long time: Lincoln's the Great Emancipator. Others also played a role—Congress through its legislation and Union generals in the military who took the possibility of freedom deep into the South.

But more and more the argument has been that none of this really would have taken place had not untold numbers of slaves taken it upon themselves to flee from their plantations or farms or wherever they were, to flee to Northern military lines during the war and confront the North with the problem of what to do with them: Okay, here we are. We were slaves. Now we're under the control of the United States Army. Are we still slaves? Are we free? What are you going to do with us? How are you going to deal with our presence here?

These people are emancipating themselves, goes an argument. From a small trickle early in the war until the end of the war, the best estimates suggest that perhaps a half a million slaves in the South made their way to Union lines. That's about one in seven of all the slaves in the Confederacy. We should talk less about whether the white Congress freed them or the white generals freed them or Abraham Lincoln freed them, argued many scholars, and talk more about how slaves did so much to free themselves.

Now, virtually all scholars agree that the black role in the process was largely ignored for many, many, many decades. They're essentially invisible. People would talk about Congress and talk about Lincoln and talk about generals and not ever talk about what black people were doing. But these scholars say that it's equally a distortion to say that black people alone pretty much freed themselves, that you have to keep all the other elements of this equation in place or the picture doesn't really make sense. You have to admit that Lincoln played a key role; you have to admit that Congress did and that the army did. It's all of these different actors coming together in the end to achieve emancipation. It's not just self-emancipation or just the white leaders in the North achieving emancipation. I think that whatever the merits of the different historians' arguments, there's absolutely no doubt that runaway slaves weakened slavery in the Confederacy. They weakened the institution. They hurt the Confederate economy by running away from their masters and making their way to Union lines. And their presence did force the United States government to deal with the problem. We'll talk more about that in our next lecture. Their presence did make Congress and Lincoln choose to do this or to do that.

But I think it would be a big mistake if we ever lost sight of the fact that the absolutely critical component in the process of emancipation is the presence of the United States Army. If the United States Army wasn't in the neighborhood, slaves had no place to run to. They couldn't emancipate themselves if not for the United States Army. That's the key thing. As the army penetrates deeper and deeper into the Confederacy, it brings the potential of freedom to an ever-widening group of enslaved African Americans. It's the army with its guns and its bayonets and its cannons that really does bring the promise of emancipation into the Confederacy during the war. So we need to, I think, look at all of these factors in helping to bring emancipation. And that is precisely what we're going to do in the next lecture. We're going to look at the roles of abolitionists and of Union generals and of Congress and of Abraham Lincoln as well as of the slaves themselves in making emancipation a major element of the Northern war effort.

Emancipation Completed
Lecture 17

This lecture will continue our examination of the process by which emancipation became an integral part of the North's national strategy. Within a chronological framework extending from the outbreak of the war through January 1, 1863, we'll look at the actions and attitudes of various players in this drama.

Emancipation moved forward on several fronts simultaneously. Abolitionists pressed for emancipation from the outset of the war. They acknowledged that the Constitution protected slavery in the loyal states and argued that slavery was a military necessity to the South and should be attacked on that basis. Several Union generals attempted to strike at slavery in 1861–1862.

Benjamin F. Butler, a so-called "political general," refused to return runaway slaves to their masters on the Virginia peninsula in May 1861, declaring them to be "contraband of war" and, thus, liable to seizure under international law. This action meant that the conflict was a war between two nations, not just a rebellion or civil war. Butler set a precedent followed by many other commanders. For example, John C. Frémont declared slaves of all rebels in Missouri free in August

Union general David Hunter, who attempted to strike at slavery in 1861–1862.

1861. Abolitionists hailed Frémont as a hero, but Lincoln forced him to amend the order to bring it into line with congressional legislation regarding rebel property (and to keep the border states in the Union).

David Hunter ordered all slaves to be freed along the South Carolina, Georgia, and Florida Atlantic coasts in May 1862. Lincoln likewise ordered him to revoke the order, because it overstepped Hunter's authority. Abolitionists roundly condemned Lincoln's action.

Congress passed several antislavery measures in 1861–1862. The first Confiscation Act (6 August 1861) stipulated that owners of slaves engaged in Confederate military service forfeited ownership of those slaves. In March 1862, Congress prohibited the use of military power to return escaped slaves to rebel masters. In April 1862, Congress abolished slavery in the District of Columbia, with compensation to the owners.

On 19 June 1862, Congress emancipated all slaves in the territories without compensation to the owners, thus fulfilling a plank of the 1860 Republican platform. In July 1862, Congress passed the second Confiscation Act, which freed all slaves who escaped from rebel owners to Union lines.

Lincoln decided by the spring of 1862 that the war would bring emancipation, which he had clearly mapped out:

- As a "domestic institution," slavery would have to be abolished by the states.

- Owners should be compensated for the loss of property, and the Federal government should help pay for the cost.

- The process should be gradual to avoid social dislocation, and freed slaves should be urged to colonize abroad.

In March and May 1862, Lincoln pressed the border states to adopt a plan along these lines, first by arguing that they would be compensated and later, in July, by warning that they would lose everything if they dragged their feet. By 22 July 1862, Lincoln announced to his Cabinet that he had decided to issue his proclamation but held off making a public announcement until he had a military victory (this was right after the reverses of the Seven Days' Battles).

He issued the preliminary proclamation on September 22, 1862, after the Battle of Antietam, explaining his reasons to his Cabinet:

- The border states would never take the initiative, as the events of March through July had shown.

- Increasing numbers of black people in Union lines demanded attention on their status.

- Great Britain and France would be favorably impressed.

- Most of the Northern people were ready to wage a harsher kind of war against the Confederacy.

- Northern Democrats would oppose whatever course he took and, thus, could be ignored.

The final Emancipation Proclamation of January 1, 1863, was offered as a measure of military necessity. It freed only slaves in rebel territory not controlled by U.S. troops. Lincoln lacked the constitutional power to free slaves in loyal states. He interpreted any area under Union military control (e.g., northern Virginia) as a loyal part of the United States. He had the Constitutional power to strike at rebel slaves as a war measure.

The Emancipation Proclamation meant that, if the North eventually did triumph over the Confederacy, there would be a new type of Union, not a slightly modified version of the old Union.

Lincoln's announcement was criticized by a variety of people as an empty gesture. Abolitionists and many foreign observers said it did not go far enough. Democrats said it went too far and that Lincoln was being hypocritical. Confederates said it was designed to incite servile insurrection.

The Emancipation Proclamation's real importance lay in the fact that it marked the addition of emancipation to the Union's war strategy and meant that Union armies would carry freedom with them as they penetrated into the Confederate heartland. Even if the men in the armies weren't that concerned about freeing slaves, the fact that the Emancipation Proclamation was in place meant that, as they marched southward, freedom marched with them. ∎

Essential Reading

McPherson, *Battle Cry of Freedom: The Civil War Era*, chapter 16.

Supplementary Reading

Franklin, *The Emancipation Proclamation*.

Questions to Consider

1. Does Lincoln deserve his reputation as the "Great Emancipator"?

2. Were Union armies the practical agents for emancipation?

Emancipation Completed
Lecture 17—Transcript

This lecture will continue our examination of the process by which emancipation became an integral part of the North's national strategy. Within a chronological framework extending from the outbreak of the war through January 1, 1863, we'll look at the actions and attitudes of various players in this drama.

We'll look at black and white abolitionists to begin with, and then we'll move on to several Union generals who figured prominently in the development of policy regarding emancipation. We'll look at Congress, and we'll look at Abraham Lincoln, and we'll close with a close look at the final version of Lincoln's famous Proclamation of Emancipation.

Let's start with the abolitionists. Among groups in the North, only abolitionists—black and white abolitionists—called for freedom as a war aim from the very beginning. Frederick Douglass predicted in May 1861 that whatever most Northerners chose to think the war was about, it was really a war for and against slavery, and should the North win, said Douglass, slavery would die. Other abolitionists took the same view. Wendell Phillips, one of the most prominent white abolitionists from the antebellum years and into the war, at the beginning of the war reminded secessionists, "The moment you tread outside the Constitution, the black man is not three-fifths of a man; he is a whole man." The three-fifths reference, of course, was to the three-fifths clause in the Constitution.

A general named Daniel Allman, who commanded a brigade of black troops during the war, put the matter with very vivid language. He said the first gun that was fired at Fort Sumter sounded the death knell of slavery. They who fired it were the greatest practical abolitionists the nation has produced. So these people believed that, from the very beginning, from the moment that it was clear that there would be shooting and that this would be a war, emancipation was going to be part of the North strategy.

Abolitionists acknowledge that the Constitution did protect slavery in the United States, but they got around that by saying slavery was a military necessity for the South and therefore could be targeted under the war powers clause of the Constitution. Abolition is going to be necessary if we're going to win the war, they said. We have to strike at this very important component of the Confederate war effort. That argument that it should be put in terms of helping us win the war, abolitionists believed, was necessary in order to rally as many white Northerners as possible to the cause of emancipation. Everyone who favored the Union, they thought, could accept the military need to do away with slavery in order to hurt the Confederate war effort.

The abolitionists wanted emancipation because it was right, because that was the moral high ground to take: We have to kill slavery; slavery's a great evil. But they understood that many of their fellow white Northerners didn't think it was a great evil, and, therefore, they said, let's put it in terms of a military necessity. That will convince our fellow white Northerners that we need it. Let them support it for whatever reasons. The end result will be the end of slavery, and that's all that counts.

Senator Charles Sumner, whom we've talked about before, wrote in November 1861 to a fellow abolitionist, "You will observe that I propose no crusade for abolition. Emancipation is to be presented strictly as a measure of military necessity. Abolition is not to be the object of the war but simply one of its agencies." Now, for Sumner it was the object of the war, really, the most important object, but he understood that it couldn't be presented that way. This was the only practical strategy for the abolitionists to take because, as we have seen, there was certainly no consensus in the white North on the issue of emancipation.

Several generals attempted to strike at slavery in 1861 and 1862. These are men on the front lines. They're actually at the point where the United States military power is bumping up against slavery. They're the ones who, in many ways, are in the best position to do something, and a number of them acted. We're going to look at three of them, beginning with Benjamin F. Butler.

By way of background, let me just say briefly that a number of members of Congress and individual military leaders took a series of what might be called halting steps toward emancipation. There would a step forward.

Sometimes you'd have to retreat from that step, but then you'd advance beyond that.

Both generals and Congress contributed to this process, and many of them had in mind the fact that international law possibly could be applied to the question of whether or not the United States would be able to strike at slavery in the Confederacy. There's a provision of international law that says, in wartime, an enemy's property is subject to confiscation, property that can be used to sustain the enemy's war effort. If you get access to it, you can take it because that is something that would give aid and comfort to the military side of your enemy.

Advocates of confiscation argued that the blockade and the treatment of captured Confederate soldiers as prisoners of war indicated that this was, in fact, a war between two nations rather than simply an insurrection on the part of Southerners who were still inside the United States. If it's a war between two nations, they said, international law can apply. If it's merely an insurrection on the part of some white Southerners, international law won't apply. The Constitution would apply.

Sometimes Abraham Lincoln treated it as a war between nations, as when he called for a blockade. You can't really blockade yourself. That really is a concession that you're fighting against another nation when you institute a blockade. If you say that you're going to treat soldiers from your enemy's armies as prisoners of war, you're conceding that they're really soldiers for another nation; otherwise, you'd just treat them as Rebels or as traitors rather than as prisoners of war. At other times, Lincoln would argue that the states hadn't really left the Union. They're really still in it—they're just temporarily under the control of evil people.

Well, those who wanted to strike at slavery tended to argue that, no, the states are gone. We're fighting another nation, and here international law can apply. The first person who did that was General Benjamin Franklin Butler of Massachusetts, an absolutely fascinating character. He was a political general, one of the North's political generals. He was in command someplace or another through the entire war although he had almost no military ability.

He showed his lack of ability wherever he went, his military ability, but he was a very astute politician. He belonged to virtually all the major political parties of his time at one time or another. He was a Democrat, he was a Republican, he was a liberal Republican, he was a radical Republican. Ben Butler was one of those people who wakes up in the morning, sort of goes like this, figures out which way the wind is going, and trims his sails beautifully and goes right along with that wind. And, to mix my metaphors, he always landed on his feet when he switched parties, so he was an able politician.

He was a pioneer in arming blacks to fight for the Union and also one of the most hated Northern figures of the war. He was hated for two reasons, really. One had to do with his being the Union commander in New Orleans in 1862, when he issued an order saying that Southern women who had been in the habit of, from second-story windows and balconies, dumping their chamber pots onto Union officers, spitting on them, or yelling things at them—he said that women who did that would be treated as women of the evening pursuing their avocation.

Well, the white South thought, he's calling our women prostitutes. He's a monster. He's a beast. He was accused of stealing spoons and silver in New Orleans. They hated him for that. They also hated him because of what he did relating to slavery on the Peninsula, which is what we'll look at now.

In May 1861, he commanded at Fort Monroe at the tip of the Peninsula, and a few African Americans who'd been working on Confederate fortifications escaped to Butler's lines. He refused to return them to their masters, and he said, "These men are contraband of war, and I will not return them." That phrase stuck, and, for the rest of the war, slaves who made their way to Federal lines were called contrabands. Now, here's an example of the idea of self-emancipation, of course, too. These men took it upon themselves to go to Union lines, and then Ben Butler said, I'm not going to send them back. I'm not going to send them back.

A second military commander who had an impact in this area was John C. Frémont. In August 1861, as commander of the Department of Missouri, Frémont issued an order confiscating the property and freeing the slaves of all Rebels in Missouri. Abolitionists and many Republicans made Frémont a hero because of this. They said, yes, this is what we should be doing. Strike at the slaveholders. But Lincoln said, no. You can't do this. He told Frémont to withdraw this order. Lincoln was afraid that it would have a pernicious effect in terms of the loyalty of the border states. He said to Frémont, you've gone way out in front. You can't do that. So Frémont backed off. Many of the radical Republicans and the abolitionists in the North were very upset with Lincoln because he reined Frémont in.

The same thing happened again in May of 1862 when a Union commander named David Hunter, who was in charge of a section of the South Atlantic coast, issued an order freeing all slaves in his department. It was called the Department of the South. It embraced parts of South Carolina and Georgia and Florida. Hunter freed all the slaves in his department. He didn't really have the power to make that stick, but he issued the order. Lincoln revoked that order as well. He said, only I, the president, have the power to issue that kind of a proclamation or order. You do not have that power. Once again, abolitionists and radical Republicans roundly condemned Lincoln for this as they had when he revoked Frémont's earlier order in Missouri.

The point is that there are generals in the field who are against slavery, and they're using their positions as commanders on the scene to try to strike at the institution of slavery. Butler did it quite effectively and, in fact, put in place a policy that was carried out by many other commanders—not sending back the slaves who came into your lines. Remember, Stone, the officer who got in trouble after Ball's Bluff, had sent slaves back when they came into his lines. He was a Democratic general doing that. Here's a Republican general taking the opposite approach. So there are generals who are making their presence felt.

Congress, of course, also contributed to this halting march toward emancipation. Let's look at some of their antislavery measures in 1861 and 1862. Shortly after Ben Butler made his contraband statement on the Peninsula, Congress passed what was called the First Confiscation Act on August 6, 1861. The First Confiscation Act stipulated that owners of slaves engaged in military service for the Confederacy forfeited their ownership of those slaves, that is, slaves who were directly helping the Confederate war effort, digging trenches or fortifications or acting as teamsters in some support role with the army. They had to be directly involved in the Confederate military effort. If you were a slave owner and you had slaves who were doing those kinds of things, your slaves could be confiscated by the United States government. This was an early step toward emancipation.

In March of 1862, Congress prohibited the use of military power to return escaped slaves to their masters. That had been up in the air, as we've seen before. Some would be returned; some wouldn't. Here Congress says, no, you will not return slaves to their masters. Now, what this didn't clear up was the status of those slaves. All right, we make our way to Union lines. If we're slaves, we're not going to be sent back, but this law doesn't say that we're free. It just says that we won't be sent back. So it left that part of the puzzle uncompleted. That act of March 18, 1862, was a clear response to the fact that many, many black slaves were making their way to Union lines. Again, this is support for the notion of self-emancipation.

In April 1862, Congress abolished slavery in the District of Columbia with compensation to the owners. So, if you're a slave owner and you lose slaves in the District of Columbia, you're compensated monetarily for that loss. On June 19, 1862, Congress emancipated all slaves in the territories without compensation. Congress had the power to kill slavery in the territories because, unlike the states, where it was considered under the Constitution—slavery was a domestic institution; Congress doesn't have power over the states there—over the Federal territories Congress does have power, and slavery is ended there in June of 1862.

That, of course, fulfilled that Republican plank from the election of 1860, which had said, no more slavery in the territories. That's finally taken care of in June of 1862. Just before that, the debate had heated up in Congress about the possibility of strengthening the Confiscation Act, and that resulted in July of 1862 with what was called the Second Confiscation Act. This was much tougher than the First Confiscation Act, much broader. It said you couldn't return any escaped slave to a master and said that any slave that escaped from a Rebel owner was free.

So here it takes care of that gray area that was left by the March 1862 legislation. If you're a slave of a master loyal to the Confederacy and you make your way to Union lines, you not only won't be sent back but you will be liberated. It didn't say loyal masters in the Confederacy. This is only the slaves of masters who were Confederates, not masters who were loyal to the United States. They're the ones covered by the Second Confiscation Act. This is much, much tougher.

In all of these pieces of legislation, Congress is sort of groping its way toward a position where the North is going to be firmly on record against slavery. It's not there yet. None of this says anything about slavery in the United States, in the border states that are still in the United States. None of it says anything about the allegedly loyal slaveholders in the Confederacy. So it's not a clear, broad statement yet that we have from Congress but a group of congressional acts that are leading toward the end of slavery.

Congress certainly would have gone further down this road, but, before they could, Abraham Lincoln stepped in and seized the stage from them, and he really, after that point, would be the principal actor. Let's move to Abraham Lincoln. Let's look at him in the spring of 1862 when he's trying to decide whether emancipation is necessary to win the war.

At that point he, as I said earlier, was against slavery, and his plan at that stage of the war had five main parts: Slavery's a domestic institution, which means that it must be abolished by the states. That's number one. Second, the owners should be compensated for the loss of their property. Third, the Federal government should pay part of that cost by providing grants and aid to the states. Fourth, he said, the process should be gradual to avoid too much dislocation, social dislocation. Fifth, he said, those slaves should be colonized abroad. So Lincoln wanted gradual, compensated emancipation accompanied by colonization.

He asked Congress in March of 1862 for funds to support compensation of owners, and Congress agreed. Lincoln then went to the border states and said, listen, we have some money. I want you to come up with a plan to end slavery in your states. You'll be compensated for your property. Now please give me a blueprint to accomplish this. But in March and again in May, the border states refused to come up with a plan. Lincoln had told them that this would cushion the shock of emancipation. It would let the United States come to terms with it gradually. They didn't come up with a plan.

On July 12, 1862, Lincoln tried again with the border states. This time he included a warning when he talked to them. He said he would much rather see them come up with a plan. That would be the best way to do it. But, he said, if you don't, I can't control how this war goes. The war may spin out of any limits that we can see now. Your slaves may be taken away from you without compensation, so it's to your selfish advantage to come up with a plan. He mentioned David Hunter's order and what he had tried to do. I'm sure he mentioned Frémont's as well. Again the border states' representatives refused. They voted by more than two to one not to come up with a plan for compensated emancipation.

That night Lincoln decided to issue an Emancipation Proclamation, and, on July 22, he told his Cabinet that he had decided to do that. But he was persuaded by some of his advisors that he couldn't issue it immediately because it would look like an act of desperation. This was right after the Seven Days reverse on the battlefield. He was persuaded to wait until Union military forces gave him a clear victory; then he could issue the proclamation. It would seem like he was doing it from a position of strength rather than weakness.

Well, McClellan gave him the opportunity at Antietam. Lincoln had to wait through the rest of July, through all of August, and through about half of September before he got his victory. He called the Cabinet together on September 22, five days after the Battle of Antietam, and told them that he was going to issue his preliminary proclamation.

Many factors, I think, motivated him, including the failure of the border states to come through with their own plan. He'd given them three tries and they hadn't done it. I think he was also concerned about the increasing numbers of contraband behind the lines in the Union armies. They really had forced him to focus more on this. He also was aware of a growing sense on the part of both some of his advisors and members of Congress and others with whom he spoke, that, if he issued this kind of proclamation, it would make it very difficult for England and France to come into the war on the side of the Confederacy.

The border states had been more important to him than England and France back in the summer of 1861 and the fall of 1861, but the war has progressed to the point where he is quite concerned with those overseas, and he doesn't think the border states are going to be brought around anyway, so the foreign dimension looms a little larger. He also detects an increasing belief in the North that the South should be punished more severely. The war engenders more bitterness, a much deeper enmity, and more hatred, if you like, as the casualty lists grow longer and longer and longer and month after month goes by with no resolution.

Many people in the North believed that you should hurt the Confederates more, and what better way to hurt them than to take their slaves away from them? Lincoln detected that sentiment in the North. He also came to believe, finally, that whatever he did on emancipation would alienate the Democrats in the North, so he shouldn't worry about them. He tried to keep them in the tent—the big tent approach, so to speak—earlier in the war. By now he's just decided that if he makes any move at all on emancipation they won't like it, so he just won't worry about them.

The preliminary proclamation did this: First, it ordered the freeing of all slaves held within states still in rebellion against the United States on January 1, 1863. So it looks ahead just a few weeks. All slaves held at that time will be free. Lincoln justified it solely on grounds of military necessity—solely. There's not talk of taking the moral high ground, no talk of slavery as a monstrous institution. This is based on military necessity.

The preliminary proclamation also endorsed the idea of voluntary colonization of free slaves—not enforced but voluntary—and it included one last plea from Lincoln to the border states to come up their own plan. If they could come up with a plan before January 1, he would consider it. This was a very conservative approach, and it was conservative because Lincoln still didn't know how the North would react to emancipation, and thus he emphasized it as a war measure.

Let's move to the final proclamation now of January 1, 1863. It freed all the slaves in those portions of the Confederacy not controlled by Federal troops, and that's important—only in the parts of the Confederacy not controlled by Federal troops. It went beyond the Second Confiscation Act, however. Remember, it had only struck at slaves belonging to disloyal masters. Lincoln's proclamation makes no distinction between loyal and disloyal masters, so, if you're a Confederate slave owner living in an area not controlled by the Federal army, your slaves are going to be freed by the Emancipation Proclamation.

The excluded areas included parts of Virginia, several Louisiana parishes, and the entire state of Tennessee. The Union army controlled most of west and middle Tennessee, and Lincoln considered east Tennessee to be such strong Unionist territory that he really saw it as having been loyal to the United States all along. Lincoln exempted the areas under Federal control because he said they were, in effect, parts of the Union, parts of the United States, and, as parts of the United States, slavery was protected there because of the Constitution.

The Constitution still protects slavery. Lincoln can't just strike at something that the Constitution protects. He can only strike at it in those areas where the Rebels are in control because he's doing it as a war measure. His war powers give him the right to do that but not with the loyal slaveholders. Well, the fact that no slaves were freed where Lincoln actually had the control to free them brought tremendous criticism both then and later of the proclamation as an empty gesture. White Southerners said Lincoln was completely hypocritical. They said, if he really is against slavery, if he really wants to emancipate slaves, why doesn't he emancipate them in Missouri or Maryland or Kentucky? No, he only emancipates our slaves. They said, what his real goal is is to incite slave rebellion in the Confederate states. That's what Lincoln is really up to.

Many Democrats in the North agreed. They said Lincoln was being hypocritical. Some radicals and abolitionists were also disappointed. They found it hard to answer some foreign critics who agreed with a sneering London newspaper that observed that the principle behind the proclamation was not that one human being could not own another. That's wasn't the principle, said this paper. The principle was that only human beings loyal to the Union could own another, and this seemed to them to be wrong. But I think these critics missed the point of the proclamation. It was a war measure aimed at the war-making capacity and resources of the Confederacy. Under the Constitution Lincoln could do that. He couldn't take property from loyal citizens.

Lincoln's proclamation really reaffirmed and then moved beyond all the acts that Congress had passed to that point. It did so in a dramatic way, a very dramatic way. It, in effect, announced a new Union war aim. Lincoln had that advantage of being president. Whatever a president does, almost anything a president does, gets more attention than individual acts of Congress. Lincoln understood that, and this was a clear attempt on his part to take the lead on this issue.

Nearly 100,000 ex-slaves had already achieved freedom by fleeing to Union lines in Virginia and Louisiana and Tennessee. West Virginia would soon be entering the Union on the condition that it abolish slavery. That was one of the stipulations that Congress made when West Virginia would come into the Union later in 1863. Movements to abolish slavery would soon grow in Missouri and Tennessee and Maryland. All of those states would get rid of slavery before the war was over. Only Kentucky resisted. Kentucky would not get rid of slavery until it was forced to.

The key thing about the proclamation is that it meant that, whenever Federal armies occupied more Confederate territory—every mile that Union forces penetrated into the Confederacy now—they would take freedom with them. Freedom would go wherever the army went. The number of freed slaves would grow. Northern armies now marched not only to restore the Union but also to free slaves. That was the practical effect. Even if the men in the armies weren't that concerned about freeing slaves, the fact that the Emancipation Proclamation was in place meant that, as they marched southward, freedom marched with them. The Emancipation Proclamation meant that, if the North eventually did triumph over the Confederacy, there would be a new type of Union, not a slightly modified version of the old Union. Lincoln had, very wisely, I think, yoked emancipation to the North's military effort against the Confederacy. We must do this, he said, in effect, if we're to win the war and restore the Union. Do you want to restore the Union? Well, then, we have to take this step on emancipation if we're going to be successful.

The vast majority of Northerners who cared passionately about the Union could accept emancipation if presented on these terms as a means to the larger end of union. Many of them would have resisted any attempt to push emancipation forward as a goal on its own, worthy of pursuit by the entire power of the United States, a goal that could stand separately from union as something that men should fight and die for and the United States should expend its treasure for. I think it was an excellent example of Lincoln's political acumen. He read the Northern temper accurately, and he acted accordingly. Well, at the same time that Abraham Lincoln was wrestling with the question of how best to deal with emancipation in the summer of 1862, he also faced another enormous problem, and that was the problem of keeping sufficient men in uniform to carry out the North strategic plans that would lead both to reunion and to emancipation. What we will do in our next lecture is take a look at the subject of how both armies pursued their efforts to fill the armies and keep the war going.

Filling the Ranks
Lecture 18

As the war dragged on and increased in fury, both sides sought to cope with a seemingly insatiable demand for more soldiers, ever larger numbers of soldiers, to keep the ranks in the armies filled. This lecture will examine that search for manpower in the Confederacy and in the Union, and we'll start with the Confederacy.

Roughly three million men served during the war, more than two million in Northern forces and 750,000 to 900,000 in Confederate forces. A huge number of men volunteered during the first year of the conflict, after which both sides used a combination of incentives and the threat of compulsory service to keep the ranks filled. Facing a disadvantage in manpower of five to two, the Confederacy resorted to extreme measures sooner than the North.

The Confederate Congress passed a national conscription act in April 1862 that extended the service of all men then in uniform and made all other military-age white males between the ages of 18 and 35 eligible to be drafted for three years of service. Subsequent legislation expanded the pool to include all men between the ages of 17 and 50. The Confederate draft allowed individuals to avoid service by purchasing a substitute until the end of 1863; various occupations were also exempt. The conscription act passed in April 1862 was the first in U.S. history and providing for the following:

- All white males between the ages of 18 and 35 were conscripted for three years.

- All original twelve-month enlistees were retained in the service. This led to a rise in the number of desertions.

- Men in war production industries, the civil service, and the clergy and teachers were exempted from service.

- Men were allowed to hire substitutes.

The North instituted its national draft in March 1863, creating a pool of men between the ages of 20 and 45. The North allowed men to hire substitutes or pay a commutation fee. The Federal government, states, and localities in the North also offered bounties to attract volunteers. Both drafts were designed to spur enlistment rather than compel service, and they operated quite effectively in that relatively few men were conscripted on either side.

Although complaints about a "rich man's war but a poor man's fight" arose in both the North and South and the drafts triggered significant opposition (the New York City draft riots being the most extreme example), all classes were well represented in Union and Confederate armies. Overall, the Confederacy mobilized about 80 percent of its available manpower (only the presence of slaves to keep the economy going allowed this impressive mobilization), and the North mobilized about 50 percent of its military-age men.

The South fought the war without a regular army, per se. For one thing, the South had no professional military in place when the war began, although some professional former United States Army officers served the Confederacy. The South relied on volunteers for national service who would return to private life at the end of the war.

Volunteers were plentiful early in the war, but less so within a year. Hundreds of thousands volunteered in 1861—about half for three years and half for twelve months. These twelve-month men were eligible to get out of the army as the second spring's campaign approached in 1862. Incentives (e.g., $50 bonuses, one month's leave, and transfers to other units) passed by the Confederate Congress in December 1861 failed to inspire reenlistment.

The Confederate Conscription Act of 1862 was controversial but necessary for the Southern war effort. As noted, it retained in service for three years all those who had volunteered for twelve months in 1861, thus averting a potential military problem in early 1862. Revisions of the 1862 Act extended the age limits to 17 to 50, added new categories of exemptions (e.g., blacksmiths, tanners, and salt workers), ended substitution, and extended service of all men in uniform to the duration of the war.

Opponents attacked conscription as contrary to individual and state rights and unduly favorable to wealthy people. A provision exempting one white male on any plantation with twenty or more slaves was especially unpopular. Groups of draft resisters and deserters found refuge in remote parts of the Confederacy. Some governors appointed hundreds of their friends to the civil service to help them avoid the draft.

The draft spurred enlistment and helped keep the Confederate armies strong. Approximately 80 percent of the Confederacy's soldiers volunteered for service. The continuance of slavery behind the lines was one factor that enabled this figure to be reached.

Although far richer in manpower, the North, too, experienced difficulty keeping its ranks filled. Hundreds of thousands of men volunteered in 1861, after which the number declined markedly. The first call to arms was for 75,000 men for three months. Subsequent calls sought many more men for much longer terms of service.

In July and August 1862, the Lincoln Administration sought more volunteers. It issued a call for states to supply 300,000 three-year men. In August, the Administration ordered states to supply 300,000 nine-month militiamen or face the prospect of a militia draft. States used bounties and other means to meet the July–August quotas. These measures did yield a large number of voluntary enlistments.

The North resorted to a national draft in 1863 that proved as controversial as the Confederate version. The Enrollment Act of March 1863 cast a wide net but allowed many men to avoid service. All males between 18 and 45 were eligible. States were given a grace period before each draft call in which to meet their quotas. Men could purchase a substitute and be released from all obligations or pay a $300 commutation fee to avoid any one draft call (this provision was abolished in 1864).

Bounties also played a prominent role in the operation of the Northern draft. Federal, state, and local bounties were offered. Bounty brokers acted as middlemen, and bounty jumpers collected their money, then deserted. Draft resistance broke out across the North. Thousands of men fled to Canada, and riots occurred in New York City and elsewhere.

Despite problems, the draft operated largely as intended. Nearly one million men volunteered during the period of the draft. Only 162,000 were conscripted or purchased substitutes.

It is instructive to investigate some differences between the Northern and Southern experiences with manning their armies. Confederates had proportionally more veterans in their ranks, because the North had, over time, more manpower flooding in. The Confederates, as attrition occurred, usually filled up their original regiments, mingling recruits with veterans. The North usually created new regiments with new recruits. This practice often led to high casualties when new regiments encountered veteran regiments on the battlefield. ■

Essential Reading

McPherson, *Battle Cry of Freedom: The Civil War Era*, chapters 14, 20.

Supplementary Reading

Cook, *The Armies of the Streets: The New York City Draft Riots of 1863*.

Geary, *We Need Men: The Union Draft in the Civil War*.

Moore, *Conscription and Conflict in the Confederacy*.

Questions to Consider

1. Do you find it ironic that the Confederacy, with its rhetoric about the sanctity of state rights, would embrace a national draft to help maintain its independence?

2. Can you imagine a crisis that would allow the modern United States to mobilize its citizenry in a way comparable to Civil War mobilization?

Filling the Ranks
Lecture 18—Transcript

As the war dragged on and increased in fury, both sides sought to cope with a seemingly insatiable demand for more soldiers, ever larger numbers of soldiers, to keep the ranks in the armies filled. This lecture will examine that search for manpower in the Confederacy and in the Union, and we'll start with the Confederacy.

The Confederacy began the war with no regular army, as we've seen before, and it never really set one up. The South fought the war with volunteer soldiers overwhelmingly, almost exclusively. Only some of the regular officers who had resigned from the United States Army and a handful of enlisted men expected to make the military their permanent profession in the Confederacy. Almost all of the men who fought went into the army to do their duty during the war with the expectation that they would be going back home as soon as the war was settled.

There were state militias in each of the states of the Confederacy, organizations that made all able-bodied white men of draft age liable for service at the request of the governor. The Southern state militias played only a minor role in the war however—their services generally being restricted to meeting emergencies as Federal armies penetrated into the Confederacy. They did not play a mainline role in the great battles of the war and the great campaigns of the war. That burden fell on volunteers, the volunteers, who, as I said just a minute ago, expected to return to civilian life as soon as fighting ended. This was the United States tradition. Those kinds of volunteers traditionally had done the bulk of the fighting in America's wars. Most recently that had been the case in the war against Mexico.

There was no shortage of soldiers at the beginning of the war. On March 6, 1861, which is six weeks before Fort Sumter was fired upon, the Confederate Congress authorized 100,000 volunteers, and many more than that responded. Men poured to the recruiting stations. Hundreds of thousands of men, in fact, offered themselves in the first few months of the war. They came in such numbers that the governments, both the local governments, the state governments, and the national government, couldn't arm and equip them efficiently. They couldn't begin to train them efficiently in the beginning. The Confederacy was awash in potential soldiers as the war loomed just ahead.

Two laws in May 1861 provided for an additional 400,000 men, bringing the total to half a million. Roughly half of those men volunteered for 12 months of service. The rest of them volunteered for a three-year hitch, which meant that, by early summer 1862, about half of the men wearing Confederate uniforms would be eligible to leave the army. By the fall of 1861, Confederate political and military leaders were nervously eyeing the following spring with the notion in mind that their armies might dwindle considerably as those 12-month volunteers exited from the service.

Enlistments by that time, by the fall of 1861, were slowing noticeably in the South. The great rush had come and gone. One Confederate general in Virginia wrote, in late October 1861, "The first flush of patriotism led many a man to join who now regrets it. The prospect of winter here is making the men very restless, and they are beginning to resort to all sorts of means to get home."

In early 1862, Jefferson Davis and his advisors recognized that they had to take action to keep the ranks filled in the upcoming spring campaign. The departure of all those 12-months men would leave the Confederacy extremely vulnerable to major Northern advances. In December of 1861, the Confederate Congress had offered a $50 bounty, a month's leave, and the opportunity to join new regiments, if they wanted to, as inducements to have men reenlist, but those measures failed to achieve very much. Only a trickle of soldiers decided to reenlist as a result of those measures.

By March 1862, Robert E. Lee, who was then President Davis's chief military advisor, together with Davis and a number of others in the Confederate administration, including the Secretary of War, pushed for a national conscription law—a draft, a countrywide draft—which would be the first of its kind in American history. This was the only solution to the problem they thought. There's no other way to get enough men into the ranks. The Confederate Congress agreed with this estimate and, in April of 1862, passed legislation.

That legislation, number one, made all white males 18 to 35 years old liable for three years service. The second provision was even more important in a sense because it retained in the army all of those men who had enlisted for one year of service back in 1861. It really changed the rules in the middle of the game on these men who had enlisted in good faith back in 1861. Their terms of service are about to expire; now they're told that they're going to be kept in the army. There was a spike in desertion right after passage of the Confederate conscription law. Many of the men who'd gone in as 12-months men believed that they'd been cheated by their government and many of them deserted.

Another provision of this Confederate draft exempted several classes of potential soldiers. Among those were men who worked in war production jobs, civil servants, militia officers, clergymen, and teachers with 20 pupils or more. A number of wry observers noted that there seemed to be a special call to become a teacher among young men that they hadn't noticed before this provision of the draft law went into effect.

The final provision of this piece of legislation that I'll mention allowed draftees to escape service by hiring a substitute. If your name came up and you were drafted, you could pay money to someone else to go serve in your place. This wasn't something new with the Confederacy. The notion of substitution in this kind of circumstance was an old tradition in the United States.

Now, this entire resort to a draft was at least mildly ironic in the Confederacy because this was a South that allegedly was dedicated to preserving individual rights and state rights against a centralized government that might reach down and perform in inequitable ways with its citizenry. And here is the Confederate States government reaching down and telling men they have to serve in the military. It went very much against the notion of state rights, but it had been necessary. This was the only way that the Confederacy could keep men in uniform. National conscription was the only option.

The odds made this necessary. The North was working with a manpower pool of more than four million men. The Confederacy was working with a manpower pool of slightly more than a million men. There was no way the South could match the North if it were left entirely to volunteering.

A second set of exemptions went into effect in October 1862, excusing many other trades such as blacksmiths and salt workers and then tanners. These were occupations that were vitally necessary behind the lines. The government had learned this in the course of the early operation of the draft law. You had to have these kinds of people behind the lines or society would fall apart. You had to give them the opportunity to do the things that every community needed to have done. In the instance of salt workers, you needed that salt for the national war effort.

The most important new exemption was that one white man on any plantation with more than 20 slaves was exempted. This exemption, together with the provision allowing the hiring of substitutes, caused many bitter protests. Many poorer whites in the South said that this was a rich man's war but a poor man's fight. A poor man couldn't avoid military service. A rich man could avoid it by hiring a substitute or could be that one white man on plantations or farms with 20 slaves who was exempted from service. The cost of substitutes eventually reached about $6,000 in Confederate money, about $300 in gold. There was so much opposition to substitution that the Confederate Congress abolished it in December of 1863.

As the war went on, the Confederate draft was further amended. In September 1862, the upper age limit was raised to 45 years old. So now it's everyone 18 to 45. In February 1864, the age spread was expanded again. It was lowered to 17 years on the younger end and raised to 50 years on the upper end—17 to 50 years. And, in that February 1864 legislation, all men then in the army were required to stay in the army until the war was over. Even those now who had joined for three years back in 1861 are in the army for the duration. If you're a Confederate soldier, the practical effect of this is you never do get out. Your term never runs out. Congress keeps changing the rules to keep everybody in the ranks. All Confederate soldiers, unless they were wounded or invalided out for some other reason, were essentially in the war for the duration.

Conscription became very unpopular in the Confederacy. State rights advocates attacked it, saying it was contrary to the principles—individual rights, state rights—upon which the Confederacy had been founded. Poorer men continued to attack it as favoring wealthy slaveholders. One Alabama hill farmer expressed the feelings of many in this latter group, this group of poorer men, when he wrote, and I'll quote from his letter, "All they want is to get you all pumped up and go fight for their infernal Negroes, and after you do their fighting you may kiss their hind parts for all they care." There's a poorer man's take on what's going on here.

By 1864, parts of western North Carolina, northern Alabama, northern Arkansas, and the hill country of Texas harbored large numbers of draft evaders or deserters. Some governors appointed hundreds of friends to civil service positions in order to let them escape the draft. A number of historians have focused on this kind of resistance to the draft to indicate that really the Confederate society was falling apart from within because of legislation such as the draft.

But there's another way to look at this—and, I think, the more accurate one—and that is that most white males of military age in the Confederacy did go into the service. The overwhelming majority of them did. They didn't try to evade the draft; they didn't desert. They went in and they served. There are some interesting documents relating to this very question.

In Virginia in 1864, an officer who was surveying the state to see what resources remained in the way of manpower reported that virtually everyone who could go had already gone. Most of those who weren't in the service were in jobs that were legitimately related to the war. He said that, in his view, conscription was going to be beside the point in Virginia by the middle of 1864. Everybody was either already in the army or doing some kind of job related to the war or wasn't up to military service.

Overall, as we've seen before, the Confederacy put about four out of five draft-age men into the army, about 800,000, probably, of the slightly more than a million available. Only slavery behind the lines made this possible. We've talked about that before. But the various conscription laws made certain that once a man was in the army he remained there, and that in the end helped the Confederacy last as long as it did. It would not have lasted nearly as long as it did without this national conscription.

Of these 800,000 or so Confederate soldiers, about 80 percent volunteered freely. The draft produced 82,000 conscripts, about 10 percent, and another 80,000 or so enlisted in order to avoid the stigma of being conscripted. Once again, without the centralized mobilization of the manpower resources of the Confederacy, the war would have ended much sooner. So the South turns to conscription first.

Let's see what the story is in the North. It's a similar story but not an identical one. The North had far more men of military age. We've said that more than once. Yet it also experienced difficulties keeping its armies' ranks filled. Traditionally, there were three types of military service in the United States. There was the regular army, which was always very small. The regular army never was the principal fighting force in a major conflict. It hadn't been in the war with Mexico; it wouldn't be in the Civil War.

A second source for manpower, as in the Southern states, was the militia, a state and federal institution going all the way back to earliest colonial days and with roots in the English militia system. It was created by state law. Its officers were appointed by state authority, and the militia served at the request of the governors, but there was a uniform drill and organization for all the militias prescribed by Congress, and the Constitution provided for the militia being called into national service in certain kinds of emergencies.

If one of those emergencies came up, the militia would be under the command of the president. If it were responding to a threat more local in nature, it would serve under the command of the governor. The militia never could be commanded by both. It was either in national service or in local service. The militia in the North, as in the South, did not play a major role in the Civil War. Professional soldiers had a very low opinion of militiamen. They had throughout United States history. It was true in the War of 1812, true in the war with Mexico, and certainly true in the Civil War. So the militia is not a key component of the North's military machine.

As in the Confederacy, it's the volunteers, the Federal volunteers, as they would be called, those who volunteered for service in the national forces during this time of national crisis. That's the traditional way Americans raised their armies, and it was true in the North. These again are men who are coming to their country's defense voluntarily with the expectation of going back to their regular jobs as soon as the war is over.

During the Mexican War, volunteers had numbered nearly 75,000 in the United States forces. The regular army during that war had been increased to about 30,000. So in Mexico there were more than two to one volunteers as against regulars. We've seen how, in the wake of the firing on Fort Sumter, Abraham Lincoln issued a call for 75,000 three-month militiamen to put down the rebellion. All the professional soldiers in the North knew that this would be far too few men and they would be in service for far too short a time to accomplish the job. William Tecumseh Sherman, for example, snorted that Lincoln might as well "attempt to put out the flames of a burning building with a squirt gun."

Various congressional and presidential actions through the rest of 1861 brought about three-quarters of a million volunteers into the Union army, most of them for a three-year term. Most of these were in regiments raised by the various states, officered by locally prominent men with commissions from the governor of the state, and many of the regiments came from a single town or county. We're talked about this before. There were a number of ethnic regiments, regiments that were almost entirely made up of Germans or of Irish soldiers. This was much more common in the North. That's not very common in the South, although there were some of those ethnic units in the South as well.

The clock was ticking in terms of the manpower pool in the North just as it was in the South. Men who hadn't enlisted for three years in 1861 would be facing the opportunity to get out of the army in the late spring of 1862. Lincoln knew that the North would need more soldiers to reinforce the Federal armies for a big round of offensives in the spring of 1862, and, as in the Confederacy, recruiting had dropped off dramatically in the North.

In July 1862, Lincoln called on the states to provide 300,000 three-year volunteers. Each state had a quota based on its population. Well, the 300,000 didn't step forward. The early volunteers had stepped forward; they're no longer doing that. Some newspapers and some politicians began to call for a draft. Lincoln knew how unpopular a draft would be in many segments of the North and hoped to avoid it. He wanted to exhaust all other possibilities. He had seen and read about reaction to the Confederate draft and didn't want that experience to be played out in the North.

On August 4, 1862, Secretary of War Stanton told the states to supply 300,000 nine-month militiamen. This is in addition to the 300,000 three-year soldiers that they wanted. Any state failing to meet its quota, said Stanton, would be subject to a militia draft. For the most part, the states avoided the militia draft and met the quotas, often by offering bounties, $100 in many instances, to volunteers. This was the beginning of a system that would get worse as the war went on, the offering of bounties. The bounties got larger and larger as the war went on, and it really gave a mercenary flavor to Northern volunteering and recruiting that wasn't present in the Confederacy.

In the end, the July and August 1862 calls produced 420,000 three-year enlistments and nearly 100,000 nine-month enlistments. There hadn't been a draft, but there had been the threat of a draft. But the North couldn't avoid a national draft forever, and let's turn now to the first conscription act in United States history, as opposed to American history (with the Confederate draft).

In March of 1863, the North finally did take this momentous step. Thousands of men would be eligible to get out of the service in the summer of 1863, so replacements had to be found. The nine-month men who'd come in during the preceding fall, for example, were going to be able to get out of service in the summer of 1863. What resulted was the Enrollment Act of March 3, 1863. It made all males between the ages of 20 and 45 eligible for the draft.

The real goal of this legislation was not to reach down directly and pull men into the army. The real goal was to encourage volunteering. The same had been true in the Confederacy. Let's encourage men to volunteer by threatening them with a draft rather than actually going out and pulling them into the army. Before each of the Union draft calls—there was one in July of 1863 and then three in 1864, in March, July, and December—the War Department assigned a target number of men to each congressional district, and the district was given 50 days to supply the requisite number of bodies to meet the quota before any men would actually be drafted.

The states worked very hard to meet their quotas because they wanted to keep their populations happy. They didn't want actual drafting going on, so they worked to meet their quotas. They used bounties, mainly, and this became, as I said earlier, a real problem. There was often a Federal bounty, a state bounty, there might be a local bounty, and sometimes these bounties would amount to several hundred dollars.

Bounty brokers went into business to find volunteers for the areas that were short of their quotas. The men for your quota didn't actually have to come from your area. They just had to be credited to your area. So if you're a county in Pennsylvania and you're not meeting your quota, you could take men from Ohio and count them against your quota as long as they're coming through your part of the picture.

Bounty brokers would go out to find these men. Rich districts outbid poorer districts. They offered bigger bounties and got more men. A group called "bounty jumpers" came into existence—men who would enlist, take the bounty, and then desert, and then go enlist somewhere else and take the bounty and desert again. One man claimed to have done this 32 times before he was finally imprisoned. The bounties eventually reached as high as $1,000, and the North paid out more than half a billion in money inducing men to join.

There were other problems beyond bounties with the Northern draft. There were no occupational exemptions as there were in the Confederacy, but there was substitution as there was in the South and something called commutation. In the North, if you were drafted, you could pay what was called commutation money to be excused from that call, just that one call. Three hundred dollars, a flat $300, would keep you out. Or you could buy a substitute and be exempted from all of the draft calls.

Poorer men didn't like this. The average working man's wage was about $600 a year. They didn't have $300. They couldn't pay a half a year's wages to get out of one draft call. Most of the substitutes who were purchased in the North were either teenagers or recent immigrants. There was such an outcry over commutation that, in July of 1864, the United States Congress abolished it, but substitution continued. Veteran volunteers bitterly resented a system that paid men a lot of money to come in and do their duty, duty that these men, the veterans, said they were doing out of sheer patriotism.

As in the South, there was a lot of opposition to the draft in the North. Many men fled to Canada, scores of thousands, perhaps. One estimate has put the number as high as 90,000 men who fled to Canada to avoid the draft. Many Democrats encouraged draft evasion. There were violent outbursts against the draft in many places in the North, the most famous being the New York City Draft Riots of July 1863.

Mobs in New York made up mainly of working men, many foreign laborers, rampaged for three days. More than 100 people were killed. The riots turned very ugly early on. They began to target black people especially. Many black men were hanged; some were burned. A black orphanage was burned down, and the mob drove back the firefighters who tried to come and put out the fire. It was a very, very ugly scene in New York City when the first draft call went into effect. Only the arrival of troops from the Army of the Potomac, fresh from the battlefield of Gettysburg, finally brought order in the streets of New York City. One Northern newspaper, in reaction to the rioting, exclaimed in a headline, "Great God, what is this nation coming to?"

So there was violent reaction to the draft, and then there was the less violent reaction of simply fleeing to Canada or somewhere else. Many others feigned illnesses. Some actually mutilated themselves. They would cut off a trigger finger; they would shoot off toes; they would knock out teeth. You had to be able to bite a cartridge, if you were a Civil War soldier, to get the end of it off and pour the powder down. There's one story about a member of the Ohio legislature who found a note on his desk saying that he had been drafted. He immediately went home and knocked all his teeth out, came back, and found out some of his friends had put the note on his desk as a joke and he hadn't been drafted at all.

My point is that there is, in the North, as there was in the South, resistance to the draft, a wide-scale resistance. The scope of opposition suggests that huge numbers of men must have been affected by the draft, but only 46,000 Northern men were drafted directly into service—46,000 out of more than two million who served. Another 118,000 furnished substitutes for a total of 162,000 men contributed directly or indirectly by the draft. That's about 6 percent of all those who served.

But, during the period of the draft, from the spring of 1863 to the spring of 1865, nearly a million men volunteered for Union service, many of them—perhaps most of them—lured by the offer of bounties of varying amounts. So while the draft might appear on the surface to be a failure, it actually did stimulate a great deal of volunteering and largely accomplished its purpose. Those 2.1 or 2.2 million soldiers who served in the Union army, as we've seen earlier, represented just about one in two of the military-age white population in the North, a much smaller percentage than in the South. Remember again the influence of slavery in that regard to free up the white men to fight in the South.

The North never did follow the South's lead in keeping veterans in service for the duration. They never took that final step to make sure that they had soldiers in the ranks. This meant that, at any given time, there was probably a higher proportion of veterans in the Confederate armies than in the Union armies, which was a distinct advantage for the Confederates on the battlefield.

One other difference between the two armies is worth mentioning. The South tended to replace losses in original regiments. If your regiment had 500 men and it suffered 150 casualties in one season of campaigning, many of those men would often be replaced in that same regiment to bring it back up to strength. So there was always a core of veterans present in these Confederate regiments to show the newcomers the ropes and steady them in battle.

The North, in contrast, tended to bleed its units right down virtually to extinction and then simply raise new regiments. The enlistments of whole regiments often ended at the same time. Sometimes whole regiments would pass out of Union service and new regiments would come in to replace them.

This meant that there would be green regiments or even brigades in Union service quite late in the war, which would have been extremely unusual on the Confederate side. These men would have seen very little service, and they might not function as effectively as their Southern counterparts.

There are many instances of these units in the Northern army being butchered on battlefields where they came up against more veteran Confederate units. Because group identity and spirit in units was important, the Confederate practice of constantly putting new men in with the veterans worked very well. It helped keep those regiments effective in battle. It helped have a nice leavening of veteran soldiers with these new men who came in.

Once men were in the ranks, once you had these soldiers in the ranks, the two nations, of course, had to find the fiscal resources to arm them and to equip them and to feed them. The war demanded national spending on an absolutely unprecedented scale in American history to achieve these goals. It extended the resources of the Confederacy right to the breaking point to arm and clothe and feed its soldiers. The North managed to do so more effectively.

Our next lecture will look at the ways in which each side sought to finance the war, and we'll look at the relative success and failure they had in giving the soldiers all they needed to fight and campaign.

Sinews of War—Finance and Supply
Lecture 19

We'll now look at how the two sides raised the money necessary to maintain those armies in the field through a long and grueling war. We'll also assess the relative quality and abundance of the weapons, clothing, and food supplied to soldiers in the opposing armies.

The conflict forced both contestants to undertake spending on an unprecedented scale. The Federal budget in 1860 was less than $65,000,000; in 1865 the North's budget alone totaled more than $1,250,000,000. Both sides resorted to selling bonds, taxing their citizens, and printing paper money to meet financial obligations; however, the Confederacy proved far less able than the North to do so without suffering economic hardship. Lacking a well-developed prewar financial infrastructure and without substantial reserves of hard money, the Confederacy relied too heavily on paper currency and experienced spiraling inflation that eventually reached more than 9,000 percent.

The Confederacy struggled to finance its war effort. Its antebellum economy had not been geared to support a modern technological war. Most Southern capital was invested in land and slaves, and the South lacked a substantial financial infrastructure.

The Confederacy resorted to three methods of financing the war:

- A series of property, income, consumer, and profits taxes contributed about 5 percent of the needed funds. Christopher Memminger, CSA secretary of the treasury, supported this option, but the Confederate Congress resisted it early in the war.

- Various bond issues brought in another 35 percent.

- Paper Treasury notes constituted the final 60 percent and proved disastrous.

Several factors contributed to soaring inflation, including over-reliance on paper currency, shortages of goods caused by the Union blockade, the presence of invading armies, and disruption of the transportation network. By the end of the war, it took $92 to buy what $1 had purchased at the outset in 1861.

The North, by contrast, easily met the test of financing the war and producing all necessary goods. During the war, the Federal budget grew from 2 percent to approximately 15 percent of the GNP. The North used the same three methods of financing the war as the Confederacy did, but with far more success. Various types of government bonds (many sold to individuals rather than to banks) raised 66 percent of needed funds and tied investors to the national effort. The bond most widely used was the "5/20" bond at 6 percent interest. Over one million people bought Northern bonds.

So overall, Union soldiers were a bit better armed, often a bit better fed—sometimes much more than a bit better—and also better clothed than their Southern counterparts.

Treasury notes, known as "greenbacks" and guaranteed as legal tender by the Legal Tender Act passed on February 25, 1862, accounted for another 13 percent. This money did not devalue like the money in the Confederacy. It was initially issued when the Union Army was doing well in the Western Theater. Income, excise, and other taxes made up the final 21 percent of revenue.

The Republican Congress enacted legislation designed to help foster a modern capitalist system. The aforementioned Legal Tender Act of 1862 created a stable paper currency. The National Bank Act of 1863 sought to drive state bank notes (of which there were over 7,000 different ones) out of circulation and replace them with more stable national bank notes. Northern inflation during the war was only 80 percent, compared to the 9,000 percent experienced in the South.

The Confederacy fought at a disadvantage in most areas of supply but managed to keep its armies adequately armed, clothed, and provisioned. Neither side had a decisive edge in shoulder weapons. Most Union and Confederate soldiers had rifled muskets by 1863 (the South produced some of its own and obtained others by capture or import). The North produced 160,000 breech-loading and 175,000 repeating weapons for a small percentage of its troops, an amount that the Confederacy could not match.

The North enjoyed a wider edge in ordnance. Confederate production was sufficient, but its quality was not (this was especially true for artillery ammunition). Josiah Gorgas was in charge of Southern ordnance, and his major factories were in Augusta, Georgia; Selma, Alabama; Richmond, Virginia; and Charleston, South Carolina. Union ordnance was almost always abundant and of much higher quality.

Prints and Photographs Division, Library of Congress.

The capitol building at Richmond, Virginia.

The North also enjoyed distinct advantages in clothing and feeding its soldiers. Breakdowns in transportation infrastructure hurt the Confederacy, as did damage to its agricultural areas as Union forces pushed into the interior of the Southern states. Union armies began an American pattern of overwhelming opponents through massive production. Confederate soldiers sometimes found themselves poorly clad and with skimpy rations. ■

Essential Reading

McPherson, *Battle Cry of Freedom: The Civil War Era*, chapter 14.

Goff, *Confederate Supply*.

Nevins, *The War for the Union: The Organized War, 1863–1864*, chapter 1.

Paludan, *"A People's Contest": The Union and the Civil War, 1861–1865*, part 2.

1. Do you believe the disparity in resources or a smaller pool of manpower was more damaging to the Confederacy?

2. Given its advantages, should the North have won the war more quickly? Or did compensating factors offset some of the material superiority?

Sinews of War—Finance and Supply
Lecture 19—Transcript

In our last lecture we discussed Union and Confederate efforts to keep the ranks of their armies filled. We'll now look at how the two sides raised the money necessary to maintain those armies in the field through a long and grueling war. We'll also assess the relative quality and abundance of the weapons, clothing, and food supplied to soldiers in the opposing armies.

We'll start with the Confederates. The Confederacy struggled mightily to finance its war effort. The key problem lay in the nature of the Southern economy, the antebellum Southern economy that was in place when the war began. Most Confederate capital was invested in land and slaves, as we've talked about before. It wasn't the kind of economy structured to fight what was a modern technological war in the mid-nineteenth century. It was not an economy geared to produce all the things that that kind of a war would demand. It couldn't produce the railroad tracks, never mind the engines and the rolling stock and all of the other material of war that each side would need.

The South had no financial system capable of meeting the demands of a large-scale war as well, as we also talked about earlier. The South did most of its financial business either in the North or in Europe. They didn't have that kind of a financial infrastructure in their own borders. So, as they surveyed the fiscal landscape of the war, Jefferson Davis and his principal advisors, they realized as the war went on that there were three ways that they could go about raising money, and we'll look at each one of those in turn.

The most obvious way, the way that would probably occur to any of us first, is to tax the citizenry. We'll raise money by levying taxes on our citizens, and we'll in essence pay for the war as we go along. Christopher Memminger was the Secretary of the Treasury in the Confederacy, and that is what he pushed for. He said, the only sound way to finance this war is to levy taxes on our citizens. But Congress, as with all Congresses, was reluctant to do something that would be unpopular with the voters and the citizenry. Congress was very resistant, the Confederate Congress, to passing taxes, especially early in the war.

It's important to remember that there had not been taxes in the United States—these kinds of direct taxes intended to raise money—for about three and a half decades before the Civil War. There had been no internal taxes levied by the federal government because revenues from tariffs and from the sale of western lands had brought enough monies into the federal coffers in those antebellum decades to take care of all the expenses of the United States government. So we're not dealing with a citizenry that's used to being taxed by the central government, and that was another problem that the Confederates were facing.

Nonetheless, the Congress did pass a small property tax in August of 1861, a very modest one. As conditions grew more serious later, a comprehensive tax law was put into effect. This included an income tax that had a scale that went from 1 percent to 15 percent. There was also an 8 percent sales tax on consumer goods and a 10 percent profits tax on wholesalers. But all of these taxes together didn't begin to cover the expenses of a mushrooming war, didn't come even within shouting distance of it. When you put all the taxes together, they yielded only about 5 percent of the money the Confederacy needed to fight the war.

They did show, however, just as the National Conscription Act had shown, that the Confederate people were willing to endure the kinds of intrusions from their central government that seemed to be at odds with the state rights/individual freedoms philosophy that they had espoused at the beginning of the war. They're accepting these taxes. The taxes aren't paying for the war, but it shows that the notion of state rights was taking a beating on another front in the Confederacy. So we have taxes; about 5 percent of the money comes from those taxes.

A second way to raise money is by floating bond issues. Sell bonds and get money into the treasury that way. That's more palatable to the citizenry because you don't have to buy bonds. It's an option on your part. The Confederacy sold a good number of bonds, in the end enough to pay for about 30 percent, perhaps as much as 35 percent, of the war. There're the kind of bonds that show up in the movie *Gone with the Wind*, for example, where Gerald O'Hara comes home and he pulls all his bonds out of his desk. He's invested his money in the future of the Confederacy, he says.

That's what other people are doing. They're counting on the Confederacy's success, and they're showing their belief in the ability of the South to win by investing their money in the national war effort. So there you have taxation and loans.

The third way to get money was simply to print it—to print treasury notes, to print paper money. Paper money brought in the remaining 60 percent or so of the funds that the Confederacy needed, and this proved to be an absolute disaster. Inflation soared as the government printed more and more and more paper money and as goods at the same time became scarcer because the Union blockade became more effective and because Union armies penetrated deeper and deeper into the Confederacy and caused greater and greater dislocation, not only of the Confederate economy but more especially of the transportation network that could deliver goods from one part of the Confederacy to another.

So you have these two factors working at the same time in deadly combination, an abundance of paper money and a shortage of goods. The result is awful inflation. Inflation soared all across the Confederacy. By 1864, it took $46 to buy what $1 had bought in 1861 of many kinds of goods. By the end of the war the ratio was $92 to buy what $1 had bought back at the beginning of the war.

So there was a combination of factors that came together to produce financial disarray in the South: the blockade, the Northern military, and the failure of Europe to recognize the Confederacy. Had Europe recognized the Confederacy, there might have been a number of other options that would have helped the South. A key one would have been the Royal Navy helping to break the blockade, which would have eased the scarcities, at least a bit. All of those are factors, but the most important one is simply the nature of the Southern economy. The Southern economy, so overwhelmingly agricultural, had so much wealth tied up in slaves and in land. That kind of an economy was simply not up to paying for an expensive and prolonged modern war.

Let's move to the North now. It's a very different picture in the North. The North had a much easier time of coming up with the money necessary to fight its war. Just as the South did, the North used a variety of measures to finance its war effort. At the beginning there's no national financial structure, as we would understand it now, in the North. There were more than 7,000 types of bank notes circulating in the North. Local banks would issue their own paper notes, and state banks would issue their paper notes, and those notes might only be good in a fairly small range from the bank that issued them. You couldn't get a note from your bank in Ohio that would be accepted by a merchant in New York City, necessarily. It was a very chaotic system in the North at the beginning of the war.

Federal budgets in the 1850s had averaged about 2 percent of the gross national product. During the war that percentage would shoot up to 15 percent of the gross national product, a huge increase that showed the magnitude of the problem that Lincoln and his advisors had to deal with.

Well, the North used the same three methods of raising money that the Confederacy used, but they used them in different combinations and different proportions, and they didn't have the same problems that plagued the Confederacy. Let's start with war bonds in the North.

The North sold a variety of war bonds. The most common one was called a "5/20" Bond. It paid 6 percent interest, and it was redeemable in not less than 5 and not more than 20 years. The North pursued the novel idea of having the people buy government bonds rather than having banks buy them. Really the ancestor, if you will, of the practice during World War I and World War II in the United States of having these huge bond drives where individual citizens purchase bonds came from this Union effort in the Civil War. Jay Cooke, a prominent banker from Philadelphia, was the prime mover behind pushing these war bonds in the North. His banking house became very successful during the war. He became one of the most powerful financial figures in the United States.

Eventually more than a million Northerners bought government bonds, and that tied them to their government. Alexander Hamilton had argued this back in debates over the nature of the Federal Constitution—how you should tie people to their new government. Hamilton said, people with a financial interest in their government are going to be tied to it. That's one way to help ensure the loyalty of your citizenry. He wanted people to be tied to the government in that sense, and that's what's happening in the Civil War.

Millions of Northern people in the end feel a direct tie because they've made a financial investment in the war effort beyond their hope to save the Union or beyond—if they happen to be abolitionists—their hope to see the war kill slavery. They actually have this other way in which they're tied to the national government and to the national war effort. This also represented a step, this system of loans, toward modernizing the nation's capitalist system. It's something that suited the Republican vision of what kind of a nation the United States should be.

In the last three years of the war, the North sold one and a half billion dollars worth of these bonds. To put that in perspective, the United States government's entire budget in 1860 was $63 million. Sixty-three million dollars ran the entire United States government. Here they're selling $1.5 billion worth of bonds during the war. So that's one method for the North to raise money.

They also issued treasury notes in the North. In late 1861 and early 1862, the United States government was running out of money—out of hard money, out of gold and silver. There simply wasn't enough to pay for all the war-related supplies that were needed. Congress, in response to this, authorized what the Confederacy had already resorted to, and that was the printing of paper money.

This was a difficult decision because many people only trusted silver and gold. They only trusted something that would clink when it hit the ground. They wanted something they could feel rattle around in their pocket or hear jangle in their pocket. That was money to them. Paper, the notion of paper money, brought back terrible memories of the Revolutionary War when the Continental Congress printed what turned out to be worthless paper money. "Not worth a Continental" was still an expression in the United States, meaning, what could be more worthless than this piece of paper money? That memory of the Revolution was still quite strong in the United States, and many Northerners were wary of the government's issuing paper money. They wanted hard money.

But money was so desperately needed that Congress passed legislation on February 25, 1862, called the Legal Tender Act, and it authorized the issuance of $150 million in treasury notes that came to be called "greenbacks." Our green money that we use now is descended from these original treasury notes issued during the Civil War, the greenbacks. Their money was bigger than ours, but that color was put in place then, and we're still going with it.

Federal paper money did not devalue nearly as badly as the Confederate paper money did, and there are several reasons for this. First, unlike the Confederate paper money, these greenbacks were made legal tender. They were receivable for all debts, public or private, with just a very few exceptions. Two of the main exceptions were that you couldn't use these to pay import duties, and you couldn't use them to pay the interest on the national debt. Well, most citizens weren't worried about paying the interest on the national debt. They just wanted to make sure that their paper money would be accepted for the normal things that you would have to pay for. So that's one strength of this paper money in the North. It is legal tender.

Secondly, it was issued in the winter and spring of 1862 at a time when the Northern army was achieving success out in the west. It was winning in Tennessee, and it was seen to be doing well almost across the board. In other words, it wasn't a period of despair in the North when the Union armies were in retreat. There was a good deal of optimism, and so this seemed to be a measure that might work. All other things were going well; this didn't seem to be any kind of a harbinger of bad tidings for the North. Strong confidence in the war effort helped ease the shock of this paper money.

Finally, Congress also levied taxes at the same time that it announced that these greenbacks would be put into circulation, and that helped relieve part of the inflationary pressures on the wartime economy. By the end of the war, the North had issued nearly half a billion dollars worth of greenbacks, nearly half a billion. All right—paper money, bonds. The third way to raise money is taxes, just as in the Confederacy, and the North levied a variety of taxes. The North also had an income tax, just as the South did. The brackets went from 3 percent to 10 percent in the North.

There were also excise taxes on a wide range of products: tobacco, liquor, yachts. There was increased revenue coming in from tariffs. Higher tariffs were placed on goods to protect the industries of the United States, the domestic industries, from the burden of the new internal taxes. All together, these taxes brought in about $600 million in the last three years of the war. So the North is using the same methods to raise money, but it's using those methods more effectively.

The Republican Congress also turned its attention to creating a national banking system. It tried to bring rationality to a national financial system that had been, as we said earlier, rather chaotic. It passed in February 1863 what was called the National Bank Act. It was supplemented by a second act in June of 1864. What this act did was set up guidelines under which a bank could get a federal charter and issue national bank notes up to 90 percent of the value of the government bonds that that bank held. If the bank bought a million dollars worth of government bonds, it could issue $900,000 worth of bank notes against those bonds.

This was designed to replace the hundreds of state banks and that welter of paper currency that had been in place when the war began. The process went slowly at first. All the state banks didn't rush to convert, but Congress decided to add an incentive, and the incentive was—this was from legislation in early 1865—that there would be in the future a 10 percent tax on all state bank notes. Well, that's a hefty tax. That got the attention of bankers all across the United States, and the result was that, by the end of 1865, there were nearly 1,300 federally chartered banks in the United States and just 350 state banks.

By 1873, state bank notes had virtually disappeared from the United States, so this was a very successful piece of legislation, from the Republican point of view. All of this legislation, the Legal Tender Act, the National Bank Act, and so forth, was the work of the Republicans in Congress. They supported it overwhelmingly. The Democrats tended to oppose all of this legislation.

On the whole, the Northern financial measures, as I've said, were very successful. Union policymakers were able to avoid the terrible inflation that plagued the South. Southern inflation soared to about 9,000 percent, as we've seen. Union inflation only reached about 80 percent. In World War II and World War I, inflation in the United States was about 72 percent in each case.

Union financing broke down this way: 13 percent of revenues came in from paper money. That's opposed to about 60 percent for the Confederates. Twenty-one percent came from taxes as opposed to about 5 percent from the Confederates, and 66 percent came in from loans as opposed to about 35 percent for the Confederates.

The Union economy, the Northern economy, was so robust during the war that it was able to provide all of the military goods that were needed and all of the domestic goods that its citizenry needed behind the lines. It produced both guns and butter without rationing or price controls. It's really a quite astonishing feat for the Northern economy, and it presents an enormous contrast, of course, with what was going on behind the lines in the Confederacy.

So they have their money raised. Let's see what they did with their money. What kinds of goods did they produce? How well did they feed and equip their armies?

You can say from the beginning that Confederate soldiers—this is a very general statement—fought at at least a slight disadvantage in most areas in terms of what they fired, the kind of ammunition they had, what they ate, and what they wore. But they're very slight disadvantages. It's easy to overstate this. You often get a sense, from reading accounts of the Civil War, that you have shivering Confederates in ragged uniforms with no shoes and outmoded weapons trying to hold back an absolutely brilliantly supplied Northern foe—Northern soldiers with full uniforms, and overcoats over those, and raincoats over those, and new shoes, and so much food in their haversacks that it sort of weighs them down, and brand-new weaponry.

It's David against Goliath in much of the literature, and that simply isn't accurate. The Confederates weren't woefully disadvantaged vis à vis their Northern opponents.

But let's look at several categories, and let's start with arms. Almost all Confederate soldiers had rifle muskets by the middle of the war. That is they had up-to-date, modern shoulder weapons. That isn't to say that all of them did. Well past the middle point of the war there were still Confederate units armed with the old-fashioned smoothbores. The unit that fired the volley that wounded Stonewall Jackson at Chancellorsville, for example, on May 2, 1863, was armed with smoothbores. Some of the biggest Confederate units at Gettysburg were still armed with smoothbores.

So they don't all have modern weapons, but the vast majority of them, by the midpoint of the war, have rifle muskets. A quarter of a million of these muskets were produced in the South, about 100,000 were captured from Northern soldiers, and another 600,000 were imported from somewhere in Europe. The most popular of those imported from Europe were Enfield muskets produced in England. They were very good muskets, a little bit lighter than many of the American ones and very accurate. They were popular both in the Confederate army and the Union army.

Northern soldiers were armed with rifle muskets on average a little bit earlier than the Confederates but not a great deal sooner than the Confederates, and some Union units also had smoothbores quite late in the war. The Irish brigade, the famous Irish brigade in the Union army, got rifle muskets rather late in the war, for example. About two and a half million rifle muskets were produced in the North; another million were purchased in Europe.

The North also produced modern kinds of weapons that the Confederacy didn't produce at all. In the North they produced 175,000 repeating arms, together with about 160,000 breech-loading arms. The Confederacy couldn't make these kinds of weapons. The repeating arms—the Spencer is the most famous example of that—could fire seven shots without stopping to reload. That's an enormous technological advance over the single-shot, muzzle-loading rifle musket.

The North could have armed a good number of its soldiers with these, but there was resistance within the army bureaucracy toward doing this. They thought that soldiers armed with repeating weapons would shoot up their ammunition too quickly and put a great burden on the ordnance department and maybe place themselves in peril on some battlefield. So mainly cavalrymen were armed with repeating weapons in the North and not all the cavalrymen. The same was true with the breech-loading carbines, that is, carbines that would load from the back rather than from the muzzle.

The Confederacy lacked the brass to make cartridges for many of these weapons, so even if they captured them from the North they weren't very useful. Breech-loaders and repeaters were mainly cavalry weapons for the North. But the most important weapon on both sides is that rifle musket, and both sides pretty much had armed their soldiers with them by the middle of the war.

All right, what about ordnance? What about the powder and the ammunition that both sides used? This was one area where the Southern arms never really were at a disadvantage in terms of quantity. The Confederacy produced all of the powder that it needed for its armies, but the quality of its artillery ammunition—not the infantry ammunition but the artillery ammunition—was much lower on average than Northern artillery ammunition.

Civil War artillery rounds, many of them, had fuses. They were designed to explode in the air. You'd estimate the distance and you'd cut the fuse. It's not like a cartoon fuse that sticks out of the round—it's an internal fuse. You'd estimate the distance, you'd cut the fuse, and you'd fire the round, and theoretically it would explode at the right place and hit the target. The Confederates never could get the fuses right. They had many, many rounds that either exploded prematurely or didn't explode at all. They would go all the way over the target and just plow into the dirt.

One Confederate artillerist at the Battle of Chancellorsville in May 1863 estimated that only one round in ten that his battery fired had fuses that worked correctly. So you had the phenomenon of Confederate gunners not being sure where their rounds were going to explode. Confederate infantry did not like their artillery firing over their heads because the rounds would often explode too soon. There are a couple of instances of Confederate infantry units turning around, pointing their muskets at the artillerists behind them, and saying, stop shooting over our heads. Your rounds are exploding. We're going to fire on you if you keep doing that. I don't think they really would have, but they were making a point, and it was a point that the artillerists took.

Union artillery ammunition on the whole was much more reliable. The Confederates had plenty of it, but it wasn't nearly as good. The Confederacy did have a man who can only be called a genius—Josiah Gorgas. He was a Northerner living in the South. He presided over the Confederate ordnance effort, and he kept ordnance flowing to Southern armies. The South melted church bells down on occasion to turn them into cannons. The women even, on occasion, were asked to save the contents of their chamber pots to be collected by government agents, and those contents then were leeched to extract the niter to produce gunpowder.

Stills were seized to be melted down for their copper—a tremendous hardship on some localities to see a really treasured still go, but anything for the cause, I suppose was the attitude among many of the Confederates. A huge powder mill was built at Augusta, Georgia. In fact, it was the largest in North America. There was no powder mill as large in the North. Arsenals and ironworks were built in Selma, Alabama. During 1863, more than 10,000 people in Selma were engaged in war-related production—10,000 in Selma, Alabama. There were also arsenals and ironworks in Richmond and Charleston and other places.

Many women were employed in these war industries in the Confederacy. Many of them wrapped the paper cartridges that the soldiers would carry. That involved close handwork, and women performed a lot of that. Sixty-nine women were killed in March of 1863 when an ordnance laboratory exploded in Richmond, Virginia.

It's really quite a record that the agricultural rural South compiled in the area of gearing up to reach a war industry level that would support the massive armies that they had in the field. It was quite astonishing and quite effective. In 1864, for example, Alabama produced four times as much iron as any state in the antebellum years had produced, but it's nothing like the Northern war machine, of course.

Northern industry far exceeded the Confederates, and it didn't take the heroic efforts to put it in place in the North. The industry was already in place. It just needed to be retooled, in many cases. Northern armies almost always had abundant ordnance and almost always had very high-quality ordnance. There's only a difference in quality, not in quantity. If you're a Confederate soldier, you can count on having enough powder; you can count on having enough ammunition. If you're a gunner it might not be very good ammunition.

What about commissary, that is, food, and quartermaster, clothing? What are the dimensions of these areas? Here the North had a distinct advantage. The breakdown of the Southern rail system as the war went on, the loss of food-growing areas to advancing Union armies, but especially the breakdown of the transportation infrastructure, which prevented the delivery of food from areas where it could be grown to areas where it was needed, really hurt the Confederacy.

Lee's army, for example, went long stretches with a daily ration of two to four ounces of meat and a pint of cornmeal. That meat was often fat bacon. That's the precooked weight of that ration. Many of the soldiers didn't even cook their meat ration because it essentially cooked away. So they would eat either raw or just barely cooked bacon with their cornmeal. It was a very rough diet. There were not heavy Confederate soldiers. Very early into the war it was a very lean group of men. Their calorie intake was quite low.

Northern soldiers were fed much better. On the whole, clothing was also better for the typical Northern soldier. Confederates often suffered from shortages of shoes, but not to the degree that many of the accounts would make you think. Most Confederate soldiers had shoes; Northern soldiers had better shoes generally and less often lacked shoes all together.

The Northern army really represents the beginning of another trend in United States military history, which is to produce massive quantities of goods— so many that there was tremendous wastage, but your armies were almost always better clothed and fed and provisioned than your opponent. As one Union general admitted somewhat sheepishly, "A French army half the size of ours could be supplied with what we waste." Many other armies that have fought the United States in the twentieth century, I think, could make that same claim. The Northern war economy, as I said, proved perfectly capable of providing all of these things while at the same time providing the consumer goods.

So overall, Union soldiers were a bit better armed, often a bit better fed—sometimes much more than a bit better—and also better clothed than their Southern counterparts. And, although the South never lost a battle for want of arms or powder or sufficient food and clothing, I think it's fair to say that superior supply must be counted as a factor that ultimately helped tip the balance of the war in favor of the North.

The War in the West, Winter 1862–63

Lecture 20

As we move into the winter of 1862, the North would enter a period of minimal good news from the battlefield that would test Union resolve, both civilian resolve and military resolve.

We left the armies in the wake of Perryville and Antietam, a period that seemed to hold great promise for Union forces and that could harry retreating Confederates. But weeks passed with no decisive movements in the West or in Virginia, which bred dissatisfaction in the North. While McClellan remained immobile north of the Potomac in Maryland, Don Carlos Buell engaged in a most tepid pursuit of Braxton Bragg's army as it left Kentucky and marched into Tennessee. Lincoln understood the importance of positive news from the battlefield and implored his generals to act. Eventually, he replaced both McClellan and Buell, promoting Ambrose E. Burnside to command the Army of the Potomac and William S. Rosecrans to oversee the effort against Bragg. Lincoln made it clear that he expected action before the year ended.

General Philip Sheridan.

Rosecrans and Bragg fought one of the biggest battles of the war near Murfreesboro (Stone's River) in middle Tennessee on December 31, 1862, and January 2, 1863. In late December, just after Christmas, Rosecrans's Army of the Cumberland marched toward Bragg's Army of Tennessee, which lay a short distance southeast of Nashville near Murfreesboro. The Confederate cavalry harassed his advance. Rosecrans nevertheless made rapid progress in this unusual (for the Civil War) winter campaign.

The armies made contact on December 30. Both commanders planned to hit the other's right flank. Fighting on December 31 favored the Confederates. Bragg launched his attacks first and drove Rosecrans's army back. Rosecrans exhibited great courage and steadiness in putting together a defensive line, and one of his subordinates, Philip Sheridan, held his division together to stabilize the line. Bragg notified Richmond that he had won a victory.

After a day of tense inaction, fighting on January 2 favored the Union. Bragg ordered desperate frontal assaults that were easily repulsed. Bragg decided to retreat deeper into southeast Tennessee on January 3–4, 1863.

Stones River or Murfreesboro was a bloody, but essentially indecisive, military contest. Casualties for the Union (13,000, or 31 percent) and Confederacy (12,000, or 33 percent) made up the highest combined percentage for any major battle of the war. The two armies settled into winter quarters and left the strategic situation in middle Tennessee similar to what it was before the battle. Lincoln praised Rosecrans because this was the best news from any major Union commander during the winter of 1862.

Ulysses S. Grant attempted without success to mount a major offensive against Vicksburg in December 1862. He planned for a two-pronged approach. He would move overland from Tennessee through northern Mississippi. William Tecumseh Sherman would move down the Mississippi River against Vicksburg from the north.

Confederates frustrated both prongs of the offensive. Cavalry raids under Nathan Bedform Forrest disrupted Grant's supply lines and forced his retreat back into Tennessee; Grant learned a lesson on this retreat about subsisting off the land. General Earl Van Dorn destroyed a major Union supply base at Holly Springs on 20 December. Confederates easily repulsed Sherman's assaults north of Vicksburg at Chickasaw Bayou on 29 December 1862.

Grant spent the remainder of the winter mounting a series of failed attempts to get at Vicksburg from the south and east. He tried unsuccessfully to dig canals to bypass the city's four miles of gun batteries that commanded the river and to maneuver through tributaries of the Mississippi River to attain the same end. He also mounted a failed attempt to approach Vicksburg via Yazoo Pass.

Finally, he decided to run his naval forces past the batteries of Vicksburg and shift his infantry across to the west bank of the Mississippi beyond the range of Confederate guns and troops. His subordinates opposed the plan as too risky. Success in the maneuver would allow Grant to shift his army back to the east bank of the Mississippi below Vicksburg, where he could live off the land. On 16 April, David Dixon Porter ran his gunboats past the defenses of Vicksburg, despite suffering hits on all thirteen vessels and having one sunk. Troop transports ran the batteries a few nights later. Grant now had the capability to get his forces back across the Mississippi. ■

Essential Reading

Hattaway and Jones, *How the North Won: A Military History of the Civil War*, chapters 11–12.

McPherson, *Battle Cry of Freedom: The Civil War Era*, chapter 19.

Supplementary Reading

Bearss, *The Campaign for Vicksburg: Vicksburg Is the Key*.

Cozzens, *No Better Place to Die: The Battle of Stones River*.

Questions to Consider

1. Try to imagine the state of Union civilian morale after the high hopes raised by Antietam and Perryville dissolved in the disappointments of the winter of 1862–1863. What would you have done as Commander-in-Chief to turn this situation around? What if these battles had occurred before the elections?

2. What does the first phase of the Vicksburg campaign tell us about Grant as a general?

The War in the West, Winter 1862–63
Lecture 20—Transcript

With this lecture we return to the military front after several lectures away from it. We last looked at armies and battles in the autumn of 1862, leaving the Western Theater with Braxton Bragg and Edmund Kirby Smith retreating from Kentucky after the Battle of Perryville, and the Eastern Theater with Robert E. Lee occupying a position just south of the Potomac River, having withdrawn from the bloody battlefield at Antietam.

As we move into the winter of 1862, the North would enter a period of minimal good news from the battlefield that would test Union resolve, both civilian resolve and military resolve. In this lecture we'll do several things. We'll look at Northern morale in the autumn of 1862 before this next round of campaigning began. Then we'll look at a winter campaign in Tennessee that climaxed in the Battle of Murfreesboro or Stone's River, another one of those battles with two names. Finally, we'll look at Ulysses S. Grant's early attempts to capture the Confederate stronghold at Vicksburg on the Mississippi River.

Let's start by looking at the sentiment in the North in the autumn of 1862, the sentiment that looked to the battlefield with a sense that things were going wrong for the North—or at least not as right as they should be going for the North—and that looked to the battlefield with the hope that things would turn around.

There's considerable dissatisfaction, both in the civilian and the military sectors of the North in the late fall of 1862. As Northerners looked across the strategic map of the war, they saw that, in the east, George B. McClellan had failed to follow up the Battle of Antietam. He hadn't pushed the Army of Northern Virginia after that battle. Lee had been allowed to retreat. He had retreated almost at leisure away from the battlefield at Sharpsburg. He'd gotten back across the Potomac River without any damage being done—any significant damage—by George B. McClellan. After Lee had retreated, McClellan had just waited and waited near the old battlefield at Antietam, and the Northern people were unhappy about that. Abraham Lincoln was very unhappy about it.

In the West, Don Carlos Buell had behaved the same way after the Battle of Perryville. He'd just let Braxton Bragg go, and Braxton Bragg, after reuniting with Edmund Kirby Smith, had left Kentucky absolutely unmolested by Don Carlos Buell's much larger United States army. Similarly, there was no follow-up to the Union victory at Corinth in northern Mississippi, which had taken place, as we saw earlier, during the first week of October 1862. So nothing had come, in a dramatic sense, of the Union successes at Antietam, Perryville, and Corinth. This is in the minds of many people in the North. It seemed that so much more could have been accomplished, and there was disappointment that more was not.

Abraham Lincoln was acutely aware of the fact that positive results on the battlefield were necessary to keep the Northern people inspirited, to keep the broadest possible portion of the North tied to the war effort. He had to have positive results from the battlefield. He eventually decided that he was simply not going to be able to prod either McClellan or Buell into action and that he would have to make changes in command at the top of his major armies in the west—one of his major armies in the west—and his major army in the east.

In the end that is exactly what he did. He removed Buell and replaced him with William Stark Rosecrans, and he replaced McClellan with Ambrose Everett Burnside. He made it clear to both of those men, to both Rosecrans and Burnside, that he expected action before the year was out. Now, this is unusual because, as we've said before, there are rhythms to campaigning in the mid-nineteenth century during the Civil War. You campaigned in the spring and in the summer and in the fall, but it was most unusual to campaign in the winter.

It's a measure of how important Lincoln believed it was to have good news from the battlefield that we're going to see winter campaigning in December and January of 1862-1863. Lincoln believed it was necessary to produce the kinds of success on the battlefield that would allow the Northern people to take heart and would sustain the Union cause.

We'll start by looking at a battle, one of the largest battles of the war, that Rosecrans and Braxton Bragg fought in middle Tennessee, near

Murfreesboro, the Battle of Stone's River or Murfreesboro. Braxton Bragg had withdrawn into middle Tennessee following the Kentucky campaign and had taken up a position just a few dozen miles from Nashville, southeast of Nashville. He commanded what was now called the Army of Tennessee. It had been the old Army of Mississippi; now it's the Army of Tennessee. This will be, together with the Army of Northern Virginia, one of the two principal Confederate field armies for the rest of the war.

Bragg's army had about 36,000 men. He faced the Union Army of the Cumberland. Again, it was the usual pattern of naming armies. Bragg's army is named after the state of Tennessee, and I think it was an optimistic gesture on the part of the Confederacy, indicating that the Confederacy meant to hold onto Tennessee or to reclaim Tennessee. They've decided to name this major army in the west after a state that was largely in Union control at this stage of the war. So it's named after the state and, as was the pattern with the North, the other army is the Army of the Cumberland, named after the Cumberland River. Commanded by Rosecrans, it numbered about 42,000 men.

Rosecrans understood very well that Lincoln expected action from him. Rosecrans is a man who had been on the scene for a good part of the war. He's an intelligent, competent graduate of West Point. He'd had a lackluster career in the old army. That's perhaps a generous way to describe it. He'd resigned his commission in the 1850s. We've seen how many of these soldiers got out of the army in the mid 1850s because there really wasn't much chance for advancement, certainly not much chance to make very much money in the army.

He ended up heading a kerosene refinery in Cincinnati at the time of the outbreak of war. He came back into federal service, as so many West Pointers did, and he'd participated in the campaigning in western Virginia in 1861, those campaigns that had made George B. McClellan one of the early Union war heroes. Much of the fighting and accomplishment had come from McClellan lieutenants, Rosecrans among them, but McClellan had gotten most of the credit. After that action in western Virginia, Rosecrans had been sent out to the Western Theater, where he had campaigned under Halleck and Grant before receiving command now of the Army of the Cumberland.

So here he is, new in field command and with instructions to make something happen, and that's what he proceeded to do. He moved south out of Nashville the day after Christmas in 1862 and embarked on this unusual winter campaign. He moved toward Murfreesboro, which is about 30 miles southeast of Nashville. That's where Bragg's army was reported. As he moved, he was harassed—his supply lines were harassed, I should say—by Confederate cavalry under Nathan Bedford Forrest and John Hunt Morgan and Joseph Wheeler. Again, this is a pattern that we've seen before. As Union armies moved deeper into the Confederacy, their supply lines, sometimes very tenuous, were subject to being hit and broken by Confederate cavalry.

That's happening to Rosecrans, but Rosecrans moved ahead anyway. He moved, in fact, quite spectacularly well, especially when compared to what his predecessor Buell had been used to doing. Ahead of him was Braxton Bragg's Army of Tennessee, positioned behind Stone's River, a little northwest of the town of Murfreesboro. The armies came together, very close to one another, less than a mile apart, on the night of December 30, 1862, and you had one of those scenes, those really memorable scenes, from the war that certainly stuck in the minds of everybody who was present.

Apparently a band on one side or the other started to play patriotic tunes that night. It was very quiet, a quiet winter night. The Northern band played the "Battle Hymn of the Republic" or some such song like "Yankee Doodle." When it finished, a Confederate band answered by playing "Dixie" or "The Bonnie Blue Flag" or "Maryland, My Maryland," or some patriotic Confederate song. When it finished, the Union band answered, and then a Confederate band answered, and you had this battle of the bands, so to speak, going on into the night as men on both sides listened.

Toward the end of this, one side's band began to play "Home Sweet Home," which was the most popular song in both armies during the war (it was very sentimental and put men in a very much thinking-of-home frame of mind), and all the bands began to play "Home Sweet Home" together, soldiers on both sides singing along and undoubtedly thinking about their homes and loved ones. This was one of the many occasions in the war when the soldiers were reminded that they did share a great deal, that they were all at least in some sense Americans.

It's the kind of incident that many historians of the war have liked to emphasize to show, these are all Americans. Isn't it a tragedy that they're fighting each other? They're really so much more alike than they are different. But I would caution you not to make too much of this. They were all Americans, but they also believed that there were tremendous differences between them, and there was a great deal of enmity, there was a great deal of hatred, between the soldiers on one side or the other.

Examples of fraternization, and examples such as this duel between the bands before the Battle of Murfreesboro should not be taken as evidence that there were really only surface differences and it was almost an accident that they ended up fighting each other. There's a tremendous amount of very deep-seated antagonism between the sides, but much of that fell aside on the evening of December 30, in those woods and fields in middle Tennessee.

Bragg and Rosecrans both planned for the battle the next day, and just as Beauregard and McDowell had planned to do the same thing before the Battle of First Manassas, they both came up with the same plan as well. Each of them was going to attack the other's right flank. At Manassas, each was going to attack the other's left flank, but here they both intend to attack the other's right flank. No frontal assault will get around the flank.

In this instance, the Confederates launched their assaults first. Braxton Bragg's men got going at dawn on December 31, 1862, hoping to pin Rosecrans's army against Stone's River and cut Rosecrans off from his direct route to Nashville. The Confederate assaults went well at first. Two Federal divisions were essentially swept from the field. It was very hard fighting.

Rosecrans behaved in an absolutely exemplary way during the fight. He moved up toward the fighting. He took a very active role in trying to keep his troops together. At one point he was riding with his chief of staff near him, and a Confederate cannonball decapitated his chief of staff, splattering blood and gray matter all over Rosecrans, but he was oblivious to it. He was so focused on what needed to be done to keep the Union lines intact that he wasn't even really aware at the time of what had happened to his staff officer.

One key stand was made by a Union division commanded by a young soldier named Philip H. Sheridan. This is the first time we've really talked about Sheridan on a battlefield. He's commanding an infantry division here and doing very well. He would end up as one of the great Union soldiers of the war. He'd end up moving east with Grant when Grant went east in 1864 and would become the commander of all of Grant's cavalry during the Overland campaign and eventually would be an army commander in the Shenandoah Valley. Well, here's Philip Sheridan holding his division together in the face of massive Confederate attacks. Three of his brigade commanders were killed, and a third of his men were shot down, but Sheridan helped keep the Union line intact. One little piece of the landscape here, four acres of forest, became known as Hell's Half Acre because the fighting was so fierce.

Well, in the end Bragg was not able to smash Rosecrans's army, although he did push it back and make Rosercrans reconfigure his lines. Bragg thought he'd won a victory. He'd done something of the sort at Perryville. Although he hadn't really understood everything that was happening at Perryville, he thought briefly that he'd won a victory there. He was quite certain that he'd won a victory here on the first day of fighting at Murfreesboro, and he sent a telegram that night to Richmond announcing that he'd had a great success.

On the Union side, some of Rosecrans's officers suggested that the Army of the Cumberland retreat. They thought that they had been beaten as well. But Rosecrans held fast, and the next day each side shifted some troops to the east side across Stone's River. Not much fighting took place. This is New Year's Day—shifting and realignment are going on.

Bragg expected Rosecrans to retreat. Rosecrans didn't, and when January 2 came, Bragg decided to renew his assaults. He talked to his subordinates about this. He wanted to attack a part of Rosecrans's line on the east side of Stone's River that had considerable artillery support, that clearly had artillery support. Bragg's lieutenants said, no. Don't attack. It looks like too strong a position. We don't think that you should attack that. Bragg overruled them. This was going to cause tension that lingered long after the battle. There were going to be recriminations after the battle directed toward Bragg by his lieutenants, who said that this attack should not have been launched.

But the attack was launched, and it was an abysmal failure. The Southern brigades attacked into a strong Union position. Fifty-eight Union cannons raked the attackers at one time or another, and the assaults produced nothing but piles of Confederate casualties. This is another instance of Bragg's being aggressive, and we'll see others. He could be aggressive, but he seemed not to be able to be aggressive in a way that yielded results on a battlefield, results beyond significant casualties.

Bragg drew back after this second day of hard fighting on January 2 and decided that his position near Murfreesboro was no longer tenable. He worried about his supplies, he worried about the level of casualties, and he also, I think, must have known that he didn't really have the confidence either of his principal subordinates or of the men in the ranks. It was an army, officers and men, without much faith in its commander, and Bragg decided to retreat. The Army of Tennessee fell back about 35 miles to the south on January 3 and 4. So it was another instance of Bragg having announced success and then having to retreat. This is something that people remembered as well. We've won, and then we're going to retreat on Bragg's part.

He left behind incredible carnage. In terms of percentages of the armies lost as casualties, this is the bloodiest battle of the Civil War, the Battle of Stone's River. The combined casualty rate was simply staggering: 12,000 Confederate casualties, a third of Braxton Bragg's army, and 13,000 Federal casualties, more than 30 percent of Rosecrans's army, and it didn't yield a decisive result.

Bragg was still in middle Tennessee. Rosecrans didn't pursue him. Bragg simply fell back to a position a bit closer to the Georgia border. But still it was much better than a defeat. It was much better than what might have happened in this instance, and Lincoln was actually pleased, or at least cautiously pleased, with what had happened. He sent a message to Rosecrans saying that, if this had been a real defeat, and I'll quote him here, "the nation could scarcely have lived through it." You can almost see Lincoln breathing a sigh of relief. Here is a battle that resulted in a Confederate retreat. That at least can be construed as a Union victory even if it isn't a clear-cut and decisive Union victory.

The strategic situation didn't change at all as a result of the Battle of Murfreesboro or Stone's River, but at least it wasn't a Union retreat. It's the last fighting in this theater during that winter. It will be even past the spring before Rosecrans and Bragg will engage one another again in significant fighting.

All right, let's shift to the Mississippi River, and let's look at the initial phase of Ulysses S. Grant's operations against Vicksburg. Vicksburg was the great remaining Confederate stronghold on the Mississippi River. As you'll remember, the Federals had already taken control of the upper reaches of the Mississippi. They controlled Columbus, Kentucky, all the way down to Memphis, Tennessee. That part of the river was solidly in Union hands, as was the lower stretch of the river from the gulf up to New Orleans and then on north of New Orleans toward Baton Rouge.

The Confederates only controlled this middle piece of the river, really between Vicksburg and Port Hudson, Louisiana. Those are their two remaining strong points, but Vicksburg is the more important of the two. It is the key to Union control of the entire sweep of the Mississippi River. Until Vicksburg fell, Union plans to control the river could not be completed, and so that is Grant's charge in this campaign. How is he going to get at Vicksburg? How is he going to complete this part of old Winfield Scott's Anaconda campaign—take control of the Mississippi?

He hoped to threaten a stronghold primarily from two directions. He would come out of Tennessee overland with an army, marching southward into Mississippi, and try to put himself in a position to come against Vicksburg from the east. A second force, under his friend William Tecumseh Sherman, would try to put itself in a position to threaten the city from the north. So you'd have this two-pronged Union offensive: coming against the city from the northern reaches along the Mississippi River and the waterways that branched off of it to the north, and Grant trying to swing in from the east against Vicksburg.

Most of the defenses at Vicksburg, of course, had been built with the intention of stopping passage of Union vessels past the city on the Mississippi River. Those batteries, the entrenchments, the placement of cannons and so forth, faced away from the city toward the water. Grant is hoping to get himself in a position to come at the city from the other direction where the defenses would not be as strong. So that's the plan, but things went wrong with the plan from the very beginning.

Grant's portion of the offensive ran into trouble with Confederate cavalry. Again, this is a light motif we've seen in campaigning in the west. Confederate cavalry is going to play havoc with the rear echelons of Union armies trying to march deeper into Southern territory, and that's what happened to Grant. Confederate cavalry under Nathan Bedford Forrest disrupted his communications in Tennessee. Forrest's cavalry tore up several dozen miles of track that Grant was using. Even more damaging than that was a raid carried out by the Confederate cavalryman Earl Van Dorn. Van Dorn's force destroyed a huge Union supply base at Holly Springs, Mississippi, on December 20, 1862, and the combination of these two strikes by Nathan Bedford Forrest and by Earl Van Dorn convinced Grant that he was going to have to abandon his plans to come overland from Tennessee and try to get at Vicksburg from the east.

As Grant retreated, however, he learned a lesson, as he later observed in his memoirs. He noted during the return to Tennessee that there was a great deal of food and fodder that his army could have siphoned off from the Confederate countryside, and he put it this way: "It showed that we could have subsisted off the country for two months. This taught me a lesson." He would remember that lesson for the next phase of the Vicksburg campaign, but that's the end of Grant's portion of the first approach to Vicksburg.

His friend Sherman also ran into trouble. Sherman's part of the plan was predicated on the Confederates having to divide their attention between the different Union threats to Vicksburg. With Grant removed from the board, the Confederates were able to concentrate on Sherman, and Sherman worked himself into a position to attack the Confederates, but the attacks were a dismal failure in the Battle of Chickasaw Bayou on December 29, 1862. There were nearly 2,000 Union casualties; only about 200 Confederate casualties were suffered by troops under John C. Pemberton, the Confederate who opposed Sherman there.

So the entire first phase of the campaign had ended in failure for Grant. He'd come up with a plan, the plan had not worked, and he had to go back to the drawing board during the winter and into the spring of 1863. He had to try to figure out a way to get his men and supplies into what he considered the best ground across which to approach the city. That ground was south of the city on the same side of the river, that is, the east side of the Mississippi, or to come in from east of Vicksburg. There was good terrain there and bad terrain—very rugged, hilly, formidable terrain—north of the city. The best way was from the south or from the east. The question was how to get his troops into a position to do that.

He tried various things through that winter. The Union engineers and the soldiers did a lot of planning and digging and expended great effort trying to find alternate routes that would avoid key Confederate defenses, especially the four miles of batteries at Vicksburg, and yet allow the Federal troops to have either a good position north of the city or a good position south of the city. They tried finding alternate waterways, following little tributaries of the Mississippi. They tried to use the Yazoo River and its tributaries as routes to get into a favorable position to get at the city. They even tried to dig canals. That might be a way, Grant thought, to put together some successful approach to Vicksburg.

But none of these things worked out in the end, and by late March he decided that what he was going to have to do was have the naval forces cooperating with him, commanded by David Dixon Porter, run past the batteries at Vicksburg and get into a position south of the city so that Grant—who would have shifted his infantry to the west side of the river and marched them downriver—those troops then could march to a point below Vicksburg. They would have the Union vessels, which had run past the batteries, ferry them over the east side of the river, and then Grant would be in position to launch his campaign.

It was a campaign, as he envisioned it, that would not need supply lines. Once he was east of the river, he would strike toward Jackson, Mississippi, and then back toward Vicksburg from the east. It was a very daring plan. It went against much of the military convention, but he believed he could live off the land. He had, as we've just seen, decided that was the case when he retreated back to Tennessee. He also probably had in mind the fact that Winfield Scott had conducted just that kind of campaign in the last phase of his march against Mexico City during the Mexican War.

So that is Grant's plan. Well, he shared his plan with his principal subordinates, with William Tecumseh Sherman and with David Dixon Porter, and they didn't like the idea. They thought that it was too risky. If fact, Sherman recommended returning to Memphis, Tennessee. He said, let's just go back to Memphis. Let's pull everybody into Memphis, go through another round of planning, and start afresh with a solid supply line.

Grant said, no, we can't seem to retreat that way. That would be too hard on Northern morale. That simply won't work. Lincoln also had doubts about whether this idea of running past the Vicksburg batteries would work, and Porter and the navy men were quite understandably reluctant to do this. They were the ones who were going to be in the ships. They thought that perhaps it wasn't the very best idea.

But Grant decided to go with it. He was capable of this kind of decisive decision making. He's much like Lee in that regard. So ahead he went, and, on April 16, the Union naval vessels, many of them with cotton bales stacked along their sides to protect them, ran past the Vicksburg batteries. They did it at night. The Confederates went down to the river and lit huge bonfires that illuminated the evening. One of Grant's children remembered later in life—he'd been there as a boy on the west side of the river—that it seemed like daylight, the fires were so bright.

The Confederate gunners found their marks. Every Union vessel was hit, most of them were set afire, and one sank, but the rest of the 12 got past the battery safely. A few nights later, on April 22, six transports and 12 barges tried their luck. One transport and six of the barges were sunk. The vessel carrying the medical supplies for Grant's troops went down, but the other ones got through, and Grant now had a fair amount of material below Vicksburg.

He moved his infantry, just as he had planned, from the west side of the river to the east, and he had accomplished what he had sought in this phase of the campaign. As he later wrote in his memoirs, "I was on dry ground on the same side of the river as the enemy." All the campaign's labors, hardships, and exposures from the month of December 1862 onward were for the accomplishment of this one object. By May 1, Grant had 23,000 infantry at Port Gibson, Mississippi, and he was prepared to go to the next phase of his campaign.

This was an accomplishment that had been born of desperation, really. Grant had tried so many other things, none of which had worked. Now this bold move, this great risk that he had taken, had paid off by at least putting him in a good starting position. But it wasn't clear by any means that he would be successful from here. All he had done is put himself in a position where he might be successful. The North, in other words, couldn't take great heart from this. This isn't a great victory that will inspirit the North. It's just a continuation, a positive one, but a continuation, of Grant's campaign.

There's going to have to be a period of waiting and seeing, in other words, whether Grant will be successful, whether Grant will in the end deliver the kind of victory at Vicksburg that the Northern people so desperately needed. What we will do in our next lecture is turn our attention to what had been transpiring in Virginia during this same period.

There had been enormously important events going on in Virginia even as Grant was trying to maneuver and get his way into position to take Vicksburg from December until May of 1863. From December 1862 to May of 1863, Grant is maneuvering in the west. In the east there will be two large battles in that same period, and it is to those two large battles that we will turn our attention next time.

The War in Virginia, Winter and Spring 1862–63
Lecture 21

This lecture will continue our examination of military events in the late autumn and winter of 1862 and the spring of 1863. Our topics will be two major campaigns in the Eastern Theater that unfolded while William S. Rosecrans and Ulysses S. Grant were campaigning in Tennessee and along the Mississippi River out west.

Our last lecture examined the Union's frustrating campaigning in the winter of 1862 and spring of 1863 along the Mississippi River and in middle Tennessee. Now we turn our attention to Virginia, where Northern arms suffered two devastating setbacks along the Rappahannock River that sent tremors of doubt and anger through the North. Ambrose E. Burnside, whom Lincoln had selected to replace McClellan in early November 1862, understood that he was expected to move against Lee.

On 11 December, Union engineers began to push pontoon bridges across the river. Union artillery largely destroyed the old city of Fredericksburg, but the Battle of Fredericksburg on December 13 was a Union disaster. Burnside's hopes to get around Lee's right flank (held by Stonewall Jackson) came to nothing because of poor execution, although the Union forces very nearly broke through.

The Federal commander resorted to unimaginative frontal assaults against a very strong Confederate position on Marye's Heights. The Union lost heavily (12,000 casualties) and gained nothing tactically or strategically as the result of this battle. The army returned to its pre-battle lines, and the Northern public expressed great indignation about the battle and the Republican direction of the war. The series of seemingly pointless frontal assaults against well-positioned Confederates made the defeat at Fredericksburg all the more bitter, and the infamous "Mud March"

On the Confederate side, perhaps the greatest result of the campaign was that it sealed Lee's position as the great military idol of the Confederacy.

in January ended Burnside's brief tenure at army headquarters. The aftermath of Fredericksburg marked a low point for the Army of the Potomac.

Some of Burnside's subordinates, including Joseph Hooker, lobbied with Congress for a change of command. Lincoln replaced Burnside with "Fighting Joe" Hooker. Hooker initially showed great promise as commander of the Army of the Potomac. He brought a combination of talent and extreme ambition to his post. He displayed formidable organizational skills, reinvigorated the Army of the Potomac, and planned a brilliant offensive that got off to a promising start in late April. Correcting Burnside's shortcomings in many areas, Hook improved delivery of supplies and medical care.

General Joseph "Fighting Joe" Hooker.

He also developed a strategic plan that shifted the bulk of his army to an advantageous position behind the Confederate lines at Fredericksburg by the end of April. Lincoln wanted him to focus on Lee's army, not on Richmond. Hook planned a cavalry raid toward Richmond, demonstrating with a large force in Lee's front and swinging the bulk of his army around Lee's left flank and in behind his positions.

But Lee and "Stonewall" Jackson countered Hooker's moves with a dazzling response that seemed to drain all energy and daring from the Federal commander. Having seized the initiative, the badly outnumbered Confederates won a remarkable victory that sent the Union army reeling back across the Rappahannock River in early May.

Hooker's planning and splendid early movements reach a shattering climax in the Battle of Chancellorsville on May 1–4. Hooker abandoned his offensive intentions when Lee (after dividing his forces) attacked on May 1 instead of retreating toward Richmond. On May 2, Lee split his army again as "Stonewall" Jackson marched around Hooker's right flank and delivered a crushing attack against the XI Corps (commanded by O. O. Howard). Jackson was wounded by his own men while returning from nighttime reconnaissance. On May 3–4, Confederate attacks against two parts of Hooker's army persuaded the Union commander to retreat back across the Rappahannock.

The Battle of Chancellorsville, with 17,000 Union and 13,000 Confederate casualties, had significant short- and long-term consequences:

- It depressed Northern civilian morale and gave impetus to critics of the Lincoln Administration.

- Jackson's death on May 10 dealt a blow to the Confederacy.

- The manner in which Lee won the victory made him and his Army of Northern Virginia the focus of Confederate national morale. ■

Essential Reading

Hattaway and Jones, *How the North Won: A Military History of the Civil War*, chapters 11–13.

McPherson, *Battle Cry of Freedom: The Civil War Era*, chapters 19, 21.

Supplementary Reading

Catton, *Glory Road*, parts 1–4.

Freeman, *Lee's Lieutenants: A Study in Command*, vol. 2, chapters 20–23.

Gallagher, ed., *The Fredericksburg Campaign: Decision on the Rappahannock*.

Sears, *Chancellorsville*.

1. Lee expressed disappointment with the battles of Fredericksburg and Chancellorsville, because he did not inflict crippling damage on the Army of the Potomac. Was this a reasonable evaluation? Or did Lee overlook the positive nonmilitary effects of his victories?

2. How do you think you would have reacted to events in Virginia during the winter of 1862 and the spring of 1863 as a Union soldier? As a Northern civilian?

The War in Virginia, Winter and Spring 1862–63
Lecture 21—Transcript

This lecture will continue our examination of military events in the late autumn and winter of 1862 and the spring of 1863. Our topics will be two major campaigns in the Eastern Theater that unfolded while William S. Rosecrans and Ulysses S. Grant were campaigning in Tennessee and along the Mississippi River out west.

We'll begin by looking at Abraham Lincoln's decision to remove George B. McClellan as commander of the Army of the Potomac and replace him with Ambrose C. Burnside. Then we'll examine Burnside's strategic planning and the disastrous Union Defeat at Fredericksburg and its bitter aftermath for the North. We'll finish up with a discussion of Burnside's successor, Joseph Hooker, known as "Fighting Joe" Hooker, and Hooker's ignominious defeat at the hands of Lee and Stonewall Jackson in the Chancellorsville campaign.

We'll start with a look at the Lincoln administration and its attempts in the fall of 1862 to come up with a winning commander and a winning strategy in the Eastern Theater. Lincoln, who'd been impatient with McClellan at many points during his relationship with that troublesome general, finally lost all faith in McClellan in the aftermath of the Battle of Antietam, and this time he decided to remove him once and for all.

The reason he did it is because McClellan was simply not showing any indication that he would go after Robert E. Lee and try to deal a real blow to the Army of Northern Virginia.

McClellan was a Democrat, as we've seen, and he was becoming, in the eyes of Republicans—not just Lincoln but Republicans in Congress—far more obnoxious in his willingness to say that he thought emancipation was a mistake, to say that the Republicans were running the war in the wrong way. He was crossing the line that military figures should not cross. He should have stayed in the military sphere believed many Republicans, but he insisted on making known his views about political issues. That was a problem.

But a bigger problem, from Lincoln's point of view, was that McClellan waited a month before he began to pursue Lee after the Battle of Antietam, and when he did begin his pursuit, he moved very slowly. It took his army six days to cross the Potomac River. Lee's army had crossed in one night after the Battle of Antietam. At one point McClellan telegraphed Washington, saying that he couldn't go after Lee until he had replacements for a number of his horses, horses that were worn out. An exasperated Lincoln sarcastically replied, in one of his famous notes to a general, "Will you pardon me for asking what the horses of your army have done since the Battle of Antietam that fatigues anything?"

There clearly was a problem between the Commander-in-Chief and his general. In the end, Lincoln got rid of McClellan. He waited until the day after the elections in November of 1862 because he was afraid that, if he removed McClellan earlier, it might alienate Democratic voters. At any rate, McClellan was gone.

On November 7, 1862, Ambrose E. Burnside was the new commander of the biggest army of the United States. Burnside was reluctant to take this high command. He probably had a better understanding of his own limitations than Lincoln did. He didn't think that this should have been his position, but he accepted it.

He was relatively young—38 years old—and a graduate of West Point who had had a really uneventful pre-war career. He resigned in 1853 and took up residence in Rhode Island. (He'd later be a prominent politician in Rhode Island after the war.) There he designed a breech-loading rifle. It was called the Burnside rifle. It was a weapon that was used fairly widely during the Civil War. He was nominated to Congress as a Democrat. He eventually went into the railroad business, as George B. McClellan had in that period before the war.

Burnside, by all accounts, was a very affable, popular man. He had many friends, and his friends were loyal to him. He'd won several victories early in the war off the North Carolina coast. He had won promotion and quite a reputation with those victories. He had fought at Antietam as one of McClellan's principal subordinates. He was an uncomplicated, straightforward man in many ways. About six feet tall, he was massive in appearance. He was bald, and he wore his whiskers in a famous cut. His whiskers swept down his chin and then up to form his mustache. His chin was clean-shaven. This was called, at the time, "the Burnside cut," and we get our expression "sideburns" from Ambrose Burnside's whiskers.

A telling assessment of him, and it's one that could be taken different ways, of course, was, "Burnside is a brick." Now, that could either mean that he's solid, or it could mean that he's immovable or dense. It could mean a lot of things, but that is what one observer said about him. His personal courage was unquestioned. His intellectual capacity to command an army of more than 100,000 men, however, was something else entirely. I think Burnside, on some level, knew that he probably wasn't up to it.

He certainly understood that his civilian superiors expected action from him, a winter campaign just as Rosecrans had carried out in Tennessee, and he put together a plan quite quickly. He tried to think of this in a very straightforward way. His army was spread out near Warrenton on the Orange and Alexandria Railroad. He decided to move rapidly toward Fredericksburg, Virginia, to try to beat Lee's army to Fredericksburg. Lee's army was spread out near Culpepper, part of it in the Shenandoah Valley. He would get to Fredericksburg before Lee did and then be in a position to move straight toward Richmond around the Richmond, Fredericksburg, and Potomac Railroad. If he could beat Lee to Fredericksburg, he'd put Lee in a difficult position.

He thought he could march swiftly and come up a success, and his campaign began very well. He did march swiftly to Fredericksburg. He beat Lee to Fredericksburg. He was at that old colonial city by November 19, 1862, but he needed pontoon boats so that he could build bridges and get his army across the river. He was on the east bank of the river; he needed to get to the western side.

It wasn't his fault that the pontoon boats weren't there. It was a mix-up on the logistical side for the Federals, but the bottom line was that he sat and waited at Fredericksburg—and waited and waited. The days went by; the pontoon boats didn't arrive. By the time the boats did arrive so that the bridges could be built, Lee had reacted to Burnside's move, and Lee had put the bulk of his army into very strong positions west of the Rappahannock on a series of hills that paralleled the river. When his entire army was concentrated, which was just before the Battle of Fredericksburg, Lee would have 75,000 men. Burnside's army was probably close to 120,000.

Well, Burnside probably should have adjusted his plan when the pontoon boats didn't come and when Lee's army went into position, but he didn't. He stuck with his original plan to cross at Fredericksburg, and that is what he did. Beginning on December 11, 1862, in the morning, the Union engineers pushed out into the river and began to construct their pontoon bridges. Confederate soldiers firing from the shelter of buildings in Fredericksburg drove them back time and again. The Union artillery from the east bank of the Rappahannock responded by shelling the old city of Fredericksburg, and much of Fredericksburg was destroyed in this shelling.

The pontoon boats eventually were laid. Union troops went across in boats—sort of assault boats—and formed beachheads on the Confederate side of the river, and that permitted the engineers to finish the pontoon bridges, and the Army of the Potomac began to cross the river.

It was an incredible panorama that day, according to all the witnesses. These two enormous armies very close to one another. The terrain was bare. It was a natural amphitheater, really, with the Confederates on the high ground west of the river and the Federals on Stafford Heights, even higher ground east of the river. Both sides could see the movement of huge numbers of troops. There were Federal balloons up in the air on their side of the river, observing the Confederates, and it was just a scene that people remembered. More men probably were visible to soldiers on each side at Fredericksburg than on any other battlefield of the war.

By the end of the day on December 12, the bulk of Burnside's men were in position. Lee had grown very angry during the Union bombardment of Fredericksburg on the eleventh. He said that this was making war on civilians, but Lee's soldiers were using the town for shelter to fire against the Federals, so it seems that it was probably inevitable that the Federals would fire on the city.

What Burnside hoped to accomplish with his battle plan was to apply pressure to the front of Lee's line and try to find a way to get around Lee's right flank or southern flank. If he could do that—interpose part of the Army of the Potomac between Lee's right flank and Richmond, he thought that good things might come of this plan. As fog lifted on the morning of December 13, Burnside ordered assaults along a five-mile front. Stonewall Jackson held the Confederate right flank. The Confederate line was more than six miles long, anchored on the Rappahannock on the left and extending well down toward Hamilton's Crossing on the right.

Jackson commanded the right flank, James Longstreet the left. Longstreet's position was much the stronger of the two. He held high ground. He had ample artillery supporting his infantry. It was an extremely strong position. The first major attacks were against Jackson on the right, and the Federals actually made a breakthrough. They found their way to a swampy piece of ground that wasn't adequately defended. They made a lodgment, but in the end the Union commander on that stretch of the Union line, William Buell Franklin, performed very timidly, I think is not too strong a word. He did not support the breakthrough. He didn't really try with any energy to carry out Burnside's plan to get around Lee's right flank.

The Confederates were able to seal that break on Jackson's end of the line, and fighting died down to the south. The focus of the battle then shifted to the high ground immediately west of Fredericksburg, Marye's Heights, the center of Longstreet's part of the line. For the rest of the day, there were Union assaults by brigades—one after another up a gentle slope, an open plain—right at the Confederates defending Marye's Heights. It was such a strong position that, at one point, a Confederate officer talking with Longstreet earlier in the day—this was a Confederate artillerist—said that he thought a chicken couldn't live on the open field approaching the Confederate line, such was the strength of the Confederate position.

Lee expressed concern to Longstreet at one point. Longstreet said, you might be in trouble on Jackson's end of the line, but, if you give me enough ammunition, I will kill every Union soldier in that army opposing us before they can get to my position. And that is essentially what happened. As wave after wave of Union soldiers went forward, they suffered fearfully. "It was a great slaughter pen," wrote a Federal general. "They might as well have tried to take hell." This was Longstreet's kind of battle. He was on the defensive in a good, sound position, and he very efficiently presided over this part of the fight.

The early winter evening finally brought an end to the sickening spectacle. More than 12,500 Federals had fallen, as well as about 5,500 Confederates, and most of those Confederate casualties were on Jackson's end of the line, not on Longstreet's. That night the temperature dropped to almost freezing. It got down to 34 degrees. It was a very uncomfortable evening for many of the wounded men who were out without any shelter or cover, lying on the field in front of Longstreet's lines. It was a grim and very dramatically negative day for the Army of the Potomac. It was a very bad day for the Army of the Potomac.

Poor Burnside was beside himself as the day went on. He really felt for his men, although he seemed incapable of changing his plans. He at one point thought that he would lead assaults the next day, that he would renew the assaults on December 14 and lead them personally. His generals talked him out of that—that would have been a silly thing to do—and the Army of the Potomac retreated back across the Rappahannock River on December 15.

News of Fredericksburg thoroughly depressed the North. *Harpers Weekly*, a very popular Northern publication at the time, said that the Northern people couldn't take much more. This is how *Harpers Weekly* put it: "The Northern people have borne silently and grimly imbecility, treachery, failure, privation, loss of friends and means, almost every suffering which can afflict a brave people. But they cannot be expected to suffer that such massacres as this at Fredericksburg shall be repeated."

It wasn't just that the Federals had been defeated at Fredericksburg—it was the way they had been defeated. It was the apparent stupidity of sending troops straight at powerfully entrenched and well-positioned Confederate defenders. That kind of a defeat—all those casualties—it all seemed pointless to the people in the North. Lincoln came in for very heavy criticism for his conduct of the war effort. Both Democrats and Republicans criticized him. When he learned of the slaughter at Fredericksburg, Lincoln turned to a friend and said, "If there's a worse place than hell, I am in it." This was a very dark moment for the North, and it got worse in the aftermath of the battle.

Let's just look at the aftermath in the army for a while. Burnside was not a good administrator. Apart from not being a good battlefield tactician, he didn't do the things that you need to do as an army commander. He failed to have supplies flow to the army the way they should. His men actually ran short of uniforms and food and medicine. They weren't paid on time. There was tremendous administrative chaos in the Army of the Potomac in late December and into January 1863. Desertions reached 200 men a day in the Union army, and the men somehow knew that, although there were warehouses nearby bulging with goods, their army commander couldn't get those supplies to them.

Discipline was lax. Many of Burnside's subordinates began to complain behind his back. They talked to members of Congress. They sent word to Lincoln that they weren't happy with how Burnside was doing as an army commander. One of the principal lieutenants doing this was Joseph Hooker, who was letting it be known in Washington that he thought he would do a whole lot better job than Burnside was doing.

In the end, Lincoln decided that Burnside had to go, and he replaced him with Joseph Hooker, "Fighting Joe," as he was known in the press. It was a nickname that he hated. He absolutely detested it. It had come from a typographical error in a newspaper account earlier in the war. The account had meant to read, "Fighting—Joe Hooker [did this or that]." They omitted the dash, and it came out "Fighting Joe Hooker [did whatever it was he was doing]," and the name stuck, much to Hooker's chagrin.

Hooker had intrigued against Burnside. He'd made rash statements about how the nation needed a dictator to win the war, the implication being that perhaps he'd be a fine one if he were selected. Lincoln let Hooker know that he was aware of all of this, that he was aware of the maneuvering, that he was aware of the statements Hooker was making. He added, did Lincoln, "Only generals who gain success can set up dictators. What I now ask of you is military success. I will risk the dictatorship."

Let's move on to Hooker's tenure as army commander. He was a West Pointer, another one of our West Pointers. He was a handsome man, a bachelor. He cut a wide swath through the social scene of the army. He liked women very much. He was seen in the company of good-looking women so often, in fact, that the rumor spread in the army that the term "hooker" to apply to a prostitute came from Joseph Hooker's name. It didn't—that term much predates Hooker—but the point is people believed it did because Hooker ran a very convivial headquarters and seemed to be a man who wasn't adverse to having a good time himself or letting other people have a good time.

He had showed himself to be a hard fighter in the past, and he'd been wounded at Antietam. He'd fought in the Seven Days. Now he proved to be a brilliant organizer. He was good at all the things that Burnside had showed himself not to be good at. Food and medicine flowed to the army. Camps were cleaned up. Medical care improved dramatically. The number of men on sick leave dropped dramatically. Pay came to the soldiers. Drill was increased and improved, and the men's spirits lifted.

Soon Hooker bragged that he had the finest army on the planet. "This is the very best one," he said, "in this continent or any other continent." He said that it really wasn't a question of whether he was going to capture Richmond; it was only a question of when he was going to capture Richmond. He said he hoped God would have mercy on Robert E. Lee because he, Joe Hooker, was not going to have mercy on Robert E. Lee.

These kinds of statements raised a red flag with Abraham Lincoln and many people behind the lines. Lincoln resorted to one of his sort of rural stories to make his point when he heard that Hooker had been talking this way, bragging about all the great things that he was going to do. Lincoln said that it always had been his experience that, and I'll quote his anecdote here, "The hen is the wisest of all the animal creation because she never cackles until the egg is laid. A hen at least will wait 'til she's produced something. Hooker's cackling plenty, and he hasn't produced anything on the battlefield yet."

The one point that Lincoln emphasized to Hooker was that, when you do come to grips with the enemy, put in all of your men. We're giving you this magnificent army—use it. Use all of it. Lincoln and Halleck also urged Hooker to make Lee's army, rather than Richmond, his chief objective. Lincoln knew how important victories were to the Northern public, and he knew especially how much they looked toward what happened in the east to decide whether the war was going well or not. What he wanted from Hooker was a clear victory over Lee's army, a victory that would give the Northern people a sense that the war was going well in Virginia.

Hooker put together an excellent plan for his campaign, really one of the best plans that any Union commander put together during the war. These were its main components. First, the armies are where they were right after the Battle of Fredericksburg: Lee and those works, those six to seven miles of works, west of the river overlooking Fredericksburg, and the Army of the Potomac right across the river. Hooker said that he would send his cavalry on a great raid behind Lee's army toward Richmond where it could disrupt communications between Lee and his capital. He would leave 40,000 infantry under John Sedgwick in front of Lee at Fredericksburg. Sedgwick would hold Lee's attention at Fredericksburg.

Sedgwick would make demonstrations and try to convince Lee that perhaps the Federals were going to try again what they had tried at the Battle of Fredericksburg back in December. Hooker himself would take the bulk of his infantry, more than 70,000 of them, on a long turning movement. They would march up the Rappahannock River, get behind Lee's left flank, and then cross the Rappahannock and the Rapidan River and come in against the rear of the Army of Northern Virginia. That was the plan. Hooker's hammer, so to speak, would crush Lee's army against Sedgwick's anvil at Fredericksburg, or Lee would have to retreat southward, in which case Hooker would harass him as he went toward Richmond.

Hooker had nearly 120,000 men to carry out this plan. Lee had only about 60,000 to oppose him. It had been a very tough winter on the Confederates. The fodder over the countryside of central Virginia, northern Virginia, had been stripped clean of forage for animals and food for men, and Lee had been forced to disperse his army rather widely. Much of the cavalry of Jeb

Stuart's cavalry wasn't even with the army. It had been sent far away so the animals could have enough forage. And James Longstreet and two of his four divisions had been sent to southside Virginia toward Suffolk on what was, in effect, a large-scale foraging expedition. They wouldn't even be present for the battle that was looming with Hooker. So Lee has only about 60,000 men—very long odds.

All right, let's look at how the campaign unfolded. Hooker made a good beginning. He got around Lee's flank just as he hoped he would. This is in late April. He crossed the Rappahannock, crossed the Rapidan, and got behind Lee. By the evening of April 30, thousands of Federals were in front of Lee at Fredericksburg—that's Sedgwick's men—but Hooker with the bulk of the army was about 10 miles in Lee's rear at a crossroads called Chancellorsville. This wasn't a town. It was just an old inn on a main road that came into Fredericksburg from the west.

Hooker thought he had Lee right where he wanted him. He thought Lee would either retreat toward Richmond, thus exposing his army to attacks from the Federals, or he would have to turn around and try to fight Hooker, in which case he would be vulnerable to Sedgwick coming from the other direction. Whatever Lee tries to do, reasoned Hooker, he's going to be in bad shape.

But, typically, Lee did not do what was expected. He decided to split his own army. He left about 10,000 men in the works at Fredericksburg to watch Sedgwick, and he hurried the rest of his army westward to confront Joe Hooker. Lee hoped that he could stymie Hooker in an area that was called the "wilderness of Spotsylvania" or just the "wilderness." It was several dozen square miles of scrub oak and other scrub vegetation. It was an area that had been cut over more than once—the big trees cut to feed charcoaling operations tied to iron furnaces in the area. There were very few farms and very few clearings in this wooded area and not very many roads.

It was an area where the Union numbers might not be brought fully to bear and where Union artillery really wouldn't be much of a factor at all. If Hooker were pinned in the wilderness and fought in the wilderness, the difference in numbers wouldn't matter as much. What Hooker needed to do was just march a few miles east (about three) of Chancellorsville and break into the open where his numbers really could tell.

On the morning of May 1, that's just what he started to do. The Union troops took three roads to the east. Marching eastward, they were just about clear of the wilderness when they ran into Stonewall Jackson's troops near a place called Zoan Church. At the first contact Hooker ordered a withdrawal. He called all his troops back down into the wilderness to Chancellorsville. That is the key moment of the entire campaign. There hadn't been much fighting—just a few shots exchanged, in fact—but Hooker had absolutely lost his nerve. There's no other way to explain it. At the first contact with Lee, he lost his nerve. He pulled his army back and put it into a defensive position.

That is when the Battle of Chancellorsville was decided. There were going to be three days of very hard fighting ahead, but Hooker, I believe, was already a beaten man on the morning of May 1, 1863. Lee now had the initiative, and he decided to split his army again. He and Stonewall Jackson met on the night of May 1 and decided to try to send Jackson's part of the army around Hooker's right flank and roll up Hooker's right flank with a massive assault. Local people helped them find a network of roads that would allow them to do that, and, on May 2, Lee, with just 14,000 men, held Hooker's attention at Chancellorsville while Jackson took about 28,000 and, in the most famous flanking march of the war, put his second corps astride Hooker's right flank and launched a very famous assault about five o'clock on the afternoon of the second.

He shattered the Union 11th Corps, commanded by O. O. Howard. The poor Union soldiers should have been warned, but they weren't. They were caught by surprise and driven back about two miles. Nightfall came, however, and the Confederate attack lost its momentum. Jackson rode forward to try to find a way to maintain that momentum, and, in the darkness and the smoke and the confusion of the wilderness, his party rode into the path of a Confederate regiment that was firing a volley, not at them but in another direction, and a number of the missiles from that volley hit Jackson. He was carried to the rear with three wounds. His left arm was amputated that night. When Jackson went down, the attack lost all of its steam. When Lee learned that his great lieutenant had been wounded, he said, "He has lost his left arm, but I have lost my right," and he, in fact, had lost his greatest lieutenant.

The Confederates were still divided at Chancellorsville. The bulk of Hooker's army was still in between Jackson's part of the force and Lee's part of the force. But, on the morning of May 3, hard fighting by the Confederates enabled Lee to unite those two wings of his army. Hooker had no offensive thoughts whatsoever, although he vastly outnumbered Lee. Meanwhile, Sedgwick had pushed the 10,000 Confederates out of Fredericksburg and was marching toward Chancellorsville.

So, for a third time, Lee divided his army. He left about 25,000 men to hold Hooker near Chancellorsville and took the rest of his troops eastward to deal with Sedgwick. On May 3 and 4, in the Battle of Salem Church, Sedgwick's part of the Union army was defeated as well, and, by night of May 6, the Army of the Potomac had retreated back across the Rappahannock. It had been a bloody campaign: 17,000 Federal casualties; 13,000 Confederate casualties. By far the most important of those 13,000 was Stonewall Jackson.

This was Lee's most brilliant victory, a primer on the bold use of veteran troops in the face of a superior foe in numbers but a foe that didn't have as good a leadership. It was also perhaps the South's most costly victory, for, on May 10, Stonewall Jackson died of pneumonia that probably arose from complications related to his wounds on May 2.

News of Chancellorsville hit the North very, very hard. Lincoln's face literally went pale, according to witnesses, when he learned that Lee had again defeated the Army of the Potomac. "My God," he said. "My God, what will the country say?" Coming so soon after the defeat at Fredericksburg, this seemed to be an enormously bad piece of news for the North. Antiwar elements in the North, the Copperheads among the Democrats, and others took heart. It became a much more difficult situation for Lincoln.

On the Confederate side, perhaps the greatest result of the campaign was that it sealed Lee's position as the great military idol of the Confederacy. He'd had a year now in command, and, from the Seven Days to Second Manassas, through the Maryland campaign and Fredericksburg and Chancellorsville, he had demonstrated to the Confederate people that he and his army would win the kind of victories that they craved, the forward-moving, aggressive victories. They became by far the most important national institution in the Confederacy. They would be, for the rest of the war, the great rallying point for the Confederate people. Chancellorsville, as much as anything else that Lee did, sealed his reputation as a great commander.

So we'll leave the armies here in Virginia now. In our next lecture we'll continue with our military narrative of 1863, and we'll look at Lee's attempt to build on his success at Fredericksburg and Chancellorsville by taking the war across the Potomac River for a second time.

Gettysburg
Lecture 22

We'll look at the Gettysburg campaign and then consider the impact of Gettysburg at the time. How did people view it at the time as opposed to how we do now? We'll finish by considering the question of whether Gettysburg should be seen as the great turning point of the Civil War.

The Gettysburg campaign took place against a background of uncertainty and unrest in the North prompted by defeats at Fredericksburg and Chancellorsville in the Eastern Theater, stalemate in Tennessee, and failure along the Mississippi River. Antiwar sentiment among civilians was growing, and the antiwar Democrats ("Copperheads") became more vociferous. The new Union draft law of 1863 (see Lecture 18) alienated many Northerners. And Lincoln had little faith in Hooker after Chancellorsville.

As Lincoln looked for good news from some theater, Jefferson Davis and his advisers discussed how best to allocate precious Southern military resources. Many Confederates argued for weakening Lee's army to reinforce commands west of the Appalachians, but Lee successfully lobbied for a second invasion across the Potomac. Many politicians and generals favored stripping troops from Lee to reinforce Braxton Bragg in Tennessee or John C. Pemberton at Vicksburg. But Lee argued for concentration of troops in Virginia for an invasion of the North.

Lee won the debate and promised a range of possible benefits: The invasion would relieve pressure against Richmond, strengthen antiwar sentiment in the North, and allow the army to provision itself in the rich Pennsylvania countryside and take pressure off Southern agriculture. It also might compel the Federals to shift troops from the West to deal with Lee's army. The campaign carried

Union success, Confederate disaster [in the Gettysburg campaign]—it simply wasn't that simple at the time. It did not mark the decisive turning point of the war.

out in June and July 1863 resulted in a clash at Gettysburg, Pennsylvania, that turned out to be the war's largest battle and the last major engagement fought on Northern soil.

The initial phase of the campaign generally went well for the Confederates. Lee reorganized the army after Stonewall Jackson's death in May. There were now three corps: the First, under Longstreet; the Second, under Ewell; and the Third, under A. P. Hill. A huge cavalry battle at Brandy Station on June 9 caused a short delay in Lee's advance. This battle was the first time that the Union cavalry had fought on even terms with the Confederate cavalry. Southern papers criticized the cavalry commander, J. E. B. Stuart, after this battle.

Confederate cavalry commander General J. E. B. Stuart.

Lee's infantry marched quickly northward after Brandy Station. The Confederates won a small victory at Second Winchester en route to the Potomac. By the third week of June, the Army of Northern Virginia was spread out across southern Pennsylvania, almost as far north as Harrisburg. Lee was moving without firm intelligence because "Jeb" Stuart and much of his cavalry lost contact with the army. Meanwhile, Lincoln replaced Hooker with George G. Meade on 27 June 1863. He was the fourth commander in seven months for the Army of the Potomac. He was an engineer and a capable, but not brilliant, professional officer.

The armies made contact near Gettysburg on June 30 and fought the largest battle of the war on July 1–3, 1863. The first day was a striking Confederate success, despite the fact that Lee's forces were not concentrated or coordinated. Two Union infantry corps were badly mauled. The Federals just managed to hang on to high ground south of Gettysburg. Meade himself arrived on the field that night; more troops from both sides also arrived.

Lee continued the tactical offensive on the second day (July 2). He has been much criticized for this decision. Despite poor execution, Lee's attacks pushed the Union defenders to the limit on both ends of Meade's line. Lee mounted a last major tactical offensive known as Pickett's Charge on the third day. But this charge against the Union center was not his first plan. It failed completely, and nearly one-half of the attackers became casualties.

Overall, casualties in the battle were enormous. At least 25,000 Confederates fell, representing nearly one-third of the army. One-third (12 out of 53) of Lee's generals were killed, wounded, or captured. More than 20,000 Federals fell; Meade's subordinate command also suffered heavy losses.

Lee retreated on July 4 and crossed the Potomac into Virginia a few days later. Meade drew criticism for not pressing Lee's beaten army. The Confederates hoped Meade would counterattack near the Potomac.

At the time, Gettysburg was seen as an important, but not necessarily decisive, battle. The North expressed a mixture of happiness and disappointment. Lee undoubtedly had been beaten and driven from Union soil. Lincoln and many others believed Meade should have hounded the Confederates after July 3.

Most Confederates did not consider the battle an unequivocal disaster. Confederates maintained faith in Lee and saw Gettysburg as a big and bloody battle that represented a temporary setback at worst. Some Confederates did express disappointment in Lee, but overall his reputation did not suffer.

Gettysburg was not the great turning point of the conflict, but it did represent a setback to the Confederacy and stop the momentum in the Eastern Theater generated by Fredericksburg and Chancellorsville. Lee's losses could not be replaced easily. The campaign probably killed any hope that European powers would intervene in the war. It gave the Army of the Potomac a badly needed victory over Lee's army, which nonetheless remained strong and helped carry the Confederacy to the brink of success a year later during the Overland campaign (see Lecture 36).

A number of factors combined to make Gettysburg seem more important in retrospect: It turned out to be the bloodiest battle of the war, and it represented the last major Confederate invasion of the North. Lincoln's benediction over the Union dead in November 1863 gave Gettysburg a special status. The battlefield is now the most visited Civil War site in America. ■

Essential Reading

Hattaway and Jones, *How the North Won: A Military History of the Civil War*, chapter 13.

McPherson, *Battle Cry of Freedom: The Civil War Era*, chapter 21.

Supplementary Reading

Catton, *Glory Road*, parts 5–6.

Coddington, *The Gettysburg Campaign: A Study in Command*.

Freeman, *Lee's Lieutenants: A Study in Command*, vol. 3, chapters 1–10.

Questions to Consider

1. How did your previous understanding of Gettysburg compare to what you have heard in this lecture?

2. Do you think it is important for Americans to have one Civil War event that is considered to be the watershed of the conflict?

Gettysburg
Lecture 22—Transcript

In our last lecture we looked at the dark Union winter and spring of 1862-63, when Fredericksburg and Chancellorsville and Grant's failure to take Vicksburg sent Union morale plunging to one of its lowest points for the entire war. Now we'll follow military events in the Eastern Theater forward into the summer of 1863. We will examine first the strategic situation in May and June. Then we'll look at the Confederate planning sessions that resulted in the invasion of Pennsylvania in mid-June. We'll look at the Gettysburg campaign and then consider the impact of Gettysburg at the time. How did people view it at the time as opposed to how we do now? We'll finish by considering the question of whether Gettysburg should be seen as the great turning point of the Civil War.

Let's look first at May and June 1863, a time that was seen as very dangerous in the North—dangerous for the cause of the Union by those who were devoted to the Union and also a period of major strategic debate in the Confederacy. The Lincoln government faced both military and political problems in this period of the war. On the military side the absence of victories is the clear problem, Chancellorsville being the most recent example of the failure of a major Union army. But beyond the military side there were serious problems on the Northern political front. The failure of Union armies had encouraged the antiwar sentiment in the North. The Copperheads, the part of the Democratic Party that argued for an end to the war, said that the war was going a way that no one had anticipated. We had supported a war just for the Union, said many of the Copperheads early on, but now you're turning it into a war for emancipation, and we will not support that. We need to end this war and then negotiate with the Confederates.

Lincoln was very concerned about that kind of sentiment in the North, and that kind of sentiment was drawing strength from the inability of Union military forces to deliver the kinds of clear-cut victories on the battlefield that the North needed. The Union draft, which went into effect in the spring of 1863, made the situation worse because it seemed to be a desperate move. Those who were against the war anyway could say, look, not only aren't we winning the war but our government is imposing this tyrannical system whereby they can force us to go fight this war even if we don't want to. The draft helped on the Copperhead side of the ledger. And Lincoln, of course, was floundering in the east in the sense that he didn't have a commander at the head of the Army of the Potomac whom he really trusted. He didn't think that Joseph Hooker was going to deliver the kind of victories that the North would need in the long run. So it's a very cloudy and troubling picture for the North in this stage.

On the Confederate side it's a period of planning. The Confederate civilian and military leaders are trying to figure out what strategy to use against the Union troops in Virginia and the west. Hooker's army still lies opposite Lee's army in northern Virginia along the Rappahannock River near Fredericksburg. Braxton Bragg and William Starke Rosecrans still face each other in the Tennessee Theater where they had been, and, of course, Grant's operations continue against Vicksburg.

In each of these theaters, the Union army was larger than its Confederate opponent, as was almost always the case, and there were other threats on the board as well for the Confederates. There would be a Union campaign against Port Hudson and Nathaniel Banks as May moved along, and the North was also planning a major naval action at Charleston. So the question for the Confederates was, how do we use our resources to best advantage in this very difficult situation?

Well, many of the Confederate leaders said that Virginia's not the most important place. We need to either take troops from Lee's army and reinforce Bragg or take troops from Lee's army and reinforce John C. Pemberton, who was commanding at Vicksburg. In fact, a plan was put forward to that. It was supported by a number of soldiers. Braxton Bragg supported it, P. G. T. Beauregard and James Longstreet in Lee's army supported it, and so did Jefferson Davis. But Lee said, no. That is not the way to look at this.

He, in effect, said this: I can do more good in Virginia by invading the north than anything that our commanders in the west can do even if reinforced from my army. And this is what I think my campaign will do. It will let me pull the war out of Virginia. If I go north the enemy will have to follow me. It will allow us to gather the logistical bounty from our farmers this summer.

It will take the pressure off Virginia, and I can gather supplies north of the Potomac River. This is much like he argued during the Antietam campaign.

He also believed that he could strengthen the peace Democrats in the North. Lee read the newspapers. He knew the Copperheads were a problem for Lincoln. He thought the presence of his army would help. Almost at the bottom of his list, but nonetheless on Lee's list, was at least a slim hope that a really successful campaign north of the Potomac might actually rekindle chances that either England or France would decide to help the Confederacy.

As a sop to those who argued that he should send troops west, Lee said that if he were really successful that maybe Grant and Rosecrans would have to weaken their armies to strengthen Union armies in the east. Now, Lee's been heavily criticized for this. He's been called a man who had Virginia blinders on. He didn't understand the big picture of the war. He always was just thinking of his own army. But, in fact, I think he realized better than any of his critics that the east was more important psychologically. It was more important in terms of morale. Lee knew that his army by that point had become the most important national institution in the Confederacy and that anything he did would likely resonate more powerfully both in a positive sense with the Confederates and a negative sense with the North.

Well, in the end Jefferson Davis decided not to go against Lee's wishes. He went along with his best commander, and the result would be the second invasion of the North by Lee and the Army of Northern Virginia, and let's look at the initial stage of that campaign.

It initially went well. Lee's army was back up to 75,000 men. James Longstreet had rejoined the army after the Battle of Chancellorsville. The army's now divided into three pieces. It had been Longstreet and Stonewall Jackson before. Now it's Longstreet commanding the First Corps, a man named Richard Ewell commanding most of Jackson's old Second Corps, and A. P. Hill, not to be confused with D. H. Hill—there're two Hills who've been fighting in the east—would command the new Third Corps.

By early June the army was ready to move, and just before it went north on June 9, there was a huge cavalry battle near Culpepper, Virginia, where the army was staging for its invasion. Union cavalry under Alfred Pleasanton surprised Jeb Stuart and his Confederate cavalry and fought in this Battle of Brandy Station, an enormous sprawling cavalry action, the biggest ever in the Western hemisphere.

Part of this action took place with troopers fighting on foot, but part of it was an old-fashioned swinging sabers and firing revolvers at each other kind of fight. It involved 10,000 men on each side. In the end, Jeb Stuart was able to hold on and drive the Federals back, but it was a very close call for his command, and it would have repercussions. Southern newspapers said Stuart had been surprised. That was humiliating for Stuart. Stuart had always had his own way with the Federal cavalry, and the Battle of Brandy Station seemed to be, at least to many Confederates behind the lines, almost a defeat for Stuart and his cavalry.

A few words about Stuart are in order here. He's a very important figure in the war in the Eastern Theater. He's a Virginian, a young man, 30 years old at this stage of the war. A West Pointer, he had fought in the Indian Wars in the 1850s. He was a very romantic figure and a real contrast in some ways. He was, on the one hand, a man thoroughly caught up in the romance of war. The women loved Jeb Stuart. They would put garlands on his horse. They'd strew petals in front of his horse when he went by. He was a very romantic figure. He liked to go to balls and stage them. He had a banjo player who accompanied his staff, and they would pick out music on the banjo and sing. He affected a gaudy uniform. He wore very high boots. He wore a plume in his hat. He had a scarlet-lined cape and a big gold sash. He cut a very dashing figure.

He was very well armed. He had a big LaMat revolver and a saber and God knows what else hooked onto his saddle somewhere. He made quite an impression. But with that on the one side, on the other side you have a very capable, hard-bitten cavalryman who was absolutely brilliant at the things cavalry was supposed to do during the Civil War, and that was screening your own army so the enemy doesn't know what you're doing and going out and gathering intelligence about what the enemy is doing. Stuart did not have anyone on either side who exceeded his talents in those areas.

He was probably the best cavalryman, I think, of the war in those classic cavalry functions.

He'd made spectacular rides clear around George McClellan's army twice earlier in the war. He had gotten lots of headlines for it, and now his pride had been stung by Brandy Station. I think that it had an effect—this experience of Brandy—almost immediately in that Stuart determined that he was going to ride around Joseph Hooker's army when he got the chance. His decision to do that was going to mean that Lee would march into Pennsylvania without the benefit of Stuart's intelligence because as Stuart started to ride around Hooker's army, Hooker's army started to march northward, and Stuart found himself on the far side of Hooker's army, moving north as Hooker moved north, and the bulk of Lee's army was to the west of Hooker. So he's going to leave Lee without good intelligence for about three weeks.

Still, the campaign began well for the Confederates. They marched rapidly north. There was a battle called the Second Battle of Winchester in mid-June on the way north. Richard Ewell won a tidy little victory there and captured several thousand Union prisoners. The Confederates made their way to the Potomac River and crossed the river, and, as the third week in June passed, Lee's army was spread out in a big fan-shaped pattern across much of southern Pennsylvania, a part of it at Chambersburg, another part of it under Ewell all the way to the Susquehanna River, not far from Harrisburg, Pennsylvania.

As Lee was marching north, Hooker told Lincoln, now's a great time for me to go capture Richmond, and Lincoln reminded Hooker that he didn't really care about Richmond at this point. The biggest Rebel army was marching toward Union territory. That was Hooker's target, not Richmond. And Lincoln made a mental note that Hooker did not seem anxious to engage Lee in battle again. There was a little quibbling back and forth about just what the best Union response to Lee's movement would be, and at one point there was debate about what to do at Harper's Ferry. Hooker wanted to do one thing, others in the War Department something else, and, in a snit, Hooker submitted his resignation in a quarrel with Henry W. Halleck, and Lincoln accepted it.

So the Army of the Potomac has a change of command in the midst of these very important operations. On June 27, Lincoln named George Gordon Meade, who was commanding the Fifth Corps in the Army of the Potomac, to be the army's chief. This is the fourth commander in just seven months for the Army of the Potomac. They've had McClellan and then Burnside and then Hooker and now Meade—no continuity at the top.

Meade learned of his appointment in the predawn hours of June 28, 1863. Meade wasn't Lincoln's first choice, and he didn't really want the job, and who can blame him? Here he's thrust into command in the midst of circumstances he doesn't fully understand and with orders to take care of the threat to the Republic posed by Lee and his army, the premier Rebel army. He had to act immediately.

He'd been born in Spain into the family of a wealthy American merchant. He was 47 years old, a graduate of West Point, and a veteran of the Mexican War. When I describe all these army commanders, you can fill out the blocks by now. There're all pretty much the same ones. They're all West Pointers; most of them fought in the Mexican War.

Meade had a good enough record from the Mexican War. He was primarily an engineer before the war. He's not one of the men who got out of the army. He commanded different levels from the beginning of the war, the Civil War, on. He was a brigade commander and then a division commander and then a corps commander. He had led at each level with skill, if not brilliance. He was tall and thin, with very heavy bags under his eyes. He was balding. He wore glasses.

He was very touchy and given to outbursts of anger. His temper would go off very, very quickly. He had a tendency to lash out in the heat of the moment. That temper, together with the glasses and the bags under his eyes, caused some people to give him a very unusual nickname. They called him a "damned old goggle-eyed snapping turtle." It's too long a nickname to really work. A good nickname has to be shorter, but that's what some soldiers called Meade.

He was a Democrat, as were most of the top commanders in the Army of the Potomac, but he had the good sense to keep his political opinions private. He talked about politics with his wife, but he didn't parade the fact that he disagreed with the Republican administration about various things.

As a soldier he had several strengths. He was a master of logistics, which is important. He had a very well-developed ability to grasp how many troops were engaged on a battlefield. He had a good sense on the battlefield of following the ebb and flow, and he had a great eye for ground as an engineer. He really did have a grasp of topography. He was not brilliant but a thoroughly sound soldier who was likely to do at least a competent job as commander of the Army of the Potomac.

Well, as Lee marched north he'd thought that the antiwar faction in the North would benefit from his presence in Pennsylvania. My presence will give them ammunition in their work against the Lincoln administration. But it really didn't work out that way. The North grew closer together for the most part in the face of an invading enemy. They were defending home soil and so forth.

The only state that really didn't do well was Pennsylvania itself, which did not forge a really praiseworthy record with Lee and his army inside the borders of the commonwealth. Pittsburgh said it would contribute more troops if Philadelphia would, and Philadelphia said it would if Harrisburg would, and Harrisburg said it would if Pittsburgh would. There wasn't a rush to the colors in Pennsylvania, and there was a good deal of antipathy toward Pennsylvania on the part of other Northern states, which argued, we're doing our bit to save Pennsylvania and the Pennsylvanians themselves aren't doing what they should.

Lee felt Stuart's absence more and more as the campaign went on. Lee, in fact, thought Hooker was still back in Virginia at a time when the Army of the Potomac had been in motion for a long time. It wasn't until June 28 that Lee found out that the Army of the Potomac had crossed the Potomac River and that George Meade was now in command. And he didn't learn it from Stuart—he learned it from Longstreet, who had heard it from a man named Harrison, who was a paid spy for Longstreet.

Once Lee found out that the Army of the Potomac was in pursuit, he ordered his army to come together. He didn't want it to be spread out across all of Pennsylvania, part of Pennsylvania, as it had been. He wanted it to come back together so that he could face the Federals as a powerful body. The place he selected was an area between Gettysburg and the South Mountain range, just a few miles to the west of Gettysburg. A number of roads led in there, so Lee gave orders on the twenty-eighth for his army to reconcentrate, and the army began to march, the pieces of it, toward that concentration. Lee didn't want to fight a battle until his army was back together.

But let's move on now to see how the battle was actually fought. It did take place before all of the army was back together. The armies made contact on June 30, brief contact. The real battle started on July 1, when one of Lee's divisions under Henry Heath, part of A. P. Hill's Third Corps, sort of wandered toward Gettysburg to see what was there and ran into some Federal cavalry under John Buford, two brigades of cavalry under Buford. If Jeb Stuart had been there doing his job, this never would have happened because Stuart would have known the Federal cavalry was there.

As it was, that Confederate infantry blundered into the cavalry, and what began as a clash between a much stronger Confederate infantry unit and Federal cavalry escalated very rapidly into a full-scale battle as both sides poured reinforcements in. The Confederates were very lucky on July 1 because A. P. Hill came in from the west toward Gettysburg, and, in a very absolutely serendipitous piece of luck, Richard Ewell's Second Corps of the Confederate army approached from the north just a little bit past noon in the perfect position to come in on the flank of the main defending Union force, the Union First Corps, which was facing west—west of Gettysburg—facing Hill's troops.

Lee rode onto the field early in the afternoon. He hadn't wanted a big battle, but, as he stood on Herr Ridge and then on Seminary Ridge and looked at the battle unfolding in front of him, he saw a great opportunity. There were two Union corps on the field, the First Corps facing west and the Eleventh Corps facing north. Lee saw that his troops were coming in in a position to threaten that Federal line that curved in a big arc around Gettysburg, north and west of Gettysburg. Lee gave the orders to push the assaults, and, by the end of the day on July 1, two Federal corps had been shattered. Outnumbered Union soldiers in those corps put up a stout defense, especially the Union First Corps. Half of the First Corps became casualties on the first day at Gettysburg.

The famous Iron Brigade, the most famous unit in the Army of the Potomac, lost two-thirds of its men—1,200 out of 1,800—in fighting on July 1. The Federal troops were driven back through Gettysburg, and they clung to high ground south of town, Cemetery Hill, East Cemetery Hill, by the evening of July 1. Many argued later that the Confederates could have accomplished more, and Lee hoped that at the time. He'd instructed Richard Ewell, who was over on the Confederate left flank, to push against that high ground where the Federal troops were rallying, if practicable. Ewell decided that there were factors that militated against his attacking, and he didn't in the end. I think he had good reasons for that.

But what really matters is that the first day ended as a striking Confederate tactical success, one of the best tactical days in all the history of the Army of Northern Virginia, Lee's army having pushed the Federals through town into that high ground. That night George Meade arrived on the field, Union reinforcements poured into the area, and James Longstreet's troops approached the field as well. All were there but George Pickett's division, which was in the rear.

The question for Lee on the night of the first was, all right, I've won a victory today. Now, do I keep attacking, or do I go on the defensive and let the Federals attack me? Meade would almost certainly have to attack Lee to drive him out of Pennsylvania. But Lee, always the audacious commander, decided to continue his assaults on the second day. Longstreet didn't like the idea, and Longstreet would sulk for the rest of the battle. But Lee decided on the second to try to attack both ends of the Union line, the Union right at Culps Hill and the Union left flank, which, at that point, was somewhere, as far as Lee knew, on Cemetery Ridge.

Lee did not get what he wanted on the second day. He wanted early assaults. It was late in the afternoon before the Confederates got going, partly because Longstreet had dallied in putting his troops in position. When the attacks did come, Longstreet attacked, the Union left and almost captured the high ground at Little Round Top, and Richard Ewell's troops almost captured the high ground on Culps Hill. It was a very frustrating day for Lee. He was close on both ends of the line, but he didn't quite succeed.

He was, on the night of the second of July, confronting the same question: Do I keep attacking now? I've tried it for two days. Or do I take up a defensive position now? He decided yet again to attack, using the same plan he'd had on the second, pressure against both ends of the Union line. But factors on the morning of July 3, the third day of the battle, prevented that plan from being carried out. The Federals attacked before Lee could get going on the Culps Hill end of the line, so that wouldn't work, and Longstreet argued that his divisions, which had fought so hard on July 2 on the Union left, weren't up to fighting again.

And Lee fell back to another plan, which came to be known as Pickett's Charge. This was a major assault against the center of the Union line on Cemetery Ridge. Thirteen thousand Confederates of George Pickett's division and two other divisions, commanded on the third by Isaac Ridgeway Trimble and Johnston Pettigrew, would cover about seven-tenths of a mile in the most famous infantry assault of the war against the center of Meade's position.

And they would fail, of course. It was, in retrospect, this gallant, doomed assault. About half of the men in the assault were shot down. Most of the field officers and many of the brigadier generals became casualties. It was a complete failure, this assault on July 3, 1863, at Gettysburg. Lee immediately rode out among the survivors of this assault and said, it's all my fault. He took immediate responsibility on the scene, and it *was* his fault. It had been his decision. It hadn't worked. He patched together a defensive line.

Poor Meade, I think, was in a state of at least partial shock because of the scale of this battle and the chaos of it and the fact that he'd just repulsed this major Confederate attack. He didn't try to launch a counterattack. There might have been some opportunity then, but, at any rate, he didn't, and that was the end of the fighting at Gettysburg.

363

The casualties were simply enormous. There were at least 25,000 Confederate casualties; at least a third of Lee's army had been shot down. Meade's army had been larger, more than 85,000 men. He lost more than 20,000, probably 23,000. The casualties were near or perhaps a bit more than 50,000 killed, wounded, and missing for the three-day battle. It had been a hard battle on general officers. Lee took 52 generals into the campaign with him; 17 of them were killed, wounded, or missing. On the Union side, there were terrible losses among the commanders, even the corps commanders. Winfield Scott Hancock of the Second Corps was wounded. Daniel Sickles of the Third Corps lost a leg in the fighting on the second. It was a horrible, brutal battle at Gettysburg with absolutely enormous casualties.

Lee retreated on the 4th of July, the 4th of July. Northerners read a lot into that, that they had a victory on the anniversary of the Declaration of Independence, and Meade allowed him to get away. I think that there was only a very narrow window for Meade to do much to hurt Lee, and I think that probably was right after the Pickett/Pettigrew assault. Once Lee disengaged from Meade's army and got down near the Potomac River, I think Union attacks would not have been a good thing. At any rate, the Confederates got away from the battlefield and settled into a strong position along the Potomac River, and that was the end of the fighting in the campaign.

Well, how was it seen at the time? We see Gettysburg now as this enormous battle, perhaps the most important battle of the war. At the time, it was a much more mixed view. The North was certainly happy about it on the one hand. Lee had been driven out of Pennsylvania. It was clearly a victory for the North. But many people in the North believed that it should have been and could have been a bigger victory. Meade should have followed up his success on July 3. He should have inflicted greater damage on the Confederate army, perhaps even destroyed the Confederate army believed many Northerners. I'm not saying this was possible, but this is how it was interpreted at the time. Lincoln was very much disappointed that Meade didn't do more damage to the Confederate army.

On the Confederate side, Gettysburg was not seen as an unequivocal disaster. It simply was not. It was seen as a battle where the Confederates won the first day's fighting clearly, attacked gallantly and almost succeeded on the second day, and then attacked and fought well again on the third day. They weren't driven from the field, argued Confederates behind the lines. They left of their own volition. They weren't pursued. So it wasn't a success, but it was not a disaster.

And Gettysburg did not have any significant negative influence on Lee's reputation in the Confederacy. Some Confederates expressed disappointment. Some criticized Lee. Wade Hampton, a cavalry officer in Lee's army, criticized Lee for launching assaults against that strong Union line on the third, for example. But, for the most part, Confederates did not see Gettysburg as a great defeat that in any way tarnished Lee's reputation. Confederates, writing months after Gettysburg, still in their letters and diaries, would describe Lee as unbeaten as a commander and a man who would never be vanquished.

So we need to be careful about interpreting Gettysburg's importance at the time and not see it as a great Union victory that cast gloom across the Confederacy and convinced many Confederates they were about to lose the war, which brings us to our last point here.

Was Gettysburg the great turning point of the conflict? It's often presented, at least in tandem with Vicksburg, as a sort of fulcrum. The war is tipping one way before Gettysburg and Vicksburg, and then, after those Confederate defeats, the fulcrum tips the other way, and it points straight toward Appomattox. Appomattox is inevitable after Gettysburg. That is a very common notion. Well, it did represent a setback. It stopped Lee's string of victories, so, in that sense, it's a noteworthy campaign. I'm not arguing that it wasn't an important campaign; it was.

It stopped Confederate momentum in the Eastern Theater that had been generated by Fredericksburg and Chancellorsville. Lee's losses couldn't be replaced easily. They were horrible losses. And it probably killed any chance that Europe might intervene in the war. That's probably true as well. It gave the Federals a badly needed victory and boosted Northern morale, as we've seen. But Lee's army remained strong, and it remained a major force in the field for nearly two more years.

Now we think Gettysburg probably should be seen as the turning point because we know a number of things about it that people didn't know at the time. We know that it was, for example, the biggest battle of the war. There wasn't going to be a bigger one. Nobody knew that at the time. They knew it was a big battle; they didn't know it was going to be the biggest battle. We know now it was the last time that Lee invaded the North. No one knew that at the time. We know that now. We know that Lincoln gave his eloquent benediction over the Union dead at Gettysburg. That makes it seem more important. Again, that was in the future at the time. That wasn't part of the balance of how to assess it within the context of the summer of 1863.

We also know, beyond those things, that it's the most visited Civil War site in the United States now by far, which also seems to give it a special position as an especially important Civil War battle. All of the things we know about it now make Gettysburg drift up in our estimation as a great turning point. I'll just say again that, at the time, it did not loom as large as it does to us now. It was a more gray matter of deciding how important it was than black and white. Union success, Confederate disaster—it simply wasn't that simple at the time. It did not mark the decisive turning point of the war. Even in tandem with Vicksburg it did not. The war would go on; the Confederacy would still have chances to win the war.

We'll next turn our attention to that other battle often yoked with Gettysburg, that is, Vicksburg, and see how Grant successfully completed his campaign against that Southern stronghold.

Vicksburg, Port Hudson, and Tullahoma
Lecture 23

We continue our military focus on the summer of 1863 with this lecture on campaigning along the Mississippi River and in Tennessee. We'll begin with a survey of the strategic situation in the West in the spring of 1863, and then we'll move on to examine Grant's successful campaign against Vicksburg. ... Then we'll look at the Port Hudson campaign.

As spring approached in 1863, Grant continued his efforts to capture the Confederate stronghold at Vicksburg, and Rosecrans and Bragg faced each other in middle Tennessee (they had engaged in no major action since the battle of Stones River). A third Union force, under Nathaniel P. Banks, was closing in on Port Hudson, Louisiana, the Confederacy's other remaining strong point on the Mississippi River. Lincoln and Union planners believed the Mississippi, which figured prominently in the Anaconda strategy laid out by Winfield Scott two years earlier, along with middle Tennessee, would witness the crucial action that summer.

Undaunted by his previous lack of success against Vicksburg, Grant put together one of the war's most impressive military campaigns between mid-April and early July. His two main opponents would be John C. Pemberton, who had about 32,000 men, the principal army defending Vicksburg, and Joseph E. Johnston, who had recovered from the terrible wound that he received in the Battle of Seven Pines back in May of 1862.

Against the advice of many subordinates, Grant ordered supporting naval vessels to run past the powerful Vicksburg batteries; mustered his troops south of the city; marched inland to seize Jackson, Mississippi; and advanced against Vicksburg from the east. Part of Grant's greatness lay in his willingness to take chances. The Navy passed the batteries with minimal losses.

Grant then crossed to the eastern bank and marched inland toward Jackson before moving against Vicksburg from the east. Confederates failed to unite their forces, while Grant and Sherman did hook up successfully. Grant cast off from his base and won victories over various parts of Johnston's force of 16,000 and Pemberton's army of 32,000 at Port Gibson (May 1), Raymond (May 12), Jackson (May 14), Champion Hill (May 16), and the Big Black River (May 17) before pinning Pemberton inside the defenses of Vicksburg. (Pemberton was a Pennsylvanian who had married a Virginian and cast his lot with the South. He was not a particularly capable general officer.)

The siege of Vicksburg.

Federal assaults against Vicksburg failed on May 19 and 22, after which Grant laid siege to the city. Grant thoroughly defeated Pemberton in this battle. There were nearly 4,000 Confederate casualties and about 2,500 Federal casualties, but the key thing is that Pemberton was pushed westward, back toward Vicksburg. Grant had Pemberton back on his heels. The next day, the two forces fought again at the Big Black River, 10 miles east of Vicksburg. Again, Grant won the battle. A six-week siege ended in Pemberton's surrender of the city and his entire army on July 4, 1863. Grant thoroughly defeated Pemberton in this battle.

Shortly after the six-week siege, Banks captured Port Hudson, which together with Grant's success fulfilled a major part of the Anaconda Plan by establishing Northern control of the entire Mississippi River. Rosecrans's Tullahoma campaign in late June added to the roster of Union successes. In a series of deft maneuvers carried out with minimal losses, Rosecrans forced Bragg's army into Chattanooga and set the stage for a strike against that city and into Georgia. A dismal winter and spring for the North had given way to a splendid summer.

These three campaigns together—Vicksburg and Port Hudson and Tullahoma—gave the North a splendid boost in national morale and conveyed enormous strategic advantage to the North.

The Northern populace took heart from events in the West, which together with Meade's victory at Gettysburg seemed to promise a successful end to the war. Grant's campaign ranks among the most brilliant in American history. He abandoned his supply lines in moving toward Jackson. He marched quickly and defeated the enemy in detail (first Johnston, then Pemberton), capturing a 30,000-man army and vast Confederate military material. His victory achieved one of the North's major strategic goals.

On the Confederate side, there was backbiting and recrimination. President Jefferson Davis blamed General Joseph Johnston, while most others blamed Pemberton. Confederate morale sank after this complete defeat of their arms in the West. ■

Essential Reading

Hattaway and Jones, *How the North Won: A Military History of the Civil War*, chapter 13.

McPherson, *Battle Cry of Freedom: The Civil War Era*, chapter 21.

Bearss, *The Campaign for Vicksburg: Grant Strikes a Fatal Blow*.

——, *The Campaign for Vicksburg: Unvexed to the Sea*.

Connelly, *Autumn of Glory: The Army of Tennessee, 1862–1865*, chapters 4–6.

Hewitt, *Port Hudson: Confederate Bastion on the Mississippi*.

Questions to Consider

1. Ulysses S. Grant is often referred to as a straight-ahead slugging general who overwhelmed his opponents with superior resources. How does this image square with his conduct of the campaign against Vicksburg?

2. If you were asked to project the outcome of the war based on an accurate understanding of the military and political situations in late July 1863, what would you predict? Support your answer.

Vicksburg, Port Hudson, and Tullahoma
Lecture 23—Transcript

We continue our military focus on the summer of 1863 with this lecture on campaigning along the Mississippi River and in Tennessee. We'll begin with a survey of the strategic situation in the west in the spring of 1863, and then we'll move on to examine Grant's successful campaign against Vicksburg, the second phase, if you like, or the ultimate phase, of his campaigning against Vicksburg. Then we'll look at the Port Hudson campaign that resulted in the loss of that other major Confederate position on the Mississippi, and we'll finish with what was called the Tullahoma campaign, which was carried out by William S. Rosecrans against Braxton Bragg in Tennessee.

Let's start with a quick look at the major Union forces and what they were preparing to do in the west in the spring of 1863. There are three armies that we need to be concerned with and three elements to the overall strategic operation in the west for the North.

The first is Grant. This is by far the most important of the different elements. It's his continuing campaign against Vicksburg. It's very important in terms of visibility on the civilian front, both in the North and the South. It's very important in terms of its psychological importance; it's important in the sense of morale for the civilians behind the lines in the North and South.

There're several reasons for that. It had been underway for a long time. This had been an operation that had been unfolding in fits and starts, with advances and retreats, since December of 1862. So people were conditioned to look at their newspapers and see what was going on in the campaigning along the Mississippi. It was on their radar screen, in other words, quite prominently. They were conditioned to check and see how it was going. It was made more prominent by the fact that they'd been thinking about it since the Anaconda Plan had first been discussed in the newspapers. Everyone knew the North wanted to gain control of the Mississippi River. Vicksburg had come to be the most important point on the river, so it had great importance because of that.

Newspapers had given it a lot of play, and the people read about it frequently. The fact that it had been in the news for so long made it seem quite important to the North. The whole Gettysburg campaign would be played out in less than a month—not really time enough for people to look forward to reading about it every day over the long term. Vicksburg was different. Finally, Vicksburg, I think, was very important because it presented a very dramatic and easily grasped image: Vicksburg, a citadel on the Mississippi River.

One of two things would happen with this citadel. It would either be captured by the North, which would be a vastly important success for the North, or the Confederates would drive Grant away and the Mississippi River would remain partially in Confederate hands. It seemed to be pretty much a black and white verdict that would come from this effort. It would either fall to Grant, or it would resist his efforts. There was nothing equivocal about that. We saw in our last lecture that the outcome of Gettysburg did seem equivocal to people in the North and South. Vicksburg was not going to be that way, and I think people realized that as they watched their papers and talked with each other about what Grant was doing.

If you read newspapers and letters and diaries from the spring and into the summer of 1863 on both sides, Union and Confederate, you will see that people have a great interest in what is happening at Vicksburg. It's a great focal point. It's not exactly like Fort Sumter in 1861 as it became the great focal point, but it really is similar. More and more people are giving more and more attention to Vicksburg. Grant's opponents in this operation would be John C. Pemberton and Joseph E. Johnston, and we'll talk about both of them a bit more in a few minutes. So that's the first of these Northern advances, the first of the Northern armies in the west.

The second was the force under Nathaniel Prentice Banks, which would move up the Mississippi River against Port Hudson, Louisiana, the second Confederate strongpoint on the river. And the third operation would be William S. Rosecrans's Army of the Cumberland marching into southeastern Tennessee to confront Braxton Bragg's Army of Tennessee. Chattanooga would be the prize here. That's the ultimate goal for this part of the campaigning. The North wants Chattanooga; the Confederacy wants to deny the North control of Chattanooga.

Those are the strategic points and the elements of the Northern military that we'll talk about now in this lecture: Grant and Banks and Rosecrans. Let's look first at Grant and how Grant moved forward in his Vicksburg campaign. This campaign would show Grant at his absolute best, and I think it's worthwhile to take just a minute or two here and emphasize that the Grant of the Vicksburg campaign is far different from the man described in much of the literature on the Civil War.

The predominant image of Grant in much of what's been written about the war is that of a clumsy, head-on fighter who didn't know how to do anything except find where the enemy was, go straight at the enemy with as much power as possible, and try to club the enemy into submission. He won battles simply because he piled his men in relentlessly. That is a very common image—he overwhelmed his opponents. The shorthand description of Grant is "Grant the butcher." You see that image used again and again and again in the literature. That's the Grant that people think of, and that image comes from the Overland campaign of 1864, the battles from the wilderness to Spotsylvania, to Cold Harbor, and so forth.

I think part of the emphasis on this element of Grant's generalship is that these events took place in Virginia, and most things that took place in Virginia have been magnified. They seem to be more important than what happened anywhere else. The same is true with Grant. People stress that part of Grant's record, the Virginia part of his record. Lost Cause writers helped spread that image after the war especially. They didn't make it up, because, even during the war, there was criticism of Grant in the North as being a man who had too many casualties and did too much of this straight-ahead fighting during the Overland campaign.

But the Lost Cause writers certainly enhanced that image, and they did it specifically to make Lee look better. They, in essence, said, here we have Lee, a gallant, very capable officer with his little Army of Northern Virginia, fighting off Grant, this clumsy butcher who has so many men that he can just keep relentlessly pressing against Lee until he finally wears Lee and his troops down. Jubal Early, a Confederate general who became one of the most prominent Lost Cause writers, is a perfect example of those who tried to portray Grant as minimally talented. In one of his publications, he specifically asked, should I compare Lee to Grant? And his answer was, I might as well compare the pyramids in their majesty along the Nile to a pigmy perched on the shoulders of Atlas. So, for Early, Grant's this pigmy and Lee, of course, is the grand figure. All Grant can do is pile in his men.

Well, in fact, Grant didn't prefer that kind of fighting. That wasn't the kind of general he would have been if he had had his way. Vicksburg shows Grant more in the milieu that he preferred, and that is as a soldier who can maneuver, who can think, and who can use guile and swift movement and only the least fighting possible to defeat his enemy. Grant was daring, resourceful, and willing to take risks, all qualities that we'll see clearly in our account of the Vicksburg campaign's climactic scenes. His decision, for example—we've touched on this; I'll just reiterate here—to have the naval vessels run past the batteries at Vicksburg is a perfect example of this, an example of his daring. As we saw earlier, most of his subordinates said, don't do it. They opposed it. He went ahead with it, and he achieved success.

And now he finds himself where we left him last time, south of Vicksburg, east of the river—of the Mississippi River—right where he wanted to be. He's near Bruinsburg with slightly more than 20,000 men. He's ready to abandon his supply lines and strike into the interior of Mississippi, where he'll live off the land for this short campaign.

Over the first three weeks of May, he moved very rapidly and succeeded, time after time after time, against a variety of Confederate opponents. His 23,000 men, as we said last time, were at Port Gibson, Mississippi, on May 1. They defeated 8,000 Confederates there in the first battle of the last phase of the Vicksburg campaign. William Tecumseh Sherman then marched downriver, down the west side of the river, to join Grant and ferried over to join Grant, bringing Grant's strength to 44,000 men in Mississippi.

His two main opponents would be John C. Pemberton, who had about 32,000 men, the principal army defending Vicksburg, and Joseph E. Johnston, who had recovered from his wound, that terrible wound that he received in the Battle of Seven Pines back at the end of May in 1862. He'd recovered from that wound and, by very late in 1862, had reported himself ready for duty, and Jefferson Davis had given Johnston command, overall command, of a big section of the Western Theater that included Vicksburg. So Johnston is technically Pemberton's superior, but Johnston also commands about 16,000 Confederates in a small army just east of Vicksburg at Jackson, Mississippi, the state capital.

A crucial feature of the campaign that we'll look at now was the failure of the Confederates to combine these two armies. They had potentially nearly 50,000 soldiers in Mississippi there, but they never got those two forces together to present a united front to Grant. Grant was going to have the luxury, partially because he moved so effectively, of facing each of these Confederate forces in detail rather than facing a larger Confederate army all in one place.

Pemberton was an interesting character. He was a Northerner; he was born in Pennsylvania. Another West Pointer, he was a veteran of the Mexican War who had married a Virginia woman in the late 1840s. And almost certainly because of that marriage, he had decided to cast his lot with the Confederacy. A number of Northern officers who were married to Southern women fought with the Confederacy, and some Southern officers who were married to Northern women fought for the North. Pemberton is one of the Northerners who fought for the South.

He compiled a less than brilliant record early in the war. Part of his service was as commander in Charleston for a time, and it's really a mystery to historians—it's never really been answered satisfactorily—why Jefferson Davis selected John C. Pemberton to command in such a crucial place, Vicksburg. Davis thought Vicksburg was one of the most important places in the Confederacy, and he put a man in command there who really hadn't demonstrated great ability at any point in the Civil War.

Some historians have suggested that part of Davis's thinking was that he needed a place to stick Gustave Toutant Beauregard, who had also reported himself able to take up duties again. Beauregard ended up at Charleston, Pemberton's old post, and Pemberton in Vicksburg. Beauregard almost certainly would have been a better choice for Vicksburg, but that's not the decision that Jefferson Davis made. Pemberton was a lieutenant general by October 1862, and now he's commanding the principal army defending Vicksburg.

After Sherman joins Grant's army, Grant disappears into the interior of the state of Mississippi. The North has no idea what is going on with Grant's army from this point until Grant will show up at Vicksburg a number of days later. Lincoln doesn't know what he's doing, Secretary of War Stanton doesn't know what he's doing, and Henry W. Halleck doesn't know what Grant's doing. Grant has dropped off the map, as far as they're concerned, for about two weeks.

During that two weeks, Grant marched 180 miles, he and his army, fought and won four battles, and then reappeared on the map at the outskirts of Vicksburg. During that period he confused the Confederates by first marching east into the interior of Mississippi. Instead of just northward toward the city of Vicksburg, he marched seemingly away from Vicksburg, away from the river, toward Jackson. Grant's idea was to defeat Joe Johnston first near Jackson, make sure that the Confederates couldn't unite, and then turn back toward Vicksburg, and that's what he did.

Let's look now at how he carried out this campaign. On May 12, the advance elements of Grant's army defeated a small Confederate force in the Battle of Raymond, which was just west of Jackson. Two days later, on May 14, Grant drove Johnston out of Jackson, and Sherman and his troops had a little practice session for what they would do later in Georgia. They very enthusiastically destroyed a number of industrial facilities in Jackson, tore up the railroads, destroyed rolling stock, and so forth. They did a very quick job of it because Grant quickly turned west toward Vicksburg.

So he's pushed Johnston out of the way, he's made sure the Confederate forces are going to be separated, at least for the moment, and now he's heading toward Vicksburg. By that point John Pemberton had decided that he'd better come out and strike Grant. What he thought he was going to do initially was interrupt Grant's supply line. He didn't know that Grant didn't have a supply line. His idea was, this is a more conventional operation on Grant's part; I might be able to slow him down.

That wasn't the case. The two forces came together on May 16 in the climatic battle, the decisive battle, of this campaign at Champion's Hill. It's about halfway between Jackson and Vicksburg. Grant thoroughly defeated Pemberton in this battle. There were nearly 4,000 Confederate casualties and about 2,500 Federal casualties, but the key thing is that Pemberton was pushed westward, back toward Vicksburg. Grant had Pemberton on his heels, back on his heels. The next day, on the seventeenth of May, the two forces fought again at the Big Black River, 10 miles east of Vicksburg. Again, Grant won the battle. It was another loss for Pemberton—1,700 Confederate casualties to just 200 Union casualties. Most of those Confederates were captured.

After the battle at the Big Black River, Pemberton retreated into the defenses of Vicksburg. He did so despite the fact that Joseph E. Johnston had sent a really rather passionate appeal to him not to retreat into the defenses of Vicksburg. Johnston said, take your forces away from Vicksburg and march northward. Let's unite our forces and see if together we can deal with Grant. That's our best move. I think Johnston understood very well that, if Pemberton hunkered down in the defenses at Vicksburg, Grant would lay siege to the place and that, between Grant's power and the Union navy, the outcome would be Confederate defeat.

Johnston tried to get Pemberton not to go to Vicksburg, but he failed. Pemberton explained, as he put it, this is the most important point in the Confederacy. I won't abandon it. Consequently, Pemberton concentrated his men within the works.

Grant had achieved what he wanted to achieve. Those in Grant's army were beginning to get a glimmer of what their commander was up to. A lot of them hadn't understood what Grant was up to. Even William Tecumseh Sherman, who was an extremely bright guy, hadn't understood what Grant was up to, how brilliantly Grant had been performing. Sherman wrote his friend a letter on May 18, in the midst of this campaign. He said, until this moment, I never thought your expedition a success. I never could see the end clearly until now, but this is a campaign, this is a success, even if we never take the town. That is Sherman to Grant on May 18.

Grant's army surrounded the stronghold at Vicksburg on the land side. The Union navy guaranteed that they would have predominance on the water side. There's no Confederate navy at Vicksburg, no Confederate strength on the naval side. Grant thought that Pemberton's troops were probably demoralized by their recent defeats, and I think that's understandable. They'd been defeated both at Champion's Hill and at the Big Black River. He thought that frontal assaults might actually allow him to take Vicksburg quickly and avoid the necessity of a siege. And he launched those assaults against the city on May 19 and May 22, but they failed completely with heavy casualties, more than 4,000 casualties, as many casualties as he'd suffered in all the other battles leading up to Vicksburg since he had gotten on the east side of the river.

Sobered by those losses, Grant decided that the only way to capture the place was to settle for a siege, and that's what he did. Well, as Joseph Johnston, I think, understood, and, as many others understood, there was really only one way that this kind of a siege could end, but the defenders and the citizens of Vicksburg put up an admirable struggle. They held out for six weeks. They put up with around-the-clock bombardment from the encircling Federal forces—sniper fire day and night. Threats of assaults all along the line kept the Confederate defenders off guard. It was hard to sleep. It kept the civilians off guard, in a state of constant anxiety.

Food became very scarce in the city. The people scooped caves out of the hillsides and moved into the caves to be safe from the bombardment. Soldiers dug into the sides of the hills and then draped little pieces of cloth above the entrances to keep the broiling summer heat off of them, to get in where it was cooler, back into the hills. What they hadn't exactly counted on was the number of snakes that would be in those hillsides as well. There are a lot of accounts of the snakes and the people mixing as the population of Vicksburg dug into the hills and the soldiers dug into the hills.

The defenders and the citizens of Vicksburg ate the horses, ate the mules, ate the dogs and cats, and eventually ate the rats inside their lines—anything to get protein. As the siege went on, they tried to keep their strength up. Grant increased his army to 70,000 men in the course of the siege. No reinforcements are coming in to the Confederates, of course. Grant knew that he was going to win. Pemberton knew that he was going to lose probably, that he, Pemberton, would lose. Joe Johnston stood by at a distance, helpless to do anything about it. He would have liked to have ridden to the rescue, but he couldn't.

On July the 4th, the day that Lee retreated from the Battle of Gettysburg, John Pemberton surrendered his entire force of 30,000 men. Grant's campaign ranks among the most brilliant, not only of the Civil War, I think, but among the most brilliant military campaigns carried out by any United States officer in our history. He suffered fewer than 10,000 casualties. His army killed or wounded 10,000 Confederates and captured another 37,000—30,000 at Vicksburg and 7,000 in the battles preceding. Fifteen generals were among the prisoners on the Confederate side, together with 172 cannons and 60,000 shoulder arms. It was just an enormous success.

And it came on July the 4th. This, even more than Lee's retreat on July the 4th, seemed to be a providential message to people in the North. This wonderful victory, this city that we have focused on for so long, falls into United States hands on July the 4th, on the anniversary of the Declaration of Independence.

Lincoln fully appreciated the way Grant had driven through to a decisive victory. Unlike McClellan or Meade or his other generals, Grant had not just won a partial victory, he had won a complete victory here, just as he had at Fort Donelson back in February of 1862. He not only won a battle, he captured an entire army. Grant is my man, said Lincoln, and I am his, the rest of the war. Lincoln really had found his general here. He'd known Grant was good before; Grant is really his man now.

On the Confederate side it's a very different story, a very different story. There was tremendous backbiting on the Confederate side, finger pointing and blaming of one person or another. Jefferson Davis waded right into the middle of this. He picked Joseph Johnston as his great villain in this whole piece. He said Johnston should have supported Pemberton. It was Johnston who didn't do his job. Now, that was completely unfair on Davis's part. Johnston actually tried to unite the Confederate forces in this operation, but

Pemberton hadn't cooperated. But such was the enmity between Davis and Johnston that Davis settled on Joseph Johnston as his villain.

Most of the Confederates, however, settled on Pemberton as the villain. There are untold references in writings of the time about how this Yankee had lost Vicksburg, this Yankee who never should have been trusted with the command in the first place. People said he was either an inept Yankee or maybe even a treasonous Yankee. Maybe he had meant to lose Vicksburg, just as many of the Republicans had wondered whether McClellan was losing on purpose in the Peninsula back when he was approaching Richmond and facing Robert E. Lee.

Confederate morale took a nosedive. Unlike Gettysburg again, there's no way to try to dress up the loss of Vicksburg and pretend that it's anything except a complete defeat. You lost the big citadel on the river; you lost an entire army. There's no way to make that look any better than it was, and so it's a tremendous blow to the Confederacy and one of the most important campaigns of the Civil War. It has achieved one of the great strategic goals of the North—not quite but almost. We'll see in just a minute, when Port Hudson falls, that's really the complete control of the river. But people interpreted Vicksburg's fall as the end of Confederate control over any part of the river.

Well, let's look at the last pieces of our western puzzle here now. Let's look quickly at Banks and at Rosecrans, and we'll start with Port Hudson. Port Hudson resembled Vicksburg in many ways. Here's Banks, moving against a strong point on the Mississippi River, facing the determined Confederate garrison. He also was supported by Union warships. Porter had been the naval man at Vicksburg; David Glasgow Farragut was the Union naval man accompanying Nathaniel Prentice Banks.

Farragut and Banks moved against Port Hudson in late May, and Banks laid siege to the place. His army had an enormous advantage in numbers, more than two to one over the defenders, but the defenders fought tenaciously, and the defenses were formidable at Port Hudson. This wasn't a minor defensive work on the river. It was a very impressive Southern defensive position. Like

Grant, Banks tried frontal assaults twice at Port Hudson. Two times he tried to just overrun these defenses, on May 27 and again on June 14.

During the first assaults, black soldiers from Louisiana distinguished themselves. This is one of the first times in the war when black soldiers got into combat in a significant way. Many of their white comrades had been very skeptical about whether these black soldiers would fight well or not. They were tremendously impressed. Again, testimony from the time, from the white witnesses who saw these black men assault the Confederate works at Port Hudson, contained phrases like, we weren't sure how they would perform, but they performed every bit as gallantly as any white troops. It really was a turning point in terms of attitudes on the part of white soldiers, in this army anyway, toward their black comrades in that first set of assaults on May 27 at Port Hudson.

Well, like Grant after these failed assaults, the two sets of failed assaults, Banks just settled into a regular siege, and the defenders suffered at Port Hudson just as they had at Vicksburg. They began to eat everything that moved, just as they had at Vicksburg, and the siege dragged on just as it had at Vicksburg. The key point in the Port Hudson operation came when news made its way downriver that Vicksburg had fallen. When the commander at Port Hudson, the Confederate commander, learned that Vicksburg was gone, he saw no reason to continue in his resistance, and he surrendered on July 9, 1863.

Port Hudson is gone, and that means the true end of any Confederate hold on the Mississippi River. That is the end of it. The Mississippi now belongs to the Union. The entire length of the greatest river in the country belongs to the United States. In its defense of that stretch of the river, the Confederacy lost 45,000 soldiers—surrendered 45,000. It is a catastrophic loss for the Confederacy, which brings us to William S. Rosecrans in Tennessee. One last disaster awaits the Confederacy here, and we'll take care of it now.

Rosecrans and Bragg had been sitting facing each other ever since the Battle of Murfreesboro or Stones River, all the way back at the first of the year. They really hadn't been doing anything. Rosecrans had been reluctant to move, and Lincoln was beginning to think that perhaps he had another Don Carlos

Buell on his hands here, someone who simply couldn't get his act together and move against the Rebels. Rosecrans resisted Lincoln's blandishments to move more quickly until he was ready. When he was ready, however, he moved very efficiently.

On June 24, he began his campaign against Braxton Bragg, and he marched his 63,000 men very effectively in what became known as the Tullahoma campaign. It's a campaign of maneuver, not a campaign of battles. Rosecrans used a series of flanking movements that befuddled Bragg, and in just two weeks he pushed the Army of Tennessee's 45,000 men all the way back into Chattanooga, which, of course, sits on the Tennessee/Georgia border. He did this at a cost of fewer than 600 casualties—fewer than 600, a remarkable performance.

And he didn't get much credit for it at the time. He was upset. Washington had issued grand pronouncements regarding the victories at Gettysburg and Vicksburg. There was thundering silence from Washington about what Rosecrans had accomplished, and it wounded him badly. He said he hoped he wouldn't be slighted—he said this in a message—just because what I've done is not written in letters of blood. But, of course, there's something about a big battle that catches people's attention more than nice maneuvering. It was a nice performance on Rosecrans's part, but it was not nearly as prominent as what had happened at Vicksburg and Gettysburg.

These three campaigns together—Vicksburg and Port Hudson and Tullahoma—gave the North a splendid boost in national morale and conveyed enormous strategic advantage to the North. The war seemed to be well on track toward Union victory.

In our next lecture we'll see how both sides experienced a mixture of success and frustration in the next round of campaigning, which occurred in the late summer and early autumn of 1863.

A Season of Uncertainty, Summer and Fall 1863
Lecture 24

This lecture will continue our look at military events in 1863. We'll examine the relatively quiescent fronts along the Mississippi River and in Virginia as well as the Battle of Chickamauga, which took place in north Georgia and ranks as the largest battle of the entire war in the Western Theater.

Union victories at Gettysburg, Vicksburg, and Port Hudson and in the Tullahoma campaign seemingly had prepared the way for knockout blows in both Virginia and the West. Lincoln and Union war planners labored diligently to achieve this result, only to see their efforts end in stalemate in Virginia and a major defeat at Chickamauga in the Western Theater.

Lee's and Meade's armies settled into positions along the Rappahannock River, testing each other on several occasions but avoiding a full-blown battle. Well before the end of the year, Lincoln had given up on Meade's accomplishing anything noteworthy and hoped merely that the Army of the Potomac would keep Lee pinned down. Far to the west, Grant found himself without a major goal after the fall of Vicksburg. Union leaders debated their next move in Grant's theater. Halleck wanted to concentrate on the Trans-Mississippi region, which embraces Arkansas, Texas, and parts of Louisiana. Lincoln also favored the Trans-Mississippi for a combination of political, diplomatic, and military reasons. Grant and Banks unsuccessfully argued for the capture of Mobile, Alabama, the last major Confederate port on the Gulf of Mexico. Grant eventually busied himself with an expedition against Jackson, Mississippi (commanded by William Tecumseh Sherman) and a number of small operations.

The principal military action that autumn developed near Chattanooga. Rosecrans maneuvered Bragg out of that city and marched into northern Georgia in early September (a smaller Union force under Ambrose Burnside captured Knoxville on September 3, thus "liberating" heavily Unionist East Tennessee). Given reinforcements from Joseph Johnston's forces in Mississippi and from Lee's army in Virginia, Bragg responded with a counteroffensive that resulted in the Battle of Chickamauga on September 19–20. The two days of heavy fighting gave Bragg the Confederacy's only tactical victory on an important western battlefield. Slow to realize what his soldiers had accomplished, Bragg allowed Rosecrans's army to regroup in Chattanooga. Chickamauga temporarily slowed the Union momentum generated by the summer's earlier triumphs, but the final fate of Chattanooga remained uncertain.

Union officer William Tecumseh Sherman.

The Davis Administration had decided to reinforce Bragg in preparation for a counteroffensive. Two divisions from Joseph Johnston's army joined Bragg. Two divisions (Hood's and McLaw's) from the Army of Northern Virginia were ordered to north Georgia by rail. Rosecrans entered north Georgia after the capture of Chattanooga on 9 September and placed his army in a somewhat scattered and vulnerable position.

The Battle of Chickamauga gave Bragg a striking tactical victory. Rosecrans concentrated his army just south of Chattanooga in the valley of Chickamauga Creek by 18 September. Bragg's reinforced Army of Tennessee, which with its almost 70,000 men outnumbered Rosecrans's Army of the Cumberland, attacked on September 19 and 20. Bragg wanted to cut Rosecrans off from Chattanooga. Then Bragg planned to trap and envelop Rosecrans. Fighting started on the 19th as it had at Gettysburg, with a cavalry and infantry skirmish that escalated into a general engagement. There was no decisive result after the first day.

Chickamauga, as I said, was the largest battle fought in the West during the war. There were enormous casualties—staggering—18,500 for the Confederates; 16,000 for the Federals.

Confederate assaults on the 20th, although not developing as planned, shattered part of the Union line; the breakthrough was spearheaded by Longstreet's forces. After Rosecrans and about one-third of the Union army fled the field, George H. Thomas conducted a tenacious defense on Snodgrass Hill on the Union left and withdrew in good order. Bragg was not certain of his victory. Casualties numbered 18,500 CSA and 16,000 Federal.

Although it was a tactical victory, Chickamauga failed to convey any long-term advantage to the Confederates. Bragg allowed the Union army to reach Chattanooga and begin to dig in. Confederate civilian morale experienced only a momentary rise. The ultimate fate of Chattanooga remained uncertain. ∎

Essential Reading

Hattaway and Jones, *How the North Won: A Military History of the Civil War*, chapter 14.

McPherson, *Battle Cry of Freedom: The Civil War Era*, chapter 22.

Catton, *Grant Takes Command*, chapters 1–2.

Connelly, *Autumn of Glory: The Army of Tennessee, 1862–1865*, chapters 8–9.

Cozzens, *This Terrible Sound: The Battle of Chickamauga*.

Freeman, *Lee's Lieutenants: A Study in Command*, vol. 3, chapters 11–15.

Questions to Consider

1. In Jefferson Davis's position, would you have elected to weaken Lee's army to reinforce Bragg's in late summer 1863?

2. Can the battle of Chickamauga be used as support for an argument that Civil War military engagements often had little real impact on the course of the war? Would shifting the lens to include all major battles between April and September 1863 change your answer?

A Season of Uncertainty, Summer and Fall 1863
Lecture 24—Transcript

This lecture will continue our look at military events in 1863. We'll examine the relatively quiescent fronts along the Mississippi River and in Virginia as well as the Battle of Chickamauga, which took place in north Georgia and ranks as the largest battle of the entire war in the Western Theater.

We'll begin in Virginia and along the Mississippi River. We've seen in our recent lectures how much success had come to the North in each of the major theaters in 1863. We've seen George Gordon Meade's victory at Gettysburg, Grant's victory at Vicksburg, Nathaniel P. Banks's reduction of the Confederate stronghold at Port Hudson, and William Rosecrans's successful Tullahoma campaign, which pushed Braxton Bragg and the Army of Tennessee back into the vital city of Chattanooga.

The tide seemed to have swung decisively against the South, and the task, it seemed for Lincoln and his group of planners, was to come up with a strategy that would build on this Northern success and perhaps bring the war to an end within a few months. As we'll see, that didn't end up being the case. They were not able to get any kind of decisive action in Virginia; they really couldn't decide on a quick target out in the far Western Theater; and the only major battle that took place in the Middle Theater, the Tennessee/ North Georgia Theater, proved to be a major disappointment for the North.

Lincoln and Halleck, as they looked at the map in Virginia in the wake of Gettysburg, grew more disenchanted with George Gordon Meade. Lincoln had hoped for a rapid follow-up to the Union success at Gettysburg. He wanted something almost immediately after the battle. He hadn't gotten that but had still hoped that Meade somehow would bring Lee to a showdown battle, perhaps before Lee was able to get back across the Potomac River. The river's waters were very high after Gettysburg, and Lee was, in effect, trapped north of the Potomac for a while. That seemed to open an opportunity for Meade, but in the end Lee was able to dig in along the river. Meade did not attack him, and the Confederates escaped.

Meade later explained that he didn't want to attack Lee's strong defensive positions near the river—it was probably a good move on his part—because he feared having to fight a Gettysburg in reverse, with the Confederates being in a good defensive position and the Federal attackers being slaughtered as they tried to carry that position. Still, it probably would have been wise for Meade to try to attempt some kind of pressure against Lee. In the end, though, he didn't.

Lee's crippled army, severely crippled army, limped back into Virginia, and eventually the armies in the Eastern Theater settled into an uneasy period of watching each other warily along that military frontier. Lincoln, I think, rather quickly gave up hope that he would have any dramatic results in Virginia. His level of confidence in Meade was dropping at this point. Meade had done well enough, at least in the actual fighting on the second and third at Gettysburg, but after that he had proved to be a disappointment, and Lincoln's confidence was dropping. He decided in the end not to ask very much of Meade in Virginia.

He in essence asked Meade only to keep an eye on Lee and not to push for any kind of dramatic showdown with the Army of Northern Virginia. In fact, Lincoln suggested that Meade probably shouldn't even attack Lee's army but just make sure that Lee didn't pull some kind of maneuver that might hurt Federal chances elsewhere. Lincoln reasoned that if Meade had failed to hit Lee when the Army of Northern Virginia was in a precarious position right after Gettysburg, it was highly unlikely that Meade would be able to accomplish much now that Lee had time to dig in, or at least sort of dig in, in a much stronger position in Virginia.

This might have been an overreaction on Lincoln's part to Meade's earlier failure, but it meant that Union planning for the Virginia Theater was considered secondary to Union planning in the west. Lincoln was not expecting that the war would be won or even advanced very much in the east. He took pretty much the same attitude he had taken when Joseph Hooker first came into power in the Army of the Potomac: I'm hoping that nothing bad happens in Virginia, but I'm expecting that something good will happen out west.

Now, Meade finally did express an interest in taking the attack to Lee. Lincoln told him no. He said, keep up a threatening attitude but do not advance. Well, while this was going on on the Union side, the Confederate planners in Richmond decided to detach two divisions from the Army of Northern Virginia, James Longstreet's divisions under Lafayette McLaws and John Bell Hood, and shift them westward to reinforce Braxton Bragg's army in north Georgia. That indicated that, on the Confederate as on the Union side, Virginia had dropped to a position where it was considered less important than what was going on out west. So that's what's happening in Virginia. Not much is the bottom line.

What about out along the Mississippi River? Well, Grant and the Federals found themselves in a position of having accomplished everything they had been hoping to accomplish for a long time, taking control of the Mississippi River, and they were somewhat at a loss as to how to follow that up. What should be our next target out west? What can we do to best build on this success that we've had at Vicksburg and at Port Hudson?

Now the North had the advantage, the wonderful luxury, really, of being able to pick a target anywhere up and down the Mississippi River because their naval power could project Union strength to any point along the river, supply Union armies at any point along the river, and therefore open up that entire vast stretch of the Confederacy to military operations that might end up with a Union victory. No worry about secure water transportation and supply lines as long as they operated near the river. They had the plus of interior lines all along the line of the Mississippi because their naval power was absolutely paramount. The Confederacy was severed in two.

Now they could go one of two directions. They could either focus their power westward toward what was called the Trans-Mississippi Theater—Arkansas, Indian territory, Texas, and the bulk of Louisiana—or they could try to find a target east of the river or on the gulf coast that made sense as the next logical place to strike. Henry W. Halleck wanted to concentrate on the Trans-Mississippi region. He argued that Confederate forces there were relatively small and scattered. The states of Arkansas, Louisiana, and Texas, he thought, might be driven out of the war entirely if the North focused enough resources on them and just took them off the board completely.

Grant and Banks, in contrast, both wanted to attack Mobile, the last major Confederate port on the gulf. If we could seal Mobile, they said, not only would that hurt the South in terms of costing them one more port, but it would also put us in a position—and this is especially Grant thinking—to strike into the heartland of Alabama and perhaps from there even into the heartland of Georgia.

But, like Halleck, Lincoln preferred the Trans-Mississippi, and Lincoln had a number of political reasons for wanting to look in that direction rather than toward Mobile. First, he wanted to open up cotton cultivation in Texas to free labor. If we can get control of Texas, all of those cotton lands in Texas will come under our control, and we can make a good cotton crop there.

He and Secretary of State William Henry Seward also thought that if the Northern forces were successful in Texas, they could make a show of strength that would prevent France from trying to pull some kind of military operation—or at least entertaining thoughts of marching French troops out of Mexico—to help the Confederacy. We'll talk more about this later, but for now it's enough to say that taking advantage of the great war in the United States, Napoleon III in Mexico had sent 35,000 French troops to Mexico, and Mexico was now a puppet regime controlled by French interests. The United States worried that perhaps some of those French troops might wander north, and they didn't want that to happen. Union strength in Texas could help blunt that.

Lincoln also reasoned that if Louisiana and Arkansas and Texas were freed of Southern military forces, they might be brought back into the Union. They might be reconstructed virtually immediately.

Well, the final result was that Grant didn't get his way in this instance. He would have to wait to strike at Mobile. The final plan was that a Union army would advance into Arkansas—Nathaniel Banks would be reinforced and ordered to move into Texas. He was told to march up the Red River to get to Texas, but, in fact, he would take another approach. He would go by sea to points along the Texas coast. And Grant would occupy himself by driving Joseph Johnston eastward out of Jackson, Mississippi. Johnston had come back into Jackson after Grant had moved on to Vicksburg. Generally, Grant would also try to clean the Rebels out of western Mississippi and make Union control of the river absolutely secure.

Grant gave the task of dealing with Jackson to William Tecumseh Sherman. He said, go over, push the Confederates out of Jackson, tear up the railroads there, and come back. And that's just what Sherman did. He had a tidy little campaign. He went to Jackson, he tore up the railroads, and he pushed the Confederates out. His men got to practice a process of tearing up railroads that became standard during the war.

They would march along a railroad bed, taking up the rails one by one. They'd stack the ties up in a heap, lay the rails over the top, set fire to the ties, and, when the fire blazed and the rails were heated, they'd then get a hold of each end of the rail and bend the rails around a tree or some other solid object so that they would be unusable for the Confederates. The Confederates couldn't produce rails to replace the ones that were destroyed this way. These twisted rails became known later in the war as "Sherman's neckties" or "Sherman's bowties."

Grant also sent out a few other expeditions that destroyed supplies and wrecked railroads elsewhere in Mississippi, but basically he didn't have a major goal. He was underutilized at this stage of the war. There simply wasn't a major target for him to focus on in the Mississippi Theater. So Grant awaited further orders from Washington.

That brings us to the North Georgia/Chattanooga, Tennessee Theater. This assumed center stage in the late summer and early fall as the most important theater of the war. The major Federal army, of course, was Rosecrans's Army of the Cumberland, stationed just outside Chattanooga, resting there after the Tullahoma campaign, which had been so successful.

Halleck and Lincoln wanted Rosecrans to continue the movement that had forced Bragg to relinquish the last piece of middle Tennessee that the Confederates held at the end of June. They thought speed was imperative because they feared that Joseph Johnston might march to join Bragg and unite those two Confederate forces and present the Union with a formidable army, either somewhere in North Georgia or even in Tennessee. Rosecrans, however, wouldn't be hurried. Again, the tendency he'd shown before the Tullahoma campaign, he showed that part of his military personality once more. He would not be rushed, and it was late July before he finally got into motion.

At the same time that he began his movement, another Union force marched into Tennessee, and that was one commanded by Ambrose E. Burnside, our old friend from the Battle of Fredericksburg. Burnside had had various adventures or misadventures, some of which we'll talk about later in the course, but now he's back out in field command again. He'd been out of field command for a while. He's taking charge of an army that has Knoxville, Tennessee, as its goal—Knoxville, the most important city in east Tennessee.

East Tennessee, as you'll remember, is a part of the Confederacy that Lincoln, from the very beginning of the war, had wanted to liberate, as Lincoln put it. All those loyal Unionists waiting there in the mountains of eastern Tennessee, said Lincoln, they deserve our attention. They deserve our sending a United States army into that area so that they can fly their true colors, those loyal Unionists, as citizens of the United States. Lincoln has high hopes yet again that east Tennessee will be added to the Union column.

The Confederates, for their part, hope to be able to seize the initiative in this theater. All Confederate eyes weren't focused on this part of the war map, but many of the pairs of eyes that counted were focused on it. That's why the decision had been made to pull strength around Virginia, central Virginia, pull it out of that theater and send it west to reinforce Bragg. The prime thinker or mover behind this idea was Gustave Toutant Beauregard. He had advocated the idea back in the wake of the victory at Chancellorsville before Lee moved toward Gettysburg, and now he brings that idea up again.

It's the revival of a plan that the Confederates had already debated and argued back in May of 1863. But now we're after Gettysburg, after Lee's failure in his invasion across the Potomac River in June and early July, and the terms of the debate are different. Davis supported the idea, Secretary of War James Seddon supported the idea, Braxton Bragg supported the idea, and James Longstreet supported the idea, as did many other military and political figures. A very strong cast, in other words, is saying, yes, what we need to do is reinforce Bragg, and this time Lee went along. He really didn't have arguments with which to counter this plan, and so he agreed that his army would be weakened in the hope of accomplishing something in the vicinity of Chattanooga.

As I said earlier, the troops that were selected to go were James Longstreet's First Corps divisions, the only two that were left with the army. George Pickett's division had been so battered at Gettysburg that it was off trying to be rebuilt at this stage of the war. It wasn't considered a viable military organization. So Longstreet had only two divisions, John Bell Hood's and Lafayette McLaws's. Those two divisions would head west together with the artillery that belonged to Longstreet's corps.

Meanwhile, Rosecrans and his Army of the Cumberland repeated their success of June by maneuvering Bragg out of Chattanooga without a fight, a brilliant follow-up to the Tullahoma campaign. Chattanooga was a critically important city. It lay at the junction of two major east-west Southern railroads, and it served as the gateway not only to eastern Tennessee if you're coming from the south, but also to the industrial centers of Georgia because a railroad ran from Chattanooga down to the important city of Atlanta in northern Georgia. A move from Chattanooga to Atlanta would split the Confederacy again. It's the type of move that old Winfield Scott had envisioned back in his early planning in the first spring of the war, this major strike into the heart of the Confederacy. So the Federal capture of Chattanooga was a very good piece of news for the North.

Rosecrans began his advance on August 16. He demonstrated in front of the city, in front of Bragg's force, with one of his army corps and then crossed the Tennessee River above the city with the rest of his strength and thus came in behind Bragg's left flank. Bragg had no choice but to abandon the city of Chattanooga, which he did on September 9. He retreated completely out of Tennessee now. The Army of Tennessee is no longer in Tennessee; it is in north Georgia. Burnside at the same time had moved fairly efficiently toward Knoxville, and, six days before Rosecrans marched into Chattanooga, Burnside had captured Knoxville. Knoxville had fallen on the third.

So here is tremendous Union success in the last two important cities left in Tennessee that hadn't been under Union control. All of Tennessee is now under Union control, all the major cities. Nashville is long gone, Memphis is gone, and now Chattanooga and Knoxville both belong to the United States. Lincoln's long-cherished wish to free east Tennessee had been accomplished. Rosecrans telegraphed Lincoln on the ninth, "Chattanooga is ours without a struggle, and east Tennessee is free. Our move on the enemy's flank and rear progresses."

Rosecrans wants to push his advantage to keep going after Bragg here. Rosecrans believed at this stage of the campaign that the Confederates were completely disorganized and demoralized. This is an army that he's pushed completely out of Tennessee without even having to fight basically, and I think that Rosecrans thought the Army of Tennessee was, if not on its last legs, approaching that position, retreating into central Georgia seemingly with no offensive notions in mind. He acted on that belief by scattering his army on an arc from Chattanooga down into north Georgia, spreading them out on a wide front, unaware of the fact that the Confederates, in fact, were planning a major counterblow in this part of the strategic landscape.

Bragg did have offensive notions of his own. He'd been reinforced by two divisions from Joseph Johnston's army. He'd been reinforced by troops under Simon Bolivar Buckner that had been stationed in east Tennessee, and he would soon receive the reinforcements from Lee's army, those two veteran divisions from the Army of Northern Virginia, used to success and victors on a number of battlefields. They were on their way via rail. They had to take a very roundabout route, these two divisions from Virginia did, because the Southern rail system was in such a decrepit state by this point in the war.

They had to take roundabout ways; they had to go way out of what would seem to be the direct route. The rolling stock wasn't in good shape; there was delay after delay; locomotives would break down; the right cars wouldn't be available. In the end, only about two-thirds of Longstreet's men would get to Bragg in time for the next fight, but it was still a fairly impressive use of railroads on the Confederacy's part to shift a significant piece of one army to reinforce another. Federal intelligence picked up this movement of the reinforcements from Lee to Bragg but picked it up a little too late. Troops ordered to Rosecrans to counter these reinforcements for Bragg wouldn't arrive in time to participate in the big battle that was looming not far ahead.

What Bragg hoped to do—he knew that Rosecrans was scattered around a good part of north Georgia—was to hit pieces of the Union army before those pieces could come together, in other words, to strike in detail at his opponent's army. Get in behind the Federals, he hoped, and cut them off from access to Chattanooga and the Tennessee River. Isolate them in the rugged country of northwest Georgia. That's what each side is trying to do.

Let's move on now to the Battle of Chickamauga. Rosecrans figured out just in time that he might be in some danger, and he pulled his army back together. By September 17, he had about 58,000 men in position a few miles south of Chattanooga in the valley of Chickamauga Creek. Chickamauga's an Indian word. You'll read in many of the accounts that it's an Indian word that means "river of death." Well, I really wonder about that. It seems that most of the Indian words that have any meaning in the Civil War mean "river of death" or "ledge of death" or "place where people die" or something like that, and I wonder whether that is people naming those in retrospect or giving a meaning to those words in retrospect. I'm doubtful whether that's what Chickamauga really means, but that's what soldiers later pretended that it meant. For our purposes it doesn't matter what the word really meant; all that matters is that is where Rosecrans is marshaling his army, in the valley of Chickamauga Creek.

When Longstreet's men, the two-thirds of them that got up in time to fight in the battle, were present, Bragg had nearly 70,000 soldiers. It's one of the very unusual times in the war when a major Confederate army outnumbers its Union opponent in one of the big battles of the conflict. Bragg's plan called for an advance through part of Rosecrans's line to interpose the Army of Tennessee between the Federals in Chattanooga, after which the Confederates would try to drive the Federals into a place called McClemore's Cove, a cul-de-sac where the Union troops would have a very difficult time escaping from the encircling Confederates.

The terrain around Chickamauga Creek was heavily wooded, much like the terrain at Shiloh. There was light skirmishing on September 18. The battle proper began on September 19, and it began much the way the Battle of Gettysburg had begun. Nathan Bedford Forrest's cavalry, some of it, ran into Union infantry, and, as at Gettysburg, each side hurried reinforcements forward, and what had begun as a skirmish escalated into a battle as the fighting spread and intensified. The Confederates kept trying to get around the Union left flank, to get in between the Federals and the road to Chattanooga. But the action was confused because of the terrain. There were nasty little fights between brigades, even regiments, sometimes divisions, that would flare up and then die down.

John Hood's division from Lee's army had a little bit of success on that day, but neither side really gained the upper hand, and the fighting came to a halt at the end of the day on the nineteenth as each side braced for an even bigger battle the next day. Longstreet arrived that night—sort of stumbled through the dark. There was no one to meet him at the little train station. He didn't know where Bragg's headquarters were. He got in late, and he made his way through the dark, he and a staff officer. He finally found Bragg's headquarters and had a discussion, and Bragg announced that Longstreet would be given half of the army on the next day.

Longstreet doesn't even know what's going on basically, but he's going to command the left wing of Bragg's army, Bishop Polk will command the right, and the plan is that the assaults, the Confederate assaults on the twentieth, would begin on Polk's flank and work their way down the line toward Longstreet's end of the line, engaging the Federals all along this very extensive battle line.

That was the plan; that's not how the fight worked out on the twentieth. Bragg woke up—he'd hoped to have the assaults begin early—and he listened, and there was no sound of firing from his right flank. And he waited and no sound. He sent couriers; he couldn't find out what was happening with Polk. Finally, a staff officer found Polk at his headquarters. Polk and a coterie of his people were sitting around tables having an enormous breakfast. And the staff officer, barely containing his anger, said, "We thought the attacks would be going now. General Bragg thought the attacks would be going now." And

Polk answered something like, "Yes, my heart is overflowing with anxiety about these attacks."

Well, Polk was in charge of the attacks. He's the one who could make the attacks go. He was not doing his job here. In the end, Bragg stepped in and ordered the assaults to begin, and the Confederates began to attack the Union line. The attacks were not making much headway until, by sheer luck, one Union officer thought that he spotted a gap in Rosecrans's line. Rosecrans ordered a division to pull out of the line at another point to plug the gap. In fact, there hadn't been an original gap, but, when the division pulled out, there was one, and James Longstreet's troops, right at the moment that the gap appeared, drove a powerful assault right through that gap in the Union lines.

It was a piece of tremendous luck for the Confederates. They shattered the right third of the Army of the Cumberland—drove it from the field. They absolutely drove a third of the Union army from the field. Rosecrans's entire right wing, in essence, sprinted for safety. One Northern witness said, "I saw our lines break and melt away like leaves before the wind." A man on the spot said that he saw Rosecrans, who was a Catholic, make the sign of the cross, and he said, parenthetically, he didn't see that was a good sign probably, that the commanding general was making a sign of the cross.

At any rate, a big chunk of the Union army is leaving the field, Rosecrans along with it, and many of those Federals didn't stop until they reached the outskirts of Chattanooga. Confederates captured 8,000 men, 15,000 muskets, 51 cannons, and a huge amount of material. It's a shattering defeat for that end of the Union line.

The Confederates renewed their pressure on the Union left. It's the Union right that's gone, and their officers urged them forward to finish the job. One officer, Benjamin Franklin Cheetum, a Confederate major general, and a tremendously hard-swearing man, was urging his men forward, "give 'em hell," and lots of other, much more profane language than that. Polk, the Bishop of Louisiana, of the Southwest, couldn't bring himself to curse that way, but he was riding along, and he hollered out at his men to "give 'em what General Cheetum says to give them." Even with that kind of sterling leadership on Leonidas Polk's part, the Confederates couldn't finish the job against the Federals.

This is another example of how resilient Civil War armies were. The key was George H. Thomas, who pulled together the left part of the Union army, the fragments that had not been driven from the field. He brought them into a tight horseshoe-shaped position centered on a place called Snodgrass Hill and held off the Confederate assaults for the rest of the day. Thomas, we'll learn more about him later. He's a Virginian who stayed loyal to the Union. He paid a terrible price for it. His family read him out of the family when he left to stay with the North and not to go with Virginia. When word came to his family later that he had died after the war, his sisters announced, "Our brother died in 1861." There was no contact between his family and him when he remained with the Union.

But he did a splendid job of fighting on the afternoon of the twentieth. He earned the nickname the "Rock of Chickamauga." He held the army together, what was left of it, and withdrew in good order toward Chattanooga. He would later become one of the great Union war heroes.

Well, the Confederates sensed their first great battlefield victory. They raised an enormous Rebel yell that swept from one end of the line to the other. Bragg wasn't quite sure that he'd won a victory. He couldn't quite believe that he'd won a victory when a Confederate soldier, who had been captured early in the battle and then escaped and made his way back to Confederate lines, saw Bragg and said, "Yes, we have won a victory, general, a great victory." The man said that the Federals were in retreat all along the line, and Bragg looked at him and said, "Do you know what a retreat looks like?" and the man replied, "Yes, general. I ought to know. I've been with you during your whole campaign" and then slipped off into the underbrush.

Chickamauga, as I said, was the largest battle fought in the west during the war. There were enormous casualties—staggering—18,500 for the Confederates; 16,000 for the Federals. It's the Confederacy's greatest tactical victory in the west and the last major battlefield victory for the Confederacy in the entire war. It gave a momentary lift to Southern morale. Rosecrans himself wired Washington, "We have met with a severe disaster." But the victory came at a terrible cost to the South and brought no strategic reward because Bragg failed to follow it up. He did not make any attempt to press the Federals toward Chattanooga.

The next major action in the war would come at Chattanooga and would result in Grant's elevation to supreme Northern command. That is what we will look at next time.

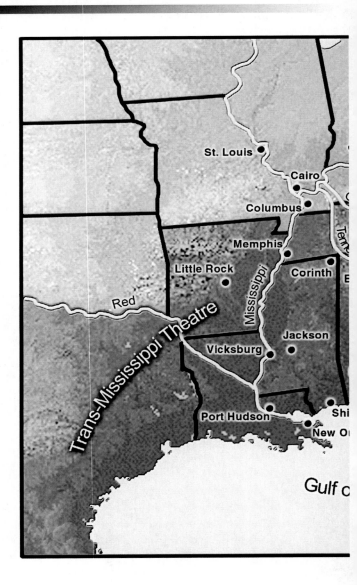

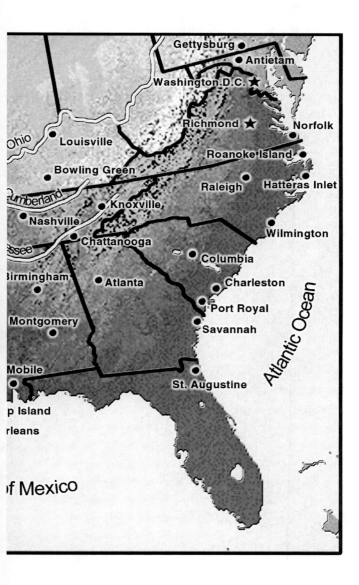

Gettysburg
Antietam
Washington.D.C. ★
Richmond ★
Norfolk
Roanoke Island
Louisville
Bowling Green
Raleigh
Hatteras Inlet
Ohio
Cumberland
Knoxville
Nashville
Wilmington
Chattanooga
Tennessee
Columbia
Birmingham
Atlanta
Charleston
Port Royal
Montgomery
Savannah
Mobile
St. Augustine
Atlantic Ocean
p Island
rleans
of Mexico

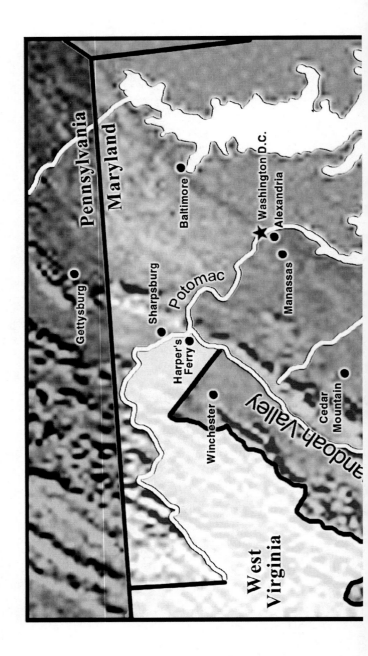

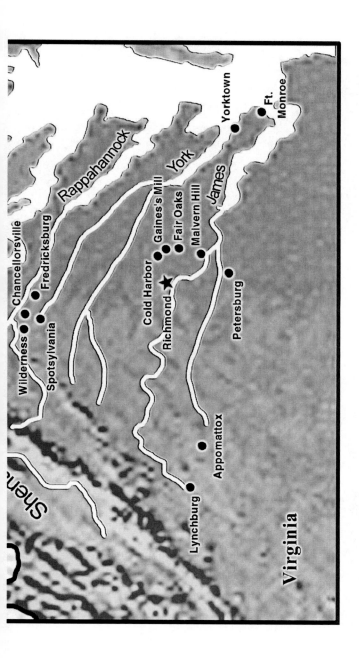

Timeline

General

1787... Framers of the Constitution compromise
on issues related to slavery.

1820... Missouri Compromise admits Missouri
as a slave state but prohibits slavery
elsewhere in the Louisiana Purchase
territory above 36°36' north latitude.

1831... Nat Turner's rebellion in Virginia sends
shockwaves through the South.

1831... William Lloyd Garrison founds his
abolitionist newspaper *The Liberator*.

1840... Liberty Party fields a
presidential candidate.

1845... Texas admitted to the Union.

1846–48.. War between the United States
and Mexico.

1846... Wilmot Proviso calls for barring slavery
from lands acquired from Mexico.

1848... Free Soil Party fields a presidential
candidate.

1850... Compromise of 1850 includes
admission of California as a free
state (giving free states a permanent
majority in the United States Senate)
and enactment of a tough Fugitive
Slave Law.

1861

Jan. 9–Feb. 1 .... The remaining six states of the Lower South secede (Mississippi, Jan. 9; Florida, Jan. 10; Alabama, Jan. 11; Georgia, Jan. 19, Louisiana, Jan. 26; Texas, Feb. 1).

Feb. 4–March 11 .... A convention of delegates from the seven seceded states, meeting in Montgomery, Alabama, writes a constitution and selects Jefferson Davis and Alexander H. Stephens as provisional President and Vice President of a new slaveholding republic called the Confederate States of America.

March 4 .... Lincoln's First Inaugural Address declares that the "momentous issue of civil war" lay in the hands of secessionists.

April 12–13 .... Confederate bombardment results in the surrender of Fort Sumter in Charleston, South Carolina.

April 15 .... Lincoln calls for 75,000 volunteers to suppress the rebellion.

April 17–June 8 .... Four states of the Upper South secede in response to Lincoln's call for volunteers (Virginia, April 17; Arkansas, May 6; North Carolina, May 20; Tennessee, June 8).

April 19 .... The Sixth Massachusetts Infantry is attacked by a mob in Baltimore.

Early May .... General Winfield Scott briefs President Lincoln and others about a strategy that came to be known as the "Anaconda Plan."

May 20 .... Confederate Congress votes to move the national government from Montgomery to Richmond.

May 24 .... Benjamin F. Butler declares fugitive slaves at Fort Monroe, Virginia, "contraband of war" and refuses to return them to their Confederate owners.

June 11 .... Unionist delegates from 26 counties convene in Wheeling, Virginia, to begin a process that eventually results in the creation of the state of West Virginia.

July 21 .... Battle of First Manassas or Bull Run yields a flashy Confederate victory that builds confidence in the South and convinces many Northerners that the war will be longer and harder than first thought.

Aug. 6 .... U.S. Congress passes the first Confiscation Act, which frees fugitive slaves who have been employed in the Confederate war effort.

Aug. 10 .... Battle of Wilson's Creek, Missouri, delivers a blow to anti-secessionists in the state.

Aug. 30 .... John C. Frémont declares free the slaves of pro-Confederate owners in Missouri; Lincoln instructs him to modify the order to make it conform with existing congressional legislation.

Sept. 3 .... Confederate military forces enter Kentucky to occupy the strong position at Columbus, an act that spurs Kentucky to stand firmly with the Union.

Oct. 21 .... Union forces suffer a debacle at Ball's Bluff, near Leesburg, Virginia, that helps prompt creation of the Joint Committee on the Conduct of the War.

Nov. 1 .... George B. McClellan replaces Winfield Scott as general-in-chief of the U.S. Army.

Nov. 8 .... Confederate diplomats James M. Mason and John Slidell are removed from the British vessel *Trent*, precipitating a diplomatic crisis between the United States and Great Britain.

1862

Feb. 6 .... U. S. Grant captures Fort Henry on the Tennessee River.

Feb. 16 .... U. S. Grant captures Fort Donelson on the Cumberland River.

Feb. 25 .... Union forces occupy Nashville, Tennessee.

Feb. 25 .... President Lincoln signs the Legal Tender Act, which creates national treasury notes, soon dubbed "greenbacks."

March 6–7 .... Union victory at Pea Ridge, Arkansas, helps solidify Missouri's status as a loyal state.

March 9 .... U.S.S. *Monitor* and C.S.S. *Virginia* fight the first naval engagement between ironclad vessels.

Timeline

March 16 .... U.S. Congress abolishes slavery in the District of Columbia, offering compensation to loyal owners.

April 5 .... George B. McClellan begins a month-long siege of Yorktown, Virginia, marking the first important event in his Peninsula campaign.

April 6–7 .... U. S. Grant wins the Battle of Shiloh (Pittsburg Landing), completing a series of Union triumphs that denies the Confederacy control of major sections of Tennessee.

April 16 .... C.S. Congress passes the first national conscription act in American history; acts passed on Sept. 27, 1862, and Feb. 17, 1864, supplement the original legislation.

April 25 .... New Orleans falls to Union forces under David G. Farragut, giving the United States control of the lower Mississippi River.

May 8 .... "Stonewall" Jackson wins the Battle of McDowell, the first of several victories in his Shenandoah Valley campaign; triumphs at Front Royal (May 23), First Winchester (May 25), Cross Keys (June 8), and Port Republic (June 9) follow.

May 9 .... General David Hunter declares free all slaves in South Carolina, Georgia, and Florida; President Lincoln nullifies Hunter's proclamation ten days later.

May 15 .... U.S. Congress passes the Homestead Bill.

May 30 .... Confederates abandon the key railroad center of Corinth, Mississippi.

May 31–June 1 .... The Battle of Seven Pines or Fair Oaks is fought near Richmond; Joseph E. Johnston is wounded on the first day of action, and command of the Confederate army defending Richmond against George B. McClellan's Army of the Potomac passes to Robert E. Lee.

June 6 .... Memphis, Tennessee, falls to Union military forces.

June 17 .... U.S. Congress passes the Land Grant College Bill (Morrill Act).

June 19 .... U.S. Congress prohibits slavery in the territories.

June 25–July 1 .... The Seven B reverses a tide of Union military success as Robert E. Lee drives George B. McClellan away from Richmond in action at Mechanicsville (June 26), Gaines's Mill (June 27), Savage Station (June 29), Glendale or Frayser's Farm (June 30), and Malvern Hill (July 1).

July 12 .... Lincoln appeals to the border state congressmen to support gradual, compensated emancipation, warning that the war may destroy slavery without compensation if they do not act; two days later, they reject his proposal.

July 17 .... U.S. Congress passes the Second Confiscation Act, which frees all slaves of owners who support the Confederacy.

July 22 .... Lincoln tells his cabinet that he intends to issue an emancipation proclamation.

July 22 .... The Union and the Confederacy agree to a cartel providing for the exchange of prisoners of war and the parole of excess captives held by either side.

Aug. 28–30 .... Robert E. Lee wins a victory over John Pope's Army of Virginia at the Battle of Second Manassas or Bull Run.

Sept. 17 .... Union victory at the Battle of Antietam or Sharpsburg ends Robert E. Lee's first invasion of the North.

Sept. 22 .... Lincoln issues his preliminary Emancipation Proclamation.

Oct. 8 .... The Battle of Perryville marks the climax of a Confederate invasion into Kentucky by armies under Braxton Bragg and E. Kirby Smith; the Confederates withdraw from the state after the battle.

Oct. 11 .... C.S. Congress exempts from conscription one white male on each plantation that has twenty or more slaves; this alienates many non-slaveholding white Southerners.

Nov. 4 .... Democrats score gains in the Northern off-year elections.

Nov. 5 .... Lincoln replaces George B. McClellan with Ambrose E. Burnside as Commander of the Army of the Potomac.

Dec. 13 .... Robert E. Lee defeats Burnside at the Battle of Fredericksburg.

Dec. 20–30 .... Destruction of U. S. Grant's supply
base at Holly Springs, Mississippi, and
William Tecumseh Sherman's repulse
in the Battle of Chickasaw Bayou
frustrate an initial attempt to capture the
Confederate stronghold at Vicksburg.

Dec. 31–Jan. 2, 1863 .... Battle of Stones River, or Murfreesboro,
fought in middle Tennessee, results
in the retreat of Braxton Bragg's
Confederate army and the beginning of
six months of inactivity on this front.

1863

Jan. 1 .... Lincoln issues his
Emancipation Proclamation.

Feb. 25... U.S. Congress passes the National
Banking Act.

March 3 .... U.S. Congress passes the Enrollment
Act, which institutes a national draft;
the Union will issue four calls under
this legislation, in July 1863 and March,
July, and December 1864.

April 2 .... Women take to the streets in the
Richmond "bread riot" to protest
food shortages.

April 24 .... C.S. Congress enacts the
tax-in-kind law, a highly unpopular
measure requiring agricultural
producers to give a portion of the
annual production of various crops to
the national government.

May 1–4 .... Robert E. Lee defeats Joseph Hooker (who had replaced Ambrose E. Burnside as commander of the Army of the Potomac in late January 1863) in the Battle of Chancellorsville.

May 1–17 .... U. S. Grant wins battles at Port Gibson (May 1), Raymond (May 12), Jackson (May 14), Champion Hill (May 16), and the Big Black River (May 17) en route to bottling up John C. Pemberton's army in the Vicksburg defenses.

May 26 .... Anti-war Democrat Clement L. Vallandigham of Ohio is banished to Confederate lines near Murfreesboro, Tennessee.

June 20 .... West Virginia joins the Union as a new state.

June 23–July 3 .... William S. Rosecrans's Tullahoma campaign compels Braxton Bragg's Army of Tennessee to withdraw from middle Tennessee.

July 1–3 .... George G. Meade's victory in the Battle of Gettysburg ends Robert E. Lee's second invasion of the North.

July 4 .... The Confederate army at Vicksburg surrenders to U. S. Grant.

July 8 .... The Confederate garrison at Port Hudson, Louisiana, surrenders, opening the Mississippi River to full Union control.

July 13 .... Anti-draft riots begin in New York City and rage for several days.

Sept. 2 .... Union forces under Ambrose E. Burnside occupy Knoxville, Tennessee.

Sept. 5 .... The British government decides to detain the Laird rams being built for the Confederacy, thus averting a diplomatic crisis with the United States.

Sept. 9 .... Union forces under William S. Rosecrans occupy Chattanooga, Tennessee.

Sept. 19–20 .... The Battle of Chickamauga, just south of Chattanooga, gives the Confederacy its greatest tactical victory in the Western Theater and compels William S. Rosecrans's Army of the Cumberland to retreat to Chattanooga.

Nov. 23–25 .... Union victory at the Battle of Chattanooga lifts the Confederate siege and opens the way for a campaign against Atlanta.

Dec. 8 .... Lincoln issues his Proclamation of Amnesty and Reconstruction as a blueprint for restoring the Union; this first presented the President's "10 percent plan" for reconstruction.

1864

Jan. 2 .... Confederate General Patrick R. Cleburne circulates a proposal that would free large numbers of slaves and enroll thousands of them in the Confederate Army; his proposal meets with staunch opposition.

Timeline

March 12 .... U. S. Grant named general-in-chief of Union forces; he plans simultaneous offensives designed to pressure Confederate military forces on a broad front.

April 8–9 .... Battles of Mansfield, or Sabine Crossroads, and Pleasant Hill, fought near Shreveport, Louisiana, mark the climax of Nathaniel P. Banks's unsuccessful Red River campaign.

April 12 .... Confederates under Nathan Bedford Forrest capture Fort Pillow, Tennessee, killing a number of black and white Union troops who try to surrender.

April 17 .... U. S. Grant ends the prisoner exchange agreement.

May 5–6 .... Battle of the Wilderness opens the "Overland campaign" between U. S. Grant and Robert E. Lee; Grant's goal is the destruction of the Army of Northern Virginia.

May 7 .... William Tecumseh Sherman begins his Atlanta campaign against Joseph E. Johnston's Army of Tennessee.

May 8–20 .... Battles around Spotsylvania Court House, Virginia, continue the struggle between Grant and Lee; heaviest fighting occurs on May 12 in the Confederate salient known as the "Mule Shoe."

May 15 .... Battle of New Market blunts Franz Sigel's Union campaign in the Shenandoah Valley; this battle included the famous charge of the cadets from the Virginia Military Academy.

May 16 .... Battle of Drewry's Bluff stops progress toward Richmond of Benjamin F. Butler's Union Army of the James; Butler retreats to Bermuda Hundred and is effectively bottled up.

June 1–3 .... Battles at Cold Harbor between Grant and Lee include massive and unsuccessful Union assaults (the heaviest attacks occurred on June 3).

June 12–18 .... Grant orchestrates a brilliant crossing of the James River but fails to capture Petersburg; his troops begin what will become a nine-month siege.

June 15 .... U.S. Congress makes pay for black and white soldiers equal.

June 19 .... U.S.S *Kearsarge* sinks C.S.S. *Alabama* off Cherbourg, France, ending the career of the most successful Confederate commerce raider.

June 27 .... Bloody repulse of Union attacks at Kennesaw Mountain, Georgia, after which Sherman resumes his campaign of maneuver against Johnston as he closes in on Atlanta.

July 2 .... The Wade-Davis Bill passes the U.S. Senate, presenting an alternative to President Lincoln's "10 per-cent Plan" for reconstruction; Lincoln kills it with a pocket veto on July 4, and supporters of the bill answer with the "Wade-Davis Manifesto," criticizing the President's actions.

July 17 .... Jefferson Davis replaces Joseph E. Johnston with John Bell Hood as commander of the Confederate army defending Atlanta; Hood launches unsuccessful offensives against Sherman's investing forces in the battles of Peachtree Creek (July 20), Atlanta (July 22), and Ezra Church (July 28), before the two armies settle into a siege.

July 30 .... The Union loses a good opportunity at the Battle of the Crater to break the stalemate at Petersburg.

Aug. 5 .... David G. Farragut's Union fleet wins the Battle of Mobile Bay, closing the last major Confederate port on the Gulf of Mexico.

Sept. 2 .... Sherman's Union forces enter Atlanta, providing a critical Union victory that virtually guarantees President Lincoln's reelection in November.

Sept. 19–Oct. 19............................ Climactic phase of the 1864 Shenandoah Valley campaign, during which Philip H. Sheridan wins decisive victories over Jubal A. Early's Confederate army in the battles of Third Winchester (Sept. 19), Fisher's Hill (Sept. 22), and Cedar Creek (Oct. 19).

Nov. 1 .... A new Maryland state constitution abolishing slavery takes effect.

Nov. 7 .... Jefferson Davis proposes enrolling slaves in the Confederate military and freeing all who served faithfully; this touches off an acrimonious debate that continues for several months.

Nov. 8 .... Abraham Lincoln reelected; Republicans gain large majorities in both houses of Congress and do well in Northern state races.

Nov. 16–Dec. 21 .... Sherman's army makes its famous "March to the Sea" from Atlanta to Savannah, leaving a wide path of destruction in its wake.

Nov. 30 .... John M. Schofield wins a Union victory over John Bell Hood's Army of Tennessee at the Battle of Franklin, a short distance south of Nashville.

Dec. 15–16 .... George H. Thomas routs Hood's Army of Tennessee in the Battle of Nashville, the final significant engagement in Tennessee.

1865

Jan. 11 .... The Missouri state constitutional
convention abolishes slavery.

Jan. 19 .... William Tecumseh Sherman begins
his march from Savannah into
the Carolinas.

Jan. 31 .... U.S. House of Representatives
approves a constitutional amendment
abolishing slavery.

Feb. 17... Columbia, South Carolina, falls
to Sherman's army; fires sweep
through the city.

Feb. 17... Charleston, South Carolina, evacuated
by Confederate military forces.

Feb. 22... Amendment to Tennessee's state
constitution abolishes slavery.

March 13 .... C.S. Congress authorizes President
Davis to recruit slaves as soldiers (but
not to offer them freedom if they serve).

March 19–21 .... Battle of Bentonville near Raleigh,
North Carolina, marks the end of
significant fighting on Sherman's front.

April 1 .... Union victory in the Battle of Five
Forks sets the stage for the Union
capture of Richmond and Petersburg.

April 2... Confederate government
abandons Richmond; Robert E. Lee's
Army of Northern Virginia evacuates
Richmond-Petersburg lines and begins
its retreat westward.

April 9 .... Lee surrenders the Army of Northern Virginia to U. S. Grant at Appomattox Court House.

April 14 .... President Lincoln is shot in Ford's Theater; he dies the next morning.

April 26 .... Joseph E. Johnston surrenders his army to Sherman at Durham Station, North Carolina.

May 4 .... Richard Taylor surrenders Confederate forces in Alabama, Mississippi, and East Louisiana to E. R. S. Canby at Citronelle, Alabama.

May 10 .... Jefferson Davis is captured near Irwinville, Georgia.

May 12–13 .... The final land battle of the war takes place at Palmito Ranch, near Brownsville, Texas.

May 26 .... Confederate forces in the Trans-Mississippi Theater are surrendered in an agreement signed in New Orleans.

Dec. 18 .... The Thirteenth Amendment is ratified; it abolishes slavery throughout the United States.

Glossary

abatis: A tangle of felled trees or brush in front of an entrenched position, with branches facing the enemy's lines to retard an attacking force.

blockade: A force of naval vessels placed to intercept shipping into or out of an enemy's ports.

bounty: A cash payment by the national, state, or local government designed to attract volunteers to the armed forces.

breastworks: A barricade of dirt, logs, sandbags, or other materials designed to protect soldiers fighting on the defensive.

breechloader: A shoulder weapon that is loaded at the breech, or rear of the barrel.

brevet rank: An honorary promotion of a military officer to a rank above his regular rank, given to reward exceptional service but conveying no increase in authority.

bummer: A soldier in William Tecumseh Sherman's army during the Georgia and Carolinas campaigns who operated beyond the effective control of superiors, often confiscating civilian property without regard to its possible military value.

cavalry screen: A body of cavalrymen charged with protecting the front and flanks of an army from probes by the enemy's cavalry.

commissary: The military department dealing with the supply of food.

company-grade officers: Those who hold the commissioned ranks of captain or lower.

contraband: Material belonging to an enemy subject to seizure by a belligerent power in time of war. During the Civil War, the term most often applied to slaves in the Confederacy who made their way to Union lines.

demonstration: A military term for a maneuver intended to hold the enemy's attention while a major assault or movement is made elsewhere.

earthworks: Fortifications constructed of dirt, sand, and other materials (a term often used interchangeably with breastworks or field works).

enfilade: To fire against an enemy's position from the side or flank. Such fire is especially effective, because the defenders are unable to bring a large volume of counterfire to bear.

entrenchments: Defensive works prepared either in the field or as part of more permanent fortifications around cities or other crucial positions (also often called, simply, trenches).

envelop: To move around an enemy's flank, placing troops in position to render a defensive posture untenable.

feint: A movement intended to hold the enemy's attention while a larger attack or maneuver is carried out on another part of the field (a term often used interchangeably with "demonstration").

field-grade officers: Those who hold the commissioned ranks of colonel, lieutenant colonel, or major.

fire-eaters: Outspoken advocates of Southern rights who took extreme positions regarding the protection of slavery. Many of them, such as Edmund Ruffin, played a prominent role in the secession movement.

flank: The end of a line of troops on the field of battle or in a fortified position. To "flank" an enemy's position involves placing troops on its side or rear. A "flanking march" is a maneuver designed to give the troops in motion either a tactical or a strategic advantage.

fleet: A group of naval warships and support vessels operating as a unified force.

flotilla: Similar to a fleet but usually consisting of a smaller number of vessels.

forage: The feed for horses and mules. As a verb, "to forage" means to procure hay, grains, or grass necessary to feed an army's animals. The verb also applied to soldiers' search for food to feed themselves.

forced march: A movement made at a rapid pace to meet a dire threat (either real or perceived).

guerrilla: A combatant who operates in small units or bands beyond the control of major organized military forces. These men often carried out raids and small attacks behind enemy lines.

logistics: Military activity dealing with the physical support, maintenance, and supply of an army.

martial law: Temporary government of civilians by military authorities, typically involving the suspension of some civil liberties.

minié ball: More properly called a minié bullet, this hollow-base lead projectile of cylindro-conoidal shape was the standard round for infantrymen on both sides who were armed with rifle shoulder weapons.

mortar: An artillery piece designed to fire projectiles in a high arc that could strike targets behind fortifications. Mortar boats deployed this type of artillery piece in naval actions.

muzzleloader: A shoulder weapon that is loaded at the muzzle, or front of the barrel. *

non-commissioned officers: Those who hold the ranks of sergeant and corporal.

ordnance: The military department responsible for the supply of arms and ammunition.

parole: An oath taken by a captured soldier not to bear arms again until formally exchanged for one of the captor's soldiers; given in return for release from captivity. As a verb, "to parole" means to obtain such an oath from a prisoner as a condition of releasing him.

partisan: A combatant operating in small groups beyond the control of major military forces. Sometimes used interchangeably with "guerrilla" but during the Civil War, partisans often were viewed as better disciplined and less likely to commit outrages against civilians or enemy soldiers.

picket: A soldier assigned to the perimeter of an army camp or position to give warning of enemy movements.

popular sovereignty: The doctrine that provided for the voters in a federal territory to decide whether they would accept slavery (rather than having Congress decide for them). An attempt to find a middle ground between those who wanted to exclude slavery from all territories and those who wanted it protected by Congress, the doctrine figured prominently in the Compromise of 1850 and the Kansas-Nebraska Act.

prisoner cartel: An agreement between warring governments to exchange captured soldiers rather than sending them to prisoner-of-war camps. If one side had a surplus of prisoners, those men would typically be paroled until a sufficient number of the enemy's troops was captured to make an exchange.

prize: An enemy vessel or neutral ship carrying contraband captured by a privateer or naval vessel. Prizes were taken to a port controlled by the captor.

quartermaster: The military department responsible for the supply of clothing, shoes, and other equipment.

reconnaissance-in-force: A probing movement by a large body of troops intended to reveal the enemy's position and likely intentions.

repeating firearm: A weapon that can be fired more than once without reloading.

salient: A portion of a defensive line that protrudes toward the enemy and is thus potentially vulnerable on three sides.

specie: Coined money, usually gold or silver. Specie payments are payments in coin, or the redemption of paper money on demand with coin equivalent.

strategy: The branch of warfare involving the movement of armies to (1) bring about combat with an enemy under favorable circumstances or (2) force the retreat of an enemy.

tactics: The branch of warfare involving actual combat between attackers and defenders.

trains: The wagons accompanying armies that carried food, forage, ammunition, and other supplies (not to be confused with railroad rolling stock).

transport: An unarmed vessel carrying troops or supplies.

trooper: A cavalryman.

volley: The simultaneous firing of their weapons by a number of soldiers in one unit.

works: A generic term applied to defensive fortifications of all types.

* One of the most common muzzleloaders used by both sides in the Civil War was the Enfield rifled musket. The replica .58 calibre Enfield ("three-bander") visible on the set in the video version of the course was graciously provided by Mrs. Mary Ritenour of Fairfax, VA in memory of her late husband, Corporal Ken Ritenour of the 3rd U.S. Infantry, Inc., a major re-enacting group.

Biographical Notes

Baker, Edward Dickinson (1811–1861). Republican senator from Oregon and friend of Abraham Lincoln, he was killed at the battle of Ball's Bluff in October 1861. His death helped spur creation of the Joint Committee on the Conduct of the War, which spent much of the conflict investigating Democratic generals.

Banks, Nathaniel Prentice (1816–1894). One of the most prominent Union political generals, he served throughout the war without achieving any distinction on the battlefield. No match for Stonewall Jackson in the Shenandoah Valley in 1862, he similarly came to grief during the 1864 Red River campaign.

Barton, Clara (1821–1912). The most famous Northern nurse, her excellent work at Antietam and elsewhere earned her the nickname "Angel of the Battlefield." Appointed head nurse of Benjamin F. Butler's Army of the James in 1864, she later helped identify and mark the graves of Union dead at Andersonville. She is most famous as the founder of the American Red Cross.

Beauregard, Pierre Gustave Toutant (1818–1893). One of the ranking officers in the Confederacy, he presided over the bombardment of Fort Sumter in April 1861, led the Southern army at the opening of the battle of First Bull Run or Manassas, and later held various commands in the Western and Eastern Theaters.

Bell, John (1797–1869). Tennesseean who ran as the presidential candidate of the Constitutional Union Party in 1860. A former Whig with moderate views, he gave lukewarm support to the Confederacy after Lincoln's call for 75,000 volunteers to suppress the rebellion.

Booth, John Wilkes (1838–1865). Member of the most celebrated family of actors in the United States and a staunch Southern sympathizer. He first planned to kidnap Abraham Lincoln, subsequently deciding to assassinate him. He mortally wounded the president on April 14, 1865, and was himself killed shortly thereafter by pursuing Union cavalry.

Bragg, Braxton (1817–1876). A controversial military figure who led the Confederate Army of Tennessee at Stones River, Chickamauga, and Chattanooga. Intensely unpopular with many of his soldiers and subordinates, he finished the war as an adviser to Jefferson Davis in Richmond.

Breckinridge, John Cabell (1821–1875). Vice President of the United States under James Buchanan and the Southern Democratic candidate for president in 1860, he served the Confederacy as a general and Secretary of War. He fought in the Eastern and Western Theaters, winning the battle of New Market in May 1864.

Brown, John (1800–1859). Abolitionist whose violent activities during the mid-1850s in Kansas Territory and raid on Harpers Ferry in October 1859 gained him wide notoriety. He was hanged after his capture at Harpers Ferry, becoming a martyr to many in the North.

Buchanan, James (1791–1868). Long-time Democratic politician who was elected president in 1856 and watched helplessly as the nation broke up during the winter of 1860–1861. During the last months of his presidency, he sought without success to find a way to entice the seceded states back into the Union.

Buell, Don Carlos (1818–1898). Union army commander in the Western Theater in 1861–1862 who fought at Shiloh and led the Northern forces at Perryville. Reluctant to conduct vigorous campaigns against the Confederates, he was relieved of command in the autumn of 1862.

Burnside, Ambrose Everett (1824–1881). Union general best known for commanding the Army of the Potomac at the battle of Fredericksburg in December 1862. His wartime career also included early service along the North Carolina coast and later action with Grant's army during the Overland campaign. After the war he served Rhode Island as governor and United States senator.

Butler, Benjamin Franklin (1818–1893). Union general who coined the term "contraband" for runaway slaves in 1861 and commanded the army that approached Richmond by moving up the James River during U. S. Grant's grand offensive of May 1864. A prewar Democrat who supported John C. Breckinridge in 1860, he became a Radical Republican during the war.

Cleburne, Patrick Ronayne (1828–1864). Confederate general who compiled a sterling record as a division commander in the Western Theater before his death at the battle of Franklin in November 1864. He caused a major controversy in 1864 with his famous circular recommending that slaves be armed and placed in Confederate service.

Cooke, Jay (1821–1905). A brilliant financier who raised hundreds of millions of dollars for the Union war effort through the sale of government bonds. Sometimes accused of receiving special treatment from the Lincoln Administration, he had powerful defenders who insisted that his actions helped keep Northern armies in the field.

Crittenden, John Jordan (1787–1863). Politician from Kentucky who worked hard to avoid the break-up of the Union in 1860–1861. He proposed reinstating the Missouri Compromise line, called for a national convention to discuss the secession crisis, and later worked hard to keep Kentucky in the Union.

Davis, Jefferson (1808–1889). Colonel during the war with Mexico, Secretary of War under Franklin Pierce, and prominent senator from Mississippi in the 1840s and 1850s, he served as the Confederacy's only president. He and his nationalist policies triggered great political debate among Confederates.

Dix, Dorothea Lynde (1802–1887). An antebellum advocate of improved care for the mentally ill, she served as superintendent of Union army nurses during the war. She rendered solid service, despite a personality that often placed her at odds with both subordinates and superiors.

Douglas, Stephen Arnold (1812–1861). Prominent senator from Illinois in the 1850s who favored the doctrine of popular sovereignty and ran unsuccessfully as the regular Democratic candidate for president in 1860.

Douglass, Frederick (1817 or 1818–1895). Born a slave, he escaped to freedom in 1838, became an abolitionist and newspaper editor, and by 1860 was the most prominent African American leader in the United States. He pressed tirelessly to add freedom as a war aim in the North.

Early, Jubal Anderson (1816–1894). Confederate general who compiled a solid record as an officer in the Army of Northern Virginia. He ended the war a disgraced figure in the Confederacy because of his defeats in the 1864 Shenandoah Valley campaign. After the war, he became one of the leading architects of the Lost Cause interpretation of the conflict.

Farragut, David Glasgow (1801–1870). The most famous Union naval figure of the war, he was promoted to rear admiral in 1862 (the first officer to hold that rank). He led naval forces in successful operations against New Orleans in 1862, Port Hudson in 1863, and Mobile Bay in 1864.

Forrest, Nathan Bedford (1821–1877). Although completely without formal military training, he became one of the best Confederate cavalry generals and proved to be a major thorn in the side of numerous Union commanders in the Western Theater. After the war, he became the first grand wizard of the Ku Klux Klan.

Frémont, John Charles (1813–1890). Famous as an antebellum western explorer, he ran as the first Republican candidate for president in 1856 and served as a Union general in Missouri and Virginia during the war. While commanding in Missouri in 1861, he attempted to free the state's slaves by issuing a proclamation that abolitionists applauded but Lincoln ordered him to rescind.

Grant, Ulysses S. (1822–1885). The most successful Union military commander, serving as general-in-chief for the last fourteen months of the war and twice winning election as president during the postwar years.

Greenhow, Rose O'Neal (1815–1864). A well-known resident of Washington, D.C., who became a Confederate spy. She supplied useful information to the Confederates before the battle of First Manassas, was later jailed in Washington, and eventually was released and sent to the Confederacy. She published an account of her imprisonment in 1863 and died when the vessel on which she was a passenger ran aground off North Carolina.

Halleck, Henry W. (1815–1872). An important Union military figure who presided over striking successes in the Western Theater in 1862, served as general-in-chief of the Union army in 1862–1864, and was demoted to chief of staff when Grant assumed the top military position in March 1864. His administrative skills outstripped his abilities as a field commander.

Hood, John Bell (1831–1879). Confederate commander who fought effectively in the Army of Northern Virginia in 1862–1863 but is best known for his unsuccessful defense of Atlanta against Sherman's army and the disastrous campaign in Tennessee that culminated in the battle of Nashville in mid-December 1864.

Hooker, Joseph (1814–1879). Union general nicknamed "Fighting Joe" who commanded the Army of the Potomac at the battle of Chancellorsville. Replaced by George G. Meade during the Gettysburg campaign, he later fought at Chattanooga and in the opening phase of the 1864 Atlanta campaign.

Hunter, David (1802–1886). A Union general who, as commander along the south Atlantic coast, tried to free all slaves in his department in May 1862, only to see Lincoln revoke his order. He later led an army in the Shenandoah Valley in 1864.

Jackson, Thomas Jonathan (1824–1863). Nicknamed "Stonewall" and second only to Lee as a popular Confederate hero, he was celebrated for his 1862 Shenandoah Valley campaign and his achievements as Lee's trusted subordinate. He died at the peak of his fame, succumbing to pneumonia after being wounded at the battle of Chancellorsville.

Johnston, Albert Sidney (1803–1862). A prominent antebellum military figure from whom much was expected as a Confederate general. He compiled a mixed record in the Western Theater before being mortally wounded on April 6, 1862, at the battle of Shiloh.

Johnston, Joseph Eggleston (1807–1891). A Confederate army commander who served in both Virginia and the Western Theater. Notoriously prickly about rank and privileges, he feuded with Jefferson Davis and compiled a record that demonstrated his preference for defensive over offensive operations. His wound at the battle of Seven Pines in May 1862 opened the way for R. E. Lee to assume field command. (He and A. S. Johnston were not related.)

Lee, Robert Edward (1807–1870). Southern military officer who commanded the Army of Northern Virginia for most of the war and became the most admired figure in the Confederacy.

Lincoln, Abraham (1809–1865). Elected in 1860 as the first Republican to hold the presidency, he provided superior leadership for the Northern war effort and was reelected in 1864 before being assassinated at Ford's Theater on the eve of complete Union victory.

Longstreet, James (1821–1904). Lee's senior subordinate from 1862 until the end of the war, he compiled a generally excellent record while under Lee's eye but proved unequal to the demands of independent command during the East Tennessee campaign of 1863–1864. He became a controversial figure in the South after the war, because he refused to embrace Lost Cause ideas.

McClellan, George Brinton (1826–1885). One of the most important military figures of the war, he built the Army of the Potomac into a formidable force and led it during the Peninsula campaign, during the Seven Days battles, and at Antietam. Often at odds with Lincoln because of his unwillingness to press the enemy, he was relieved of command in November 1862 and ran as the Democratic candidate for president in 1864.

McDowell, Irvin (1818–1885). Military officer who commanded the Union army at the battle of First Bull Run or Manassas. The remainder of his wartime career was anticlimactic.

Meade, George Gordon (1815–1872). Union general who fought throughout the war in the Eastern Theater, commanding the Army of the Potomac at Gettysburg and for the rest of the war. U. S. Grant's presence with the army after April 1864 placed Meade in a difficult position.

Pope, John (1822–1892). Union general who won several small successes in the Western Theater before being transferred to the Eastern Theater to command the Army of Virginia. His defeat at the battle of Second Bull Run or Manassas in August 1862 ended his important service during the war.

Porter, David Dixon (1813–1891). Union naval officer who commanded the Mississippi River Squadron during 1862–1863 in support of various army operations, including the campaign against Vicksburg. He later served along the Atlantic coast and on the James and York Rivers in Virginia.

Rosecrans, William Starke (1819–1898). Union military commander who fought in the Western Theater and led the Army of the Cumberland at the battle of Chickamauga and during the early phase of the siege of Chattanooga. His removal from command at Chattanooga by Grant in mid-October 1863 ended his important wartime service.

Schofield, John McAllister (1831–1906). Union general who fought in the Western Theater, commanding the Army of Ohio during the Atlanta campaign and winning the battle of Franklin on November 30, 1864.

Scott, Dred (1795 [?]–1858). Slave who stood at the center of legal proceedings that culminated in 1857 in the Supreme Court's landmark *Dred Scott v. Sanford* decision. The Court declared that, as an African American, Scott was not a citizen and, therefore, could not institute a suit. The Court also declared the Missouri Compromise unconstitutional and seemingly opened all federal territories to slavery.

Scott, Winfield (1786–1866). One of the great soldiers in United States history, he performed brilliantly in the war with Mexico and remained the ranking officer in the army at the outbreak of the Civil War. He devised the "Anaconda Plan" in the spring of 1861, a strategy that anticipated the way the North would win the conflict.

Semmes, Raphael (1809–1877). The most celebrated Confederate naval officer, he captained the commerce raiders *Sumter* and *Alabama*, the two of which captured more than 70 Northern ships, and later commanded the James River Naval Squadron.

Sheridan, Philip Henry (1831–1888). Ranked behind only Grant and Sherman as a Union war hero, Sheridan fought in both the Western and Eastern Theaters. His most famous victories came in the 1864 Shenandoah Valley campaign; at the battle of Five Forks on April 1, 1865; and during the Appomattox campaign.

Sherman, William Tecumseh (1820–1891). Union military officer who overcame difficulties early in the war to become Grant's primary subordinate. An advocate of "hard" war, he is best known for his capture of Atlanta and the "March to the Sea" in 1864.

Sigel, Franz (1824–1902). German-born Union general who was popular among German-speaking troops but ineffective as a field commander. His most famous service came in the Shenandoah Valley in 1864, ending in defeat at the battle of New Market on May 15.

Smith, Edmund Kirby (1824–1893). A Confederate general who participated in the 1862 Kentucky campaign and later commanded Southern forces in the vast Trans-Mississippi Theater.

Stephens, Alexander Hamilton (1812–1883). A moderate Democrat from Georgia who supported Stephen A. Douglas in the 1860 presidential campaign and embraced secession reluctantly, he served throughout the war as Vice President of the Confederacy. Increasingly at odds with Jefferson Davis over issues related to growing central power, he became an embittered public critic of the President and his policies.

Stevens, Thaddeus (1792–1868). Radical Republican congressman from Pennsylvania who chaired the House Ways and Means Committee. He favored harsh penalties for slaveholding Confederates and pushed to make emancipation a major focus of the Union war effort.

Stuart, James Ewell Brown (1833–1864). Known as "Jeb," he commanded the cavalry in the Army of Northern Virginia from June 1862 until his death at the battle of Yellow Tavern in May 1864. His role in the Gettysburg campaign generated a great deal of controversy, but overall he compiled a superb record as the "eyes and ears" of Lee's army.

Sumner, Charles (1811–1874). Radical Republican senator from Massachusetts who was caned on the floor of the Senate by Congressman Preston Brooks of South Carolina after delivering his famous "Crime against Kansas" speech in 1856. During the war, he chaired the Senate Committee on Foreign Affairs and consistently pressed for emancipation.

Taney, Roger Brooke (1777–1864). Chief Justice of the Supreme Court from 1835–1864, he antagonized abolitionists with the *Dred Scott* decision in 1857. During the war, he sought to curb Abraham Lincoln's power to suspend the *writ of habeas corpus*, opposed Northern conscription, and argued that governmental assaults on civil liberties posed a greater threat to the nation than secession of the Southern states.

Thomas, George Henry (1816–1870). A leading Union military officer who spent his entire Civil War career in the Western Theater. Earning the nickname "Rock of Chickamauga" for exceptional service on that battlefield, he later commanded the Army of the Cumberland during the siege of Chattanooga and decisively defeated John Bell Hood's Army of Tennessee at the battle of Nashville. A Virginian outside Grant's inner circle, he never received his full measure of credit for superior accomplishments.

Tompkins, Sally L. (1833–1916). Established Robertson Hospital in Richmond, Virginia, in July 1861 and supervised it for the duration of the war. Commissioned a captain in the Confederate army when all private hospitals were placed under military control, she was the only woman to hold official rank in the Southern armed forces. Her hospital earned the distinction of returning the highest percentage of its patients to active service.

Vallandigham, Clement Laird (1820–1871). Congressman from Ohio and a leading Copperhead who staunchly opposed emancipation and most of the rest of the Republican legislative agenda. Exiled to the Confederacy by Lincoln in 1863, he returned to the United States and helped draft the peace platform at the 1864 Democratic national convention.

Wade, Benjamin Franklin (1800–1878). Radical Republican senator from Ohio who chaired the Joint Committee on the Conduct of the War, urged Abraham Lincoln to dismiss George B. McClellan, and called for the emancipation of all slaves. In 1864, he co-authored the Wade-Davis Bill and the Wade-Davis Manifesto that attacked Lincoln's actions relating to Reconstruction.

Yancey, William Lowndes (1814–1863). Prominent Alabama fire-eater whose "Yancey Platform," calling for the protection of slavery in all federal territories, helped break up the Democratic Party in 1860.

Bibliography

Essential Reading:

Berlin, Ira, et al., eds. *Free at Last: A Documentary History of Slavery, Freedom, and the Civil War*. New York: The New Press, 1992. Reprinted in paperback. A basic collection of primary testimony relating to black participation in the Civil War. The editors provide excellent introductory essays to sections dealing with black military service, the process of emancipation, and the transition from slave to free labor in the Upper and Lower South.

Clinton, Catherine, and Silber, Nina, eds. *Divided Houses: Gender and the Civil War*. New York: Oxford University Press, 1992. Reprinted in paperback. Includes essays by eighteen scholars on various facets of women's wartime experience, conceptions of manhood, and other aspects of gender history.

Foner, Eric. *Reconstruction: America's Unfinished Journey, 1863–1877*. New York: Harper & Row, 1988. Reprinted in paperback. This standard survey includes material on wartime reconstruction.

Gallagher, Gary W. *The Confederate War*. Cambridge, Mass.: Harvard University Press, 1997. Reprinted in paperback. A concise treatment that focuses on popular will, nationalism, and military strategy in the Confederacy.

———. *Lee and His Generals in War and Memory*. Baton Rouge: Louisiana State University Press, 1998. Includes essays on the ways in which modern Americans have tried to understand the meaning of the war.

Hattaway, Herman, and Jones, Archer. *How the North Won: A Military History of the Civil War*. Urbana: University of Illinois Press, 1983. Reprinted in paperback. The best one-volume military history of the Civil War, this study pays rigorous attention to all theaters and places campaigns and battles in a broad political context.

McPherson, James M. *Battle Cry of Freedom: The Civil War Era.* New York: Oxford University Press, 1988. Reprinted in paperback. Equally well written and researched, this Pulitzer Prize-winning analytical narrative is the best one-volume treatment of the subject. It gives full attention to the background of the conflict, as well as to the military and nonmilitary aspects of the war.

————. *Drawn with the Sword: Reflections on the American Civil War.* New York: Oxford University Press, 1996. Includes excellent essays on the continuing popularity of the Civil War as a topic for study by modern Americans.

————, and Cooper, William J., eds., *Writing the Civil War: The Quest to Understand.* Columbia: University of South Carolina Press, 1998. Includes essays by Emory M. Thomas, Reid Mitchell, Joseph T. Glatthaar, Gary W. Gallagher, Drew Gilpin Faust, Mark E. Neely, Jr., and six other scholars on various aspects of the conflict. The essays evaluate important historical literature and discuss areas in need of further exploration.

Nevins, Allan. *The War for the Union: The Improvised War, 1861–1862.* New York: Scribner's, 1959. The first of Nevins's four volumes on the history of the Civil War. Nevins interpreted the conflict as a transforming event that helped make the United States a powerful modern state.

Paludan, Philip Shaw. *"A People's Contest": The Union and the Civil War, 1861–1865.* New York: Harper & Row, 1988. The best one-volume treatment of the nonmilitary side of the Northern war experience, this volume emphasizes how the conflict pushed the North toward modern nationhood.

Potter, David M. *The Impending Crisis, 1848–1861.* New York: Harper & Row, 1976. Reprinted in paperback. A fine analytical narrative of the political events and sectional controversies that preceded the Civil War.

Thomas, Emory M. *The Confederate Nation, 1861–1865.* New York: Harper & Row, 1979. Reprinted in paperback. A superior one-volume history of the subject, well researched and well written.

Supplementary Reading:

Adams, Michael C. C. *Our Masters the Rebels: A Speculation on Union Military Failure in the East, 1861–1865*. Cambridge, Mass.: Harvard University Press, 1978. Reprinted in paperback under the title *Fighting for Defeat*. This interesting study argues that a Northern belief in the superiority of Southern fighting prowess hampered Union military operations in the Eastern Theater.

Attie, Jeanie. *Patriotic Toil: Northern Women and the American Civil War*. Ithaca, N.Y.: Cornell University Press, 1998. A rigorous scholarly treatment of the impact of the war on Northern women.

Bearss, Edwin Cole. *The Campaign for Vicksburg*. 3 vols. Dayton, Ohio: Morningside, 1985–86. A massively detailed narrative of the protracted campaign that resulted in the Union capture of Vicksburg in July 1863.

Bensel, Richard Franklin. *Yankee Leviathan: The Origins of Central State Authority in America, 1859–1877*. Cambridge: Cambridge University Press, 1990. Reprinted in paperback. A densely written but important book that sees secession and the Civil War as crucial events in spurring the formation of the modern American state.

Bergeron, Arthur W., Jr. *Confederate Mobile*. Jackson: University Press of Mississippi, 1991. Contains considerable material on the battle of Mobile Bay, as well as on the city's experience during the Civil War.

Beringer, Richard E., Hattaway, Herman, Jones, Archer, and Still, William N., Jr. *Why the South Lost the Civil War*. Athens: University of Georgia Press, 1986. A detailed study that attributes Confederate defeat to disaffection, war weariness, doubts about slavery, and religion rather than to Northern military might and industrial superiority.

Boritt, Gabor S., ed. *Why the Confederacy Lost*. New York: Oxford University Press, 1992. Reprinted in paperback. Includes essays by James M. McPherson, Archer Jones, Gary W. Gallagher, Reid Mitchell, and

Joseph T. Glatthaar that highlight the role of military events in explaining Confederate defeat.

Case, Lynn M., and Spencer, Warren F. *The United States and France: Civil War Diplomacy*. Philadelphia: University of Pennsylvania Press, 1970. A massive scholarly study of Franco-American diplomatic relations.

Castel, Albert. *Decision in the West: The Atlanta Campaign of 1864*. Lawrence: University Press of Kansas, 1992. A masterful, detailed narrative of the first phase of Sherman's critical operations in Georgia during 1864.

Catton, Bruce. *Glory Road*. Garden City, N.Y.: Doubleday, 1952. Reprinted in paperback. The second volume of Catton's brilliantly written narrative of the campaigns of the Army of the Potomac.

―――. *Grant Takes Command*. Boston: Little, Brown, 1969. A perceptive biographical treatment of Grant's career from the aftermath of Vicksburg through Appomattox.

―――. *Mr. Lincoln's Army*. Garden City, N.Y.: Doubleday, 1951. Reprinted in paperback. The first volume of Catton's history of the Army of the Potomac.

―――. *A Stillness at Appomattox*. Garden City, N.Y.: Doubleday, 1953. The Pulitzer Prize-winning third volume of Catton's history of the Army of the Potomac.

Coddington, Edwin B. *The Gettysburg Campaign: A Study in Command*. New York: Scribner's, 1968. Reprinted in paperback. The best one-volume treatment of the campaign, this provides an excellent overview for readers beginning to explore the vast literature on Gettysburg.

Connelly, Thomas Lawrence. *Army of the Heartland: The Army of Tennessee, 1861–1862*. Baton Rouge: Louisiana State University Press, 1967. A critical scholarly examination of the Confederate military effort in the Western Theater during the first eighteen months of the war.

————. *Autumn of Glory: The Army of Tennessee, 1862–1865*. Baton Rouge: Louisiana State University Press, 1971. The concluding volume in Connelly's study of Confederate military operations in the Western Theater.

Cook, Adrian. *The Armies of the Streets: The New York City Draft Riots of 1863*. Lexington: University Press of Kentucky, 1974. A sound narrative of the most famous anti-draft violence of the war.

Cooling, Benjamin Franklin. *Forts Henry and Donelson: The Key to the Confederate Heartland*. Knoxville: University of Tennessee Press, 1987. A full-scale examination of the campaign that propelled Ulysses S. Grant to prominence and set the stage for Union success in Tennessee.

Cooper, William J. *The South and the Politics of Slavery, 1828–1856*. Baton Rouge: Louisiana State University Press, 1978. Reprinted in paperback. A well-written narrative that places slavery at the center of antebellum Southern politics.

Cox, LaWanda. *Lincoln and Black Freedom: A Study in Presidential Leadership*. Columbia: University of South Carolina Press, 1981. Reprinted in paperback. A perceptive treatment that focuses on events in Louisiana.

Cozzens, Peter. *The Darkest Days of the War: The Battles of Iuka and Corinth*. Chapel Hill: University of North Carolina Press. A scholarly, well-written study of two battles in northern Mississippi that adversely affected Confederate strategic operations in the autumn of 1862. Like Cozzens's other campaign studies, it rests on solid research and boasts a strong narrative.

————. *No Better Place to Die: The Battle of Stones River*. Urbana: University of Illinois Press, 1990. Reprinted in paperback. The best study of this important battle.

————. *The Shipwreck of Their Hopes: The Battles for Chattanooga*. Urbana: University of Illinois Press, 1994. Reprinted in paperback. The best study of the campaign that helped propel Grant to overall command of all Union armies.

―――. *This Terrible Sound: The Battle of Chickamauga.* Urbana: University of Illinois Press, 1992. Reprinted in paperback. The best study of this major battle in the Western Theater.

Crook, D. P. *The North, the South, and the Powers: 1861–1865.* New York: John Wiley and Sons, 1974. A good brief overview of the diplomatic history of the war.

Current, Richard N. *Lincoln and the First Shot.* Philadelphia: Lippincott, 1963. Reprinted in paperback. A thoughtful exploration of whether Lincoln manipulated the Confederates into firing the first shot at Fort Sumter.

Curry, Leonard P. *Blueprint for Modern America: Nonmilitary Legislation of the First Civil War Congress.* Nashville: Vanderbilt University Press, 1968. Examines the Republican legislation that influenced the social, economic, and political development of the nation for the rest of the century.

Daniel, Larry J. *Shiloh: The Battle That Changed the Civil War.* New York: Simon and Schuster, 1997. Reprinted in paperback. A soundly researched narrative of the war's first massive battle.

Davis, William C. *"A Government of Our Own": The Making of the Confederacy.* New York: The Free Press, 1994. Reprinted in paperback. A detailed and engagingly written narrative of the Montgomery convention at which the Confederacy was established.

―――. *Battle at Bull Run.* Garden City, N.Y.: Doubleday, 1977. Reprinted in paperback. A concise, well-written narrative of the campaign that ended in the first major battle of the conflict.

―――. *The Battle of New Market.* Garden City, N.Y.: Doubleday, 1975. Reprinted in paperback. The best narrative of Franz Sigel's failed 1864 Union offensive in the Shenandoah Valley.

―――. *Duel Between the First Ironclads.* Garden City, N.Y.: Doubleday, 1975. Reprinted in paperback. A lively account of the historic battle between the *Monitor* and the *Virginia.*

Donald, David. *Charles Sumner and the Coming of the Civil War*. New York: Alfred A. Knopf, 1961. Reprinted in paperback (together with Donald's *Charles Sumner and the Rights of Man* in an edition containing two volumes in one). The first volume of Donald's two-volume biography of Sumner, this superbly written narrative provides numerous insights into abolitionism, sectionalism, and national politics.

Donald, David Herbert. *Lincoln*. New York: Simon & Schuster, 1995. Reprinted in paperback. The best one-volume life of Lincoln, written by a two-time winner of the Pulitzer Prize for biography.

Dowdey, Clifford, *The Seven Days: The Emergence of Lee*. Boston: Little, Brown, 1964. An immensely readable narrative only somewhat weakened by the author's obvious pro-Southern sympathies.

Durden, Robert F. *The Gray and the Black: The Confederate Debate on Emancipation*. Baton Rouge: Louisiana State University Press, 1972. Quotes extensively from wartime testimony in examining the bitter debate over whether to enroll slaves in the Confederate army.

Faust, Drew Gilpin. *Mothers of Invention: Women of the Slaveholding South in the American Civil War*. Chapel Hill: University of North Carolina Press, 1996. Reprinted in paperback. A well-written, prize-winning examination of the ways in which upper-class Southern women were influenced by and reacted to a conflict that severely disrupted their lives and society.

Fellman, Michael. *Inside War: The Guerrilla Conflict in Missouri during the American Civil War*. New York: Oxford University Press, 1989. Reprinted in paperback. The best study of guerrillas during the war, this title gives considerable attention to the social and political conditions that spawned and nourished guerrilla activity.

Foster, Gaines M. *Ghosts of the Confederacy: Defeat, the Lost Cause, and the Emergence of the New South, 1865–1913*. New York: Oxford University Press, 1987. Reprinted in paperback. The best examination of the development of Lost Cause arguments about the causes and conduct of the Civil War.

Franklin, John Hope. *The Emancipation Proclamation*. Garden City, N.Y.: Doubleday, 1963. A concise treatment of a seminal document by a leading historian of African American history.

Freeman, Douglas Southall. *Lee's Lieutenants: A Study in Command*. 3 vols. New York: Scribner's, 1942–45. Reprinted in paperback. These compellingly written volumes are the classic treatment of the Army of Northern Virginia's high command. Few studies have exerted as much influence on the military history of the Civil War.

Gallagher, Gary W., ed. *The Antietam Campaign*. Chapel Hill: University of North Carolina Press, 1999. Includes essays by Robert K. Krick, Brooks D. Simpson, Peter S. Carmichael, Lesley J. Gordon, Gallagher, and five other scholars on various military and nonmilitary aspects of this immensely important campaign.

————, ed. *The Fredericksburg Campaign: Decision on the Rappahannock*. Chapel Hill, University of North Carolina Press, 1995. Includes essays by Alan T. Nolan, William Marvel, George C. Rable, Robert K. Krick, A. Wilson Greene, William A. Blair, and Gallagher on various military and nonmilitary aspects of the campaign.

————, ed. *The Wilderness Campaign*. Chapel Hill: University of North Carolina Press, 1998. Includes essays by Brooks D. Simpson, Gordon C. Rhea, John J. Hennessy, Robert K. Krick, Gallagher, and three others on aspects of the battle, the performances of selected commanders, and the ways in which veterans chose to remember the campaign.

Geary, James W. *We Need Men: The Union Draft in the Civil War*. DeKalb: Northern Illinois University Press, 1991. The standard title on the operation and impact of the Northern draft.

Glatthaar, Joseph T. *Forged in Battle: The Civil War Alliance of Black Soldiers and White Officers*. New York: The Free Press, 1989. Reprinted in paperback. An excellent scholarly examination of the military experiences and battlefield record of the black soldiers who made up almost 10 percent of the Union army.

————. *The March to the Sea and Beyond: Sherman's Troops in the Savannah and Carolinas Campaigns.* New York: New York University Press, 1985. Reprinted in paperback. A social history of Sherman's army that emphasizes its veteran character and success in wreaking havoc in the Southern hinterlands.

Goff, Richard D. *Confederate Supply.* Durham, N.C.: Duke University Press, 1969. The best study of the Confederacy's efforts to clothe and feed its armies.

Hanchett, William. *The Lincoln Murder Conspiracies.* Urbana: University of Illinois Press, 1983. This important study exposes as baseless the many conspiracy theories about Lincoln's murder.

Harris, William C. *With Charity for All: Lincoln and the Restoration of the Union.* Lexington: University Press of Kentucky, 1998. The fullest modern treatment of wartime reconstruction, this study argues that Lincoln would have allowed Southern states a significant voice in the process, even after the end of the war.

Hennessy, John J. *Return to Bull Run: The Campaign and Battle of Second Manassas.* New York: Simon & Schuster, 1993. Reprinted in paperback. A model campaign study that combines exhaustive research and literary flair.

Hesseltine, William Best. *Civil War Prisons: A Study in War Psychology.* Columbus: Ohio State University Press, 1930. Remains the best general treatment of a subject badly in need of new scholarly attention.

————, ed. "Civil War Prisons." Special issue of the journal *Civil War History* (June 1962) with eight essays on various prison camps and other aspects of the topic.

Hewitt, Lawrence Lee. *Port Hudson: Confederate Bastion on the Mississippi.* Baton Rouge: Louisiana State University Press, 1987. Reprinted in paperback. A solid scholarly study of the campaign that resulted in the loss of the last major Confederate stronghold on the Mississippi River.

Hughes, Nathaniel Cheairs, Jr. *Bentonville: The Final Battle of Sherman and Johnston*. Chapel Hill: University of North Carolina Press, 1996. This well-researched narrative covers the last major military action in Sherman's 1865 campaign through the Carolinas.

Johnson, Ludwell H. *The Red River Campaign: Politics and Cotton in the Civil War*. Baltimore: Johns Hopkins University Press, 1958. Reprinted in paperback. This standard study of the 1864 campaign successfully places military events in a broader political and economic context.

Jones, Howard. *Union in Peril: The Crisis over British Intervention in the Civil War*. Chapel Hill: University of North Carolina Press, 1992. This excellent treatment of Anglo-American diplomatic affairs during the first twenty months of the conflict highlights the degree to which military operations influenced British leaders.

Jones, Virgil Carrington. *The Civil War at Sea*. 3 vols. New York: Henry Holt, 1960–62. An engaging, popularly written narrative of the naval war that gives attention to the struggle on Southern rivers, the blockade, and commerce raiders.

Kennett, Lee. *Marching through Georgia: The Story of Soldiers and Civilians during Sherman's Campaign*. New York: HarperCollins, 1995. Reprinted in paperback. A well-written and impressively researched study that accords full attention to the experience of soldiers and the civilians their military maneuvering and fighting affected.

Klement, Frank L. *The Limits of Dissent: Clement L. Vallandigham and the Civil War*. Lexington: University Press of Kentucky, 1970. A sound treatment of the most prominent Northern Copperhead politician.

Long, David E. *The Jewel of Liberty: Abraham Lincoln's Re-election and the End of Slavery*. Mechanicsburg, Pa.: Stackpole, 1994. A detailed account that emphasizes the importance of the slavery issue and takes the Copperheads to task for behavior that might be labeled treasonous.

Luraghi, Raimondo. *A History of the Confederate Navy*. Annapolis, Md.: Naval Institute Press, 1996. The best scholarly treatment of the topic, impressively researched and sound in its judgments.

McDonough, James Lee. *War in Kentucky: From Shiloh to Perryville*. Knoxville: University of Tennessee Press, 1994. A serviceable narrative of the strategic counteroffensive of the western portion of the Confederacy in the summer and autumn of 1862.

McPherson, James M. *For Cause and Comrades: Why Men Fought in the Civil War*. New York: Oxford University Press, 1997. Reprinted in paperback. An important study that emphasizes the role of ideology as a factor in motivating men on both sides to enlist and fight.

————, ed. *The Negro's Civil War: How American Negroes Felt and Acted during the War for the Union*. New York: Pantheon, 1965. Reprinted in paperback. A useful collection of firsthand testimony relating to the black experience during the conflict.

Marvel, William. *The Alabama and the Kearsarge: The Sailor's Civil War*. Chapel Hill: University of North Carolina Press, 1996. This deeply researched and beautifully written study of the two vessels that fought a famous duel off the French coast in 1864 includes the best treatment to date of the life of common sailors in the Union and Confederate navies.

————. *Andersonville: The Last Depot*. Chapel Hill: University of North Carolina Press, 1994. Easily the best study of any Civil War prisoner-of-war camp, this narrative reflects extensive research and careful analysis.

Massey, Mary Elizabeth. *Bonnet Brigades: American Women and the Civil War*. New York: Alfred A. Knopf, 1966. Reprinted in paperback under the title *Women in the Civil War*. A pioneering survey of women's experiences during the conflict.

————. *Refugee Life in the Confederacy*. Baton Rouge: Louisiana State University Press, 1964. The most detailed examination of white refugees in the Confederacy.

Mitchell, Reid. *Civil War Soldiers*. New York: Viking, 1988. Reprinted in paperback. A major study that explores the motivations, expectations, and experiences of Union and Confederate soldiers.

Mohr, Clarence L. *On the Threshold of Freedom: Masters and Slaves in Civil War Georgia*. Athens: University of Georgia Press, 1986. Reprinted in paperback. The best study of slavery in a Confederate state, this work emphasizes the ways in which the war weakened the hold of master over slave.

Moore, Albert Burton. *Conscription and Conflict in the Confederacy*. New York: Macmillan, 1924. Reprinted in paperback. Although more than 60 years old, this remains the only full-scale examination of the legislative background and overall effect of the Southern draft.

Nevins, Allan. *The War for the Union: The Organized War, 1863–1864*. The third of Nevins's Civil War quartet, this volume stresses the degree to which Northern organizational skills and accomplishments furthered the Union war effort.

Perry, Milton F. *Infernal Machines: The Story of Confederate Submarine and Mine Warfare*. Baton Rouge: Louisiana State University Press, 1965. Reprinted in paperback. The standard account of Confederate efforts to use technology to overcome Northern numbers and material advantages.

Potter, David M. *Lincoln and His Party in the Secession Crisis*. New Haven, Conn.: Yale University Press, 1942. Reprinted in paperback with a new preface in 1962. A durable examination of the way in which Lincoln and his party reacted to the South's actions following the 1860 presidential election.

Powell, Lawrence N. *New Masters: Northern Planters during the Civil War and Reconstruction*. New Haven, Conn.: Yale University Press, 1980. Reprinted in paperback. A careful examination of the wartime interaction between Northerners and freedmen in the context of Southern plantation agriculture.

Rable, George C. *Civil Wars: Women and the Crisis of Southern Nationalism.* Urbana: University of Illinois Press, 1989. Reprinted in paperback. Impressive research and clear writing are two of this important book's many strengths.

————. *The Confederate Republic: A Revolution against Politics.* Chapel Hill: University of North Carolina Press, 1994. The best study of politics in the Confederacy, this book analyzes the debate between those who favored and opposed granting strong war-related powers to the central government.

Rhea, Gordon C. *The Battle of the Wilderness, May 5–6, 1864.* Baton Rouge: Louisiana State University Press, 1994. The quality of research and writing are equally impressive in this detailed narrative.

————. *The Battles for Spotsylvania Court House and the Road to Yellow Tavern, May 7–12, 1864.* Baton Rouge: Louisiana State University Press, 1997. Displays the same strengths as Rhea's fine study of the battle of the Wilderness.

Richardson, Heather Cox. *The Greatest Nation of the Earth: Republican Economic Policies during the Civil War.* Cambridge, Mass.: Harvard University Press, 1997. A good study of the Republican Party's economic ideology and the process by which much of it was translated into wartime legislation.

Robertson, William Glenn. *Back Door to Richmond: The Bermuda Hundred Campaign, April–June 1864.* Newark: University of Delaware Press, 1987. A solid treatment of a failed element in U. S. Grant's 1864 strategy of simultaneous advances.

Robinson, William Morrison. *The Confederate Privateers.* New Haven: Yale University Press, 1928. The standard title on an interesting facet of Confederate naval history.

Rose, Willie Lee. *Rehearsal for Reconstruction: The Port Royal Experiment.* Indianapolis: Bobbs-Merrill, 1964. Reprinted in paperback. A classic treatment of the transition from slavery to freedom for black people on the South Carolina Sea Islands.

Sears, Stephen W. *Chancellorsville*. Boston: Houghton, Mifflin, 1996. Reprinted in paperback. A fine treatment of a complex campaign. As with all of Sears's titles, this volume is very well written and researched.

————. *Landscape Turned Red: The Battle of Antietam*. New York: Ticknor & Fields, 1983. Reprinted in paperback. The best analytical narrative of the 1862 Maryland campaign.

————. *To the Gates of Richmond: The Peninsula Campaign*. New York: Ticknor & Fields, 1992. Reprinted in paperback. The best study of George B. McClellan's Peninsula campaign and the Seven Days battles.

Silbey, Joel H. *A Respectable Minority: The Democratic Party in the Civil War Era, 1860–1868*. New York: W.W. Norton, 1977. Reprinted in paperback. A good short treatment that portrays the Democratic Party as mounting an effective opposition to Lincoln's Administration and the Republican majority in Congress.

Simpson, Brooks D. *The Reconstruction Presidents*. Lawrence: University Press of Kansas, 1998. This well-researched and provocatively argued book includes two chapters on Lincoln and wartime reconstruction.

Stampp, Kenneth M. *And the War Came: The North and the Secession Crisis, 1860–1861*. Baton Rouge: Louisiana State University Press, 1950. Reprinted in paperback. An influential study of the shifting attitudes toward the South among Northerners during the period between Lincoln's election and the firing on Fort Sumter.

Still, William N., Jr. *Iron Afloat: The Story of the Confederate Armorclads*. Nashville: Vanderbilt University Press, 1971. The standard scholarly study of the construction, deployment, and battle performance of Confederate ironclad naval vessels.

Sword, Wiley. *Embrace an Angry Wind—The Confederacy's Last Hurrah: Spring Hill, Franklin, and Nashville*. New York: HarperCollins, 1992. Reprinted in paperback. A detailed narrative of John Bell Hood's operations in Tennessee during the last three months of 1864.

Tanner, Robert G. *Stonewall in the Valley: Thomas J. "Stonewall" Jackson's Shenandoah Valley Campaign, Spring 1862*. Revised and expanded edition. Mechanicsburg, Pa.: Stackpole, 1996. The best overall narrative of Jackson's famous campaign, this volume accords the Federals relatively little attention.

Tap, Bruce. *Over Lincoln's Shoulder: The Committee on the Conduct of the War*. Lawrence: University Press of Kansas, 1998. The only book-length study of the important, highly partisan congressional committee that took an active role in investigating Union military commanders and their operations.

Tidwell, William A. *April '65: Confederate Covert Action in the American Civil War*. Kent, Ohio: Kent State University Press, 1995. A study of Confederate clandestine operations that makes a plausible case for ties between Southern agents and John Wilkes Booth in a plan to kidnap Lincoln.

Trudeau, Noah Andre. *Bloody Roads South: The Wilderness to Cold Harbor, May–June 1864*. Boston: Little, Brown, 1989. An engaging narrative that includes numerous excerpts from participants' accounts.

————. *The Last Citadel: Petersburg, Virginia, June 1864–April 1865*. Boston: Little, Brown, 1991. Reprinted in paperback. Continues the treatment begun in the author's *Bloody Roads South*.

————. *Out of the Storm: The End of the Civil War, April–June 1865*. Boston: Little, Brown, 1994. Reprinted in paperback. The final volume of Trudeau's trilogy on the last year of the war expands its coverage to embrace not only Virginia but also late-war clashes and major Confederate surrenders elsewhere.

Wert, Jeffry D. *From Winchester to Cedar Creek: The Shenandoah Campaign of 1864*. Carlisle, Pa.: South Mountain Press, 1987. Reprinted in paperback. The best narrative of the operations pitting Philip H. Sheridan against Jubal A. Early.

Wiley, Bell I. *The Life of Johnny Reb: The Common Soldier of the Confederacy*. Indianapolis: Bobbs-Merrill, 1943. Reprinted in paperback. A pioneering study of the Confederacy's common soldiers that retains considerable value after more than half a century.

———. *The Life of Billy Yank: The Common Soldier of the Union*. Indianapolis: Bobbs-Merrill, 1952. Reprinted in paperback. The companion volume to Wiley's study of Confederate soldiers.

Notes

Notes

Notes